Trial of

John Donald Merrett

(1927)

EDITED BY

William Roughead

Author of "Malice Domestic," "The Fatal Countess," &c.

EDINBURGH AND LONDON

WILLIAM HODGE & COMPANY, LIMITED

1929

MADE AND PRINTED IN GREAT BRITAIN
BY
WILLIAM HODGE AND COMPANY, LIMITED
GLASGOW AND EDINBURGH
MARCH, 1929

TO

THE RIGHT HONOURABLE

ROBERT MUNRO, LORD ALNESS, LL.D., ETC.

LORD JUSTICE-CLERK

THIS VOLUME

IS

BY KIND PERMISSION

RESPECTFULLY DEDICATED

BY

THE EDITOR

PREFACE.

THE following report has been prepared from the original record of the proceedings in the Books of Adjournal of the High Court of Justiciary, Edinburgh, and the text of the evidence and speeches is that of the official shorthand writers' notes taken in Court.

The obvious difficulties presented by the lateness of the trial and its indeterminate result have, it is hoped, been successfully surmounted; and the attempt is made to give in the Introduction, as fully and fairly as may be, an account of the whole facts and circumstances of this very remarkable case.

The Editor's labours have been lightened and the value of this report much enhanced by the facilities afforded him for insuring the accuracy of the medical evidence, the addresses of counsel, and the charge of the learned judge. The Right Hon. Lord Alness, Lord Justice-Clerk, has done him the favour to read the proof sheets of his lordship's charge to the jury; the Right Hon. William Watson, K.C., Lord Advocate, and Mr. Craigie Aitchison, K.C., have been good enough to read those of their respective speeches. The proof sheets of the late Professor Littlejohn's evidence have been obligingly read by Dr. Douglas Kerr, who was his assistant at the time of the trial; Professor Glaister has kindly read the proofs of his evidence for the Crown; Sir Bernard Spilsbury and Professor Robertson, those of their evidence for the defence.

The Editor has further received every assistance from the courtesy of the officials as well of the Crown as of the Justiciary Offices; also from Messrs. Norman Macpherson and Dunlop, S.S.C., the agents for the defence; for all of which he is duly grateful.

The several reports—medical, chirographical, and actuarial, deponed to by the skilled witnesses at the trial, are printed in the Appendix. W. R.

12 BELGRAVE CRESCENT,
EDINBURGH, *February*, 1929.

CONTENTS.

CONTENTS.

APPENDICES.

LIST OF ILLUSTRATIONS.

JOHN DONALD MERRETT.

INTRODUCTION.

THE trial of John Donald Merrett for the murder of his mother and for uttering forged cheques upon her bank account has divers claims to inclusion in the present Series. Together with those of Alfred John Monson, of Ardlamont fame, in 1893, for the shooting of Cecil Hambrough, and of Oscar Slater, in 1909, for the slaying of Marion Gilchrist, it forms one of the three outstanding Scottish murder trials of the generation. It bristles with interest, social and scientific. It abounds in psychological, evidential, and medico-legal problems whereon the learned may exercise their wits; while for the gentler reader it provides a story strange and arresting in *motif*, notable alike in character and plot. Finally, it is a mystery, which the verdict of the jury on the first charge: Not Proven—that indefensible and invidious finding—failed to resolve. As Rupert Brooke has remarked of the lost Elizabethan tragedy by Ford and Webster—"A Late Murther of the Son upon the Mother "—" What a superb combination! And on such a subject!"

The crime of parricide is rare in the judicial annals of Scotland, our murderers, however reprehensible their practices, having generally the good taste to draw the line at the home circle. Yet it is a matter of fact that within recent years three young men in Edinburgh have been severally accused of the destruction of their respective parents. Of these, the first in time, if not in interest, is John James Hutchison, aged twenty-four, who handed round the coffee at a supper party, given on Friday, 3rd February, 1911, at Bridgend, Dalkeith, on the occasion of his father and mother's silver wedding. Three only of the eighteen guests declined to participate in the fatal brew, the partakers whereof were presently seized with pain, vomiting, and purging. Mr. Charles B. Hutchison, of the Chamberlain's Office, Dalkeith Park, and Mr. Alexander Clapperton, grocer, Musselburgh (from whom the coffee had that day been bought), emptying their cups

B
1

John Donald Merrett.

at a single gulp, died after a few hours' agony. The rest, who merely sipped and, disliking the flavour, fortunately eschewed the draught, escaped with sufferings more or less severe according to the amount imbibed, and ultimately recovered. A post-mortem examination disclosed that the deaths of Mr. Hutchison and Mr. Clapperton were due to arsenic; and the presence of that poison was detected in the remains of the coffee served at supper. Inquiries resulted in the issue, a fortnight later, of a warrant for the arrest of young Hutchison upon a charge of murder. He had been assiduous in succouring the stricken guests, and afterwards attended the funerals of the two victims. It appeared that he had been for some time employed as a dispenser in the shop of his uncle, Mr. Robert Stenhouse, chemist, Musselburgh, from which a bottle containing arsenic was mysteriously missing. He had also been gambling heavily on the stock exchange, and was deep in debt. When " wanted," he was found to have gone south with a bag of sovereigns—presumably in quest of change. The authorities traced him to London and thence to the Channel Islands, where at Guernsey he was discovered living in a boarding-house under a false name. Visited by the police, Hutchison bolted upstairs to his bedroom pursued by two officers, and, draining a phial of prussic acid which he had prepared for such contingency, fell dead in the arms of his captors. From the wholesale nature of the young chemist's dealings, and the fact that his betrothed was included in the purposed massacre, one can only suppose him to have been deranged.[1]

In the second case I have in mind the accused was, after trial, unanimously found Not Guilty, and it is therefore inexpedient to recall the facts. The third case to which I have referred forms the subject of the present study.[2]

Part I.—The Tragedy.

I.

Mrs. Bertha Milner or Merrett, when she met her death in the circumstances disclosed upon the following inquiry, was fifty-

---

[1] *Dalkeith Advertiser*, 9th February-2nd March, 1911.

[2] A later case is that of James M'Kay, tried in Glasgow on 14th December, 1927, for the murder of his mother. He was convicted and hanged.

Introduction.

five years of age.[3] She was the youngest of the three daughters of the late Mr. William Henry Milner, of The Gables, Birkdale, Southport, formerly a prosperous wine and spirit merchant in Manchester. Her elder sisters married respectively the Rev. Dr. Chadwick, some time vicar of St. Peter's Church, St. Albans, and Mr. Walter E. Penn, artist, of The Whym, Bosham, near Chichester. Upwards of twenty years before the events we are about to consider Miss Bertha Milner, who all her life was fond of travel, went a voyage to Egypt with one of her sisters. On shipboard she made the acquaintance of an electrical engineer named John Alfred Merrett, then on his way to New Zealand in connection with a dry-milk factory. The friendship thus formed was maintained by correspondence, and, whether or not they then became engaged, in the end the lady went out to New Zealand, where they were married. There, at Levin, North Island, on 17th August, 1908, was born the only issue of the marriage, John Donald Merrett. Some time later the Merretts proceeded to Russia, where at St. Petersburg Mr. Merrett pursued his calling, without, as appears, much success. The climate did not suit the child, so Mrs. Merrett took him to Switzerland, where he had a governess. Presently, with the rest of Europe, they were involved in the Great War. Mrs. Merrett wired to her husband, " What am I to do? " He replied, " Stay where you are "; which she did, and later devoted herself to nursing the wounded British officers discharged from German prison camps. Thereafter she went to London, and did good work for the Ministry of Food, inventing a fireless cooker, which was known by her name. When the war was over she returned with her son to New Zealand; and, as her husband had now definitely deserted her,[4] she settled at Oamaru, South Island, where there was a good school for the boy. In 1924 Mrs. Merrett and her son came back to England in order to complete his education. He was then sixteen, a promising, clever lad; and his mother destined him for the diplomatic service. She took a cottage at Mortimer, near Reading, and sent him to

---

[3] At the trial there attached to Mrs. Merrett's life an element of mystery which I think it due to the memory of that lady, so far as is in my power, to dispel, on the authority of two witnesses from the Crown list, each of whom had known her long and intimately, the one for ten, the other for thirty years, and to whose courtesy I am indebted for such facts as I am now able to supply.

[4] She believed him to have been killed in the Russian Revolution; but as a matter of fact it was stated at the trial that he was then alive in India.

John Donald Merrett.

Malvern College, where he remained throughout the year 1925. That autumn Mrs. Merrett visited her sister at Bosham, and in December, at the end of term, her son left Malvern, being then seventeen years and four months old. He had a brilliant record for work; but, unfortunately, his conduct on one occasion was such as to cause his mother much uneasiness. She therefore decided not to let him go, as she had intended, to Oxford, but to Edinburgh University—a non-resident college—where he could live at home with her and be under her own eye. They came to Scotland accordingly, and having spent Christmas at Melrose Hydropathic —a nephew, Mrs. Penn's boy, being of the party—Mrs. Merrett and her son arrived in Edinburgh on 4th January, 1926, and took rooms at 7 Mayfield Road. There they continued till the 25th, when they left for a boarding-house, 33 and 35 Palmerston Place. Finally, Mrs. Merrett rented for four months a furnished flat at 31 Buckingham Terrace, to which they removed on Wednesday, 10th March, 1926.

Upon the testimony of those who knew her, Mrs. Merrett was a lady eminent alike in character and accomplishments. Possessed of much personal charm and many social gifts : cheerful, cultured, musical, a keen bridge player, and exceptionally capable in affairs, she was held in high esteem by all with whom she had relations. " Everything she did, she did to perfection " is the tribute of one friend; and her sister in the witness-box said of her : " She was a splendid woman." These manifold endowments were by Mrs. Merrett wholly devoted to the benefit of her son. Deserted early by his father, the burden of his upbringing had fallen upon her alone. She was, as the phrase is, bound up in her boy. His present welfare and future success formed the one great object of her life, and her constant anxiety was to do the best for the lad and his advantage, moral and material.[5] Perhaps she was, if anything, an over-anxious mother; but there is no doubt— although by the generosity of the Crown the fact was not brought out at the trial—that this maternal devotion was by its object very ill requited. Apart altogether from the fraudulent operations on her bank account which formed the subject of the second charge, Donald Merrett, during the last months of her life, habitually deceived his mother. He entered upon his arts course at the University at the commencement of the session; she paid the

---

[5] She was a religious woman, and one source of worry was the boy's refusal to be confirmed.

4

Introduction.

necessary fees, and in addition engaged for him a tutor. He attended classes during January and the early part of February; but after that date he never went near the college at all, although he left home every morning with his books ostensibly for that purpose, and his mother thought him suffering from overstudy!

By night his behaviour was equally deceptive. He locked his bedroom door so that his mother believed him to be abed, when in fact, as often as not, he was, in the Parliamentary euphemism, " in another place."[6] The venue of his irregular resort was commonly the Dunedin Palais de Danse in Picardy Place, where, unknown to his mother, he became intimate with two of the instructors, a girl named Betty Christie and a young man of the name of Scott, with whom he spent much of his too ample leisure. He was known to them familiarly as " Donnie."

Mrs. Merrett's annual income was some £700; as her son grew older and the cost of living increased, it required all her ability to maintain them both in comfort. She allowed him 10s. a week as pocket-money; and so careful was she in matters pecuniary that he had to keep an account of his expenditure. His weekly balances, however, failed to disclose such items as the " bookings out " of Miss Christie at 30s. a night and 15s. an afternoon; the £2 and £2 5s. paid for two jade and opal rings presented by him to that young lady; the cost of an A.J.S. motor bicycle and of an H.R.D. motor racing cycle with sidecar; and the price of an automatic pistol and cartridges—outlays all incurred before his mother's death and, as appears, without her knowledge. We shall see in the sequel the means whereby these extraordinary expenses were met.

II.

" We are getting on quite well, and like Edinburgh in spite of its really appalling climate," wrote Mrs. Merrett on 26th February to her banker at Boscombe, " and Donald has taken to life at the 'Varsity." And again, on 4th March, " Donald is doing well at the University, and is quite settled down to the life here." Whatever cause of disquietude she may have had, she was not going to give her boy away.

The flat at 31 Buckingham Terrace was in one of those modern

---

[6] At Buckingham Terrace he got out and in of his bedroom window by means of a rope, with which by day the window was protected, on the pretence that he walked in his sleep!

John Donald Merrett.

reconditioned houses which have suffered the fate gradually over-taking the West End mansions of Edinburgh in being, like Cæsar's Gaul, divided into three parts. It occupied the first floor above the street, and consisted of a sitting-room and small bedroom to the front, and a larger bedroom, kitchen, and bathroom to the back. There was no accommodation for servants, so Mrs. Merrett had to employ a daily maid. The person appointed to the office was Henrietta Sutherland, twenty-eight years of age, a married woman living apart from her husband and supporting herself by going out as a "help." Her duties were limited to between the hours of 9 a.m. and midday, and, except on Friday, the 12th, these were daily discharged by her throughout the week beginning Wednesday, 10th March, when Mrs. Merrett moved into the flat.

On the morning of Wednesday, the 17th, Mrs. Sutherland arrived in due course; Mrs. Merrett opened the door to her, and she noticed nothing unusual in that lady's demeanour. Mother and son had already breakfasted; Mrs. Merrett assisted her to clear the table, and then took some writing materials out of the bureau. Mrs. Sutherland was twice in the sitting-room that morn-ing, and on the last occasion she left Mrs. Merrett seated at the table writing, with the open bureau behind her on the right.[7] Merrett was then sitting in the recess on the other side of the room reading a book. The time was about 9.40. Of the subsequent happenings, so vitally important, Mrs. Sutherland regrettably varied her account, and these disparate versions will fall to be considered when we come to deal with her evidence. Meantime, to avoid confusion, we may take her original statement, to which at the trial she ultimately swore as the truth. She left the sitting-room door wide open, got a pailful of coals from the cellar in the hall, and went into the kitchen to make up the fire. Just as she was bending down to the grate she heard a shot, followed immediately by a scream and the thud of a falling body. She rose to her feet and stood still in amazement. Some few seconds later she heard Merrett coming towards the kitchen and a sound as of books falling in the hall. On reaching the kitchen he said, "Rita, my mother has shot herself." He looked much upset and as if he were going to cry. "She seemed quite all right this morning," said the maid; to which he replied that he had been

---

[7] The bureau, when closed, resembles a chest of drawers; the front of the top drawer, pulled out, folds down and forms a writing-desk, with small drawers and pigeon holes behind. See photograph reproduced herewith.

Introduction.

wasting his mother's money and she had " quarrelled " him about it; he thought she was worried over that. They then entered the sitting-room. Mrs. Merrett, bleeding from a bullet wound in the right ear, lay insensible on the floor between the table and the bureau; the chair on which she had been sitting was overset. On the top of the bureau, at the front right-hand corner, Mrs. Sutherland saw a pistol. One should have thought that the natural thing to do in the circumstances would have been to telephone for a doctor : they rang up the police. On returning to the room— the telephone was in the hall—Merrett asked the maid to help him to lift his mother on to the sofa; she replied, " I think we had best leave her." He then said, " Let's go out; I cannot stand to look at it any longer." So they went downstairs together to the street door. The police arrived with an ambulance and took Mrs. Merrett to the Royal Infirmary. Merrett accompanied them, and gave as the reason for his mother's rash act " money matters."

Had Mrs. Merrett been taken to a nursing home as a private patient, attended by her own doctor, we should doubtless have known a good deal more than we do about the matter. The question of how she came by her injury was begged by the authorities from the start. She herself was unconscious; Merrett and Mrs. Sutherland said she had shot herself; and at the Infirmary she was, after due examination, consigned to ward 3—a place with barred windows and locked doors, reserved for attempted suicides, where she remained practically under arrest until her death. The position is made quite plain by the following letter received at the Infirmary on the afternoon of her admission :—

Police Station, West End,
Edinburgh, 17th March, 1926.

Sir,

    I have the honour to inform you that Bertha Milner or Merrett, now detained in No. Three Ward, Royal Infirmary, is a prisoner charged with attempted suicide, and I am directed by the Chief Constable to ask you to be good enough to inform the Lieutenant on duty, Central Police Office, High Street, Edinburgh, the date and hour on which it is proposed to discharge the Accused, in order that arrangements may be made for taking her into custody.

I have the honour to be, Sir,
Your obedient Servant,

HUGH ROSS, Sergt.

The Superintendent,
   Royal Infirmary,
     Edinburgh.[8]

---

[8] Productions for the defence, No. 20.

John Donald Merrett.

As a result of this procedure Mrs. Merrett became the subject of a conspiracy of silence. Nurses, friends, relatives, every one who approached her, were told not to tell her what had happened, nor to discuss with her the cause and nature of her injury. Although the poor lady lived for a fortnight, and was until a few days before her death quite clear, conscious, and conversable, she in fact died—even on the medical hypothesis offered by the defence—without knowing what was the matter with her, or that she had been shot, and was suffering from a bullet wound in the head.

III.

The earliest account of the affair given by Mrs. Sutherland was the statement she made, immediately after the occurrence, to Constable Middlemiss, one of the two policemen who came with the ambulance, namely, that she was working in the kitchen when she heard the shot, and that Merrett came to her there and told her what had happened. When they had all gone away and she was left alone in the flat, Detective-Inspector Fleming, of the Criminal Investigation Department, with Detective-Sergeant Henderson, arrived about ten o'clock to make inquiries. He took a statement from Mrs. Sutherland. "She told me," says Fleming, " she had been in the kitchen about half-past nine and heard a shot, and on going into the lobby she saw Mrs. Merrett fall off the chair and on to the floor, and a revolver or pistol falling out of her hand." The case being thus obviously one of suicide, Inspector Fleming proceeded with his investigation, which, in the circumstances, would seem to have been merely formal. On the table at which Mrs. Merrett had been writing he observed an unfinished letter, which he read. " Mrs. Merrett was writing," he says, " to some friend in Stirling[9] mentioning the fact that she had got a flat at last, and that she had some trouble in getting a maid, but that she had got a maid who was coming there daily." Most unfortunately Fleming, instead of taking possession of it, left this letter lying on the table; we shall hear what became of it later. He also noticed and read, laid out open upon the desk of the bureau, two letters, dated respectively 13th and 16th March, from the Clydesdale Bank to Mrs. Merrett intimating that her account was overdrawn, which confirmed him in the belief that it was a case of suicide.

---

[9] Mrs. Anderson, her oldest friend.

8

Introduction.

Meanwhile in the Infirmary Mrs. Merrett had recovered consciousness. On the night of her admission, to Dr. Holcombe, who had charge of the case, she complained of pain in her ear and wanted to know the cause of it. " Oh," replied the doctor, " you have had a little accident," and nothing more was said. Next day, Thursday, the 18th, she again asked him the reason of her suffering; what did the X-ray show?—(she had been twice photographed and the bullet located behind the nose, but inoperable)—and could she see an ear specialist? But she got upon these points no information. That evening Mrs. Merrett asked Sister Grant, who was attending her, " What has happened? Why am I here? "—it was so extraordinary; she could not understand it. The sister answered that she didn't know; could not Mrs. Merrett tell her? She said, " She was sitting writing at the time, when suddenly a bang went off in her head like a pistol." " Was there not a pistol there? " asked the sister; upon which the patient, in great surprise, exclaimed, " No; was there? " Asked further whether she was certain she was writing when this occurred, Mrs. Merrett answered, " Yes; quite sure. Donald can tell you; he was standing beside me, waiting to post the letter." This conversation, which was confirmed by Nurse Innes, who was present, was at once reported by Sister Grant to Dr. Holcombe, who then for the first time asked the patient how her accident happened. " I was sitting down writing letters," she told him, " and my son Donald was standing beside me. I said, ' Go away, Donald, and don't annoy me '; and the next I heard was a kind of explosion, and I do not remember anything more." So important did Dr. Holcombe consider this statement that he communicated it to the police; Inspector Fleming went up to the Infirmary next day and interviewed the doctor; but though this lady was then in grave peril and was still fully conscious, Fleming neither saw nor questioned her, and no dying deposition or formal statement was taken from her at all.

That Friday Dr. Holcombe saw Merrett for the first time and asked him what had taken place. He said, " His mother was sitting down writing letters, and she said to him, ' Go away, Donald, and don't annoy me,' and he went over to the corner of the room, and the next he heard was a shot, and he looked round and saw his mother falling to the ground with a revolver falling from her hand." The coincidence of these accounts by mother and son, with one cardinal exception, should be noted.

John Donald Merrett.

The only action which the Criminal Investigation Department took upon this new and most material evidence was to send Constables Watt and Gibson to interview Mrs. Sutherland, apparently for the purpose of ascertaining to which of her discrepant statements she adhered. On Sunday, 21st March, four days after the event, these officers visited her in her own house, when she gave to them the same statement as she originally made to Middlemiss, namely, that she was at the kitchen grate when she heard the shot and saw nothing. Reminded of what she had told Fleming, she said " that she may have said that [*i.e.*, that she had seen her mistress fall]; but she was so excited at the time she could not remember." The authorities, equally oblivious, saw no reason to revise the official verdict, and there matters rested—for the time.

IV.

At the conversation with Merrett on Friday, the 19th, Dr. Holcombe told him that in view of his mother's critical condition her relatives ought to be informed. Merrett replied " that they were not on the best of terms," but the doctor said they should be given the chance to come.[1] Yet Merrett sent no word to either of his aunts as to their sister's state.

On the night of the occurrence, at his mother's request, Merrett had telegraphed to her friend, Mrs. Hill, at Brighton that his mother was " ill " and was asking for her. That lady arrived in Edinburgh on the morning of Friday, the 19th. She saw Mrs. Merrett, who welcomed her with the words, " Thank you, dear, I am so grateful." Mrs. Hill, informed by Merrett that his mother had shot herself as she was in money difficulties, having received information from her bank that her account was overdrawn by £20, was naturally very much astonished. Before seeing the patient she was warned by Sister Grant not to let her know the nature of her injury; but Mrs. Merrett herself at once raised the question by saying, " Why am I here? What has happened? " Mrs. Hill, mindful of her instructions, said she had had a fall, which Mrs. Merrett denied. She said she was writing a letter to Mrs. Anderson—she remembered the name of her correspondent— " and a pistol went off under my ear." Mrs. Hill asked her,

---

[1] Sister Grant, who was present, says: " He said he would send for them. He said that it would not be much use sending for them, because they were not on friendly terms."—*Evidence of Sister Grant at the Trial.*

10

Introduction.

Did she see a pistol? Did she handle one? Was there one there? To each of these questions Mrs. Merrett answered, "No." Mrs. Hill did not pursue the subject; but in further conversation Mrs. Merrett asked her to write to her sister Mary (Mrs. Chadwick, then in Switzerland), and also to go to the flat "to see to things" there. "You know my little purse?" said she; "there are £6 in it; take what you want to go on with." The purse, she added, was at the flat. Mrs. Hill did not go to Buckingham Terrace; she had to return south that night; but she telegraphed to Mrs. Penn, Mrs. Merrett's other sister, who with her husband was then on the Riviera. They at once left for home; and in London, on their way north, met Mrs. Hill, who told them what she had learned about the matter.

Mr. and Mrs. Penn arrived in Edinburgh on the morning of Wednesday, 24th March, a week after the tragedy. They visited Mrs. Merrett that forenoon. She was delighted to see them and thanked them for coming. She asked her sister to get her an ear specialist; they—the Infirmary folk—said she had had a fall, but she doubted that. She was sitting, she said, at the table, writing, when a sudden explosion went off in her head—"as if Donald had shot me!" "That would be impossible," was Mrs. Penn's comment.[2] Mrs. Merrett then begged her to go at once to the flat and look after Donald, as Edinburgh was a particularly wicked city. She asked her further to get a present for Sister Grant, who had been so good to her, and to take her fur coat from the flat. She also recommended a certain church where the best music was to be heard.

Now, Mrs. Penn, from her intimate knowledge of her sister's character and from what she had just heard from her own lips, was firmly persuaded that, notwithstanding the official story, suicide was out of the question. On Friday, the 26th, in Sister Grant's room, her husband and Mr. Jenks, Mrs. Merrett's man of business, who had been wired for by Mr. Penn, being present, Mrs. Penn "asked Donald if he could explain matters." He said that he had not shot his mother; so they were reduced to the theory of accident. It was then proposed that the parties should adjourn to the flat for the purpose of reconstructing the "accident," which was done. "The suggestion was," says Mrs. Penn, "that the pistol was in

---

[2] Nurse Grant, who was present, reports Mrs. Merrett as saying, "Did Donald not do it? He is such a naughty boy." She did not remember Mrs. Penn's reply.—*Evidence of Nurse Grant at the Trial.*

John Donald Merrett.

the secretaire [bureau] drawer, and that it might have been taken out in some papers and gone off accidentally." That was the most they could make of it; " accident," therefore, with the family, held the field.

Meanwhile, on Thursday, the 25th, Mrs. Merrett, being supported in bed for the purpose, managed to sign a cheque; it was the first time she had held a pen since writing the unfinished letter to Mrs. Anderson.[3] Late that night she became delirious, on Friday, the 26th, she was incoherent, on Saturday, the 27th, she lost consciousness, which she never regained, and she died about one o'clock in the morning of Thursday, 1st April, a fortnight after the infliction of her injury. Dr. Holcombe certified the cause of death : " Basal Meningitis, following a bullet wound in cranium." The same day, in the mortuary of the Royal Infirmary, a post-mortem examination of the body was made by Professor Littlejohn, of Edinburgh University, in presence of Dr. Douglas Kerr, his assistant, and of Dr. Holcombe. The professor prepared a report, now printed in the present volume,[4] in the course of which he stated : " The direction of the wound, judging by the external wounds and the position of the bullet where found, was horizontal and slightly from behind forwards, the bullet lying about an inch anterior to the external wound." The conclusion at which Professor Littlejohn then arrived was this : " There was nothing to indicate the distance at which the discharge of the weapon took place, whether from a few inches or a greater distance. So far as the position of the wound is concerned, the case is consistent with suicide. There is some difficulty in attributing it to accident, although such a view cannot be wholly excluded."

This was, so to speak, the last nail in the coffin of the hapless lady; accordingly, on Saturday, 3rd April, in Piershill Cemetery, and, as I am informed, with such maimed rites as the Church accords to those who have laid violent hands upon themselves, the body of Bertha Merrett was buried. If she were in fact guiltless of her own blood, that suicide's grave was indeed the ultimate irony of Fate.

---

[3] The head injury had induced paralysis of the left side, depriving her of the use of that arm and leg. Nothing more is heard of this cheque at the trial; but it otherwise appears that it was filled in for £5 to refund Mrs. Hill's expenses. It was handed to Mr. Jenks, but was not presented for payment.

[4] Appendix I.

Introduction.

V.

We are now to consider the behaviour of Merrett during the tragic fortnight while his mother lay stricken down at death's door, which with every allowance for the unrespective character of youth, does seem to fall something short of what one should expect from an only and beloved son. Though not brought out in evidence, it otherwise appears that his mother was constantly asking for him, missing him, wondering where he was and why he was not beside her, and that his visits to her were brief, hurried, and perfunctory. Although his collegiate duties, as we have seen, sat lightly enough upon his shoulders, and his literary activities were confined to a subject of which there will be much to say, he had other calls upon his time. Old heads are not found on young shoulders; and, as at the trial his counsel put it, he was just " a big romping boy." Before the tragedy he was dancing nightly at the Dunedin Palais; after that date, while he continued to frequent the place, it is not in proof that he actually danced there.

At 2 p.m. on Wednesday, 17th March, Merrett, having seen his mother safely in ward 3, " rolled up "—if I am technically right—at the Dunedin and " booked out " Miss Christie for the day. He then took her on the pillion of his motor cycle to Queensferry, where they had tea. He told her his mother had shot herself that morning with his own pistol. In describing the affair, he said that at the time *the maid was in the kitchen*. They afterwards went to the flat, which was empty, where they were presently joined by his friend Scott, for whom he had telephoned. To him, with reference to what had happened to his mother, Merrett said, " *He had gone through to the kitchen* and told the maid about it." The three then took a taxi to the Infirmary. There Merrett asked Sister Grant whether his mother was " still alive " and, on learning that she had recovered consciousness, he said, " if his mother got better, not to tell her what had happened, as he did not wish her to know anything about it." It was arranged that Scott should engage a room for him at the County Hotel in the Lothian Road, which was conveniently situated next door to the Caley Picture House, where he and Miss Christie spent the evening. That night they again called at the Infirmary, and Merrett saw his mother, Miss Christie remaining in the corridor.

John Donald Merrett.

Thereafter Sister Grant asked him, if anything happened in the night, would she get him at Buckingham Terrace?

He said no, he was staying with friends. He hesitated, and I said, "What is the address, please?" and he said he was then staying at the County Hotel, Lothian Road. I said, "Will I find you there any time I want you?" and he said, "No," and he stepped out, and addressing the girl in the corridor, he said, "Betty, what is the number of the Dunedin Palais?" and he gave me 766 and told me to ring up to 1 a.m. any time I wanted him and ask for Mr. Scott, and I would find him there.[5]

In explanation of this and other incidents from which, in the circumstances of the case, the uncharitable might be apt to infer on the part of the accused a certain callousness and unconcern, counsel for the defence, in addressing the jury, drew a pathetic picture of the lonely lad, a stranger in a strange city, dependent for solace and companionship upon a couple of dancing instructors. But, as one happens to know, Mrs. Merrett had then good friends in Edinburgh, who would very willingly have done their best for her boy in his sad situation. To them, however, Merrett, after the event, made no approach; nor did he even advise them of his mother's illness.

His treatment of Mrs. Hill, his mother's old friend, who had known him from a child, and who, at some personal inconvenience and expense, had at once responded to her call for help, lacked both courtesy and feeling. He did not meet that lady on her arrival, though she had wired that she was coming; and she had to make her way alone to the Infirmary at 6 a.m. in order to learn where he was to be found. After breakfast at his hotel, he took her to see his mother and left her, promising to return at lunch time. Mrs. Hill waited till 2 p.m., but he never appeared. She then went back to the hotel and rang up the Infirmary several times to ask if he had been there. Sister Grant referred her to his permanent address, the Dunedin, to which Mrs. Hill telephoned in vain. Finally, he looked in at 6.30, and promised to see her off by the night express to London. He failed to do so.

That Friday, at the Infirmary, Dr. Holcombe told Merrett that his mother was very seriously ill, but she yet had " a fighting chance "; to which her son rejoined, " So it is still on the cards that she will recover?"—an expression, the defence maintained, in the circumstances natural enough. At any rate it showed more sense than sensibility.

---

[5] Evidence of Sister Grant at the trial.

14

Introduction.

VI.

Pursuant to her promise to her dying sister, Mrs. Penn and her husband occupied the flat at 31 Buckingham Terrace, where, on leaving the hotel, their nephew went to live with them. On Tuesday, 30th March, Inspector Fleming, being informed of the discovery by Mr. Penn of an empty cartridge case in the sitting-room there, called to make inquiries. Mr. Penn told him he found it on the floor, a foot from the outside angle of the bay window, on the left-hand side. It lay 6 or 8 feet straight in front of the place where Mrs. Merrett had been sitting when she received her injury.

On this occasion Fleming had an interview with Merrett—the first time he was officially interrogated—a fortnight after the event and the day before his mother died—who, having been duly cautioned, made to Fleming the statement read by him at the trial. Merrett said he acquired a pistol as they thought of going abroad at Easter.

After coming to the flat at 31 Buckingham Terrace everything [*sic*] was in good spirits and getting on all right. When in Palmerston Place she got on to me for spending too much money. She also got on to me for going out too much and neglecting my lessons. . . .

About noon on Saturday, 13th March, I had the pistol and loaded it with six cartridges, one being in the breech, and the safety catch on. I was going to the Braids to shoot rabbits. I wanted to take it on the Sunday morning, but she took it from me and put it in the small drawer in the writing bureau. I think I told my mother to be careful, that it was loaded. I never again saw the pistol.[6]

He said his mother had been worrying herself over money matters. On the morning of the 17th there arrived an intimation from the Clydesdale Bank that she had overdrawn her account. After breakfast he went into his bedroom, and on returning to the sitting-room found Mrs. Merrett writing at the table.

I saw an envelope my mother had addressed to Mrs. Anderson, 64 Murray Place, *Edinburgh*. I pointed out the mistake, and she said, "Go away, you worry me." I went to the other side of the room to get my books, when I heard a report and saw my mother in the act of falling on to the floor. I rushed over to my mother *and saw the maid in the hall*, when I said, "Mother has hurt herself." She fell on the left side and the

---

[6] Evidence of Inspector Fleming at the trial. There is no evidence except the accused's own statement that he and his mother meant to go abroad at Easter. My information is that Mrs. Merrett intended taking him to France for the summer vacation.

John Donald Merrett.

revolver was lying beside her right hand. I telephoned for the police, and they removed the body to the Royal Infirmary, where she was detained.

He said he had lifted the pistol off the floor and put it on to the corner of the bureau, and then tried to lift his mother but could not—all this before he had seen the maid. Asked what had become of the unfinished letter which Fleming had seen on the table on 17th March, he said he had destroyed it, as there were some blood marks on the letter. Yet Fleming, when he read it, saw no marks of blood.[7]

The inspector adjourned the inquiry to the kitchen for a last word with Mrs. Sutherland, whose services had been retained by Mrs. Penn in accordance with her sister's wish. She told him, with reference to her former statement to him of 17th March, that she was then so upset she did not remember what she had said. She was now, however, quite clear as to her original and final version being the truth of the matter.

Fleming then for the first time searched the premises and took possession of certain documents, the import of which we shall presently see, and also of 38 cartridges, which he found lying loose in a drawer in Merrett's bedroom. Fleming asked him where he got the pistol and ammunition. "He told me he had purchased it from Hardy Brothers in Princes Street, along with 50 cart- ridges. *He did not think his mother knew he had the pistol.* £5 was what he paid for it."[8]

Although Mrs. Merrett deemed Edinburgh "a particularly wicked city," it must, I think, be taken as a tribute to the general character and good conduct of its citizens that certain remarkable features of her case raised in the official mind no suspicion what- ever. The criminal authorities of, say, Glasgow, or of any other really abandoned burgh, would, one imagines, in such suggestive circumstances have been more swift to mark possible iniquity; but

---

[7] *Ibid.* It is strange that Mrs. Merrett should have made this mistake in addressing her old friend and constant correspondent, who lived at 64 Murray Place, *Stirling.* What became of the envelope? Inspector Fleming stated at the trial, " I saw no envelope at all on the table on 17th March." Mrs. Sutherland heard Merrett, on his way to the kitchen, drop some books, which she found later upon the hall floor. He cannot have had these in his hand while he attempted to lift his mother; he must have taken them up afterwards, before leaving the room.

[8] Now this would be a very grave admission indeed were it not for the fact that Merrett had already described to Fleming how his mother took the pistol from him and put it in the bureau drawer. A further inaccuracy attaches to the price here said to have been paid for the weapon, which was actually £1 17s. 6d.

16

Mrs. Merrett in her New Zealand Home.

Introduction.

here nine months were to elapse before anything definite was done to cast a doubt upon the question of Mrs. Merrett's suicide.

VII.

By her last will and codicil, executed at Reading in 1924, Mrs. Bertha Merrett devised her whole estate to the Public Trustee and to "William Arthur Jenks, of number 89 Calverley Road, Catford, London, S.E.6," in trust, for behoof of her son John Donald Merrett, until he should attain the age of twenty-five, the income to be applied for his maintenance and education; and the executors were thereby appointed joint guardians of her said son. Mr. Jenks having renounced Probate, the Public Trustee acted alone.[9] It was arranged that Mr. and Mrs. Penn should remain in Buckingham Terrace until the expiry of the tenancy, and that Merrett should stay with them there and continue his University course. When in June the flat fell to be vacated, other accommodation for him would need to be devised.

It must have been a strangely discomfortable household: the uncle and aunt, perplexed by the enigma of the mother's death; the nephew, who alone knew the answer; the maid, who had claimed to know, and afterwards denied it. Though now ostensibly engaged in the resumption of his studies, these proved for Merrett less exigent than those of Dr. Blimber's young gentlemen. True, he left home in the morning with his books as usual, but the college was not his objective. By night the rope and the rhone-pipe outside his bedroom window were again in requisition, whereby disturbance of the inmates at untimeous hours was tactfully avoided. The peripatetic perquisitions of the police, too—the official conscience seems to have become uneasy—must have got on every one's nerves. On Tuesday, 13th April, Merrett told his aunt that he purposed going to London to consult a famous detective—possibly Mr. Sherlock Holmes—in case of further developments regarding his mother's death. Having provided himself with money to the measure of Mrs. Penn's resources, he fared forth, along with a casual acquaintance (in civil life a taxi-driver), to

---

[9] Probate, dated 14th July, 1926. Certain references to Mr. Jenks made in the course of the trial suggest some mysterious unknown, who appeared suddenly from nowhere at Mrs. Merrett's deathbed, took possession of her last cheque, and vanished into appropriate darkness. The fact above stated disproves this myth. He came to Edinburgh on the instructions of Mr. Penn.

John Donald Merrett.

seek expert advice. He omitted to inform his aunt that they were accompanied on their quest by two young ladies,[1] one of whom, being under sixteen, when in London withdrew from the party at the instigation of the police. What was the counsel of the famous detective is not recorded; but a week or so later his two clients turned up at Buckingham Terrace in lamentable case, alleging that, their funds being exhausted, they had walked back from London! All things considered, no doubt it was rather a relief to Mr. and Mrs. Penn when their term of guardianship was over. On the evacuation of the flat Merrett removed to the students' settlement at Ramsay Lodge till the end of the summer session, when he went for a yachting holiday on the Clyde at Tighna-bruaich. It would be interesting to know if he visited Ardlamont.

The Public Trustee was now faced with the problem of what to do with his ward. The Edinburgh University authorities, in respect of Merrett's previous persistent absention from his classes, refused to permit him to resume his course. It was therefore proposed that he should have the benefit of private tuition, with a view to his going to Oxford; but before placing him with a tutor, the Trustee deemed it desirable to have the prospective pupil medically examined. Accordingly this was done by a physician and an alienist, who duly reported to the Trustee the result of their consultation. It would be improper to enter into particulars —the report was confidential—but the general conclusion at which these experts arrived may be given :—

> The lad is exceptionally developed physically for his age [seventeen] and looks at least over twenty years. He talks intelligently and confidently, and is clear and lucid in his statements on general topics. He is sound in every bodily organ, and mentally he is perfectly sane.[2]

They advised his removal from Edinburgh (that " particularly wicked city ") as the scene of his late untoward experiences, and prescribed a healthy, open-air life in the country, where he might be prepared for an academic career. Such a hygienic retreat was found for him in the vicarage of Hughenden, near High Wycombe, in Buckinghamshire, and there in August Merrett was given a fresh start.

But meanwhile in Edinburgh something had happened which, like the accolade bestowed upon the enchanted princess in the tale,

---

[1] In accordance, as appears, with the time-honoured precedent of carrying coals to Newcastle.

[2] Report, dated 1st July, 1926.

Introduction.

roused from their protracted slumbers the sentinels of the palace of justice.

On 27th November there was presented to the Sheriff of the Lothians and Peebles a petition by the Procurator-Fiscal of Midlothian, setting forth (1) that John Donald Merrett had murdered his mother, and (2) that he had " uttered as genuine "— presented for payment—29 cheques upon her bank account, " on each of which cheques the name of ' Bertha Merrett ' bore to be signed as drawer, such signatures being forged "; and therefore praying his lordship to grant warrant for the accused's apprehension. A warrant was granted on the 29th, and the ensuing arrest was effected by a local sergeant of police, who conveyed the accused by motor car to High Wycombe police station, where he was handed over to two officers from Edinburgh. There, on 3rd December, the accused appeared before Sheriff-Substitute Jameson, and, having intimated that he did not desire to emit a declaration (*i.e.*, to make any statement), was committed to the prison of Edinburgh for further examination. On 9th December Sheriff-Substitute Neish granted warrant to imprison the accused until liberated in due course of law. The indictment was served on 14th January, 1927, the pleading diet being fixed for the 21st, when the accused pleaded Not Guilty; and on Tuesday, 1st February, the trial began.

Part II.—The Trial.

I.

It was a memorable time, that February week, in the High Court of Justiciary in the Parliament Square, Edinburgh, when, at the instance of His Majesty's Advocate, John Donald Merrett stood at the bar indicted for the crimes of murder and uttering. No trial since that of Oscar Slater seventeen years before had so engaged the public interest; and, when the diet was called, the old Court-room, theatre of so many moving dramas, was crowded to its utmost limits. There attaches to Scots criminal procedure— unless I am prejudiced by patriotism—an air of dignity and distinction hardly to be found in the tribunals of less favoured lands. In the present instance our system showed at its best. The richly robed presence on the bench, holding with scrupulous hand the balance of justice; the notable fairness and moderation of the prosecutor; the brilliant and resourceful conduct of the defence;

John Donald Merrett.

the figure in the dock, surprisingly mature, detached, indifferent, suggesting rather a bored spectator of some tedious business than a lad on trial for his life :[3] these are impressions which none who then received them is likely to forget.

The Lord Justice-Clerk (the Right Hon. Lord Alness) was the presiding judge; the Lord Advocate (the Right Hon. William Watson, K.C.), assisted by the Right Hon. Lord Kinross, Advocate-Depute, conducted the prosecution, Sir John Prosser, W.S., acting as Crown agent; Mr. Craigie M. Aitchison, K.C., Mr. R. Macgregor Mitchell, K.C., and Mr. J. L. M. Clyde, advocate, instructed by Messrs. Norman Macpherson & Dunlop, S.S.C., Edinburgh, appeared for the defence. The indictment embraced two charges—

(1) On 17th March, 1926, in the flat at 31 Buckingham Terrace, Edinburgh, then occupied by Bertha Merrett, your mother, you did shoot the said Bertha Merrett in the head with a loaded pistol, whereby she was so severely injured that she died on 1st April, 1926, in the Royal Infirmary, Edinburgh, and you did murder her,

and (2) that on certain specified dates he uttered as genuine to tellers of the Clydesdale Bank 29 cheques, " each of which said cheques was payable to J. D. Merrett, and on each of which the name of the said Bertha Merrett bore to be signed as drawer, such signatures being forged," and thereby induced the tellers to pay him sums of money amounting in all to £457 13s. 6d. Annexed to the indictment were (1) schedule showing the dates and amounts of the forged cheques and the names of the bank tellers to whom they were presented for payment; (2) list of productions containing 192 items, chiefly cheques; and (3) list of witnesses, 57 in number. The accused having pleaded Not Guilty, a jury, which included six women, was empannelled, and the prosecutor adduced his proof.

I propose to take the second charge first, because with respect to it we are in a different position from that of the learned judge and the contestant counsel when they respectively dealt with it at the trial. Then the issue was yet in doubt; now, by the unanimous verdict of the jury, we are certified that the accused was guilty of that crime, for which, being convicted, he was by

---

[3] The accused was of powerful build, 6 feet in height, and broad in proportion. His features were heavy and high coloured; he wore thick horn-rimmed spectacles, and looked many years older than his age.

Introduction.

the Court sentenced to twelve months' imprisonment. The able
and ingenious character of the defence, therefore, is in this regard
no more than matter of academic interest, and as such to be
appreciated by the curious in the evidence.

Mrs. Merrett's ways of dealing with her money matters were,
for a lady, unusually methodical and exact. Her principal account
was with the Midland Bank at Boscombe, into which were paid
her dividends and other items of income; but when she came to
Edinburgh she opened, for convenience, with the George Street
branch of the Clydesdale Bank a second account, upon which it
was arranged she should draw only to the extent of £30 at one
time, and which she kept supplied by cheques drawn, as and when
required, upon her Midland Bank account. She had thus two
separate bank books, with cheque books corresponding. So particular was she to preserve a complete and regular record of her
banking transactions that not only did she keep a private account
book, in which every payment and withdrawal made by her was
duly entered and the resultant balance shown, but, further, it
was her practice to duplicate these entries by noting on the counterfoils of her cheques the balance as affected by each one drawn,
as also the increase arising from any payment into the account.
To attempt, therefore, to cheat and rob by means of forged cheques
a lady of such meticulous business habits was no easy exploit;
and yet this for many weeks the accused accomplished undetected.

Certain features common to, and characteristic of, the 29
forged cheques, not to be found in any genuine cheque of Mrs.
Merrett, were as follows:—(1) Mrs. Merrett used her cheques in
proper sequence; the forged cheques, which were taken from the
beginning and end of cheque books and the counterfoils of each
removed, were not used consecutively—until Mrs. Merrett was
safely in the Infirmary, when they were drawn in regular order;
(2) the body of every genuine cheque of Mrs. Merrett was filled in
by herself—the forged cheques alone were written entirely by the
accused; (3) no known genuine cheque was ever made payable
to J. D. Merrett—in each of the forged cheques his name appeared
as payee; (4) no trace of the forged cheques could be found either
in Mrs. Merrett's own account book or on her counterfoils, so
far as recovered; and (5) two handwriting experts, Mr. Gurrin,
in London, and Mr. Morrison Smith, in Edinburgh, examining

John Donald Merrett.

independently the whole series of cheques drawn, and purporting to be drawn by Mrs. Merrett during the year 1925 and the first three months of 1926, severally picked out the same 29 cheques as having thereon *a double signature*—one superimposed upon another—and as presenting other marked dissimilarities to her undoubted signatures. The method which, in the opinion of these experts, had been employed was this : between the cheque to be forged and a specimen of the genuine signature was placed a sheet of carbon paper, such as is used for typewriting duplication; the signature was then traced with a pencil or similar pointed instrument, to the effect that it appeared in violet outline upon the blank cheque; it was then carefully gone over—" painted," was their expression—in ink, with results superficially satisfactory. But upon examination with a microscope the double outline was plainly perceptible, as may be seen in the two enlarged signatures reproduced herewith, which, of course, do not show the difference in *colour* between the blue ink and the violet outline.[4]

Mr. Gurrin also found among certain members of the doubtful group a striking family resemblance. Following up this clue he made a tracing of one suspected signature, and superimposed it upon all the others in turn; it corresponded exactly with those on 16 of the cheques, so that 17 were practically identical. A second tracing, of slightly varying form, corresponded with other 10, showing that 11 were drawn upon the same basis. One false signature stood alone—the first, or trial, forgery, which was not repeated in that form. Thus of the 29 false signatures, 17 were reproduced from the same model, which for purposes of reference he termed A; 11 from a second model, B; and one only from a single model, C. Facsimiles of these three models are printed in the present volume. Such " coincidence " was, in Mr. Gurrin's experience, quite incompatible with genuineness, as no two signatures are, to the skilled eye, ever exactly alike. Indeed, this is common knowledge; one has only to compare one's own signatures to arrive at that conclusion. The method adopted by the forger

---

[4] I am informed that Mr. Penn found in a drawer in the accused's bedroom a fly-leaf torn out of his mother's prayer book, containing her signature " Bertha Merrett," and a coloured impression of the same upon the verso. He showed this significant *trouvaille* to Fleming, who seemingly thought it of no consequence. Mr. Penn had the leaf in his pocket at the trial, but did not produce it; yet he and his wife were by the defence regarded as hostile witnesses, and treated as such.

Introduction.

prevented any feature of his personal peculiarities of handwriting being apparent in signatures so reproduced.

This opinion, embodied by Mr. Gurrin in a report,[5] was substantiated by him in the witness-box, and corroborated by Mr. Smith. No expert evidence was led for the defence to controvert their testimony; and the trenchant cross-examination by Mr. Macgregor Mitchell, who handled this branch of the case with singular skill, while it now and then drew blood, failed to disarm his adversaries. The best that the defence could make of a bad job was to put the questioned cheques to the identifying tellers who had cashed them, and ask whether even now they saw anything wrong with the signatures or would hesitate to accept them as genuine; to which, having already passed them as such, the answer of these officials was, naturally enough, in the negative.

II.

The first we hear of the accused in relation to his mother's banking affairs is from Inspector Fleming, who made on Tuesday, 30th March, his famous investigation at the flat. The reader may remember that officer's previous visit to Buckingham Terrace on the very morning of the tragedy, when he had noticed—as even a detective could hardly have failed to do—two opened letters, displayed upon the desk of the bureau, which on perusal satisfied him that this was indeed a simple case of suicide. Here are the letters :—

(1)

The Clydesdale Bank, Limited,
George Street,
Edinburgh, 13th March, 1926.

Mrs. Bertha Merrett,
31 Buckingham Terrace.

Dear Madam,
    We beg to advise you that we have to-day paid a cheque on your account which makes the balance £22. Might we suggest the advisability of drawing on your Boscombe account a sum sufficient to put your account here in order.

Yours faithfully,

R. J. L. HENDRY,
Manager.

---

[5] Appendix IV.

John Donald Merrett.

The Clydesdale Bank, Limited,
George Street,
Edinburgh, 16th March, 1926.

Mrs. Bertha Merrett,
    31 Buckingham Terrace.

Dear Madam,

    We think it well to advise that cheques have been paid by us on your account which make it overdrawn to the extent of £6 11s. 3d.

Yours faithfully,

R. J. L. HENDRY,
Manager.[6]

The respective dates of these letters should be noted. On 30th March Fleming took possession of them—they had escaped the fate of the unfinished one to Mrs. Anderson, presumably because they were free from bloodstains. These two letters the accused now identified as having been *both* received on the morning of the 17th. In the course of his search Fleming found in a drawer in the accused's bedroom (1) a Midland Bank cheque book, from which five cheques with the corresponding counterfoils were missing; (2) an envelope, addressed to Mrs. Merrett at 35 Palmerston Place, containing her Midland bank book, with a letter from the bank enclosing same, dated 5th March, 1926, of which we shall hear again; and (3) a note book, marked " Accounts, J. D. Merrett."[7] He also found on the desk of the bureau Mrs. Merrett's private account book, and in one of the pigeon holes the counterfoils of another (Clydesdale) cheque book. The accused said he knew nothing about the missing cheques and counterfoils, neither could he tell where was his mother's Clydesdale bank book.[8] Fleming asked him to look for the five missing Midland cheques, which he promised to do. He was so far successful that on Fleming's next visit to the flat he produced from the dressing-table drawer in his mother's bedroom two blank cheques. What had become of the other three he said he did not know.

    Shortly after Mrs. Merrett's death Fleming communicated with the Hampshire police, and recovered from the Midland Bank

---

[6] Productions Nos. 15 and 16 of Crown list.

[7] This is the book before referred to, kept by the accused for his mother's satisfaction, which, regarded as a record of his expenditure, is scantly satisfactory. While disclosing such minor weekly outlays as " Collection, 6d." it makes no mention of his more formidable secular disbursements.

[8] It was discovered later in the basement of the Dunedin Palais de Danse, as aftermentioned.

Introduction.

at Boscombe a number of that lady's cheques, among which were the three missing ones. Each was payable to J. D. Merrett, bore to be signed " Bertha Merrett," and was filled in and endorsed by the accused himself. The dates and amounts were as follows :— 24th March, 1926, £30; 26th March, £30; and 27th March, £28 9s. 6d. It will be recalled that these dates fall within the second week of Mrs. Merrett's confinement to the Infirmary, during the greater part of which she was unconscious. Now, as the accused had told Fleming on 30th March that he knew nothing whatever about these cheques, the inspector naturally called upon him to explain. He then stated that his mother had signed the cheques and left them blank—with her " a customary thing," though she had omitted to sign the two found in her bedroom—and that he had appropriated the proceeds to the purchase of a motor cycle.

This explanation, in view of Mrs. Merrett's known business-like habits, does not seem to have commended itself to the authorities, for on 3rd June we find the accused at the Central Police Office, writing, by request, the name " Bertha Merrett " six times upon a piece of paper—four times in his natural hand and twice in emulation of the signature on one of the Midland cheques— whether genuine or not does not appear.

I have been thus particular to give an account of this incident as affording an example of the accused's double dealing, because I do not propose to follow in detail the intricacies of his felonious operations with bank books, cheque books, and pay-in slips, as instructed by production of the documents and by the testimony of bank officials, all which are fully set forth, and may profitably be studied in the evidence adduced at the trial. It is sufficient here to indicate generally the progress of his nefarious course. But for the guidance of the reader about to thread the labyrinth of the Crown proof certain clues may be afforded.

Of the Clydesdale cheque books, each of which contained 12 cheques, there were issued, during the three months in question, four—(1) On 12th January, 1926; three cheques from which were forged, and the rest used by Mrs. Merrett. (2) On 11th February; three forged, the others used by her. The counterfoils of this book were found in the bureau by Fleming on 30th March. It was finished on 13th March and a new one—(4)—obtained. (3) On 22nd February; six forged, none used by Mrs. Merrett, who, as appears, never saw it. (4) On 13th March; unused and not recovered. At the date of the tragedy, 17th March, the whole of the forged Clydesdale cheques, 12 in number, had been presented and cashed. They were all drawn between 2nd February and 11th March, and amounted to £87 4s. 6d.

Of the Midland Bank cheque books, each containing 30 cheques, there were issued two—(1) On 24th December, 1925; from which the last cheque drawn by Mrs. Merrett was on 4th March. This is the cheque book believed by her to have been lost in the removal to Buckingham Terrace. On 12th March she wrote to the bank for a new one, as the old " was destroyed by accident "— though as a matter of fact the accused used six forged cheques from it after that date. (2) On 15th March; from which none was used by Mrs. Merrett, and the last forged cheques were used by the accused. Thus, as at 17th March, 11 forged Midland cheques had been presented and cashed, all drawn between 8th February and that date, and amounting to £117 18s. 6d., making the total spoil secured by the accused in less than six weeks £205 3s.[9] The balance of the sum in the second charge is made up by his drawings between 17th March, when his mother was taken to the Infirmary, and 27th March, after which date his operations were suspended by the inquisitiveness of Fleming on the 30th.

The history of the two bank books is less involved and more interesting. (1) The Clydesdale pass book, made up to 13th March, was certainly in the accused's possession on Tuesday, the 16th, when he squared the £22 overdraft by a forged Midland cheque for £30, paying £25 into the account and taking £5 in cash. We hear no more of it until, on some later and unascertained date, it was found on the stairs leading to the boiler-room at the Dunedin Palais by a lad employed in that place of amusement; it was by him handed to the cashier, who, seeing Mrs. Merrett's name on it and knowing that Merrett had left the flat, put it aside for him should he call for it. Upon learning of his arrest, the cashier gave the book to the manager, who delivered it to the police.

(2) On 21st February Mrs. Merrett sent to Boscombe her Midland pass book, asking the bank to keep it for her. On 4th March she wrote requesting its return, made up, as she wished to know how she stood. It was posted to her at Palmerston Place from Boscombe on the 5th. Yet on the 12th she wrote to the bank from

---

[9] The accused's system was to pay into the Clydesdale account from time to time part of the proceeds of the forged Midland cheques, and to take the balance in cash.

Introduction.

Buckingham Terrace that she had not received it. To this letter was appended in the handwriting of the accused a postscript: "My pass book has just arrived from my old address, where they have had it some few days. It is quite in order." Now, had Mrs. Merrett seen that book, made up to date, she would have found that, so far from being "quite in order," it disclosed a startling diminution of her credit balance—no less than £88 15s.—as brought out in her private account book. But that pass book, with the bank's covering letter and envelope, was found by Fleming on 30th March in a drawer in the accused's bedroom. When they left Palmerston Place on 10th March Mrs. Merrett told the landlady that "Donald would call for letters." It would seem that he had done so.

After the removal of his mother on 17th March the accused drew steadily upon the Midland account to the maximum amount allowed—£30 a time, with one £28 9s. 6d. to give variety to the performance; and when on the 30th, alarmed by the domiciliary visit of the inspector, his operations ceased, he had reduced the credit balance on Mrs. Merrett's principal account—her sole source of revenue—to £4 3s. 4d.[1] Despite Fleming's infelicitous interference, he had not done so badly after all.

With reference to the apparent negligence of the bank officials in dealing with these cheques, it must be borne in mind how immense was the advantage derived by the perpetrator of the fraud from his relationship to its victim. He was introduced at the bank by his mother; and the mere fact of being her son was enough to disarm suspicion. Further, the forgeries were cunningly contrived and executed, and the signatures, seen singly, not compared in bulk, might well impose upon the unwary. Still, one wonders why, during that fortnight that their client lay dying in the Infirmary, the bank saw nothing strange in the extent and persistency of these drawings on her account. And it was for the Clydesdale Bank a happy chance that the Public Trustee could not sue them for restitution of funds paid wrongously on the forged signature of the drawer, their customer, to the very person in whom on the owner's death the stolen moneys vested. Mrs. Merrett, had she survived, could have compelled the bank to restore to her account the sums charged thereto as against the forged cheques. But this was not the only matter in which the accused's filiation stood him in good stead.

---

[1] Report by J. M. Geoghegan, C.A.—Appendix V.

John Donald Merrett.

III.

The first charge, which the Lord Justice-Clerk blamed as " belated " and Mr. Aitchison stigmatised as " stale," has now to be considered. (We shall have to revert once and again to the second charge, with which it is indissolubly linked.) And, indeed, it is obvious that the charge of murder was an " after-thought," although, as his lordship pointed out to the jury, it might none the less be a correct one. But there is no doubt that, had the accused's banking exercises remained undetected, he would never have been charged with murder. Whether or not the defence was prejudiced by the delay, there is, I submit, no question that the Crown case suffered. Had the suspicions which finally materialised in this prosecution been earlier aroused and acted upon, things might have worn a different aspect. As it was, during the ten months which elapsed between the tragedy and the trial, much more than time was lost. The memories of witnesses were dimmed, material facts forgotten, important circumstances obscured; and, as was justly observed by the learned judge, there resulted in vital matters relating to the issue a lack of precision highly unsatis-factory—his lordship had almost said deplorable. This defect is chiefly marked in that part of the case where one should con-fidently have expected the greatest accuracy : the evidence of the police. Two intelligent schoolboys, visiting the *locus* that morn-ing, could better have observed and reported what they saw and did than the officers responsible for that duty.

Mrs. Sutherland was, in a double sense, the prosecutor's first witness. To her alone, of the three persons present at the time, could no motive to conceal the truth be imputed. Yet, having told the two constables that she was in the kitchen and saw nothing, within an hour she tells Fleming that she ran out and saw her mistress falling with the weapon. Nay, more; the defence called a medical man, Dr. Rosa, whom she consulted on the evening of the same day, and to whom she then said that her mistress had shot herself as she (Sutherland) was leaving the sitting-room, and that, turning round, she saw her fall.[2] Finally, at the trial, she swore to the truth of her first version, from which not all Mr. Aitchison's ingenuity could persuade her to depart. These con-

---

[2] When Dr. Rosa read in the newspapers of the accused's arrest he recalled this statement, which he thought it his duty to communicate to the defence, after being legally advised that to do so was not in breach of professional etiquette.

Introduction.

flicting accounts were by the witness explained as due to confusion following upon the shock of the tragedy. Another explanation, which will occur to those familiar with the type of witness to which the maid belonged, is a desire to be in the limelight. Or, if I may borrow a scientific term from Dr. Robertson, the eminent professor of psychiatry, called for the defence, it may be that Mrs. Sutherland, like Mrs. Merrett, was suffering, after the event, from "altered consciousness." But there is one witness who, although not called, corroborates her original tale—the prisoner at the bar. On the day of the occurrence, as I have mentioned, he stated, severally to the girl Christie and to his friend Scott, that after his mother had shot herself he went to the kitchen and told the maid; wherefore Mrs. Sutherland is not, upon this point, without support, and that from the person best qualified to give it.[3] And in this connection it may here be noted—though it properly belongs to another branch of the case, to which I shall later refer—that the accused also corroborates in a very remarkable manner his mother's statement as to the last words uttered by her before the shot: "Go away, Donald, and don't annoy me." So, to that extent at least, on the testimony of the accused himself, Mrs. Merrett's consciousness is proved to have been unaltered. The accused further corroborates the maid as to the position of the pistol on the top of the bureau, after the event and before the coming of the constables, thus superseding the hazy recollections of those inadvertent officers.

So far as the evidence goes, the accused made no secret of his possession of the pistol. He bought it from Hardy Brothers, 101 Princes Street, on 13th February, 1926, having obtained from the police the requisite certificate, and paid £1 17s. 6d. for the weapon and 7s. 6d. for 50 rounds of ammunition. Both the girl Christie and his friend Scott knew that he had a pistol, but Mrs. Sutherland did not know and never saw it till after the event; as to his mother's knowledge we have only his own word.

With respect to his other sporting purchases, we learn that on Saturday, 6th March, the accused bought from a motor cycle agent in Greenside Place a second-hand A.J.S. motor cycle for £28, and, depositing a forged cheque for £30 as security, took the

---

[3] The accused also varied his version; for in his statement to Fleming on 30th March he said that after the shot he "saw the maid in the hall." Here, as with Mrs. Sutherland, the defence preferred the old proverb regarding second thoughts.

John Donald Merrett.

machine away. On Monday, the 8th, he uplifted the cheque, cashed it, and paid for the cycle. There is no evidence that Mrs. Merrett was aware of this transaction. On Monday, 22nd March, the accused ordered from Rossleigh, Limited, Shandwick Place, an H.R.D. motor racing cycle with sidecar, the price of which, with accessories, was £139. He was allowed £30 for his old A.J.S., so that the net price of the new combination was £109. The following payments to account were made by him in cash :— 23rd March, £20; 24th, £15; 26th, £20; and 27th, £15: £70 in all. After that date, as we have seen, he was prevented by circumstances from concluding the purchase. Of all this, of course, Mrs. Merrett on her deathbed knew nothing. During his visit to London, as before narrated, the accused telegraphed twice to Rossleigh to send on the cycle at once, which they prudently declined to do until the balance of the price was paid. Had the company proved more confiding, the accused and his friend might have accomplished their return journey in greater comfort.

There are many other matters spoken to by divers witnesses which it were tedious to discuss; they are fully set forth in the report of the trial, and I have given in the present narration only such facts as seemed to me most material to the issue.

IV.

The crux of the case, as I see it, is the medical evidence; for had that been clear and convincing as against murder, there would be an end of the matter : no circumstances however suspicious, no motive however pregnant, no doubts however "reasonable," could affect the question. That evidence may for our present purpose be considered in two classes—practical and theoretical. By the first I mean that of the doctors and nurses who saw and treated Mrs. Merrett's injury, attended her throughout her illness, and formed at first-hand their impressions of her mental state; together with the appearances observed by Professor Littlejohn upon the post-mortem examination, and the conclusions at which he then arrived. By the second, the professor's reconsidered judgment, formed after certain experiments, and the opinion of Professor Glaister for the Crown; and the inferences deduced from the facts of the case by Sir Bernard Spilsbury and by Professor Robertson for the defence. There are also the shoot-

Introduction.

ing experts called by each side, **Mr.** Macnaughton and **Mr.** Churchill.

On the reception of Mrs. Merrett as " a police case " in the out-patient department of the Royal Infirmary her injury was examined by Dr. Bell, to see whether there was any blackening or tattooing round the wound; he found none, nor any sign or smell of singeing.[4] In cross-examination, he admitted that there was a good deal of blood about the ear, but said he had satisfied himself as to the absence of blackening, &c. The patient was sent to the surgical theatre, where her wound was dressed by Dr. Holcombe. It was a very small wound, the size of a slate pencil. There was little destruction of the tissues, but slight reddish discoloration round the edge. He observed no blackening or tattooing. In cross-examination, he said that the external wounds were in the antehelix (inner ridge of the ear) and in the concha (the cavity above it); both were covered with blood, which he washed off with a swab, applying a good deal of pressure. In looking for blackening he did not use a hand lens. Nurse Innes said she dressed the patient's wound that evening in ward 3. The edges were red, but there were no signs of blackening.

The admission in evidence of the statements made by Mrs. Merrett to or in the presence of the nurses and the doctor, which I have already recounted, was strenuously opposed by **Mr.** Aitchison, who argued that they were incompetent on three grounds : as not forming part of the *res gestæ*; as not having been made in the accused's presence; and as not having been made before a magistrate by way of dying deposition. After discussion, the Court repelled the objections and admitted the statements. The cross-examination by Mr. Aitchison was directed to show that these Infirmary witnesses had made at the time no notes of the statements, which they were now repeating from recollection only, ten months after the event. While counsel successfully brought out certain inevitable variations in the actual words reported, these did not, if I may venture to express an opinion, abate the force, effect, and general tenor of Mrs. Merrett's averments, as sworn to by the witnesses in Court.

Regarding the mental condition of the patient when she so spoke, Dr. Holcombe said that she was in full possession of her

---

[4] The presence or absence of blackening or tattooing by particles of powder had a very important bearing upon the issue, the significance of which will presently appear.

faculties and mentally normal until the night of Thursday, 25th March. Sister Grant said that from the time she regained consciousness until the Thursday night Mrs. Merrett's conversation was quite rational. She was very clear and decided about what had happened up to the moment when she lost consciousness on the morning of 17th March. Nurse Innes corroborated. Mr. Aitchison could not, in this connection, make much of Mrs. Hill, Mrs. Merrett's old friend who came from Brighton to see her on Friday, 19th March. This lady was an admirable witness : clear, collected, and capable in expression. I have described what passed between her and Mrs. Merrett six days before the symptoms of mental disturbance developed, and the latter's emphatic denial that she either saw or handled any pistol. Counsel did better with Mrs. Penn, a witness of more emotional type, rendered doubly sensitive by relationship to the sister in her grave and to the nephew in the dock. Swearing as she did to Mrs. Merrett's arresting phrase : '' As if Donald had shot me,'' it was very necessary for the defence that she should be discredited. But to the objection that she took at the time no written note of the conversation and was speaking merely from memory, she made the cogent rejoinder : '' Her words were burnt into my mind.'' And although treated by counsel as a hostile witness, whose interest it was to have her nephew hanged in order that her own son should supplant him in the heritage of their common grandfather, she displayed in the box no animus whatsoever against the accused, and, indeed, as one happens to know, refrained from stating matters to his prejudice within her knowledge.[5] I confess to sympathy with Mrs. Penn in her painful position, to which I am glad the learned judge did justice in his charge. The conversation of Mrs. Merrett on general topics, as reported by these two ladies, so rational, connected, and particular, should, one imagines, convince any one except an expert that in describing what had happened to her she knew quite well what she was saying. We shall hear, however, the scientific view.

The comic relief which never fails to lighten the darkness of the most grave proceedings was here supplied by the appearance in the witness-box of Mr. Walter Penn. This gentleman was very

---

[5] According to my information Mrs. Penn, after the sentence had been pronounced, asked to see the convict in the cell beneath the dock, but was not allowed to do so. Her message to him was, that when he came out of prison, he would find " a kind auntie " ready to receive him——"He was Bertha's boy.''

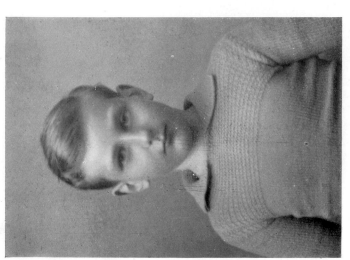

John Donald Merrett as a Small Boy.

Introduction.

deaf, and had to be questioned through an ear-phone. As a witness he was further handicapped by an irritable temper, which brought him into conflict with counsel and even with the Court. In describing to the Lord Advocate the scene in Sister Grant's room at the Infirmary, he mentioned an incident not spoken to by his wife. They had just learned from the doctor that Mrs. Merrett's case was hopeless; Mrs. Penn was greatly upset, and, looking across at her nephew, who was with them in the room, she said: " Donald, didn't you do it? " To which the accused replied: " No, Auntie, I did not do it, but if you like I will confess." In cross-examination, Mr. Penn admitted that on the occasion in question he was not, in journalistic phrase, availing himself of his auditory aids; whereupon Mr. Aitchison asked him to discard his ear-phone, and then, stepping back to the rail of the dock, dramatically repeated the words, " I will confess, if you like," three times, at varying distances from the witness-box. Only when counsel and witness were close together as before could the latter hear what was said to him. The inference was plain; and the Lord Advocate, in his address to the jury, did not found upon the alleged admission.

Retracing our steps from this digression, we now approach with delicate tread the threshold of the temple of science; and if we make bold to retain our shoes, it is from no lack of reverence, but because of the hardness of the footing. The defence called Professor George Robertson, Scotland's leading alienist, who, though he had not seen the post-mortem report, had read about the case in the newspapers, had studied the official temperature chart relating to it, and was familiar with the medical facts. He was taken in detail by Mr. Aitchison through the entire history of the illness, and gave his opinion as to the significance of the several symptoms described. In the early stage the patient was suffering from the effects of shock; after that passed off she was suffering from the effects of an inflammation surrounding the brain. The chart showed that the patient received on the first day an injection of one-sixth of a grain of morphia; on the second day, two of a quarter of a grain each : very full doses. Except in cases of persons treated for the morphia habit, witness had not ordered a quarter of a grain in one dose during the last twenty years. Full doses were given daily throughout the illness. From his experience of persons during the war rendered unconscious from explosions of various kinds, he found that such

D

33

John Donald Merrett.

injuries produced certain mental changes, which resulted in what is termed altered consciousness or dissociation. In Mrs. Merrett's case, when she regained consciousness on the afternoon of 17th March, all the conditions which usually accompany altered consciousness were present. The changes so induced might not be apparent to an ordinary observer, or even to an expert observer who had not previously known the patient.[6] There might be complete appearance of perfect normality, yet afterwards the patient would suddenly come to himself and would have no recollection of what had happened in the interval. The professor then gave as illustrations two cases in point : the one, relating to a patient who hanged himself with the cord of his own dressing-gown, was timeously cut down by his wife, and on recovery had no recollection of having attempted suicide; the other, that of a motor cyclist, rendered unconscious by collision with another motor cycle; a doctor, arriving in a motor car, attended him, and on his return home he said that the doctor had caused the accident. Only the coming forward of the cyclist responsible saved the good Samaritan from an action of damages. In view of Mrs. Merrett's condition the professor considered that any statements made by her should be received with the very greatest hesitation.

Cross-examined by the Lord Advocate, it appeared from the temperature chart that the doses of morphia were given very early in the morning or at night. It did not necessarily follow that a person suffering from hemiplegia was mentally affected. While Mrs. Merrett's condition was consistent with altered consciousness, witness did not profess to say whether it was in fact so or not. As regards the illustrations, the gentleman with the dressing-gown had been suffering from depression, and was not in perfect mental health at the time. As to the mistaken motor cyclist, the accident might have occurred at a corner or on a dark night and the man have no opportunity to see what struck him. Witness admitted that if material corroboration of what Mrs. Merrett had said were forthcoming, it was of value as evidence.

Re-examined, he knew from his experience that in the case of head injuries recollection does not, as a rule, come up to the period of the accident.

---

[6] This, surely, would not apply in the case of a sister and an intimate friend of the patient. Yet neither Mrs. Penn nor Mrs. Hill saw any difference from Mrs. Merrett's customary manner, and thought her in full possession of her faculties.

Introduction.

By the Court, his suggestion was that the interval of time that elapsed between when Mrs. Merrett found her son beside her and when the explosion took place was very much longer than was suspected, because the sense of time is one of those mental conditions which is most apt to be disturbed in unconscious cases.[7] On the facts before him witness was unable either to affirm or to deny that Mrs. Merrett was in a state of altered consciousness; and his evidence came to this, that it was necessary to proceed with caution in accepting statements made by her in such conditions.

V.

When Mrs. Merrett died a prisoner in the Infirmary under the shadow of a charge of attempted suicide, upon the signed information of her own son and servant, it fell to Professor Harvey Littlejohn, as surgeon of police, to perform the customary autopsy. The result of his examination, as already mentioned, was embodied in a report to the Procurator-Fiscal, dated 5th April, 1926.[8]

Called for the Crown, Professor Littlejohn read that report, and also a second report by him, dated 13th January, 1927 :—

The post-mortem examination made by me on the body of Mrs. Bertha Merrett showed that the bullet had entered the skull through the right ear in a direction from behind forwards at an angle of approximately 120 deg. to a line drawn longitudinally through the middle of the skull. The deceased having survived for fourteen days after the injury, there were no indications at the post-mortem examination of the distance at which the weapon had been discharged, such as injury to the surrounding skin from the action of flame of the discharge or of particles of unconsumed powder driven into the skin, appearances which are present if the discharge has taken place close to the skin, that is to say, within 3 inches. On this point I made careful inquiry from Dr. Holcombe, the house surgeon who examined her and dressed the wound on her arrival at the Infirmary, and he stated that there was only a redness around the wound and no indication of blackening or tattooing by ingrained particles of powder.[9]

---

[7] It does not appear whether Professor Robertson had in view the fact that Mrs. Merrett's recollection of her last words before the shot, " Go away, Donald, and don't annoy me," is corroborated *verbatim* by the accused, who said that he then crossed the room and immediately thereafter heard the sound of the discharge. How far this would have affected the professor's theory we have no means of judging; but, to the lay mind at least, the point seems to be, in this connection, important.

[8] Appendix I.

[9] Appendix II.

John Donald Merrett.

As regards the track of the bullet, witness stated that it proceeded in a direct line from the wound to where it was found. The brain was uninjured, and he saw no reason why Mrs. Merrett's mental condition should have been affected before symptoms of meningitis developed on the night of Thursday, 25th March. He had made certain shooting experiments since in connection with the case. The first were in August; the next in December, 1926, along with Professor Glaister; further experiments were made on 30th January, 1927, in presence of the defence experts, Sir Bernard Spilsbury and Mr. Churchill. These experiments were made with the actual weapon, with cartridges obtained from Hardy Brothers, and with those found in the accused's drawer; all the results obtained were precisely similar. The pull required to discharge the trigger of the pistol was about 6 lbs. Witness identified the pieces of white cardboard produced as those at which he had fired, as described in his report. The results may be briefly stated :—

At $\frac{1}{2}$ an inch—intense blackening around the bullet entrance measuring $1\frac{1}{4}$ inches in diameter; outside this, an area $2\frac{1}{3}$ inches in diameter of darkening by smoke, and a large number of particles of powder embedded in the cardboard.

At 1 inch—a ring of intense blackening and diffuse blackening 2 inches in diameter, tattooing 1 inch.

At 2 inches—diffuse blackening 3 inches in diameter and tattooing $\frac{3}{4}$ of an inch.

At 3 inches—ring of blackening $\frac{2}{3}$ of an inch in diameter and tattooing $\frac{1}{4}$ of an inch.

At 6 inches—a few particles of ingrained powder.

At 9 inches—showed nothing except the hole produced by the bullet.

From these facts, therefore, the professor inferred that the discharge was not a near one, i.e., within 3 inches of the head; that both suicide and accident were in the highest degree improbable; and that " the direction of the bullet wound, the position of the wound, the distance at which the discharge took place, all point to the weapon having been fired by another party." The results detailed in his report corresponded very closely with those obtained by the defence experts upon their experiments in Edinburgh with the actual weapon and cartridges, and differed from those of experiments made by them in London with similar ammunition. There was then less blackening and more yellowness, due to the different powder used. Suicide by shooting was uncommon in women. In this case, to produce the wound, " the arm has

36

Introduction.

to be put behind, bent at the elbow on itself, and held in a strained position." To do so by accident Mrs. Merrett must be supposed to take the pistol out of the bureau drawer with the butt in her palm, must turn her hand so that the muzzle points towards herself, must put her thumb or finger on the trigger, and give it a pull of not less than 5 lbs. If the safety catch were on, that also must be accidentally released. With regard to the removal of blackening or tattooing by washing or rubbing, witness tried by means of a sponge to do so on that produced at 1-inch range. Some of the surrounding blackening became less, but the central zone, always the darkest part, was quite unaffected, as appeared from the productions. Together with Professor Glaister he also experimented on a piece of human skin, shot at 3-inch range. The result was the same : the main evidence of blackness remained. Deep blackening, which immediately surrounds where the bullet enters, consists of unconsumed particles of powder driven into the skin, and cannot be washed away. Beyond this, the varying zone of blackening due to smoke is not difficult to remove by washing. In his opinion blackening, if existing, must have been observable by Dr. Holcombe and Dr. Bell on 17th March.

Professor Littlejohn was cross-examined at great length and with commensurate ability by Mr. Aitchison, and the issue of the encounter is of much interest to medical jurists. I do not propose here to follow minutely the fortunes of that forensic duel, which to be profitable should be studied in detail. Witness said that to his mind suicide was inconceivable from the facts now known to him. He agreed that if there were a doubt as to whether the weapon was discharged within a range of 3 inches, neither suicide nor accident could be excluded. His conclusions were based on (1) the unusual site and direction of the wound, (2) the absence of blackening around the wound, and (3) the evidence of the discharge being at a distance of over 3 inches. If the weapon were pointed at right angles to the head, and the head were instinctively averted at the moment of discharge, it would account for a greater angle to the longitudinal line. Women had considerable range of movement in the shoulder joint, owing to the old-time practice of putting up their hair. Counsel having read to witness several passages from recognised textbooks relating to the effects of shot wounds, with some of which he concurred and with others disagreed, witness was shown a piece of skin, fired at by Sir Bernard Spilsbury at a range of 1 inch, upon which blackness was

John Donald Merrett.

seen only on one side of the wound, the rest having been removed by a single movement of a wet cloth. Witness pointed out that this experiment was made in London with other ammunition; he had a specimen done in Edinburgh with the actual cartridges, giving a totally different result.[1] Professor Glaister and witness tried it, and could not remove by washing the blackness caused by the cartridges used in this case. If the discharge was within 2 inches of this lady's head, it was impossible by using a swab to have got rid of all the blackening. The site of wound, though not in suicide impossible, was extremely rare; suicides usually aim at the temple. Witness agreed, as regards counsel's theory of accident, that it was conceivable, but most unlikely. He refused assent to the inference that there must have been in this case intellectual disturbance; this was negatived by the deceased's conversation with Mrs. Hill. Death was due to septic poisoning: infection of the brain by an organism, entering through the course of the bullet wound. As to " altered consciousness," witness knew by experience cases of severe head injury in which the person remembered everything up to the time when the injury was received. There was no doubt that reliance could be placed on statements made by a person within twenty-four hours of an acute delirium, unless the doctors and nurses in attendance observed a marked change in the patient's mental condition.

Re-examined by the Lord Advocate, his opinion was strengthened by the fact that this lady had made similar statements on previous occasions. It was essential that all experiments be made with the actual weapon and powder in question. By the Court, the reason of his changed conclusion, as expressed in his second report, was the absence of blackening, in view of his experiments. Though these began in August, 1926, he was not asked by the Crown to make a formal report until January, 1927.

Professor Glaister, examined by the Lord Advocate, said that, on the instructions of the Crown, he had prepared a report, which he then read. The conclusions at which he arrived, as therein stated, were as follows:—

Taking all the facts of the wounding in this case, while I am unable to exclude absolutely the possibility of the production of such a wound as in this case by self-infliction, the improbabilities so outweigh in my mind the

---

[1] Why this specimen was not included in the Crown list of productions is one of the many mysteries which attend the conduct of the prosecution.

Introduction.

possibilities that I have come to the conclusion that the head-injury which caused the death of Mrs. Merrett was not self-inflicted.[2]

Witness identified the results of the several experiments made by him in conjunction with Professor Littlejohn, as before described. With regard to the blackening on the piece of skin, good hard rubbing with a sponge failed to remove it wholly. If blackening had existed, the dressing of the wound by Dr. Holcombe could not entirely have taken it away. Cross-examined by Mr. Aitchison, he relied not only upon the absence of blackening, but upon the direction of the wound. He considered the wound " barely possibly " consistent with suicide. The whole facts of the case were, witness admitted, problematical. The skin used for experiment was that of a newly amputated limb. Some of the blackening was removable, but enough remained for any one to see it had been there. The skin had been kept in water since 8th December, and the blackening was still as fresh as at the moment of production.[3] If blackening had been present originally it could not have been completely removed by the swab. It would make little difference if blood were congealed on the blackening. Re-examined, if the Infirmary doctors said that there were patches of the edge of the wound free from blood on which they saw no blackening, that would confirm his opinion.

Both sides boasted an expert in shooting. For the Crown, Mr. Macnaughton, of Edinburgh, said he had examined the pistol and cartridges in the case. He made no tests. Such a weapon was useful only for self-defence; it was no use for rabbit shooting, &c., nor for target practice, on account of the shortness of the barrel and the difficulty of taking a steady aim. In cross-examination, the explosive was a modified type of cordite called smokeless powder, which caused less discoloration than gunpowder. For the defence, Mr. Churchill, of London, examined by Mr. Aitchison, said he had conducted with Sir Bernard Spilsbury there and in Edinburgh the experiments already mentioned. The Edinburgh ammunition produced the greater degree of blackening; but with such flake powder it was purely superficial and easily removed. In the conditions of the wound in this case—bleeding, washing, &c.—it would be impossible to determine any blackness. Both

---

[2] Appendix III.

[3] I recently examined, in the laboratory of my late friend, Professor Littlejohn, the specimen in question. Though it has now been for well-nigh two years soaked in water, the blackening is as plain as ever.

suicide and accident were possible. He had experience of a case where a woman shot herself behind the right ear. He knew as a shooting instructor that women instinctively flinch at first from a discharge. Supposing the weapon pointed at the temple, an instinctive movement of the head would produce this wound exactly, without any straining of the arm. Assuming that Mrs. Merrett took up the pistol from the bureau, holding it with her thumb on the trigger and her fingers at the butt, an accidental discharge could produce such a wound. Witness demonstrated how this might have occurred. It might also have happened if she overbalanced herself while the pistol was in her hand, and, raising the hand to protect her head as she fell, discharged the weapon. Cross-examined by the Lord Advocate, it was uncommon for a woman to commit suicide with a pistol, especially if unused to firearms. The case to which he had referred was that of a woman who shot herself, for no apparent motive, in presence of her sleeping husband. Witness was not aware that there were 20 inches between the pigeon holes and the edge of the writing-slab of the bureau. It would affect his theory if Mrs. Merrett's body, in falling, were stopped by the bureau. He agreed that the tests should be carried out with the actual weapon and powder. Re-examined, the London tests were done with similar ammunition: both made by the Nobel combine.

VI.

The defence reserved for the final round their heaviest weight. Fortunate, indeed, was the accused to secure the evidence of Sir Bernard Spilsbury. Had the trial taken place in England the services of that gentleman, as Honorary Pathologist to the Home Office, would have been reserved for the Crown—I believe this is the only case in which he has appeared for the defence; and for a pannel to be able to call an expert of his calibre—of European fame, of the highest eminence in his profession, and of such un-failing fairness—was an advantage as unusual as it was inestimable.

Examined by Mr. Aitchison, Sir Bernard said he had been present in Court and heard the evidence, excepting that of the scientific witnesses, and was otherwise acquainted with the medical facts of the case. The site of the wound was inconsistent neither with suicide nor accident. He had had a case of a man who shot

Introduction.

himself behind the right ear. With regard to direction, owing to the lightness of the weapon and the shortness of the barrel, the wound could readily be produced. Witness demonstrated the requisite position. The weapon could easily be so held 1 or 2 inches from the head; personally, he could hold it 3 or 4 inches away: it depended upon the range of movement of the shoulder joint, which in women was commonly considerable. If the weapon were held across and in front of the ear, an instinctive movement of the head might alter the angle by 30 degrees or even more. With the explosive used in this case it would be unsafe, in view of the other circumstances, to draw any sure conclusion as to distance. Witness then described in detail the experiments made by him in London and in Edinburgh. In the shorter ranges blackening on skin was less distinct than that on white cardboard. One-half of the blackening on the specimen fired at 1 inch was removed by wiping with damp cotton wool. If the skin were smooth there was less lodgment for particles of powder. That of the antehelix and concha, being smooth, blackening could the more easily be removed. The hæmorrhage must have flowed over all that part of the ear, from the position in which the lady lay and during her removal to the Infirmary. A hand lens, if used, might have detected blackening. The bleeding, in conjunction with the rubbing, might well have removed any that was there. The degree of blackening obtained in the Edinburgh tests was greater than in the London experiments; but as to the ease with which it could be removed there was no difference. Taking all the facts of this case, he found nothing to exclude either suicide or accident as a possible explanation. With regard to accident, it was often impossible to reconstruct the actual conditions. Witness was then taken through the history of Mrs. Merrett's illness. The inflammatory condition of the brain must have been developing from the first rise in temperature on 22nd March. Any statements made by the patient within twenty-four hours of delirium must be accepted with great caution, and the same applied generally to cases of severe head injury resulting in death.

Cross-examined by the Lord Advocate, Sir Bernard admitted that the side of the head was not one of the usual points selected by suicides. As a rule, they held the weapon against the spot. His Edinburgh experiments corresponded closely with those of Professor Littlejohn, and both differed from the London tests. His skin experiments were made with the London powder; Professor

John Donald Merrett.

Littlejohn's, with the Edinburgh powder. As regards their different results in trying to remove blackening, witness said much depended on the degree and extent of rubbing, as well as upon the condition of the skin. As to those parts of the ear which Dr. Bell said were free from blood, that might have been washed off in the course of the patient's removal. Witness was sure that in this case the muzzle of the pistol had not been pressed against the skin—it was certainly not a discharge in contact. Sir Bernard then demonstrated how he conceived the accident might have happened by Mrs. Merrett tilting her chair, losing her balance, and, with the pistol in her hand, jerking her elbow on the projecting edge of the bureau. " Q. Would that elbow not be too low for any such possibility?—A. No, I do not think so. If she had stretched over the bureau to get something out, the arm would presumably be over that part."[4]

By the Court, in his opinion all traces of blackening may be removed by wiping or rubbing, except such as could not be detected without minute examination. If none were present, one must conclude that the muzzle of the weapon was at least 3 inches from the head.

The case for the defence was here closed, and the Lord Advocate began his address to the jury. Before referring to the speeches of counsel and the charge of the learned judge, a word may be said as to the failure of the accused to avail himself of his statutory right to give evidence on oath in his own behalf. The law upon this matter stands thus : by the Criminal Evidence Act, 1898,[5] it is provided that " The failure of any person charged with an offence . . . to give evidence shall not be made the subject of any comment by the prosecution." But, although the prosecutor be thus debarred, the Court may, in its discretion, comment upon

---

[4] With reference to this theory it may be mentioned that the desk flap of the bureau, when open, is too high for writing upon with ease in an ordinary chair, hence Mrs. Merrett's use of the table for that purpose. From the plan showing measurements of furniture in 31 Buckingham Terrace (No. 5 of the defence productions) it appears (1) that the height of the desk flap from the floor was 2 feet 10¼ inches, (2) that the flap of the desk projected 1 foot 6¾ inches beyond the front of the bureau, and (3) that Mrs. Merrett's chair, measured from the floor to the top of the seat, was 1 foot 8 inches high. To any one sitting in a chair of that height, with the open bureau behind on the right, the difficulty of reaching up and over to the drawers or pigeon holes without coming in contact with, and being prevented by, the edge of the flap, unless Mrs. Merrett had an extraordinary reach of arm, would seem to be insuperable. Such, at least, is the result of my own extrajudicial experiments with the actual bureau.

[5] 61 & 62 Vict. c. 36, sec. 1 (b).

42

Introduction.

the fact. Here his lordship did not see fit to do so; but we, to whom the provisions of the Act do not apply, may well wonder at the pannel's silence. If ever there was a case which called for such enlightenment, as he alone could give, surely it is this. Of the members of that tangled trinity—three persons in one flat—present on the fateful morning, one was in her grave, and her account of what had happened was dismissed as due to "altered consciousness"; another told two disparate and discordant tales; yet the only one who really knew the truth elected to hold his peace. Mr. Aitchison, alive to the significance of this omission and its probable effect upon the jury, in the moving peroration of his address for the defence, took occasion to thank God that there were those who would go to their death with sealed lips rather than speak a single word that would reflect upon the sacred name of mother. Whether or not his client be included in the category of these martyrs to filial piety we cannot tell; but one should like to have heard from the witness-box the authentic version.

VII.

It would serve no purpose, and indeed might savour of presumption, to analyse in this place the addresses of counsel and the judge's charge. They are printed *verbatim*, revised by the respective speakers, in the following report of the trial, where every reader can appreciate them for himself. The Lord Advocate's speech for the prosecution was in accordance with the best traditions of the Crown Office, and as such received from the Court well-merited commendation. One has known regrettable instances of a Crown prosecutor pressing for a verdict on a criminal charge with an ardour and impetuosity more proper to be employed in civil pleadings. Here was nothing of such intemperate zeal; fairness, moderation, and, as the Lord Justice-Clerk observed, even generosity, were the " notes " of the Lord Advocate's address. And his lordship was no half-hearted prosecutor : the Crown case was presented with force and clearness, and its strength was in no degree lessened by the temperate tone adopted. Yet one could not but feel, on hearing the speech delivered—and the impression is confirmed by the printed page—that his lordship had been unconscionably, as the phrase goes, " let down " by those responsible for the earlier conduct of the investigation. His chief witness had told two stories, his chief medical expert had changed his mind,

43

John Donald Merrett.

and the official handling of the case by the police, from first to last, was lamentable. Despite these manifest disadvantages, however, his lordship's presentment of the Crown case carried conviction to the jury on the second charge, and induced upon the first but a modified acquittal.

Of the speech for the defence it is hard to write without hyperbole. Only those who have studied the evidence closely, and know the measure and substance of the case the accused's counsel had to meet, can appreciate the difficulties by which the defence was faced. Mr. Aitchison is recognised as an incomparable jury pleader; but I doubt whether his great abilities were ever so severely taxed as here. Yet, notwithstanding the perils and dangers by which he was beset, his address was a triumph of forensic oratory. Not a point was missed, everything favourable to the accused was displayed in the strongest light, the thinness of the ice in parts was deftly negotiated, and he was not more felicitous in what he actually said than in what, in his wisdom, he refrained from saying. The speech might serve as a model for young aspirants to the criminal bar; they could have no better example of how a ticklish case should be tackled. In one thing only is my admiration qualified: I am unable to approve counsel's attitude to Mrs. Penn. It may be that his treatment of that lady was called for by his client's interests; if so, I still think the necessity is to be deplored.

The charge of the Lord Justice-Clerk—logical, precise, and even-handed—it is not for me to appraise. Although eminently judicial, it made plain that his lordship drew a sharp distinction between the state of the proof upon the first and second charges. On that of uttering, the summing up left little room for doubt as to the accused's guilt; but with regard to the charge of murder, it was clear that in his lordship's judgment the Crown case had failed. The vacillations of Mrs. Sutherland seemed to him fatal to the success of the prosecution, and, in the matter of Mrs. Merrett's alleged statements, were the jury not being invited to draw an inference of guilt which the Crown authorities did not do at the time? Similarly, in view of the conflicting testimony of the respective experts as to the possibilities of accident or suicide in general, and the presence and removability of blackening in particular, how could the jury decide? Professor Littlejohn was asked, "If experts differ, what are we to do?" His reply was, "I do not know." Were they, the jury, any wiser? But,

44

Introduction.

although upon this particular ample justice was rendered by the judge to the defence, I submit, with great respect, that in other branches of the case his lordship was perhaps less lenient to the prosecution.

The jury retired at twenty-five minutes to five o'clock, and returned their verdict at 5.30. Their finding was as follows :—On the first charge, murder, by a majority, Not Proven; on the second charge, uttering, unanimously, Guilty. It is noteworthy that, despite the eloquence of Mr. Aitchison and the criticisms of the Court, no single member of this jury of fifteen saw his or her way to find the pannel Not Guilty.[6] Lord Kinross, in the absence of the Lord Advocate, formally moved for sentence; and the Lord Justice-Clerk, in respect of the accused's youth, restricted the sentence of the Court to one of twelve months' imprisonment. The Court then rose.

In view of the jury's finding, and of the recency of the events, it were impertinent to say more. One may perhaps be permitted to express an opinion that the pannel was not less fortunate in his prosecutor and his defender than in his judge and jury. But there is one question, touching the very marrow of the mystery, to which I should like to have had an answer : How did the accused propose to deal with the situation which his nefarious transactions had created? He had depleted his mother's bank accounts, dissipated her current income, despoiled her temporarily of livelihood. Detection, imminent and inevitable, confronted him. He could not have counted upon a timely accident, or foreseen her suicide on the discovery of his guilt. What was he going to do about it? How was the plot to end?

---

[6] The jury consisted of 6 women and 9 men. The vote, as I am informed, was 5 for Guilty and 10 for Not Proven. It is superfluous to add that the women were of the majority.

Leading Dates in the Merrett Trial.

1926.

January	4.	Mrs. Merrett and her son arrive in Edinburgh.
,,	25.	They remove to 35 Palmerston Place.
February	2.	Merrett cashes the first forged cheque.
,,	13.	Merrett buys the pistol.
March	6.	Merrett buys second-hand motor cycle.
,,	10.	Mrs. Merrett moves into the flat, 31 Buckingham Terrace.
,,	13.	Clydesdale Bank intimates overdraft of £22.
,,	16.	Clydesdale Bank intimates overdraft of £6 11s. 3d.
,,	17.	The Catastrophe ; Mrs. Merrett taken to the Royal Infirmary.
,,	18.	Mrs. Merrett makes to Sister Grant and Dr. Holcombe her first statement.
,,	19.	Mrs. Merrett's statement communicated by the Infirmary authorities to the police ; Mrs. Hill comes to Edinburgh ; statement by Mrs. Merrett to her.
,,	22.	Merrett orders new racing motor cycle from Rossleigh.
,,	24.	Mr. and Mrs. Penn arrive in Edinburgh ; statements by Mrs. Merrett to them.
,,	25.	Mrs. Merrett develops at night symptoms of delirium.
,,	27.	Mrs. Merrett becomes unconscious ; Merrett cashes the last forged cheque.
,,	30.	Inspector Fleming's investigation at the flat ; official statement taken by him from Merrett.
April	1.	Death of Mrs. Merrett ; post-mortem examination.
,,	5.	First medical report by Professor Littlejohn.
June	3.	Merrett copies by request at the Police Office his mother's signature.
August	6.	Professor Littlejohn carries out shooting experiments with the pistol and cartridges.
November	4.	Mr. Gurrin reports upon the forgeries.
,,	29.	Warrant granted for Merrett's arrest.
December	3.	Merrett brought to Edinburgh in custody.
,,	8.	Further shooting tests conducted by Professors Littlejohn and Glaister.
,,	9.	Merrett committed for trial.
,,	10.	Medical report by Professor Glaister.

1927.

January	13.	Second medical report by Professor Littlejohn.
,,	14.	Indictment served.
February	1.	First day of trial—evidence for prosecution.
,,	2.	Second day—evidence for prosecution continued.
,,	3.	Third day—evidence for prosecution continued.
,,	4.	Fourth day—evidence for prosecution continued.
,,	5.	Fifth day—evidence for prosecution concluded.
,,	7.	Sixth day—evidence for defence ; Lord Advocate's address to jury.
,,	8.	Seventh day—Lord Advocate's address to jury concluded ; Mr. Aitchison's address for defence ; Lord Justice-Clerk's charge ; verdict and sentence.

46

THE TRIAL.

TUESDAY, 1st FEBRUARY, 1927.

Judge Presiding—

THE LORD JUSTICE-CLERK (LORD ALNESS).

Counsel for the Crown—

The LORD ADVOCATE (The Rt. Hon. William Watson, K.C.).

The Rt. Hon. Lord KINROSS, Advocate-Depute.

Agent—

Sir JOHN PROSSER, W.S.

Counsel for the Pannel—

Mr. CRAIGIE M. AITCHISON, K.C.

Mr. R. MACGREGOR MITCHELL, K.C.

Mr. J. L. M. CLYDE, Advocate.

Agents—

Messrs. NORMAN MACPHERSON & DUNLOP, S.S.C.

John Donald Merrett at the time of the Trial.

First Day.

AT EDINBURGH, the first day of February, 1927.
Present—The Right Honourable the Lord Justice-Clerk.

INTRAN.   JOHN DONALD MERRETT, prisoner in the prison of Edinburgh, pannel.

INDICTED and ACCUSED at the instance of His Majesty's Advocate of the crimes of murder and uttering in manner mentioned in the libel raised thereanent.

The Indictment.

JOHN DONALD MERRETT, prisoner in the prison of Edinburgh, you are indicted at the instance of the Right Honourable WILLIAM WATSON, His Majesty's Advocate, and the charges against you are that (1) on 17th March, 1926, in the flat at 31 Buckingham Terrace, Edinburgh, then occupied by Bertha Merrett, your mother, you did shoot the said Bertha Merrett in the head with a loaded pistol, whereby she was so severely injured that she died on 1st April, 1926, in the Royal Infirmary, Edinburgh, and you did murder her; and (2) that on the dates mentioned in column I. of the schedule annexed hereto, in the office of the Clydesdale Bank, Limited, at 29 George Street, Edinburgh, you did utter as genuine the cheques specified in column II. of said schedule opposite said dates respectively, each of which said cheques was payable to J. D. Merrett, and on each of which the name of the said Bertha Merrett bore to be signed as drawer, such signatures being forged, by presenting said cheques for payment to the persons whose names are set forth in column III. of said schedule, opposite said dates and cheques respectively, said persons being tellers in the employment of said Clydesdale Bank, Limited, at 29 George Street aforesaid, and did thereby induce said persons to pay to you the sums of money in said cheques, amounting *in cumulo* to £457 13s. 6d., and said cheques are respectively Nos. 21 to 49 inclusive of the productions lodged herewith.

KINROSS, *A.D.*

E   49

John Donald Merrett.

SCHEDULE.

Column I.	Column II.	Column III.
2nd February, 1926	Cheque on the Clydesdale Bank, Limited, Edinburgh (George Street), dated 2nd Feb., 1926, for £7 7s.	Henry James Mercer Kerr.
3rd February, 1926	Do. do. 3rd Feb., do. £2 13s.	do.
5th February, 1926	Do. do. 5th Feb., do. £3 3s.	Hugh Sutherland Ritch.
13th February, 1926	Do. do. 13th Feb., do. £10	do.
17th February, 1926	Do. do. 17th Feb., do. £5	Henry James Mercer Kerr.
20th February, 1926	Do. do. 20th Feb., do. £10 10s.	Hugh Sutherland Ritch.
22nd February, 1926	Do. do. 22nd Feb., do. £5 8s.	do.
27th February, 1926	Do. do. 27th Feb., do. £4 2s. 6d.	do.
2nd March, 1926	Do. do. 2nd Mar., do. £8 6s.	Henry James Mercer Kerr.
5th March, 1926	Do. do. 4th Mar., do. £5	Hugh Sutherland Ritch.
6th March, 1926	Do. do. 6th Mar., do. £10	do.
11th March, 1926	Do. do. 11th Mar., do. £15 15s.	do.
8th February, 1926	Cheque on the Midland Bank, Limited (Boscombe), Bournemouth, dated 8th Feb., do. £15	Henry James Mercer Kerr.
9th February, 1926	Do. do. 9th Feb., do. £5	do.
11th February, 1926	Do. do. 11th Feb., do. £8	do.
15th February, 1926	Do. do. 15th Feb., do. £15	do.
18th February, 1926	Do. do. 18th Feb., do. £10	Hugh Sutherland Ritch.
24th February, 1926	Do. do. 24th Feb., do. £20	do.
3rd March, 1926	Do. do. 3rd Mar., do. £15 15s.	do.
8th March, 1926	Do. do. 8th Mar., do. £30	do.
13th March, 1926	Do. do. 13th Mar., do. £25 14s.	Cecil George Minto Harrower.
15th March, 1926	Do. do. 15th Mar., do. £22 10s. 6d.	Hugh Sutherland Ritch.
16th March, 1926	Do. do. 16th Mar., do. £30	do.
18th March, 1926	Do. do. 18th Mar., do. £30	do.
20th March, 1926	Do. do. 20th Mar., do. £25	do.
23rd March, 1926	Do. do. 23rd Mar., do. £30	do.
24th March, 1926	Do. do. 24th Mar., do. £30	do.
26th March, 1926	Do. do. 26th Mar., do. £30	do.
27th March, 1926	Do. do. 27th Mar., do. £28 9s. 6d.	do.

KINROSS, *A.D.*

List of Productions.

1. Medical report by Harvey Littlejohn, M.B., Professor of Forensic Medicine, The University, Edinburgh, dated 5th April, 1926.

1a. Medical report by said Harvey Littlejohn, dated 13th January, 1927.

2. Medical report by John Glaister, M.D., &c., Professor of Forensic Medicine, The University, Glasgow, dated 10th December, 1926.

3. Two prints of X-ray photographs marked A and B respectively.

4. Report, dated 4th November, 1926, by Gerald Francis Gurrin, F.R.M.S., Bath House, 57-60 Holborn Viaduct, London, E.C.1, with 3 tracings of signatures " Bertha Merrett," and 3 photographic enlargements of signatures " Bertha Merrett " appended thereto.

5. Book of photographs and documents prepared by said Gerald Francis Gurrin.

6. Photographic reproductions of 5 signatures " Bertha Merrett."

7. Report by John Michael Geoghegan, chartered accountant, 13 Albany Street, Edinburgh, dated 28th December, 1926.

8. Cheque book, Midland Bank, Limited, Boscombe, Bournemouth, containing blank cheques.

9/10. Two blank cheques, Midland Bank, Limited, Boscombe,
U/A7   U/A7
Bournemouth, Nos. 307/76544 and 307/76545.

11. Envelope addressed " Mrs. B. Merrett, at 35 Palmerston Place, Edinburgh, Scotland."

11a. Bank pass book, Mrs. Bertha Merrett in account with Midland Bank, Limited, formerly London Joint City and Midland Bank, Limited, Boscombe Branch.

11b. Letter, Midland Bank, Limited, Boscombe Branch, to Mrs. B. Merrett, dated 5th March, 1926.

12. Certified excerpt from bank account of Mrs. Bertha Merrett with Boscombe Branch, the Midland Bank, Limited.

13. Excerpt copy bank account of Mrs. Bertha Merrett with the Clydesdale Bank, Limited.

14. Bank pass book, the Clydesdale Bank, Limited, George Street, Edinburgh, in account with Mrs. Bertha Merrett.

15/16. Two letters, the Clydesdale Bank, Limited, George Street, Edinburgh, to Mrs. Bertha Merrett, dated respectively 13th and 16th March, 1926.

17. Cheque book, containing counterfoils 2331 to 2339 inclusive.

51

John Donald Merrett.

18. Pay-in slip of the Clydesdale Bank, Limited, George Street, Edinburgh, dated 12th January, 1926, on account of Bertha Merrett.

19. Pay-in slip of the Clydesdale Bank, Limited, George Street, Edinburgh, dated 26th January, 1926, on account of Bertha Merrett.

20. Sheet of paper, dated 3rd June, 1926, upon which the name of Bertha Merrett is written six times.

21/32. Twelve cheques on the Clydesdale Bank, Limited, George Street, Edinburgh, signed " Bertha Merrett," all payable to " J. D. Merrett."

    (21) Cheque, dated 2nd February, 1926, for £7 7s.
    (22) Cheque, dated 3rd February, 1926, for £2 13s.
    (23) Cheque, dated 5th February, 1926, for £3 3s.
    (24) Cheque, dated 13th February, 1926, for £10.
    (25) Cheque, dated 17th February, 1926, for £5.
    (26) Cheque, dated 20th February, 1926, for £10 10s.
    (27) Cheque, dated 22nd February, 1926, for £5 8s.
    (28) Cheque, dated 27th February, 1926, for £4 2s. 6d.
    (29) Cheque, dated 2nd March, 1926, for £8 6s.
    (30) Cheque, dated 4th March, 1926, for £5.
    (31) Cheque, dated 6th March, 1926, for £10.
    (32) Cheque, dated 11th March, 1926, for £15 15s.

33/49. Seventeen cheques on the Midland Bank, Boscombe, Bournemouth, signed " Bertha Merrett," all payable to " J. D. Merrett."

    (33) Cheque, dated 8th February, 1926, for £15.
    (34) Cheque, dated 9th February, 1926, for £5.
    (35) Cheque, dated 11th February, 1926, for £8.
    (36) Cheque, dated 15th February, 1926, for £15.
    (37) Cheque, dated 18th February, 1926, for £10.
    (38) Cheque, dated 24th February, 1926, for £20.
    (39) Cheque, dated 3rd March, 1926, for £15 15s.
    (40) Cheque, dated 8th March, 1926, for £30.
    (41) Cheque, dated 13th March, 1926, for £25 14s.
    (42) Cheque, dated 15th March, 1926, for £22 10s. 6d.
    (43) Cheque, dated 16th March, 1926, for £30.
    (44) Cheque, dated 18th March, 1926, for £30.
    (45) Cheque, dated 20th March, 1926, for £25.
    (46) Cheque, dated 23rd March, 1926, for £30.
    (47) Cheque, dated 24th March, 1926, for £30.
    (48) Cheque, dated 26th March, 1926, for £30.
    (49) Cheque, dated 27th March, 1926, for £28 9s. 6d.

50/60. Eleven cheques on the Clydesdale Bank, Limited, George Street, Edinburgh, signed " Bertha Merrett."

    (50) Cheque, dated 15th January, 1926, payable to Edinburgh University, for £2 2s.
    (51) Cheque, dated 21st January, 1926, payable to Edinburgh University, for £15 15s.

List of Productions.

(52) Cheque, dated 23rd January, 1926, payable to self, for £3 3s.

(53) Cheque, dated 2nd February, 1926, payable to William King Gillies, for £4 10s.

(54) Cheque, dated 6th February, 1926, payable to "Rentons, Limited," for £3 4s. 3d.

(55) Cheque, dated 11th February, 1926, payable to self, for £5.

(56) Cheque, dated 24th February, 1926, payable to Mlle. Servien, for £3 3s.

(57) Cheque, dated 8th March, 1926, payable to self, for £10.

(58) Cheque, dated 10th March, 1926, payable to W. Forsyth, Limited, for £7 7s.

(59) Cheque, dated 12th March, 1926, payable to Robert Anderson, for £25.

(60) Cheque, dated 13th March, 1926, payable to self, for £7.

61/76. Sixteen cheques on the Midland Bank, Boscombe, Bournemouth, signed "Bertha Merrett."

(61) Cheque, dated 31st December, 1925, to Star Supplies Stores, for £1 18s.

(62) Cheque, dated 5th January, 1926, payable to self, for £10.

(63) Cheque, dated 8th January, 1926, to cash, for £10.

(64) Cheque, dated 12th January, 1926, to cash, for £30.

(65) Cheque, dated 15th January, 1926, to self, for £20.

(66) Cheque, dated 19th January, 1926, to self, for £10.

(67) Cheque, dated 26th January, 1926, to self, for £20.

(68) Cheque, dated 29th January, 1926, to self, for £5.

(69) Cheque, dated 4th February, 1926, to Mrs. Ellingham, for £1.

(70) Cheque, dated 4th February, 1926, to cash, for £20.

(71) Cheque, dated 16th February, 1926, to self, for £25.

(72) Cheque, dated 22nd February, 1926, to self, for £5.

(73) Cheque, dated 25th February, 1926, to self, for £5.

(74) Cheque, dated 2nd March, 1926, to self, for £20.

(75) Cheque, dated 2nd March, 1926, to Robert Anderson, for £25.

(76) Cheque, dated 4th March, 1926, to self, for £30.

77/83. Seven cheques on the Clydesdale Bank, Limited, George Street, Edinburgh, signed "Bertha Merrett," payable to "Mrs. Sharp."

(77) Cheque, dated 1st February, 1926, for £6 7s.

(78) Cheque, dated 8th February, 1926, for £6 10s.

(79) Cheque, dated 15th February, 1926, for £6 13s.

(80) Cheque, dated 22nd February, 1926, for £6 6s.

(81) Cheque, dated 1st March, 1926, for £6 7s. 6d.

(82) Cheque, dated 8th March, 1926, for £7 3s. 6d.

53

John Donald Merrett.

(83) Cheque, dated 10th March, 1926, for £2 15s. 6d.

84/86. Three pay-in slips of the Clydesdale Bank, Limited, George Street, Edinburgh, all signed " Bertha Merrett."

    (84) Pay-in slip, dated 15th January, 1926, for £15.

    (85) Pay-in slip, dated 16th February, 1926, for £20.

    (86) Pay-in slip, dated 2nd March, 1926, for £20.

87/147. Sixty-one cheques on the Midland Bank, Boscombe, Bournemouth, signed " Bertha Merrett."

    (87) Cheque, dated 27th June, 1925, to Kendall & Co., for £1 6s. 9d.

    (88) Cheque, dated 29th June, 1925, to Amalgamated Press (1922), Limited, for 11s.

    (89) Cheque, dated 29th June, 1925, to Baylis & Co., Limited, for £1.

    (90) Cheque, dated 30th June, 1925, to Dunlops, for £5.

    (91) Cheque, dated 1st July, 1925, to Dickins & Jones, Limited, £5 15s. 6d.

    (92) Cheque, dated 6th July, 1925, to self, for £5.

    (93) Cheque, dated 9th July, 1925, to self, for £15.

    (94) Cheque, dated 9th July, 1925, to Dunster & Hodgson, for £12 12s.

    (95) Cheque, dated 9th July, 1925, to Heelas Sons & Co., Limited, for £1 6s. 9d.

    (96) Cheque, dated 17th July, 1925, to self, for £5.

    (97) Cheque, dated 20th July, 1925, to the " Lady," for 12s. 6d.

    (98) Cheque, dated 29th July, 1925, to self, for £10.

    (99) Cheque, dated 4th August, 1925, to Lloyds Bank, Limited, for £73 18s. 6d.

  (100) Cheque, dated 4th August, 1925, to cash, for £15.

  (101) Cheque, dated 6th August, 1925, to John Lewis & Co., for £1 7s. 9d.

  (102) Cheque, dated 11th August, 1925, to cash, for £10.

  (103) Cheque, dated 13th August, 1925, to Heelas Sons & Co., Limited, for £3 6s. 5d.

  (104) Cheque, dated 15th August, 1925, to W. Edward Chadwick, for £10.

  (105) Cheque, dated 18th August, 1925, to cash, for £20.

  (106) Cheque, dated 21st August, 1925, to G. Shapter, for £1 10s.

  (107) Cheque, dated 23rd August, 1925, to self (with authorisation, dated 29/7/25, attached signed " Bertha Merrett "), for £5.

  (108) Cheque, dated 24th August, 1925, to cash, for £20.

  (109) Cheque, dated 24th August, 1925, to Heelas Sons & Co., Limited, for £3 10s. 11d.

  (110) Cheque, dated 24th August, 1925, to Read & Sons, Limited, for £7 15s.

List of Productions.

(111) Cheque, dated 26th August, 1925, to A. J. Walker, for £5.

(112) Cheque, dated 27th August, 1925, to cash, for £5.

(113) Cheque, dated 1st September, 1925, to A. J. Walker, £6 3s.

(114) Cheque, dated 1st September, 1925, to self, for £20.

(115) Cheque, dated 7th September, 1925, to Arthur New-bery, Limited, for £2 8s. 6d.

(116) Cheque, dated 11th September, 1925, to Annie E. Penn, for £1.

(117) Cheque, dated 16th September, 1925, to self, for £10.

(118) Cheque, dated 16th September, 1925, to H. & C. Collins, for £5.

(119) Cheque, dated 21st September, 1925, to Heelas Sons & Co., Limited, for £10.

(120) Cheque, dated 21st September, 1925, to A. Newbery, Limited, for £2 10s. 6d.

(121) Cheque, dated 28th September, 1925, to cash, for £20.

(122) Cheque, dated 29th September, 1925, to W. A. Jenks, for £5.

(123) Cheque, dated 29th September, 1925, to Marshall & Snelgrove, for £7 7s.

(124) Cheque, dated 30th September, 1925, to Heelas Sons & Co., Limited, for £2 9s. 6d.

(125) Cheque, dated 30th September, 1925, to E. Dennis Berry, for 10s. 6d.

(126) Cheque, dated 15th October, 1925, to W. J. Harris, for 15s. 6d.

(127) Cheque, dated 17th October, 1925, to self, for £20.

(128) Cheque, dated 22nd October, 1925, to self, for £10.

(129) Cheque, dated 26th October, 1925, to Thos. Blackburn, for £10.

(130) Cheque, dated 2nd November, 1925, to self, for £10.

(131) Cheque, dated 6th November, 1925, to Mrs. Frank Preston, for 10s. 6d.

(132) Cheque, dated 10th November, 1925, to self, for £10.

(133) Cheque, dated 19th November, 1925, to self, for £5.

(134) Cheque, dated 24th November, 1925, to Heelas Sons & Co., Limited, for £11 11s.

(135) Cheque, dated 25th November, 1925, for self, to £15.

(136) Cheque, dated 2nd December, 1925, to H. M. Robinson, for £2 2s.

(137) Cheque, dated 5th December, 1925, to self, for £5.

(138) Cheque, dated 7th December, 1925, to self, for £10.

(139) Cheque, dated 12th December, 1925, to self, for £10.

(140) Cheque, dated 14th December, 1925, to H. M. Robinson, for £1.

(141) Cheque, dated 14th December, 1925, to University of London, for £3 3s.

John Donald Merrett.

(142) Cheque, dated 16th December, 1925, to self, for £20.
(143) Cheque, dated 18th December, 1925, to H. M. Robinson, for £1.
(144) Cheque, dated 21st December, 1925, to self, for £30.
(145) Cheque, dated 21st December, 1925, to self, for £5.
(146) Cheque, dated 21st December, 1925, to Reid & Sons, Limited, for £9 17s. 6d.
(147) Cheque, dated 26th December, 1925, to Lloyds Bank, Limited, Malvern, for £17 0s. 6d.
148. Account book, Mrs. B. Merrett.
149/158. Ten pay-in slips of the Clydesdale Bank, Limited, George Street, Edinburgh, dated as follows :—
(149) 4th February, 1926, on account of Bertha Merrett, by J. D. Merrett, for £15.
(150) 8th February, 1926, on account of Bertha Merrett, by J. D. Merrett, for £10.
(151) 15th February, 1926, on account of Bertha Merrett, by J. D. Merrett, for £13.
(152) 18th February, 1926, on account of Bertha Merrett, by J. D. Merrett, for £5.
(153) 24th February, 1926, on account of Bertha Merrett, by J. D. Merrett, for £10.
(154) 3rd March, 1926, on account of Bertha Merrett, by J. D. Merrett, for £7 7s.
(155) 4th March, 1926, on account of Bertha Merrett, by J. D. Merrett, for £20.
(156) 13th March, 1926, on account of Bertha Merrett, by J. D. Merrett, for £8 14s.
(157) 16th March, 1926, on account of Bertha Merrett, by J. D. Merrett, for £25.
(158) 18th March, 1926, on account of Bertha Merrett, by J. D. Merrett, for £17.
159. Note book—accounts, J. D. Merrett.
160. Application for fire-arms certificate, dated 10th February, 1926, signed " J. D. Merrett."
161. Probate of will and codicil of Bertha Merrett.
162. Statement showing value of estate as sworn for probate and approximate value of residuary estate of the late Mrs. Bertha Merrett.
163/168. Six sheets of paper mounted on cardboard with bullet holes therein, marked respectively 1, 2, 3, 4, 5, 6.
169. Sheet of cardboard with bullet holes therein signed " Harvey Littlejohn."
170/175. Six letters beginning " Dear Mr. Rooker " and signed " Bertha Merrett."
(170) dated 8th December, 1925.
(171) dated 24th December, 1925.
(172) dated 4th January, 1926.
(173) dated 22nd January, 1926.

List of Productions.

(174) dated 26th February, 1926.

(175) dated 4th March, 1926.

176. Letter to the Manager, Midland Bank, Limited, Boscombe, Hants, dated 12th March, 1926, signed " Bertha Merrett."

177. Order for cheque book signed " Bertha Merrett," dated 21st December, 1925.

178. Post card to the Manager, Midland Bank, Limited, Boscombe, Hants, dated 23rd January, 1926, signed " B. Merrett."

179/180. Two copy advice notes of Midland Bank, Limited, Boscombe Branch, to Mrs. B. Merrett, dated respectively 23rd and 24th February, 1926.

181. Copy letter, Midland Bank, Limited, Boscombe Branch, to Mrs. B. Merrett, dated 25th January, 1926.

182. Manager's compliments form, Midland Bank, Limited, Boscombe, dated 15th March, 1926.

183. Plan of flat, 31 Buckingham Terrace.

184. Plan of flat, 31 Buckingham Terrace.

185. Extract entry of death of Bertha Merrett on 1st April, 1926.

186. Probate of the will of William Henry Milner.

Label No. 1. An automatic pistol and five live cartridges.

Label No. 2. Bullet.

Label No. 3. Empty cartridge case.

Label No. 4. Box containing cartridges.

Label No. 5. Box containing cartridges.

Label No. 6. A skull.

KINROSS, *A.D.*

List of Witnesses.

(All in Edinburgh, except Nos. 2, 8, 9, 14, 15, 16, 17, 20, 21, 30, 31, 35, 39, and 40.)

1. Mrs. Henrietta Sutherland, 107 Broughton Road.

2. Thomas Gray Middlemiss, 5 Scott Street, Galashiels.

3/7. (3) David Izatt, constable; (4) William Watt, constable; (5) Victor Gibson, constable; (6) David Fleming, detective-inspector; and (7) William Henderson, detective-sergeant—all City Police.

8. Roy Stanley Holcombe, L.R.C.P., L.R.C.S., 9 Victoria Square, Jesmond, Newcastle-on-Tyne.

9. Richard Bell, M.B., Ch.B., Holmhead, Newcastleton, Roxburghshire.

10/12. (10) Elizabeth Fraser Grant; (11) Jean Innes; and (12) Elizabeth Seaggers Wilson—all Nurses' Home, Royal Infirmary.

13. Elspeth Elliot Grant, nurse, City Hospital.

John Donald Merrett.

14. Mrs. Bertha Hill, 1 Devonshire Place, Brighton.
15/16. (15) Mrs. Annie Eliza Penn, and (16) Walter Penn, both Rumbling Bridge Hotel, near Dollar.
17. Elizabeth Helen Christie, 447 Sauchiehall Street, Glasgow.
18. James Robertson, City Engineer's Office.
19. Said Harvey Littlejohn.
20. Said John Glaister.
21. Said Gerald Francis Gurrin.
22. William Morrison Smith, 11 Forth Street.
23/29. (23) William Bethune Ferguson; (24) Henry James Mercer Kerr; (25) Hugh Sutherland Ritch; (26) Cecil George Minto Harrower; (27) John Anderson; (28) Robert Smith Henderson; and (29) Robert James Lee Hendry—all the Clydesdale Bank, Limited, 29 George Street.
30/31. (30) Charles Arthur Ridge, and (31) Arthur Sydney Rooker—both Midland Bank, Limited, Boscombe, Bournemouth.
32. Said John Michael Geoghegan.
33. Mrs. Isabella Grant, County Hotel, 21 and 27 Lothian Road.
34. Robert Anderson, 7 Drumsheugh Place.
35. Mrs. Agnes Mary Anderson, 64 Murray Place, Stirling.
36. Mrs. Elizabeth Hardie, 7 Mayfield Road.
37. Mrs. Joan Sharp, 33 and 35 Palmerston Place.
38. Major Thomas Blackburn, 20 Dick Place.
39. Emsley Mark Lee, Public Trustee Office, Kingsway, London, W.C.2.
40. James Dundas Paton, 112 Thirlestane Road.
41. James Pearson Cairns, 27 Rossie Place.
42/43. (42) William Davidson, constable, and (43) Murdo M'Lean, constable—both City Police.
44. Charles Nicol Stott, Fair-a-far, Cramond.
45. Douglas James Acworth Kerr, M.B., 16 Dreghorn Loan, Colinton.
46. John Miller Woodburn Morison, M.B., 11 Greenhill Place.
47/48. (47) George Armstrong Scott, and (48) James Aitchison Scott—both 34 Dean Park Street.
49. John Lawson, Private, Cameron Highlanders, Depot Cameron Barracks, Inverness, No. 2925491.
50. Thomas Ritchie, c/o Hardie, 26 Canaan Lane.
51. George Wilson, 537 Castlehill.
52. Evelyn Pearce, 18 Montgomery Street.
53. Allan Fairley, 60 St. Albans Road.
54. Donald Rose, inspector, City Police.
55. John Garton Appleyard, the Clydesdale Bank, Limited, 29 George Street.
56. William Johnston, detective-constable, City Police.
57. Alan Macnaughton, 18 Hanover Street.

KINROSS, *A.D.*

Copy List of Productions for the Pannel,
John Donald Merrett.

1. Telegram from Jas. Scott to the prisoner, sent on 8th January, 1927.
2. Telegram from Jas. Scott to the Public Trustee, London, sent on 8th January, 1927.
3. Letter dated 7th January, 1927, from Mr. Walter Ed. Penn to Messrs. Wood & Sons, solicitors, London.
4. Plan showing situation of furniture in room, 31 Buckingham Terrace.
5. Plan showing measurements of furniture.
6. Sketch plan showing position of furniture.
7. Ground plan of flat, 31 Buckingham Terrace.
8. Envelope containing four cards showing shooting experiments marked A, B, C, and D.
9. Envelope containing five cards showing shooting experiments marked A, B, C, D, and E.
10. Envelope containing four cards showing shooting experiments marked A, B, C, and D.
11. Envelope containing four cards showing shooting experiments marked A, B, C, and D.
12. Envelope containing two cards showing shooting experiments marked A and B.
13. Envelope containing four cards showing shooting experiments marked A, B, C, and D.
14. Envelope containing one card showing shooting experiment marked A.
15. Skull.
16. Skull bone.
17. Packet containing powder from cartridges used in London experiments.
18a. Glass box containing skin used for shooting experiments.
18b.   Do.   do.
18c.   Do.   do.
18d.   Do.   do.
18e.   Do.   do.
18f.   Do.   do.
18g.   Do.   do.
18h.   Do.   do.
18i.   Do.   do.
19. Temperature charts.
20. Letter to Col. Thom, dated 17th March, 1926.

59

John Donald Merrett.

List of Witnesses for the Pannel, John Donald Merrett.

1. Charles A. Macpherson.
2. Col. G. St. C. Thom.
3. Dr. Lewis George Rosa.
4. William Henderson.
5. Elizabeth Hardie.
6. Thomas Bowhill Gibson.
7. Professor G. M. Robertson.
8. Robert Churchill.
9 Sir Bernard Spilsbury.

The pannel, having pleaded not guilty, was remitted to an Assize, and the following jury was balloted :—

1. Norman Ferdinand William Mitchell-Innes, major, Murrayfield, Roslin.
2. James W. Campbell, 8 Leithen Road, Innerleithen.
3. John Anderson, senior, spirit merchant, 27 Park Road, Leith.
4. Herbert William Love, tobacconist, 5 Merchiston Place.
5. Clarence Bentham, engineer, 2 York Road, Trinity.
6. James Black M'Kinnon, piano tuner, 116 Gilmore Place.
7. Miss Isabella N. Cleghorn, Craigour, Gilmerton.
8. Mrs. Jane Wood, widow, 167 High Street, Musselburgh.
9. Thomas Blair, colliery manager, Dean Terrace, Rosewell.
10. Alexander Urquhart, fishmonger, 1 Lower Granton Road.
11. Miss Euphemia Arnott, teacher, 8 Comely Bank Road.
12. Andrew Chisholm Elliot, coachbuilder, 3 Windsor Street.
13. Mrs. Helen H. Nicol, 35 Meadowbank Crescent.
14. Mrs. Amelia C. Hadden, 40 Henderson Row.
15. Mrs. Helen Telfer Carmichael, Craigower, The Loan, Loanhead.

The Clerk of Court having read over to the jury the charges against the pannel, they were all lawfully sworn to try the libel.

The Court appointed the evidence to be taken down in shorthand, and appointed Messrs. Alfred Eadie, John S. Mearns, John Moran, and Ernest J. Sharp, 12 Bank Street, Edinburgh, to take the said evidence in shorthand, and the declaration *de fideli* was administered to them.

The trial then proceeded.

Evidence for the Prosecution.

Mrs. HENRIETTA SUTHERLAND (28), examined by the LORD ADVOCATE—I am the wife of Hugh Sutherland, but I left him a year or two ago on account of his habits, and I have been supporting myself since. I have no family. I go out doing work in houses through the day. I heard of work with the late Mrs. Merrett in a flat at 31 Buckingham Terrace, and I went there to do the housework in the beginning of March, 1926. It was Wednesday, 10th March, that I started. I worked from nine to twelve. I was back there the next day, Thursday, but not on the Friday, as I had another situation to go to that day. I was there, however, on the Saturday, Sunday, Monday, Tuesday, and Wednesday. That is up to Wednesday, the 17th. The flat consisted of two bedrooms, a public room, a kitchen, and a bathroom, all on the same floor. The occupants of the house were Mrs. Merrett and her son, the accused. As a rule, when I got there at nine o'clock, the Merretts had already had breakfast. My first work was to clear away the breakfast dishes. The accused was not always there when I arrived. When Mrs. Merrett engaged me, she told me she would require me up to the 10th June. I remember coming to the flat on the morning of 17th March. The flat was on the first storey, the one above the street. On the morning of 17th March I got to the flat just about nine. I did not have a key of my own, so I had to ring. I was let in by Mrs. Merrett. When I got in I went right to the kitchen to take my hat and coat off. Having taken them off, I went into the dining-room. Mr. Merrett and Mrs. Merrett were both in the room when I first went in. Mrs. Merrett was putting some of the things off the table into the drawers of the bureau—the salt cellar, sugar bowl, and such things. As you entered the flat by the front door the kitchen was along a passage to your left, and the sitting-room was along a passage to your right. As you entered the sitting-room you looked straight forward to a big bay window with three windows in it. The fireplace was in the middle of the wall to your left as you entered the door. Just behind the fireplace, on the left-hand side, there was a recess. The drawers to which I have referred, into which Mrs. Merrett was putting away things, were in a writing bureau, which stood on the right-hand side of the room as you went in, between the door and the window. The table, on which the breakfast dishes were, was near the bureau, but in the middle of the room. When I went in the first time some of the breakfast things were still on the table. I started to clear them away. I took them to the kitchen. When I left the room Mrs. Merrett was at the bureau, getting out what I thought was writing material. I cannot remember where the accused was at that time. Mrs. Merrett did her writing on the big table on

61

John Donald Merrett.

Mrs Henrietta Sutherland

which the breakfast things were. When I left the room on the first occasion Mrs. Merrett was still collecting the things. I washed up the dishes in the kitchen. Having finished with the dishes, I went into the sitting-room again to do the fireplace. There was no fire on at that time. When I went in to do the fireplace Mrs. Merrett was sitting writing at the big table, and the accused was sitting reading behind the big chair in the recess. As I went in at the door and saw Mrs. Merrett sitting writing, her left side was a little towards me. Her back would be towards the bureau, but not straight on. I did not do the fire at that time, as I saw they were both engaged in the room, so I just came out. After leaving the sitting-room I made to go to the kitchen, and on my way I opened the coal-cellar door and took out a pailful of coal that I had ready to take into the kitchen along with the ash-bucket. I then went to do the kitchen fireside. I had just got started on the kitchen grate when I heard the shot.

When you heard the shot were you standing or sitting or kneeling?—I was just making to bend down, but I got up.

As you enter the kitchen door, where is the fireplace—straight in front or to the right or left?—It is a little to the right. It is almost opposite the door, across the kitchen.

Did you hear anything else besides the shot?—I heard Mrs. Merrett scream.

Once or oftener?—Once.

How quickly after the shot would that scream occur?—Just almost immediately.

What did you do?—I just stood; I did not know what to do.

What happened next?—Then I heard a thud as of some one falling.

Did you move or did you remain standing?—I still stood still.

What happened next?—A few seconds after that the accused came out into the kitchen and said his mother had shot herself, and he seemed very much upset. He made to put his head on my shoulder. I thought he was going to cry.

Do you remember his exact words?—He just said, " Rita, my mother shot herself."

He seemed very much upset?—Yes.

And he put his head on your shoulder?—He made to do it.

Did you hear any other sound between hearing the thud of a body falling and the accused coming into the kitchen?—Some books dropped just behind the outside door, where the telephone stood.

Is the telephone in the lobby—it is not in a closed box, is it?—No, it is just standing on a table.

What happened next?—I said to the accused I thought his mother seemed quite all right when she let me in, and he said he had been wasting her money.

He said what?—He said he had been wasting his mother's money, and he thought she was worried over that.

62

Evidence for Prosecution.

Mrs Henrietta Sutherland

Was this before you moved into the other room?—Just as we were walking out of the kitchen. We both went into the sitting-room together. When I went into the sitting-room I saw Mrs. Merrett lying on the floor with her head towards the door.

What about the chair upon which she had been sitting?—The chair was at the other side where her feet were—like at the other side of her body.

Was the chair in the position where she had been sitting?—No; so far as I can remember, it was lying on its back.

From where you were looking was the chair lying on its back to the left or right of where it had been when Mrs. Merrett was in it?—To the right.

That is nearer to the window?—Yes. I did not go up to Mrs. Merrett when I saw she was bleeding so much. She never moved while I saw her. The accused was beside me at the time.

What happened next?—I went right to the telephone.

Did somebody suggest the police?—No, I just thought of it.

And you went to the telephone and rang up the police?—I just asked them to put me on to the police. I did not know the number. I got on to the police. The accused was standing at my side while I was telephoning.

When you had finished telephoning, did you go back into the sitting-room?—Donald finished the telephoning.

Did he help you with the telephoning?—Well, they asked me to spell the name, and I was not sure of the double " t," and the accused took the receiver. I remained beside him whilst he was telephoning. After he had finished telephoning we both went back to the sitting-room. Mrs. Merrett was still lying there. She had not moved. She was still bleeding. The accused asked me to help him with his mother on to the settee. The settee was to the right-hand side of the fireplace between the door and the window. I said, " Oh, I think we had best leave her."

And did you leave her?—Yes.

What did you do then? Did you stay in the room or did you go out?—We both stood in the room, and then when I said we had best leave her Donald made to take my hand and said, " Let us go out; I cannot stand to look at it any longer." We both walked out of the room, and I opened the outside door and made to go down the stair in order to meet the police. I arrived at the house about nine o'clock, and I should say it would be about twenty minutes to ten when I heard the shot and the thud.

When you first entered the room with the accused after hearing the shot, did you notice a pistol anywhere?—On the corner of the bureau.

Was the bureau open at that time?—Yes.

When you say the corner, do you mean on the flap that was turned down or on the top?—On the very top.

Was it on the corner of the bureau nearest the window or the corner nearest the door?—The corner nearest the door.

John Donald Merrett.

Mrs Henrietta Sutherland

Was that corner within reach of Mrs. Merrett while she was sitting writing where you saw her?—No.

Had you ever seen that pistol before?—No.

When you went in the first time to clear away the breakfast dishes was the bureau open then?—I cannot remember whether it was or not.

Did you notice any letters from the post that first time you went in?—I noticed one lying on the outside of the bureau on the top.

Were you close to it?—Yes.

Did you see to whom it was addressed?—Yes. It was addressed to Mrs. Merrett.

Did you see that letter again?—No. The police arrived just as the accused and I got to the foot of the stair. There were three of them, I think.

Was it you or the accused who spoke to them?—I think we both spoke, but I cannot really remember right who it was.

Did you hear the accused saying anything to them then?— No, I did not hear him. We both returned up the stair with the policemen and went into the sitting-room.

When you went back into the sitting-room did you again see the pistol?—I think I asked one of the constables to take it away.

You mean it was still there in the same place?—Yes.

And at that time did you notice the letter lying on the bureau? —I cannot say for that time.

Did you see anything of an open letter lying on the bureau?— There was a letter lying under an envelope, but I cannot say what was on it, because the envelope was lying across the letter.

When was it you saw the letter lying under the envelope?— While I was clearing the dishes off the table. That was the first time I went into the sitting-room.

That is the letter you have already told us about, addressed to Mrs. Merrett?—Yes.

Was there an open letter lying underneath it?—Yes.

Did you see what that open letter was?—I cannot say, but there was a heading on the paper. I cannot say what that heading was.

You mean a printed heading?—Yes.

You spoke about having heard some books falling in the passage; did you find the books?—Yes, I picked them up.

Where were they lying?—They were just scattered on the floor, in the passage, just about the telephone.

Was that after Mrs. Merrett had been taken away?—Yes. [Shown label No. 1]—That is like the pistol I saw lying on the top of the bureau. It was just the same size. Later on detective officers came to the flat and interviewed me. I think one was Inspector Fleming, but I do not know the other gentleman.

Did you tell them what had happened?—Well, I spoke to them, but I do not know what I said to them, because I was mixed up

No. 31 Buckingham Terrace, Edinburgh.

(The bow-window on the first flat is that of the sitting room ; the single
window with balcony is that of Merrett's bedroom.)

Evidence for Prosecution.

at that time. I had been upset by the whole incident, because I had only been there a few days, and I did not know what had happened when I heard the shot.

Did you say to the officers that you had seen the pistol falling out of Mrs. Merrett's hands?—I do not remember saying that. I certainly heard her falling, but I did not see anything.

You told us already that at the time when you heard the shot you were just getting down to the kitchen grate?—Yes.

From where you were at the kitchen grate was it possible for you to see along the passage into the sitting-room?—No, quite impossible.

Did you see, or did you not see, the pistol falling out of Mrs. Merrett's hands?—I did not.

Then you left the house a little later, about twelve o'clock?—Yes, about that time. I went back to the flat in about a fortnight's time to do some work for Mrs. Penn, Mrs. Merrett's sister.

Did Mrs. Merrett ask you at any time about a cheque book?—Yes. That was on Saturday, 13th March. She asked if I had seen a cheque book about the house, as she had lost it. I said I had not seen one. I cannot remember whether the accused was present when Mrs. Merrett asked me about the cheque book.

Did she say anything about how she had come to lose it?—She thought perhaps she had mislaid it during her removal from Palmerston Place.

You told us you went first on Wednesday, the 10th. Had Mrs. Merrett just gone into the flat that day?—Yes, she had just arrived.

On the following day did you hear a conversation between Mrs. Merrett and the accused?—On the Sunday, yes. She was asking Donald to write to some gentleman about the cheque book, to say to send on another one as she had lost hers. I think she gave the name of the gentleman, but I cannot remember. I could not say whether the accused wrote that letter or not. I cannot remember seeing him write it. I am quite sure that that occurred on Sunday, the 14th. I was not at the flat on Friday, the 12th. The accused never at any time said anything to me about the pistol.

Did he ever tell you where he was when the shot went off?—No, he never spoke of it.

Did he never say anything to you about his having moved the pistol, or anything of that kind?—No. I pointed out to Mr. James Robertson, the surveyor, the places which the furniture had occupied in the sitting-room. Production No. 183 gives a fair representation of how the room was arranged. The table on which the breakfast was taken and at which Mrs. Merrett was writing was an oval table, and it was placed at a slight angle to the window, as shown on the plan. Mrs. Merrett was sitting writing at the end nearest the bureau.

F

John Donald Merrett.

Mrs Henrietta Sutherland

Cross-examined by Mr. AITCHISON—You entered the service of Mrs. Merrett on 10th March, and, accordingly, you had only been in her service for one week when this tragedy occurred?—Yes.

I suppose during that time you had not got to know her intimately?—No.

Do you remember having a conversation with her about two days before this thing happened—on the Monday?—Yes, I had a little conversation with her.

Did she say something to you to the effect that she had had a very hard life?—Yes.

Did she seem rather down that morning?—No, she did not seem down.

Was not she a little depressed?—No, I do not think she was.

Did she ever tell you anything about her husband?—Yes, she said she lost her husband in the Russian Revolution.

Did not that seem to be preying on her mind a bit?—I could not say.

But you remember quite distinctly that being mentioned about two days before this thing occurred?—Yes.

Am I right that she seemed fond of the accused?—Yes, very fond of him.

Devoted to him?—Yes, she was.

And did he seem fond of her?—I did not see much of the accused and his mother altogether.

But, so far as you could judge, were they on perfectly happy and affectionate terms?—Yes.

On the morning of the 17th, after you arrived at the house, I understand that you entered the sitting-room where the tragedy afterwards occurred?—Yes.

Do you remember seeing Mrs. Merrett taking something out of the bureau?—Yes, she took letters and some writing material, but I could not say exactly what it was.

Did you not see her with some metal thing in her hand?—No.

Did not you form the impression at the time that she had cutlery in her hand?—She had the sugar bowl and the salt and pepper dishes.

I am talking about cutlery. Did not you form the impression at the time that she had some cutlery in her hand near the bureau?—Yes, she had the things that had been on the table.

Then do you agree that she seemed to have some metal thing in her hand, whatever it was?—I thought all the things were silver that she had.

If you cannot be certain just say so; but did you at the time get the impression that, whatever it was, she had some metal thing in her hand?—No.

At any rate, you saw her working about the bureau?—Yes.

When last you saw the accused, before the shooting occurred, was he seated at a table in the recess of the room working with books?—Yes.

Evidence for Prosecution.

Mrs Henrietta Sutherland

I show you No. 183. Is the recess shown in the south-west corner of the room, that is to say, does the recess lie to your left hand as you enter the room from the lobby?—Yes.

You say he was seated there when you last saw him?—Yes.

Was that a second or two before the shooting occurred?—Yes, just a second or two.

And when you last saw Mrs. Merrett, before the shooting occurred, was she seated on a chair between the table and the bureau?—Yes.

And is the bureau on your right-hand side as you go in at the door?—Yes.

I think it was placed up against the wall?—Yes.

In order to reach the bureau from the chair in which Mrs. Merrett was seated, would she need to stretch out her hand?—Yes.

So far as you can recollect, in order to reach the bureau, would she have required to tip up the chair on one or more legs?—I think a little.

So that if she wanted to take anything out of a drawer in the bureau she would require to tip the chair over in the direction of the bureau, and lean over in its direction?—Yes, a very little.

In order to reach the slab in front?—She would require to give her chair a good turn.

And tip it over in the direction of the bureau; and if she wished to reach the drawers in the bureau she would require to tip it all the more?—There were little drawers, and she could have reached them quite easily.

Did part of this bureau fold down in order to form a writing table?—Yes.

Now, that morning was it folded down?—Yes.

And beyond the folded-down part are there a number of drawers and pigeon holes?—Yes, little drawers.

From the position in which Mrs. Merrett was seated, in order to reach these drawers or pigeon holes, would she require to tip up her chair and to stretch over?—Not if she wanted to go into the little drawers at the left-hand side of the bureau.

Not at the left-hand part, because that was the part she was nearer?—Yes.

But if she wanted to take anything out of a drawer at the right side of the bureau, do you agree that it would have been necessary for her to tip up the chair for that purpose?—Yes.

I think when you came into the room after the shooting had occurred you found the chair had been overturned?—Yes.

Were you in the sitting-room that morning for more than a very few seconds the last time you were there prior to the shooting?—No, only a few seconds.

When you left the sitting-room did you leave the door open?—Yes.

Did you ever hear the door closed?—No.

John Donald Merrett.

Mrs Henrietta Sutherland

When you returned to the sitting-room after the shooting had occurred was the door open?—Yes.

Am I right that from the lobby which runs between the sitting-room and the kitchen you can see into the sitting-room?—No.

Supposing you come out of the kitchen door, don't you come into the lobby?—Yes.

And is not that a straight lobby that runs right through to the sitting-room?—No.

Do you say no?—It is a small lobby. The bathroom looks right into the sitting-room.

You are quite right. Is the bathroom at one end of the lobby, and at the other end of the lobby is there the sitting-room?—Yes.

As you come out of the kitchen does a couple of steps take you to the bathroom door on your left-hand side?—Yes.

And if you were there and looked along towards the sitting-room would you see into the sitting-room if the door was open?—Yes.

And from that position would you see the table at which Mrs. Merrett was writing?—Yes, from the bathroom door.

And would you also see the chair?—Yes.

And the edge of the bureau?—Yes.

I understand you to say that having left the sitting-room you went into the kitchen?—Yes.

Had you just been there a matter of seconds when the shot rang out?—Yes.

Is not it the case that on hearing the shot you at once ran into the lobby?—No.

I put it to you that it is the case?—Well, it is not the case.

I will come later to statements which you made, but meantime I put it to you that on hearing the shot, you being in the kitchen at the time, at once ran into the lobby. Is not that so?—Well, I didn't.

Have you ever said anything to the contrary?—I may have, but I did not run into the lobby.

So you say that, hearing the shot, you just stood where you were?—Yes.

How long did you stand?—A few seconds.

And then you heard a thud?—No, I heard a scream next.

And did you then run into the lobby?—No.

Then you heard a thud?—Yes.

Is it your evidence you still stood where you were?—Yes.

Do you tell us you remained exactly where you were in the kitchen until the accused came from the sitting-room towards you?—Yes.

When the accused did come, is not it the case that he was very much upset?—Yes, he was.

Was he very agitated?—Yes.

Evidence for Prosecution.

Mrs Henrietta Sutherland

Did he appear to be in great distress?—He was at the time.

I think you tried to comfort him?—I did.

Did you say to him, " Surely she will come all right "?—Before that I said, " She seemed quite all right this morning. Whatever has happened to her? "

Did he agree with you?—He did not say. He just said he had been wasting her money and she had quarrelled with him about it.

You say he said he had been wasting her money. Can you be certain that he did not say this, that his mother had worried about money being wasted?—No, he said he was wasting her money.

Can you recall whether any reference was made at that time to Mrs. Merrett's husband, that is, the accused's father?—No.

May he have said that she had worried about money being wasted?—I am sure he mentioned it was him who had been wasting the money.

That may be your opinion. You were excited, were you not?—Yes, I was excited.

May it not have been put the other way, that his mother had been worried about money matters?—I am sure he used the words " wasting her money."

That his mother had been worried about money being wasted. May it not have been put in that way?—No, I am positively sure he said he had been wasting her money.

When you went into the room, I think you have already told us that the chair in which Mrs. Merrett had been sitting was overturned?—Yes.

Was the head of Mrs. Merrett pointing in the direction of the door?—Yes, her head was just at the door as I went in.

And her feet pointing in the direction of the window?—Yes.

As she lay, was she inclining more to the left side or to the right?—A little to her left.

Did you notice that both her hands were over towards the left side?—No, she clutched with her right hand her clothing.

Her right hand, you say, was clutching her clothing?—Yes.

Did you notice that the revolver was lying just by her side?—It was up on the bureau.

I want you to try and recollect this if you can. Is it not the case that it was at a later stage that the revolver was lying on the bureau?—No, it was there the very first time I went in.

Can you be certain about that?—I am positive.

I put it to you that your recollection in that matter is wrong, and that it was at a later stage that the revolver was lying on the bureau?—No, I am positive.

Did you notice that there was blood about the revolver?—No, I did not notice that.

Did you see the revolver being moved by any one until it was taken possession of by the police?—No.

69

John Donald Merrett.

Mrs Henrietta Sutherland

Was Mrs. Merrett bleeding pretty freely?—Yes, she was.

From the right ear?—No, to me it seemed as if it was coming out of each side of her mouth.

You thought the blood was coming from her mouth?—Yes.

Was there not a good deal of blood over the face generally?—Yes, and running down.

Where was it running down from?—Down like on her arm.

Was it not coming from the right side of the head?—I cannot remember.

Do you agree there was a very considerable quantity of blood?—Yes.

And a good deal of blood lying about the floor?—Yes, on the carpet.

You have told us you heard a thud of falling books?—Yes.

Was that just a matter of seconds after the shooting occurred?—Yes.

And did you afterwards pick certain books up just about the sitting-room door?—No, the books I picked up were at the telephone behind the outside door.

About the telephone, a few paces along the lobby from the sitting-room door?—Yes.

Is it your evidence that those books were dropped by the accused as he was coming towards you?—I think so, because I cannot recollect them lying on the hall table when I was there before.

You had seen the accused working with books the last time you saw him before the shooting?—Yes.

And then you heard a thud of books falling when he came towards you?—Yes.

The whole thing, I suppose, was only a matter of seconds?—Yes, it was a few seconds.

You tell us that the accused never said anything to you about the pistol at all?—Never at any time.

Did he ever discuss with you in any way whatsoever what you had seen happen that morning?—No, never at any time.

Are you perfectly clear about that?—I am positively sure he never spoke about it to me.

He never spoke to you about the matter at all, or about what you had seen?—He never spoke to me.

Do you remember being interviewed that morning by Inspector Fleming of the Edinburgh Police?—Yes.

Did that interview take place in the house at 31 Buckingham Terrace shortly after ten in the morning?—Yes.

Did he ask you what had happened?—I said the lady had shot herself.

Did you say anything more?—I said other things that I cannot rightly remember.

But you must try to remember?—I think I said I saw the lady falling, but I did not. I had got mixed up with other things.

70

Evidence for Prosecution.

Mrs Henrietta Sutherland

I want to know first of all what you said to Inspector Fleming?—I cannot rightly remember.

Well, as near as you can remember?—I know I said the lady had shot herself.

What else did you say?—I must have said I saw her falling, instead of saying I heard her falling.

Did you make some statement to the Edinburgh Police at the time about her falling?—I certainly heard her falling, and I may have said I saw her falling.

Did you say you had been in the kitchen at the time?—Yes.

Did you say to Inspector Fleming that you had heard a report of a firearm?—Yes.

Did you say that you went into the lobby?—No, I did not.

Did you say that on going into the lobby—I will give you the exact words as I have got them—" I saw Mrs. Merrett falling on the floor in the sitting-room "?—No, I could not have said that, because I did not. I never left the kitchen until the accused came in.

Did you say to Inspector Fleming, " I saw the pistol falling out of Mrs. Merrett's right hand "?—No, I did not say any such thing.

If Inspector Fleming says you said these things, how do you account for that?—He may have picked me up wrong. I may have said it, but I am positive I did not, because I could not, because I had never seen it.

Do you remember that at the time Inspector Fleming was there asking you questions Detective-Sergeant Henderson was present?—There was another gentleman there, but I do not know who he was.

I suppose he would hear?—Well, he was standing close by.

He would hear what you said to Inspector Fleming?—Yes.

What I have put to you as being said by you to Inspector Fleming was said by you in the presence of Detective-Sergeant Henderson, who was there at the time?—Well, if I did say it, there is no truth in it.

You now say there is no truth in it?—There is no truth in it.

On the evening of 17th March did you consult Dr. Rosa?—Yes.

Is he a medical practitioner at 28 Pitt Street, Edinburgh?—Yes.

Did you consult him on the evening of 17th March at his evening consulting hour?—Yes.

I think you were feeling upset?—Yes.

Did you make a statement to him?—Yes.

What did you say?—I said I had not been feeling very well, and at the place where I was working the lady had shot herself.

What else did you say?—I said I felt very sorry for the boy, because he was so young, and that was all I said regarding the case.

John Donald Merrett.

Mrs Henrietta Sutherland

Did not you tell the doctor a great deal more than that?—No, I did not.

Did you tell the doctor that your mistress was sitting at a desk writing?—I probably said she was writing the last time I had seen her. I may have said that.

Did you tell him that the accused was sitting reading at the other end of the room?—I cannot remember. I may have said that the boy was in the room at the time.

Do you remember telling Dr. Rosa of something Mrs. Merrett had done that had struck you as peculiar?—No.

Do you remember saying to Dr. Rosa anything about Mrs. Merrett's false teeth?—I think she had them in her left hand.

What did you tell Dr. Rosa that night as to what you had observed Mrs. Merrett doing?—I did not observe her doing anything.

Did you mention her false teeth?—I don't think so. Not to that doctor.

To any doctor?—No, not to any doctor.

To any one else?—I think to the police when I was asked about her hands, but not to any doctor, and that is the only doctor I have spoken to about the case.

Did you not say that night that you had been struck by something Mrs. Merrett had done before the shot occurred?—No.

I put it to you that you said to Dr. Rosa that you noticed your mistress taking out her false teeth a few seconds before the shooting occurred, and that that struck you at the time as strange?—That is a downright lie, for I never said that.

That is what we want to get at?—I never said it.

Is it your evidence that if Dr. Rosa tells us that you mentioned some incident about Mrs. Merrett's false teeth, and you being struck with it as being strange, that is a falsehood on Dr. Rosa's part?—Yes.

Do you remember saying to Dr. Rosa that it was just as you were leaving the room that Mrs. Merrett shot herself?—I might have said I was just out of the room a few seconds, because I had just got to the kitchen; I was no more than at the door.

I put it to you that you conveyed quite clearly to Dr. Rosa the impression that it was just as you had passed the door that the shot occurred, and that you had seen Mrs. Merrett fall from her chair?—No, I did not say that to Dr. Rosa.

Do you think he just imagined that, if he says you did?—Well, he may have, but I know I did not say that to him. I know Mrs. Penn. I was in her service for some time after 17th March in the same flat at Buckingham Terrace. Mrs. Penn is a sister of the late Mrs. Merrett. I was in Mrs. Penn's service for about two months.

Did you discuss this matter with her?—No, not very often, because I tried not to talk about it to her.

Evidence for Prosecution.

Mrs Henrietta Sutherland

Was she anxious to speak to you about it?—No, she did not seem, because I always had plenty of work to do while I was there.

Is not it the case that Mrs. Penn frequently discussed this matter with you?—We talked about it, but not often.

Is not it the case that Mrs. Penn showed a good deal of hostility to the accused?—No, I do not think so.

Do you say she showed none?—Well, at times; but not as regards this case.

Did she not suggest to you on more than one occasion that it was the accused who had shot his mother?—No, she did not.

Do you say she never suggested that?—No, she never suggested that.

At any time?—No.

Did not she suggest to you that you had not seen Mrs. Merrett fall from the chair?—I did not see her fall.

I am asking you if Mrs. Penn ever suggested that to you?—No.

Can you tell me when you first said that you had not seen Mrs. Merrett fall from her chair after the shot was fired? I understand your story now is that you did not see Mrs. Merrett fall from her chair?—Yes.

When did you first tell that story?—The first time I told it, I think, was when the two police gentlemen called at my home. I think it was a fortnight after, on the Sunday morning.

And, accordingly, was it a fortnight after the occurrence that you first said you had not seen Mrs. Merrett fall from her chair? —No, but I had no occasion to say it to any one else. I was never questioned about it.

Had you not occasion to say it when you were interviewed by Inspector Fleming and Detective-Sergeant Henderson on the morning of the occurrence?—Yes; you already asked me that.

I put it to you that what you said to these officers of police on the morning of the occurrence was that you had seen Mrs. Merrett fall from her chair and the revolver fall from her hand. I put it to you that that is the truth of this matter?—There is no truth in it.

And that you know it is the truth?—If I did say it, there is no truth in it.

Are you in the habit of saying things in which there is no truth?—No, but I was very much upset that morning. I would be only too pleased to say it if it was the truth, but it is not.

I put it to you that something has occurred which made you think it right to change your story?—No. I know right from wrong, and I would not tell any lie in such a case.

If you did say it, can you account for saying it?—No, I do not know what has caused me to say it, if I did say it. I had no occasion for making a wrong statement.

John Donald Merrett.

Mrs Henrietta Sutherland

Do you know that Mrs. Penn has strongly resented throughout any suggestion of suicide?—She has often just said, " How did it happen ? "

And has not she said a great deal more than that?—She may have, but I conversed very little with her on the matter.

Has she not said to you that the idea that her sister shot herself was absurd?—No, she did not.

Did she not think the idea was absurd?—Well, she may have, but I did not hear.

Are you aware of the fact that the information supplied by you to Inspector Fleming was passed on to the Fiscal, and that a charge of attempted suicide was preferred against Mrs. Merrett?—No, I never knew it.

Are you aware of the fact that, on the information supplied by you, Mrs. Merrett was technically put under arrest on a charge of attempted suicide?—Well, I never knew of it.

You never heard of it before?—No.

Do you know that, on the information supplied by you, not only was a warrant issued, but intimation of that warrant was made to the Royal Infirmary, where Mrs. Merrett was conveyed?—Well, I expect so, if I did so.

You expect so, if you did say it?—Yes, but there is no truth in it.

Re-examined by the LORD ADVOCATE—Of course, you do not know what steps the police took as regards charging Mrs. Merrett, or on what evidence they proceeded in doing so?—No.

Do you remember a few days after 17th March two constables, Constable Watt and Constable Gibson, coming to see you about what you knew about the happening?—Two plain-clothes gentlemen, yes.

My information is that the date they came to see you about it was Sunday, 21st March, the first Sunday after the shooting?—Yes.

Did they take a statement from you?—Yes.

And did you tell them just what you have told the jury now? —Yes.

Were you asked by them about what it was suggested you had said to Inspector Fleming?—Yes, they did speak to me about it.

Was it put to you that Inspector Fleming asserted that you had said to him that you had seen Mrs. Merrett falling off a chair in the dining-room, and the revolver falling from her hand?—Yes.

What was your reply?—I said, " No; there was no truth in it."

Was that on Sunday, 21st March, just four days after the occurrence?—Yes.

Was there anything out of the ordinary about Mrs. Merrett at any time? Was she an ordinary healthy woman?—Yes, as far as I thought.

Evidence for Prosecution.

Mrs Henrietta Sutherland

An active woman?—Yes, very active.

I understand she was 55 years old?—Yes, as far as I know.

On the morning of the 17th did she appear her ordinary self? —Yes, but she seemed as if she was in a great hurry.

As you told us, you said to the accused immediately after the occurrence, " She seemed quite all right this morning "?—Yes.

That was how it had struck you?—Yes.

When you left the dining-room without doing the fire, the second time you went in that morning, you say you left the door open?—Yes.

Was it wide open, or half-open?—Wide open.

When you left the sitting-room you went, first of all, to the coal-cellar to get the ash-bucket out?—Yes.

And, having got it out, you then proceeded to the kitchen to get ready to do the kitchen grate?—Yes, I did.

It would take more than a second to do all that?—A few seconds. I just walked smartly along the lobby, and the coal-cellar was just on the way into the kitchen.

And it was just when you were bending down to start the kitchen grate that you heard the first sound?—Yes.

Namely, a shot?—Yes.

You heard a shot, and a thud as of a body falling?—Yes.

How soon after the thud would you hear the books falling in the lobby?—It was a few seconds.

And how soon after you heard the books falling did the accused appear in the kitchen?—Just immediately after.

It fitted in with his having dropped the books as he came along?—Yes.

Were you able to judge whether the accused had come straight to the kitchen as quickly as he could immediately after the thud you heard, or whether there had been some few seconds elapse?—Oh, there was a little delay.

Did he come in a hurry into the kitchen?—He walked smartly into the lobby. I heard him walking quite quickly.

But there was some delay after the thud before you heard him walking along the lobby?—Yes.

Did Mrs. Merrett have false teeth?—I did not know.

Did you ever see her false teeth?—Well, only on that day I thought she had false teeth in her left hand.

When?—When I went in along with the accused and found her on the floor.

Did you see them again?—No.

Now, at the breakfast table there would be dishes used, crockery, and, I suppose, knives and forks?—Yes.

And possibly spoons; and then there would be cruet stands, and things of that kind?—Yes.

First of all, I suppose the crockery was all kept in the kitchen, and it was your duty to wash up the crockery?—Yes. I also washed the cutlery, knives, forks, and spoons.

75

John Donald Merrett.

Mrs Henrietta Sutherland

And where were they put away after you washed them?—I had them on the kitchen table. I did not take them back to the sitting-room that morning.

On that morning did you wash up the knives and forks and spoons?—Yes, I washed them up.

When you first went in, I think it was the first time you saw Mrs. Merrett at the bureau, was not it?—Yes.

Could she have been handling any of the cutlery—knives, forks, or spoons?—Well, I think there was a big spoon, a table spoon, and a dessert spoon lying on the table for the dessert they had at breakfast, and I did not take it away, because it was clean. She may have been putting it away.

But there was a cruet stand that had some metal about it?—Yes, a little salt-cellar and pepper dish. I could not say whether it was plated.

Was it metal or glass, or had it some metal about it?—It had metal about it.

Did you see exactly what she was putting away in the bureau that first time you went in?—No, I could not say.

Did you see anything like that pistol lying about, or being handled by Mrs. Merrett at that time?—No.

By the Lord Justice-Clerk—I understand it is suggested that you told the policemen or detectives who came to the house on the morning of the tragedy that you saw Mrs. Merrett fall, and that you saw a revolver fall from her hand. Now, do you admit that you made that statement to them, or do you deny that you made that statement?—I won't contradict it.

Or do you not remember?—I may have said it, but I cannot give an account of myself for saying that, for there was certainly no truth in it.

I am asking you whether, having thought about it, you admit that you made the statement, or deny that you made it, or cannot remember whether you did or not?—I cannot remember.

But you think that you may have made it?—I may have.

Can you account for your making it?—Well, I was just sort of mixed up. I heard Mrs. Merrett fall, and then Donald said his mother had shot herself. I was mixed up with what I heard and what Donald said. That may have been the cause of my saying what I did say.

Were you on very friendly terms with the Merretts?—No.

I notice that you have three times referred to the accused as "Donald." Was that what you called him?—I called him "Mr. Merrett" until the thing happened, and it is just since that I started to call him "Donald"; but I used to call him "Mr. Merrett" when I worked there at first.

James Robertson (42), examined by the Lord Advocate—I am a surveyor in Edinburgh. On 9th November, 1926, on the instructions of the Crown, I visited the flat at 31 Buckingham

Evidence for Prosecution.

James Robertson

Terrace, accompanied by the last witness and Constable Izatt, who showed me the sitting-room and flat occupied by Mrs. Merrett. I prepared the plan of the sitting-room, which is production 183, and on that plan I marked various articles of furniture, the positions of which were pointed out to me by Mrs. Sutherland. I also prepared a corresponding plan without the articles of furniture marked upon it, which is production 184.

THOMAS GRAY MIDDLEMISS (29), examined by the LORD ADVOCATE —In March last I was a constable in the Edinburgh City Police.

And are you presently a piper in the King's Own Scottish Borderers?—I was, but I am out of them now. I intend going out to Australia in April to my brother in Sydney. On Wednesday, 17th March, at 9.30 a.m., after I had come on duty and was in Queensferry Street, a police ambulance came along, and the driver Edgar told me there had been a shooting accident at 31 Buckingham Terrace. I went with the ambulance. At the foot of the stair I met the accused and the tablemaid or kitchenmaid, Mrs. Henrietta Sutherland, the first witness. I asked what was wrong, and the accused said that his mother had shot herself. I went up the first-flat stair and into the sitting-room, and found Mrs. Merrett lying on the floor. She was lying in front of a kind of writing desk or something. I think her feet were towards the window, and her head towards the door. There was a good deal of blood about, and she was still bleeding. She was unconscious.

Did you notice any chair near Mrs. Merrett?—Yes, there was a chair there, a chair near a table.

Near the writing table, do you mean?—I could not say if it was near the writing table or not.

When you went in was Mrs. Merrett lying between you and the writing table?—No, she was not. She was lying in front of the door, and the writing table was on the right-hand side, and the window was facing looking out towards Buckingham Terrace. The writing table I refer to was against the wall.

The only writing table we know of against the wall there was a bureau?—I am not up to those names about bureaus or anything like that.

However, Mrs. Merrett was in front of that?—Yes.

Did you notice there was a flat-topped table between her and the window?—That was on her left-hand side, I think.

Well, somewhere in front of her feet?—About ten months have elapsed since I put in a report, and I have been up and down a lot of places, and I cannot just remember a lot of these things.

You spoke about a chair. Where was that chair relative to this writing desk you spoke of?—I could not really tell you. I am not clear about that.

Was the chair overturned or standing on its feet?—I could not really tell you.

John Donald Merrett.

Thomas Gray Middlemiss

Did you ask the accused any question about how this had happened?—I did. I asked him what happened, after his mother went into the out-patient surgical department at the Infirmary when I took her up there.

Did you ask him anything when you were in the sitting-room?—Not at the time, because Mrs. Merrett was lying unconscious, and I intended to see her right; that was my first duty.

Though she was unconscious, was she moving about?—She was; she was moving.

Was she making any sounds?—Like as if she was trying to get breath; she was kind of choking with the blood in her throat.

Did you see any pistol anywhere in the room?—Yes.

Where?—It was me that picked the pistol up. I do not know if I picked it up off the floor or the bureau.

Did Mrs. Sutherland ask you to take it away, do you remember?—I asked young Merrett, I think, or Mrs. Sutherland where the revolver was, and they pointed it out to me. I lifted it up and rolled it in paper and put it in my pocket.

Was there blood on the revolver?—Yes, there was blood on the revolver.

Before you picked it up?—Yes. [Witness identified the pistol produced as the pistol which he said he picked up.] We then lifted Mrs. Merrett from the floor and put her on to a stretcher and carried the stretcher down to the ambulance. The accused went with us in the ambulance to the surgical out-patients' department. I had a conversation with the accused in the corridor when Mrs. Merrett was inside being examined.

Tell us what passed in that conversation?—I said to young Merrett, " I wonder what has went wrong with your mother?" I said, " How has she come to do this?" and he said, " Money matters."

I want you to give us as exactly as you can what he said?—I said, " What do you mean by ' money matters '—too much or too little?" and he said, " No, just money matters." That was all he said to me.

Did he give you any description as to how it had happened?—Not at that time. After we had finished up there I went back to 31 Buckingham Terrace with the accused in a taxi, and while in the taxi I asked him again—because I wanted a proper statement for my report, and he told me just the same, that his mother was writing a letter at the bureau at the time, and he was sitting at the other side of the room when he heard the shot go off.

Did he say what he had done when he heard the shot?—Aye, he went to see about his mother, and then I think he went in to see Mrs. Sutherland in the kitchen, and then they telephoned for the police. I asked, " Who was the owner of the pistol?" and he said, " It was my pistol." I asked him if he had a certificate, but he could not produce the certificate at the time. He looked up and down some baggage there and got a receipt. When we

78

Evidence for Prosecution.

Thomas Gray Middlemiss

got back to Buckingham Terrace I saw Mrs. Sutherland, and I asked her what had happened. She told me she was in the pantry or kitchen, or whatever you call the place, at the time working away when she heard the report of the revolver—a report like a shot going off—and young Merrett came in and told her that his mother had shot herself.

On the information you had got, did you report the case as one of attempted suicide?—I did.

When you took the pistol to the police station, was an examination made of it?—Yes.

What did you find in it?—We found that it was loaded with five cartridges. It is an automatic pistol, and when you fire it the spent cartridge jumps out and another one comes into the breach. The pistol holds six cartridges. When examined at the police station it was found that there were four in the magazine and one in the breach, five altogether.

And, of course, the one that had been fired was not there?—It was not there; it would be automatically ejected.

Do you remember noticing whether when you went to Buckingham Terrace first and into the dining-room there were any letters or writing material lying about?—There was some writing material lying about or something.

Did you pay any particular attention to the matter?—No, I did not.

Cross-examined by Mr. AITCHISON—When you came on the scene first and found the body of Mrs. Merrett lying on the dining-room floor, was there a considerable amount of blood about?—There was a lot of blood. There was blood on her face, and particularly about her right ear.

Was the blood clotted about her right ear, did you notice, or was it flowing freely from the right ear?—It was bleeding right enough; it was bleeding from the wound.

You cannot, of course, tell us the precise position of the table and chair?—I cannot.

Do you remember picking the pistol up?—I do.

May you have picked it up from the floor?—I do not know whether I picked it up from there.

At any rate, are you clear on this, that when you did pick it up it was covered with blood?—It was covered with blood.

If it had been lying on the floor by the side of the injured woman that would account for blood being on it?—It might.

Do you remember, owing to the blood being on it, you got blood on your hands?—I did. I got a little touch of blood on my hands.

And as there was blood on the pistol, did you get a little piece of paper in which to wrap it?—Yes, I did; I wrapped it up and put it in my pocket.

Of course, going there as a constable, you naturally made some inquiries?—Yes.

John Donald Merrett.

Thomas Gray Middlemiss

And did you learn that Mrs. Merrett had shot herself?—Yes.

I think the accused went to the Infirmary with the ambulance?—Yes.

And on the way back from the Infirmary did he give you further details about the matter?—Yes, I was trying to get another statement.

Do you remember him saying to you that he had been looking at books at the other side of the room from where his mother had been writing?—Yes, he said that.

Did he say to you that on hearing the report of a firearm he turned round and saw his mother falling on the floor?—That is right.

When you asked him as to what had happened did he give you the information quite freely and willingly?—Well, he did not give it freely or willingly; but, you know, he is a fellow that I could not really tell you what he is. You know you could not read him very well. You could not sum him up. If he had been a pal——

If he had been a pal you would have known him better?—Yes.

Of course, he was very much excited?—Oh, he was a bit flurried.

And agitated?—Yes.

Did he give you the information I have just put to you?—He gave the information.

And when you asked to whom the pistol belonged, did not he at once say it belonged to him?—He did.

Did he say to you what he had it for?—Yes.

Tell us about that?—He said he bought the automatic pistol, as he was going to France on holiday. He was going a short vacation to France.

And did you ask him for his firearm certificate?—I did, and he tried his best to find it, but could not.

But did he get the receipt?—Yes.

And did he at once hand over the receipt to you?—He did, and I took the number of the receipt, and I said, " That will do me just now. We will get your certificate later on.''

Did he hunt about for the receipt?—Yes.

And when he found it, did he bring it to you at once?—Yes, he did.

And you also had some talk with Mrs. Sutherland about the matter?—Yes, Mrs. Sutherland, the kitchenmaid.

Before you had your conversation with Mrs. Sutherland, had Inspector Fleming been there?—Not to my knowledge. I think he came on the scene after us.

But, at any rate, whatever Mrs. Sutherland said to you, did you report the information you had obtained from her and from the accused to your official superiors?—Yes, at Torphichen Street, which is the West End Police Station.

80

Evidence for Prosecution.

Thomas Gray Middlemiss

Following upon your report, do you know what step was taken?—Yes. I gave the sitting sergeant my report about the statements Mrs. Sutherland and young Merrett gave us, and what happened to Mrs. Merrett as well—the times and places that everything happened.

I suppose you cannot remember the details of what Mrs. Sutherland told you?—She told me she was working away at the time and she heard a report like a shot going off, and young Merrett came in and told her his mother had shot herself.

And is that about all you remember she said? And then I asked her, " What kind of people are they?"

But apart from that, is all you have told us regarding what had happened all you can recollect of what she said?—I have told you.

But you made a report at the time?—I made a report. It was my duty.

And I suppose it was your duty to keep your eyes open?—It was, but in cases like this, when you are a policeman in uniform, you have to " get your skates on quick "; but it was reported to the C.I.D. I did my best. I could not do anything more in my duty.

There was nothing in the circumstances to arouse your suspicion?—Well, not at the time, but after——

At the time there was nothing whatsoever in the circumstances as you found them to arouse your suspicion?—(No answer).

Do you follow the question?—I follow it.

Am I right?—I was telling you at the time when you get a job like that you have to do it in quickness and try to save life.

I am not blaming you in the least, because I think you were right in your conclusion; but was your conclusion at the time that it was a case of attempted suicide?—Well, after I reported the matter I was beginning to think different things, just the same as the public.

But, at the time when you were there officially, was it your view that it was a case of attempted suicide?—I reported the case as that.

And may I take it that that was the view you formed at the time after your interview with the accused?—Yes.

And with Mrs. Sutherland?—Yes, with the statements I got I could not do anything else.

Re-examined by the LORD ADVOCATE—Are you quite clear in your recollection that Mrs. Sutherland told you that, at the time she heard the shot, she was in the kitchen or pantry, and working?—She was working there in the pantry or the kitchen.

When she heard the shot?—Yes, because it is just a straight walk through from where the thing happened—just a matter of about 10 yards or 7 or 8 yards.

And the accused came into the kitchen or pantry where she was working and told her about it?—That is what she told me.

G

John Donald Merrett.

Thomas Gray Middlemiss

By the LORD JUSTICE-CLERK—I suppose you made a written report?—Yes.

Did you not think it worth while to include in your written report, relating to a case which you thought was one of attempted suicide, where you found the revolver?—Yes, I put that in my report, but, as I told them here, I could not remember where I picked up the revolver from, because it is ten and a half months since.

But do you mean that in your report at the time you stated where you found it?—Yes, I put it in my report, but I have not seen my book for over six months, because it is the police property, and you have to hand it in.

DAVID IZATT (29), examined by the LORD ADVOCATE—I am a constable in the Edinburgh City Police attached to the West End Police Station. On the morning of Wednesday, 17th March, 1926, I was picked up by the police ambulance on its way to 31 Buckingham Terrace, and I went there along with the last witness, Constable Middlemiss. When we got there we were met at the door by the accused and the first witness, Mrs. Sutherland.

Did the accused make any statement to you when you arrived?—Middlemiss asked him if it was money matters or something, you see.

What I am asking you is, when you arrived at Buckingham Terrace, before you went up to the sitting-room, did you hear any conversation pass between Middlemiss and the accused?—I heard the accused say that his mother had shot herself, and so we went up the stairs and saw Mrs. Merrett lying on the floor of the sitting-room. We picked her up and put her on the stretcher and took her to the Infirmary.

While you were in Buckingham Terrace on that first occasion in the sitting-room did you see a pistol?—Yes, lying by the side of her body. She was lying about straight out, and the pistol was lying on her right-hand side. I never handled the pistol; Middlemiss took it.

Did he take it up from the floor or where?—Well, I believe he did.

I want to know what you remember and not what you believe?—He bent down to the floor and picked it up, as far as I noticed.

And not from the top of the bureau against the wall?—No.

Are you sure about that?—Oh, yes, I am sure. You see, when I went in first I saw him bending down, and he got a piece of paper and rolled up the revolver in a piece of paper and put it in his pocket. I did not see whether there was any blood on the revolver. I went to the Infirmary along with Middlemiss and the accused. I did not hear any conversation between Middlemiss and the accused in the corridor at the Infirmary, but I heard the conversation in the house at Buckingham Terrace the first time we were there.

Evidence for Prosecution.

David Izatt

What was said?—Middlemiss went up and asked him how this happened. He said to him, " Is there any trouble, any financial matters? " and he said, " No, I think my mother is well off." He said something to the effect that it was not money matters that was wrong with his mother.

Was that what he said?—You see, Middlemiss asked him if it was money matters which caused his mother to take her life, and he said, " Oh, no, my mother's well off." I did not notice when we first went to Buckingham Terrace whether there were any letters or writing material lying about.

WILLIAM WATT (33), examined by the LORD ADVOCATE—I am a constable in the Edinburgh City Police attached to the West End Police Station. On Sunday, 21st March last, which was the first Sunday after the shooting, I was instructed to go and see the witness, Mrs. Sutherland. My purpose was to find out if the statement she had made to the constables on the morning in question was correct.

When you say " the constables " do you mean Constables Middlemiss and Izatt, or Inspector Fleming and Inspector Henderson?—All of them.

You had seen a report of these statements?—No, I did not see any report. I took a statement from Mrs. Sutherland. She said (referring to note book), " I was employed as maid for a few hours daily at 31 Buckingham Terrace, and about 9.40 a.m. on Wednesday, 17th March, 1926, I had occasion to go into the dining-room, where I saw Mrs. Merrett, who was sitting writing, and her son, Donald, was sitting in a corner reading. I then went to the kitchen, returned to the coal-cellar, and saw Mrs. Merrett still writing, and returned to the kitchen again. When working at the grate there I heard a shot, and a sound as if some one had fallen. Then the boy came to the kitchen door and informed me that his mother had shot herself, and requested me to 'phone the police. I then entered the dining-room and saw Mrs. Merrett lying on her back with her head towards the door, and the revolver lying on the drawers near the writing table. I never at any time heard her threaten to commit suicide."

Did you put it to Mrs. Sutherland as to whether she had seen Mrs. Merrett falling off the chair?—I did. I had heard that she had made a statement to that effect to Inspector Fleming. She said she may have said that, but she was so excited at the time she could not remember.

Did she say whether in fact she had seen her falling off the chair or not?—She said she could not remember.

I am not asking you as to what Mrs. Sutherland said as to whether she had made the statement to Inspector Fleming or not, but what did she say to the suggestion that she, Mrs. Sutherland, had in fact seen Mrs. Merrett falling off the chair?—She had told Inspector Fleming that.

83

John Donald Merrett.

But did you ask Mrs. Sutherland whether it was true she had seen Mrs. Merrett?—I did.

What was her reply to that?—She said she may have said that to the policeman.

Listen to what I am asking you. I am not asking about what she said to Inspector Fleming. I am asking you about what Mrs. Sutherland said to you was the truth as to what she saw?—She never said what the truth was. You see, after I took this statement from her, I took that as her statement.

And is that statement inconsistent with her being in a position to see Mrs. Merrett falling off the chair at the time?—I could not say. I have never been in the house.

Did you not see Mrs. Sutherland at Buckingham Terrace?—No.

Then Mrs. Sutherland did not say to you whether in fact she had seen Mrs. Merrett, or had not seen her, falling off the chair?—No, she did not.

Cross-examined by Mr. AITCHISON—When you went to see Mrs. Sutherland on the Sunday what instructions did you receive from your superiors?—I was to find out if her statement was correct.

When you went to see her what exactly did you ask her?—I put several questions to her.

I want to know what they were. Do you remember?—[Referring to note book]—I asked her what occurred at 31 Buckingham Terrace on the morning in question, and then she started off with her statement.

[Note book handed to Mr. Aitchison.] I see, according to this statement, she said, " I never at any time heard her threaten suicide "?—That is right.

Did she volunteer that statement?—I asked her that question.

So that you put a series of questions to her?—I did. You see, she started with her statement and continued, and when she stopped I said, " And what happened then? " and " What occurred afterwards? " and so forth.

I understand the purpose for which you were sent to interview Mrs. Sutherland was to ascertain whether she adhered to what she had said on the morning of the 17th March?—That is right.

How is it that your note contains no account of what she said regarding that vital matter?—Well, I took this statement from her. That was her statement of what occurred on the morning in question.

But, you see, you have told us that the purpose of your visit was to find out whether what she had said on the morning of the 17th was true. Did you ever put to her what she had said on the morning of the 17th?—After I took the statement from her I said to her, " I thought you told the policemen on the morning in question that you had seen Mrs. Merrett fall from the chair

84

Evidence for Prosecution.

and the revolver drop to the side," and she said, " I may have done so, but I was too excited at the time."

Did she ever deny that she had made such a statement?—No, she never denied that. On Friday, 19th March, I was on duty at the Gorgie Police Station at 2 p.m. when a telephone message came through from the Royal Infirmary. I was told to call at the Infirmary, ward No. 16. I went to the Royal Infirmary the same afternoon and saw Dr. Holcombe. I ascertained that Mrs. Merrett was conscious.

I do not want you to tell us in any way what Dr. Holcombe said to you, but did Dr. Holcombe communicate to you a statement which Mrs. Merrett was said to have made in the Infirmary?—Yes.

Following upon that communication being made, did you report it?—I immediately telephoned the particulars to the Criminal Investigation Department.

Was any step taken, so far as you know, to take a deposition from Mrs. Merrett?—I cannot say.

Would the taking of a deposition be a matter for the Criminal Investigation Department?—Well, I asked if I would take a statement.

You must not repeat anything that Dr. Holcombe said to you, or what you said to anybody else; I merely want to know with whom lies the responsibility of taking a statement according to police practice?—I asked if I would take a statement there and then, and I got word back from the Criminal Investigation Department to say that a detective officer would be up that same afternoon to take a statement from Mrs. Merrett.

And having heard that a detective officer would be up the same afternoon to take a statement, you felt that you had done your duty in the matter?—That is correct.

Do you know that, notwithstanding the message from Dr. Holcombe, no statement was ever taken?—I could not say. I received no further instructions regarding the case.

You received no instructions to take a deposition?—No, I did not.

And, so far as you know, no deposition was ever taken?—As far as I know.

VICTOR GIBSON (32), examined by the LORD ADVOCATE—I am a constable in the Edinburgh City Police. On Sunday, 21st March, I went along with the last witness, Constable Watt, to interview Mrs. Sutherland at her house. She stated that about 9.40 a.m. on Wednesday, 17th March, 1926, she had occasion to enter the dining-room at 31 Buckingham Terrace, where she saw the now deceased Mrs. Merrett sitting at a writing desk, and her son, Donald, was sitting in a corner reading a book. She left the dining-room and returned to the kitchen. She then came from the kitchen to the coal-cellar, and returned to the

John Donald Merrett.

Victor Gibson

kitchen again, and while working at the grate there she heard a shot. The accused then came to the kitchen and asked her to telephone for the police, as his mother had shot herself. The police were summoned. I think she said that he finished the message himself. We were aware of a statement which she had made to Inspector Fleming about what she saw, and the preceding witness questioned Mrs. Sutherland as to that statement.

What did Mrs. Sutherland say about it?—She said that she might have made the statement, but she was excited at the time.

Was that statement to the effect that she had seen Mrs. Merrett falling off the chair with the pistol in her hand?—That is so.

Did she say whether in truth she had actually seen Mrs. Merrett tumbling back with the pistol in her hand?—No, she did not state that to us.

Did Constable Watt asked her whether Mrs. Merrett had ever threatened suicide?—Yes, I think he did. She said she had never heard her threaten to commit suicide.

Cross-examined by Mr. AITCHISON—Do you remember whether Constable Watt, who took the statement of Mrs. Sutherland on the occasion when you were present, put questions to her, to which she gave answers?—He put several questions.

So that the statements she made were elicited by questions put to her?—I would not say elicited.

Do you prefer another word? When Watt referred to the statement she had made to Inspector Fleming, did Mrs. Sutherland know quite well to what he was referring?—We referred to the statement she had made to Constable Middlemiss on the morning in question.

Did Watt refer to the statement which Mrs. Sutherland had made to Inspector Fleming?—I cannot remember about that.

Were you not sent to interview Mrs. Sutherland for the very purpose of finding out whether she adhered to the statement which she made to Inspector Fleming on the morning of 17th March?—The statement she had made to Constable Middlemiss.

Is that your evidence?—Yes.

Did you keep any record of what took place at that interview?—Constable Watt did. I did not.

Did you keep any record of the purpose for which you were sent by your superiors to interview Mrs. Sutherland?—No, I did not, but Constable Watt did.

And your recollection of the matter is that you were sent in order to check statements which she had made to Constable Middlemiss?—Yes.

Was she ever asked, either by you or by Watt, whether it was not the fact that she had seen Mrs. Merrett falling from her chair?—She was asked by Watt that question.

Was she pressed upon that matter?—No, he simply asked her. He said, "I thought you informed Middlemiss on the morning in question that you saw Mrs. Merrett falling from the chair

Evidence for Prosecution.

Victor Gibson

and the revolver drop from her side," and she said she might have said so, as she was excited at the time.

But she was not pressed regarding the matter in any way?—No.

Your evidence is that she was asked nothing at all as to what she had said to Fleming?—I cannot remember her being asked anything.

DAVID FLEMING, examined by the LORD ADVOCATE—I am a detective-inspector in the Edinburgh City Police. On 17th March, 1926, I got information from the West End Police Station regarding an occurrence at 31 Buckingham Terrace, and in consequence of that message I, along with Sergeant William Henderson, went to the flat at 31 Buckingham Terrace, which was occupied by Mrs. Merrett. We got there about ten o'clock in the morning. By the time we arrived there Mrs. Merrett had been removed in the police ambulance to the Royal Infirmary. Mrs. Sutherland was the only person in the house at that time. I asked Mrs. Sutherland what had happened, and she told me she had been in the kitchen about half-past nine and heard a shot, and on going into the lobby she saw Mrs. Merrett fall off the chair and on to the floor, and a revolver or pistol falling out of her hand.

What else did she say?—She had been in the room earlier in the morning removing the breakfast dishes. Mrs. Merrett at that time was sitting at the table writing, and Donald, her son, was sitting reading a book on a chair in the room, on the left of the door as you go in. That is towards where the fireplace is. Sergeant Henderson and I went into the sitting-room and saw where Mrs. Merrett had been lying on the floor. We saw the blood on the mat. Near where Mrs. Merrett had been lying there was the table they had been breakfasting at that morning. I noticed a letter lying on the table, and I looked at the letter. I believe the table was an oval gate-legged table. I saw a chair standing upright between the bureau and the table, a little towards the window. It had been removed from where the blood was lying on the floor. The letter I have spoken of was lying on the table at the end where the chair was. It was unfinished. I read the letter.

Out loud?—Not exactly out loud, but I think Sergeant Henderson would probably hear it, and the maid too. Mrs. Merrett was writing to some friend in Stirling mentioning the fact that she had got a flat at last, and that she had some trouble in getting a maid, but that she had got a maid who was coming there daily. There was nothing about money troubles in it.

Assuming that Mrs. Merrett had been sitting at the end of the table writing that letter, where were the marks of blood relative to where she would have been sitting? Were they on her right hand or her left?—On her left.

Was what you saw consistent with her having been sitting writing and having fallen off towards the left-hand side of the

87

John Donald Merrett.

chair?—Yes. There was a bureau standing against the wall behind the chair.

In appearance was it like a chest of drawers with a front that could open down?—There were four drawers, I think, in it, two just the ordinary drawers of a chest of drawers, and the third opened down and made a sort of writing desk. Inside there were some little pigeon holes for holding stationery and other things. When we first went to the flat the writing part of the bureau was open.

Assuming Mrs. Merrett was sitting writing in the chair at the end of the table, and the bureau was open, how close would the open bit be?—Quite close.

To her right or her left hand?—The larger portion would be to her left.

Then the bureau was pretty well behind her?—Yes, pretty well behind her. I saw writing material in the bureau. After I had read the letter I left it lying on the table, and I never saw it again. On the same occasion I also saw two open letters from the Clydesdale Bank, addressed to Mrs. Merrett, intimating that her account was overdrawn. One of the letters is dated 13th March and the other 16th March. These letters were lying open on the writing bureau.

Did you draw a conclusion from what you saw of the flat as to what had happened?—That Mrs. Merrett had committed suicide. I returned to the police station and gave instructions that the necessary inquiries be made with a view to the consideration of a charge.

What was the charge you were going to consider?—Attempted suicide by shooting.

I just want to know, as a matter of practice, in a case of attempted suicide, is it the ordinary course for the constables attached to the division to make the inquiries?—Plain-clothes constables, or uniformed constables sometimes.

But where there is a crime, does it then fall to the Criminal Investigation Department, of which you are a member?—Yes. On Friday, 19th March, 1926, I was informed of a communication which had come from Dr. Holcombe at the Royal Infirmary, and I called at the Infirmary, but failed to find Dr. Holcombe. I returned, however, the next day, 20th March, a Saturday forenoon, when I saw Dr. Holcombe.

I do not want you to tell me what they were, but did he report to you certain remarks which he said Mrs. Merrett had made to him?—He did.

In consequence of what you learned from Dr. Holcombe, did you send Constables Watt and Gibson to see Mrs. Sutherland?—I saw them that same afternoon in Gorgie Police Office, and I asked them if they had seen Mrs. Sutherland or the accused. They said

Evidence for Prosecution.

David Fleming

they had not, and I instructed them then to go and see Mrs. Sutherland and John Donald Merrett.

I think you were not concerned with the case until about a week later?—That is so, the 30th. On 30th March, 1926, I was informed of certain statements alleged to have been made by Mrs. Merrett to her sister, Mrs. Penn, and there was also reported to me the finding of an empty cartridge case in the flat at Buckingham Terrace. Accordingly, on that same day I, along with Constable William Johnston, went to 31 Buckingham Terrace, and found there Mr. and Mrs. Penn and the accused. Mr. Penn pointed out to us the place where he said he had found the empty cartridge. It was to the left of where Mrs. Merrett had been sitting, or rather in front—straight in front.

How far off from the chair, assuming Mrs. Merrett had been sitting writing?—Roughly speaking, 6 or 8 feet, probably. I got the empty cartridge from Mr. Penn. Label No. 3 is the cartridge. On this occasion I took a statement from the accused. I duly cautioned him and warned him before taking the statement.

What statement did he give you? Read it slowly, please?—After being duly warned and cautioned he said—" I am the only son of Bertha Milner or Merrett, about fifty-six years. We arrived in Edinburgh on 4th January, 1926, from Waverley Hydropathic, Melrose. We resided at 7 Mayfield Road, c/o Hardie, and remained there about a fortnight or three weeks, when we removed to 35 Palmerston Place, a boarding-house, and remained until we took a flat at 31 Buckingham Terrace, c/o Crooke, on 10th March, 1926. The reason for coming to Edinburgh was to attend classes at the University. In February, 1926, I applied for a certificate for an automatic pistol, as we thought of going abroad to Baileau, near Paris, at the Easter holidays. She allowed me 10s. a week, sometimes extra for outside meals. I also purchased a motor cycle three weeks ago, £27. After coming to the flat at 31 Buckingham Terrace everything was in good spirits and getting on all right. When in Palmerston Place she got on to me for spending too much money. She also got on to me for going out too much and neglecting my lessons. This was when we came to Edinburgh first. On 16th March, 1926, we had a Miss Macglashan, 7 Ann Street, visiting us, there just being the three of us. Mother went to bed, I having retired before her. About 8.30 a.m. on 17th March I got up and dressed and had breakfast. Some letters arrived in the morning, and one was an intimation from the Clydesdale Bank in George Street to the effect that she had overdrawn her account. After breakfast I went into my room, which adjoins the dining-room, and mother got the dishes removed. When I returned to the dining-room mother was sitting at the table writing, when I saw an envelope my mother had addressed to Mrs. Anderson, 64 Murray Place, Edinburgh, I pointed out the mistake,[1]

---

[1] The correct address of this lady, No. 35 of the Crown List of Witnesses, was 64 Murray Place, Stirling.—ED.

John Donald Merrett.

David Fleming

and she said, ' Go away, you worry me.' I went to the other side of the room to get my books, when I heard a report and saw my mother in the act of falling on to the floor. I rushed over to my mother and saw the maid in the hall, when I said, ' Mother has hurt herself.' She fell on the left side, and the revolver was lying beside her right hand. I telephoned for the police, and they removed the body to the Royal Infirmary, where she was detained "——

Have you not missed a sentence? Do you not say something about lifting his pistol?—No, I have nothing here. He mentioned to me afterwards that he had lifted the pistol.

Please go on?—" In the dining-room there is a writing bureau with three drawers. About noon on Saturday, 13th March, I had the pistol and loaded it with six cartridges, one being in the breach, and the safety catch on. I was going to the Braids to shoot rabbits. I wanted to take it on the Sunday morning, but she took it from me and put it in the small drawer in the writing bureau. I think I told my mother to be careful, that it was loaded. I never again saw the pistol."

Did he say something about lifting the pistol?—He said he lifted the pistol off the floor and put it on to the corner of the bureau.

Did he say at what stage he had done that?—Shortly after his mother had fallen on the floor.

Did he say whether he had tried to lift his mother?—He said he had tried to lift his mother, but could not.

Did he say whether that was before or after he had seen the maid and the maid had come into the room?—Before he had seen the maid.

Did he say anything about his mother having worries over money?—He said his mother had been worrying herself over money matters.

Look again at the two Clydesdale Bank letters (Nos. 15 and 16). Just tell us the amount of the overdraft?—The first letter is dated the 13th March, and the amount is £22. The next is dated the 16th, and the amount is £6 11s. 3d. On the same day, the 30th March, Constable Johnston and I saw Mrs. Sutherland in the kitchen at the flat. By this time I had heard what Mrs. Sutherland had said to Constable Watt and Constable Gibson, and she had varied her statement from what she told me at the beginning.

What passed between you then on this day?—I took the following statement from Mrs. Sutherland :—" Henrietta Sutherland, wife of Hugh Sutherland, residing at 107 Broughton Road. I reside with my husband at the above address. For the past eighteen months I was daily maid to a lady in Great King Street. Through a friend of mine I learned that Mrs. Merrett wanted a maid for a few hours in the morning, 9 to 12 noon. I first came on Thursday, 11th March. I did not come on Friday, 12th,

Evidence for Prosecution.

but I came every day after until the morning of the 17th inst. I arrived at 9 a.m. I heard no disagreement between the mother and son. On Sunday, 14th March, I arrived, and she told me that she could not get him up, the bedroom door was locked.''

I do not think we need take this at length. What I want to ask you is, did you ask Mrs. Sutherland about the point on which she had varied her story?—She gave no excuse at all. She said she was upset on the morning of 17th March when I saw her, and did not remember what she said.

But on 30th March was she quite clear as to the story which she gave you?—Quite clear.

On that day, 30th March, did you take possession of certain articles at the flat?—I did.

[Shown production No. 8]—Is that a Midland Bank cheque book, the numbers on the cover being 76541 to 76570?—Yes. There are five cheques wanting. I noticed that at the time.

Is it the cheques only that are wanting or the counterfoils as well?—The counterfoils as well. They are 76541 to 76545 inclusive. I asked the accused where those missing cheques and counterfoils were, and he informed me he did not know anything about them. I asked him to search for them, and he said he would.

Where did you find that cheque book?—I found that cheque book in a drawer of a table in the accused's bedroom.

[Shown productions Nos. 11, 11a, and 11b]—Did you find these three productions also in the accused's bedroom?—I did, in the same drawer. The envelope, No. 11, is an envelope addressed to Mrs. Bertha Merrett, 35 Palmerston Place, Edinburgh, and it is marked '' Private.'' It is not re-addressed in any form. No. 11a is a Midland Bank book, Boscombe, and No. 11b is a letter from that bank to Mrs. Merrett, dated 5th March, 1926. When I found them the letter and the bank book were inside an envelope. The accused was present when I found these things.

But you yourself were searching for them?—I was.

They were not produced by him?—They were not produced by him. I also found in the same drawer an account note book [production No. 159]. It is a note book marked, '' Accounts, J. D. Merrett.'' In the bureau I found another account book.

[Shown production No. 148]—Is that an account book of Mrs. Merrett's?—Yes. It was lying on the top of the writing portion of the bureau. I also found in the bureau, No. 17, a portion of a cheque book, the counterfoils left being 2331 to 2339. I found that in one of the little pigeon holes of the bureau. At the same time I asked the accused where his mother's Clydesdale Bank book was. He stated he did not know; that it had been sent from the bank two or three days before. I searched for it in the flat and failed to find it.

Did you also ask the accused on that date what had become of the unfinished letter which you had seen on the writing table

John Donald Merrett.

David Fleming

on 17th March?—I did. He said he had destroyed it, as there were some blood marks on the letter.

Had you noticed any blood marks on it?—I did not—not on the 17th March.

Had you noticed any envelope about?—I saw no envelope at all on the table on 17th March. I was back again at 31 Buckingham Terrace a few days later. On this occasion the accused told me he had found some of the cheques out of the cheque book— two cheques—and he took me to the bedroom occupied by his mother and took two cheques out of a small drawer in a dressing table there. They were two of the cheques out of the cheque book that I had taken possession of. [Shown productions Nos. 9 and 10]—I took possession of these. They are Midland Bank cheques, 76544 and 76545, but there are no counterfoils. That left three cheques and counterfoils still missing out of that book. I asked the accused again where they were, and he said he did not know. I was back several times again after that at the flat.

On one of these occasions did you ask the accused about the pistol and ammunition?—I asked him where he got them. He told me he had purchased it from Hardy Brothers in Princes Street, along with 50 cartridges.

Did he tell you whether his mother had known whether he had the pistol?—He did not think his mother knew he had the pistol.

Did he say anything about the cost of the pistol?—£5 was what he paid for it.

Did he not say whether his mother had helped him with the purchase price of the pistol?—That I cannot remember.

Did he make any statement to you about a motor cycle?—He told me that his mother had bought him a motor cycle and paid £27 for it. On Thursday, 1st April, I got information that Mrs. Merrett had died very early that morning, and she was buried on Saturday, the 3rd. I got possession of certain cheques drawn upon the Midland Bank of Boscombe, and I noticed among those cheques the three missing cheques to which I have spoken. Those are the cheques missing from the Midland Bank cheque book [production No. 8]. I questioned the accused about those three cheques on the occasion of his call at the police office about the 10th or 12th April. [Shown productions Nos. 47, 48, and 49]—Those are the cheques of which I have been speaking. The first one is dated 24th March, that is a week after Mrs. Merrett had gone to the Infirmary. It is filled in, " Pay to J. D. Merrett £30," and signed " Bertha Merrett." The next is dated 26th March, 1926, and is filled in, " Pay to J. D. Merrett £30," and signed " Bertha Merrett." The third one is dated 27th March, and is filled in, " Pay to J. D. Merrett £28 9s. 6d.," and it is signed " Bertha Merrett." That was on the 27th March, and it was on 30th March I first asked the accused where those three cheques were, and he told me he did not know.

Evidence for Prosecution.

David Fleming

When you put these cheques to him on the 10th or 12th of April, what did the accused say about them?—He said he had used two of them.

Did he say what they were used for?—For purchasing a motor cycle from the Rossleigh Company in Shandwick Place.

On this occasion did he say anything further about the signing of cheques or his mother?—He stated that his mother signed the cheques and left them blank, and he filled them in, for the amount that was drawn, at the bank, and he paid part of it to his mother's banking account and a portion towards expenses incurred by his mother, and the remainder he handed over to his mother.

Did he speak of that as being a customary thing?—Yes. When I visited the flat on 30th March I found some pistol cartridges. [Shown label No. 4]—These are the cartridges found by me. At that time there were 38 cartridges in the box. I found the cartridges lying loose in a table drawer. They have been put in this box since then.

You found the cartridges in a drawer in the accused's bedroom?—Yes.

Cross-examined by Mr. AITCHISON—When you went to the flat on the morning of 17th March did you proceed at once to make inquiries?—No, I did not.

What did you go there for?—We were informed it was a case of suicide by shooting, and we simply went down there to see what had happened. We were told what had happened, and in consequence we left the matter for divisional plain-clothes officers to make inquiries.

But you thought it right as divisional inspector to go yourself to the flat at Buckingham Terrace and see what you could see?—Yes.

When you got there and entered the room you found a good deal of blood about?—There was blood lying on the mat in front of the writing table.

Would you say it was lying between the table and the bureau?—I would.

And a very considerable quantity?—A very considerable quantity.

And on the table, I understand you to say, you found a letter?—We saw a letter lying on the table.

Can you tell me what the concluding sentence of that was?—I could not tell you.

Did you read the letter right through?—I glanced it over.

Did you notice that there was not anything in the nature of a blur or a smudge about the last word of the letter?—That is right.

Was there anything to indicate that the writer had suddenly been stopped in her writing of the letter?—No, I would not say so.

93

John Donald Merrett.

David Fleming

You say there was no blot or smudge. Was there any dragging of the pen as if the writer had been suddenly stopped?—No, I would not say that either.

As regards the position of the furniture, when you got to the flat had the chair been moved?—It had been moved.

Assuming the chair to have been at the end of the table nearest the door, would the bureau be a little behind the chair?—Yes.

But would it be more to the right-hand side of the chair than to the left-hand of the chair?—No, I would say it would be more to the left of the chair than the right.

Would it depend entirely on the precise position in which the chair was?—It would.

And you did not see it in position?—I did not.

You are quite clear when you got to the flat the front part of the bureau was lying open?—It was lying open.

You made from that time onwards a number of inquiries, and I think you took possession of various things that are here as productions?—Most of them on the 30th of March. No. 11b of the productions is a letter from the bank manager of the Midland Bank at Boscombe addressed to the late Mrs. Merrett.

And do you see there is a postscript to that letter which appears to be in the same handwriting as the signature?—It is. It reads, " Am pleased to hear that your son is getting on so well. Kind regards."

And does that letter bear to be an acknowledgment of a letter from Mrs. Merrett dated 4th instant notifying the bank manager of a change in residence?—That is so.

At one of your interviews with the accused you asked him some questions regarding the pistol which he had?—I did.

Did he not tell you that his mother had given him the money to purchase it?—Not that I can remember.

May he have said that?—He may have said it.

So far as I can see from your note book, you have made no note of any conversation regarding the pistol?—No, no note.

As regards the conversations which you had with him relating to the cheques, do you remember whether he told you that his mother had a credit with the Clydesdale Bank amounting to £30 a day?—That is so.

Did he tell you that she had agreed to purchase a motor cycle for him?—He told me she had already paid for one, and paid £27 for it.

Is your recollection right in that matter? Did he not tell you that his mother had agreed to purchase him a new motor cycle? —No, there was only the one motor cycle that I remember of, and that was the one he said he had paid £27 for.

Did he tell you his mother had given him cheques to be used on successive days, within the limit each day of the credit of £30, in payment of the cycle?—No, I cannot remember that he said so.

94

Evidence for Prosecution.

David Fleming

Following upon your visit to the flat on 17th March, was there a charge sheet made out?—Yes, there was, at the West End Police Office.

Did that charge sheet formulate a charge of attempted suicide against Mrs. Merrett?—It did.

Was one of the witnesses to that charge sheet Mrs. Sutherland?—She was.

I think information had been given to you also by the accused. Did his name also appear on the charge sheet?—Yes.

Was the statement made by Mrs. Sutherland at the time appended to the charge sheet in accordance with the usual practice?—That is so.

On the morning of the 17th did you interrogate Mrs. Sutherland as to what had occurred?—We did not.

I am not using the word "interrogate" in any sinister sense?—We simply called there and asked what had happened.

That is what I mean. Did you ask Mrs. Sutherland as to what had happened at the time of the shooting?—I did.

Did she tell you that she was in the kitchen at the time?—She told me she was in the kitchen at the time when she heard the report.

And she told you that when she heard the report she ran out into the lobby?—She did.

Did she tell you that on going out into the lobby she saw Mrs. Merrett falling from her chair?—That is quite correct.

Did she also tell you that she saw the pistol falling away from Mrs. Merrett's hand?—That is correct.

Was Mrs. Sutherland in telling you that quite clear in what she said?—She was quite clear in what she said.

Did she appear to you to know what she was saying?—Perfectly.

She was not in any way mixed?—No, I would not say she was mixed—a little excited.

But in no way mixed?—In no way.

Were you as an experienced officer of police satisfied with the statement she had given you?—I was.

Was there any reason why, so far as you could judge, you should have doubted its accuracy?—None. whatever.

I think a statement was made by the accused the terms of which you have already given us?—That is so.

I see from that statement that the accused said this at the time, "I rushed over to my mother and saw the maid in the hall." Is that statement of the accused, that he saw the maid in the hall, in accordance with what Mrs. Sutherland had told you as to her being in the lobby and seeing Mrs. Merrett fall from her chair?—No, it is not.

What do you mean by "It is not." I thought it was?—Well, Mrs. Sutherland did not tell me that she saw Donald at the time when she saw Mrs. Merrett falling.

John Donald Merrett.

David Fleming

I understand that Donald made a statement that he had seen the maid in the hall. Is that consistent with what Mrs. Sutherland told you, that she had been in the hall when Mrs. Merrett fell from her chair?—That is quite correct.

And both these statements were made to you at the time?—They were. Mrs. Sutherland made one on the 17th, but the other was made on the 30th of March. Of course, I saw Mrs. Sutherland also on the 30th of March.

Did Mrs. Sutherland make a statement to you on the 17th of March?—She did.

The LORD JUSTICE-CLERK—I do not think the witness said that on the 17th of March he took a statement from Mrs. Sutherland.

Cross-examination continued—I understand you took a statement from Mrs. Sutherland on the 17th of March?—No, I did not.

So far as the accused is concerned, did you take a statement on the 17th or the 30th of March?—On the 30th of March.

Am I right that the statement which the accused gave you at your request on 30th March harmonised with the statement which you had received from Mrs. Sutherland in the flat on the 17th of March?—With what Mrs. Sutherland told us on the 17th of March.

Did you take down in your note book, which you have referred to, all that you regarded as material in the statement which the accused gave you on 30th March?—Yes, that is so.

I understand that in your note nothing is said as to the accused having lifted the pistol from the floor?—No.

Is it not in accord with your recollection that he said nothing about that matter?—I was back the next day at the house, and I believe he mentioned then that he had lifted the pistol off the floor and put it on the corner of the bureau.

You see, there is some suggestion in the evidence which has already been led that the pistol was lifted by Constable Middlemiss?—My information was that the accused had lifted the pistol and put it on the end of the bureau, and Mrs. Sutherland also saw it there before the police arrived.

But did you know that Constable Izatt saw Middlemiss lift the pistol from the floor and put it on the bureau?—I was not aware of it until this moment.

I think, so far as the pistol is concerned, you did not make any note at the time?—I did not.

I think you also said that on the 30th of March the accused said he had tried to lift his mother before he had seen the maid in the hall?—That is so.

Are you quite clear about that?—He said so himself, that he had tried to lift his mother, but he could not, and then he went and informed the maid.

Did you take a note of that at the time?—I did not.

May he not have said that he and the maid had endeavoured

Sketch Plan of Sitting Room in 31 Buckingham Terrace.

(From the original produced in Court.)

Evidence for Prosecution.

to lift his mother, but they were unable to do so?—No, he alone, he said.

I think you were told that some letters had arrived at the house that morning, 17th March?—Two letters had arrived that morning.

Were you told two, or more, or do you remember?—Two that I remember of.

As regards the charge sheet that was made out following upon the inquiries, can you tell me if the statements of Middlemiss and Izatt would be appended to that charge sheet?—They would.

What I mean is their report?—Their statement is also attached to the charge sheet.

Do you remember the accused being asked to call at the Central Police Office on 3rd June, 1926?—Yes.

On the occasion of that visit was he asked to write out his mother's name?—He was. He was also asked to copy his mother's signature. He complied with these requests.

Willingly?—Yes, willingly.

And quite freely?—Yes, that is so.

And without hesitation?—Without hesitation.

I think you took upon a sheet of paper the name " Bertha Merrett," written six times by the accused?—Yes, that is so.

Were the first four names on that sheet of paper in the accused's own natural handwriting?—Yes.

And were the fifth and sixth intended to be copies of a signature of his mother which was placed before him by you?—That is so.

I show you No. 20 of the productions. Is that the sheet of paper dated 3rd June, 1926, containing the signatures made by the accused at your request?—That is so.

As regards the signature which he was asked to copy, where did you get it?—From some Boscombe Bank cheques we had in our possession at the time.

Can you tell what particular cheque it was?—That I could not tell. My recollection is that it was cheques that were missing from the cheque books along with the counterfoils, which we had written to the Hants police to call at the Boscombe Bank for and send on to Edinburgh.

What I want to bring out is that he at once freely acceded to your request that he should write his name and copy a signature? —That is so.

On 19th March you received a communication from Dr. Holcombe from the Royal Infirmary?—No, I did not.

Was the fact of such a communication being made communicated to you?—It was.

Did you go up to the Royal Infirmary on the following day? —I went that afternoon, but I failed to find Dr. Holcombe, and I went back on Saturday forenoon, the 20th.

H   97

John Donald Merrett.

David Fleming

The matter of the communication was a matter of importance. I do not want you to tell us what he said, but was it not a matter of some importance?—I did not think so at the time.

Did it relate to statements alleged to have been made by Mrs. Merrett?—That is so.

And thought to have some bearing on the occurrence on the morning of the 17th of March?—It might.

Did you report to any one the intimation which you had from Dr. Holcombe?—I did not.

Are you yourself attached to the Criminal Investigation Department?—Yes.

Did you know that Mrs. Merrett was suffering from a very serious head wound that might become dangerous at any moment? —I did not know at that time the extent of the injuries at all, or how serious they were.

Did you know that she had sustained a severe injury to the head which had rendered her unconscious for some time?—Yes.

Did you learn from Dr. Holcombe that, with a head injury of that kind, a condition of danger might supervene at any time?—Quite.

Did you discuss with Dr. Holcombe the question of taking a deposition?—I did not.

Did it never occur to you?—It did not.

Why not?—Because I did not consider at that time that the woman was so dangerously ill as she appears to have been. I asked Dr. Holcombe if her life was in danger, and he said it was. It was with a view to taking a statement from Mrs. Merrett we had gone to the Infirmary, to bear out what Dr. Holcombe had said.

On 20th March you were informed by the surgeon in charge of the case that Mrs. Merrett was suffering from a dangerous wound?—I knew Mrs. Merrett was in the Royal Infirmary suffering from a wound in the head by shooting.

You were informed by the surgeon in charge that it was a wound that might endanger her life?—I do not know if he said so in so many words at that time. I went out and saw him on the Saturday, and he told me what Mrs. Merrett had said.

Were you not informed by Dr. Holcombe, in answer to your own inquiry, that Mrs. Merrett's life was in danger?—No, I would not say so.

By the LORD JUSTICE-CLERK—But you have just said, " I asked if her life was in danger, and he said ' Yes.' " Is that correct or is it not?—If I recollect correctly, I do not think Dr. Holcombe mentioned her life being in danger.

According to your evidence, you yourself mentioned it?—I went to see Dr. Holcombe——

Do you want to withdraw that answer or modify it?—I went to see Dr. Holcombe, and I asked him what Mrs. Merrett had said—there had been a telephone message received—and he said she had

Evidence for Prosecution.

made a certain statement. I asked him then, " Is her life in danger," and I cannot recollect now whether he said " Yes."

You have told us already he said " Yes." Do you want to alter that?—No, I do not. He may have said " Yes."

Cross-examination continued—Did it not occur to you as important in these circumstances that a deposition should be taken in proper form by a magistrate?—Up till that time we were still of the opinion it was a case of suicide.

Whatever your opinion may have been, in view of the communication from the surgeon in charge of the case, did it not occur to you that it would be a wise precaution to have a deposition taken by a magistrate?—Yes, if the circumstances were suspicious.

And, accordingly, may I take it that on the 20th March, when you had the interview with Dr. Holcombe, there was no element of suspicion at all, so far as your knowledge went?—Not at that time.

And so far as your investigations went at that time?—That is so.

Is it within your knowledge that intimation was made to the Royal Infirmary authorities that Mrs. Merrett was under arrest on a charge of attempting suicide?—That she was a prisoner.

And was there a request made to the Royal Infirmary authorities that the prison authorities should be informed prior to her discharge, in order that she might be taken in custody?—Yes, by the police authorities.

In the matter of taking a deposition from people who are critically ill, who is that in the hands of?—The Procurator-Fiscal, the Sheriff, and the Sheriff-Clerk.

Do the officials of the Criminal Investigation Department report these matters when they think it necessary?—Yes, they do in some cases.

Is your department constantly in touch with the Procurator-Fiscal?—Well, yes.

Am I right that it is nearly always your department that sets the machinery in motion for the taking of depositions?—That is so.

Re-examined by the LORD ADVOCATE—I want to get a little more clearly if I can what the accused said to you about the pistol in question. Can you tell us what he said about whether his mother knew of his having the pistol or not?—He told me he did not think his mother knew about the pistol.

Did he suggest that his mother in any way provided the money for the pistol?—No.

Mrs. Merrett in fact was never charged with attempted suicide? —No, it was simply that the charge was prepared. She was never charged with it.

The charge sheet simply means putting down on paper the form of the charge, and then handing it to your constables to make the necessary inquiries?—No, the charge is completed with

John Donald Merrett.

David Fleming

the statements and is forwarded to the Charge Office, where it remains until such time as information is received from the Royal Infirmary as to whether the person is in a fit state to come out.

And when you get that information you enter it in the charge book?—Yes.

In fact, Mrs. Merrett was never well enough to be charged?—No. The charge was never entered in any book.

Who told you that two letters had arrived that morning, the 17th?—The accused.

Did he say what the letters were?—Referring to his mother's banking account being overdrawn.

It was you who found the two letters from the bank?—Yes, lying on the bureau. They had been opened.

Did the accused identify those two letters in your office as being the two letters received that morning?—Yes, he said these were the two letters.

Did he explain to you how a letter dated 13th in Edinburgh, and sent off in Edinburgh, did not arrive until the following Wednesday morning, the 17th?—He did not. He made no explanation.

Did you ask for an explanation?—I did not. I did not see the accused until the 30th.

It was on the 30th he told you that?—Yes, on the 30th of March. I never saw the accused until 30th March.

Had you the letters with you then?—No, I only took possession of the letters on that date.

It was on the 30th he told you this?—Yes.

He identified the two letters as being those received on the morning of 17th March?—Yes. I saw them myself on the morning of the 17th.

But I am talking of the date of their receipt, not of when you found them. I want to know when they arrived in the flat?—On the 17th.

By the Lord Justice-Clerk—On the 17th, I understood you to say, you interviewed Mrs. Sutherland?—I asked her a few questions, but I did not take any statement from her.

Among other things, you said she told you that on coming out from the kitchen she saw Mrs. Merrett falling from her chair, and saw the pistol falling from Mrs. Merrett's hand?—That is so; she told me that on the morning of the 17th.

Was that statement volunteered by her or was it in answer to particular questions put by you?—It was a statement volunteered by her. I asked her what had happened, and she told me she had been in the kitchen and heard the report of a firearm, that she went out to the lobby and saw Mrs. Merrett falling off the chair and the revolver falling from her hand.

That was in answer to a question you had put, of a general character, as to what had happened?—Yes.

Would you describe her on that occasion as being agitated?—

100

Evidence for Prosecution.

David Fleming

No, I would not say agitated. She was a little nervous, but not much.

When you saw her again on the 30th, did she admit that she had made that statement on the 17th?—She admitted to me she had made that statement and had made a mistake.

What reason did she give?—No reason whatever, except that she was excited and did not know what she was saying.

Did you see the revolver on the 17th at the flat?—I did not. It was taken possession of by the two constables before I arrived.

Dr. RICHARD BELL, examined by the LORD ADVOCATE—I am a bachelor of medicine and a bachelor of surgery, and in March last I was acting as surgeon in the out-patient department of the Royal Infirmary, Edinburgh. I remember the deceased, Mrs. Merrett, being brought in by the police in an ambulance on 17th March, 1926. She was suffering from a wound in the head. I examined the wound to see whether there was any blackening or tattooing round the wound, but I could not find any. The hair round the wound did not smell of any explosive. I examined it specially to see if it did. I cleared away some of the hair so as to get better observation. The patient's clothing was spoiled both by blood and vomiting. I knew the accused, as I had had occasion to attend him a day or two before for a slight injury to his leg. I spoke to him on the occasion when his mother was admitted to the Infirmary. His explanation to me of how it happened was that he was present in the room when he heard an explosion, and he looked up and saw his mother was wounded, or words to that effect. After I had made a preliminary examination the case was sent to ward 3, when it was then out of my hands.

Cross-examined by Mr. AITCHISON—I do not remember the nature of the injury for which I attended the accused, but I recollect that it was an injury sustained by him when on a motor cycle. I cannot remember the exact time when Mrs. Merrett was brought in to my department.

I suppose the kind of examination you make when a patient is brought in to the out-patient department is just a very brief examination with a view to determining where to send patients?—That is so. After my examination I sent the patient to the surgical theatre.

Was it quite plain from the examination you made that there had been very considerable bleeding?—As far as I remember, there was a good deal of blood about the ear.

Did you do anything to remove it?—No, I did not.

Accordingly, you were not really in a very good position to ascertain whether there was blackening or tattooing?—I satisfied myself that I could not find any. I looked for it.

If you did not remove the blood you could not see very well?—I did not remove the blood.

John Donald Merrett.

Dr Richard Bell

Do you mean in so far as the skin was not blood smeared or blood covered you did not see any sign of blackening or tattooing? —Yes. I had nothing to do with the ward into which the patient was put. She was a police case, and she would go to ward 3. It is the practice of the Infirmary to put attempted suicides into ward 3.

Is ward 3 what you call a barred ward, with barred windows and locked doors?—Yes.

So it is really a detention ward?—I do not know whether you would call it that or not—yes, practically, I suppose it is.

The Court adjourned.

Second Day—Wednesday, 2nd February, 1927.

Dr. Roy Stanley Holcombe (29), examined by the Lord Advocate—I am an L.R.C.P., L.R.C.S., of Edinburgh. On the forenoon of Wednesday, 17th March, 1926, the deceased Mrs. Merrett was admitted to ward 3 of the Royal Infirmary. I found she had a wound through the right ear which entered the skull. I dressed the wound on her admission. She was unconscious when she was admitted. I saw her conscious about half-past twelve that day.

Had you been informed what caused the wound?—I had been informed that there was a case of suicide going up immediately to the theatre. The wound was just about the size of a slate pencil—very, very small, but well defined.

Does that mean there was very little destruction of the tissues at the edge of the injury?—There was very little destruction, but there was a slight reddish discoloration.

Was there any sign of blackening or tattooing by particles of powder in the region of the wound?—No.

I assume you examined the wound very carefully before you dressed it?—I washed the blood away.

By the Lord Justice-Clerk—You have not answered the question which the Lord Advocate put to you. Did you examine the wound carefully?—Yes, I did, after I washed the blood away.

Examination continued—Was the blood all over the wound or round portions of it?—The blood hid the wound, but you could see portions of the ear.

And does what you say about the absence of blackening or tattooing apply to those portions of the ear where there was no blood?—When I looked I saw there was a definite amount of blood, and I could see parts of the ear, and I did not see tattooing or blackening.

Then you washed the wound and washed away the blood?—Yes.

You did not rub it away; you washed it away?—I got a swab. The blood was well into the ear, and I got it out well and made it quite clean.

And you still saw no signs of blackening or tattooing?—No.

Was the wound still bleeding?—It had stopped. Mrs. Merrett was under my charge until 1st April, when she died. She became definitely unconscious on Saturday, 27th, and died very early on 1st April.

From the time that she regained consciousness after midday on 17th March until she lost it again on the 27th, what do you

John Donald Merrett.

Dr R. S. Holcombe

say about her mental condition?—She was quite conscious all the time.

Was she normal mentally?—Yes. There is just one thing I would like to say. She was definitely unconscious on Saturday, 27th, but it was late on Thursday night that she went into a kind of delirium, on Friday she was incoherent, and on Saturday she was unconscious.

May I take it what you said about her being mentally clear applied up to Thursday evening, the 25th?—Yes.

Did Mrs. Merrett speak to you about what had happened?—Yes.

When was that?—At the visits from Wednesday, every time I saw her she would ask——

Mr. AITCHISON—So far as the question is, " Did she speak," I take no objection, but if the witness is going to be asked what she said I will object.

The LORD JUSTICE-CLERK—Well, raise the question.

Examination continued—Did Mrs. Merrett speak to you about what had happened?—Yes.

What did she say?——

Mr. AITCHISON objected to the question, submitting that any statement made, or alleged to have been made, by Mrs. Merrett during the period in the Infirmary prior to her death was not admissible in evidence. A statement made by a person deceased was only admissible provided it satisfied any one of three well-defined conditions. The first was that it must be part of the *res gestæ*, the second that it must be made in the presence of accused, and the third that it must be made in a dying deposition taken by a magistrate.

After hearing the arguments of counsel, and having a number of authorities quoted to him, the Lord Justice-Clerk intimated that he was not prepared to exclude the evidence.

Examination continued—What did she say?—On Wednesday night she complained of pain in the ear, and wanted to know the cause of it.

Did she ask you what the cause was?——

Mr. AITCHISON—I would rather the witness told us what she said in his own way.

Examination continued—She did not ask definitely what was the cause of it, but she could not quite make out what the pain was due to.

Tell us what happened?—I just said, " Oh, you have had a little accident, Mrs. Merrett," and that was all. I did not force the matter at all. I did not tell her straight out that I thought it was a case of suicide. At each visit on the Thursday till seven o'clock she kept on complaining of the pain. She was having great pain—there was no doubt about that—and she asked what was the cause of it—what was found in the X-ray, and she asked

104

Evidence for Prosecution.

Dr R. S. Holcombe

to see an ear specialist. On the Thursday night Sister Grant told me that Mrs. Merrett had been speaking, and, as the result of being told that, I went and saw Mrs. Merrett.

Tell us what passed between you?—I said to Mrs. Merrett, " Now, Mrs. Merrett, how did this accident happen? " and she said, " I was sitting down writing letters, and my son Donald was standing beside me——"

Mr. AITCHISON renewed his objection, upon the additional ground that it was not a statement freely made, but a statement elicited by a question.

The LORD JUSTICE-CLERK said he was not prepared to disallow the question.

Examination continued—Then please continue?—I said, " Now, Mrs. Merrett, how did this accident happen? " and she said, " I was sitting down writing letters, and my son Donald was standing beside me. I said, ' Go away, Donald, and don't annoy me,' and the next I heard was a kind of explosion, and I do not remember any more."

Was Sister Grant beside you when she was saying this?—Yes.

Was that all that was said by Mrs. Merrett that night?—No, I said, " Mrs. Merrett, who were you actually writing to at the time of the accident? " and she said (making a gesture of impatience), " Oh, I do not know." On the following day I reported the statement by Mrs. Merrett to my chief, and I know that a message was communicated to the police.

Did Mrs. Merrett on any later occasion in your presence refer to how the injury had happened?—No.

Did Mrs. Merrett mention a pistol or revolver in her statement at any time?—Not to me.

Was the accused paying visits to his mother in the Infirmary? —I saw the accused first on the Friday.

That was the third day she had been there?—Yes. I often saw him after that. I used to see him about the ward.

Did you have any conversation with him as to how it happened?—Yes, I asked him on the Friday how it happened.

What was the reply?—He said his mother was sitting down writing letters, and she said to him, " Go away, Donald, and don't annoy me," and he went over to the corner of the room, and the next he heard was a shot, and he looked round and saw his mother falling to the ground with a revolver falling from her hand.

So far as you saw, were Mrs. Merrett and the accused on quite good terms?—They were on quite good terms, as far as I knew.

On the same day, Friday, when you saw the accused, did the subject of his mother's condition come up between you?—Yes. I said that his mother was very, very seriously ill, but I said she still had a fighting chance, and he said, " So, it is still on the cards that she will recover? " and I said, " Yes. Where there's life there's hope."

John Donald Merrett.

Dr R. S. Holcombe

Did you have a conversation with the accused about relatives?
—Yes. The question arose whether Mrs. Merrett's sisters should
be informed of the fact, and I said, " Yes, I thought they should,"
and Merrett pointed out to me that they were not on the best of
terms, but I said I thought they certainly should be given the
chance to come. That was on the first occasion that I met the
accused, the Friday. I was present at the post-mortem examination which was conducted by Professor Littlejohn, and I identified
the body of Mrs. Merrett.

I want to know as to the physical condition of Mrs. Merrett
while she was in the Infirmary. Was she lying all the time?—Yes.

What would her capacity to sign cheques be, for instance?—
She would have to be given assistance to sign cheques. She would
have to be propped up, and she would have to be assisted, because
her left arm was paralysed, and her left leg also.

Could that assistance have been given by one person, or
would it need two?—I should think one person could have done it
if they were strong.

Do you know whether Mrs. Merrett signed any cheques while
she was in the Infirmary?—No. I saw none.

Cross-examined by Mr. AITCHISON—Given the necessary
assistance, she was quite able to sign cheques?—Yes, I should think
that she could write, but she would be writing under difficulties,
because she was very ill.

You did not happen to know that, in point of fact, she did?
—I know that she did sign one cheque.

Was that in the presence of an Infirmary nurse?—I do not
know.

When did you first see Mrs. Merrett after admission?—I saw
her just after she was admitted. She was sent up from the surgical
out-patient department to the theatre in ward 16, and I went up
then.

Am I right that there had been very extensive bleeding from
the wound?—Yes. The whole ear was clotted with blood, but you
could see parts of the skin inside.

But the part of the ear you could see was the part away from
the wound?—Yes. The wound in the antehelix you could not see
for the blood, and the wound in the concha was covered with blood
too. The wound in the antehelix was the first entrance wound,
and the wound in the concha was the second one.

Were both of these wounds covered with coagulated blood?—Yes.

By the LORD JUSTICE-CLERK—Tell us in ordinary language,
first, what the antehelix is, and, second, what the concha is?—The
ear has two definite ridges, the outer and the inner, and the antehelix is the continuation inwards of the inner ridge. The concha
is the cavity line above the antehelix.

Cross-examination continued—Both wounds were covered with
coagulated blood which I had to remove.

106

Evidence for Prosecution.

Dr R. S. Holcombe

In order to remove it you found it necessary to use a swab?—Yes.

Did you use water or spirit?—I used water.

And had you to apply a good deal of pressure to get the blood off.—Yes, I had to apply a good deal of pressure.

I think coagulated blood is very difficult to remove from the skin?—Yes.

It requires a certain amount of rubbing?—It was deep in, and I had to apply a certain amount of force.

Would it be accurate to say that in order to see exactly the precise position of the wound you washed the ear thoroughly?—Yes, I washed the ear well.

And was it then that you failed to discover any signs of blackening or tattooing?—Yes.

Did you examine for blackening or tattooing just with the naked eye?—Yes. I did not use a microscope.

Nor did you apply a hand lens?—No.

Can you tell me at what hour did Mrs. Merrett regain consciousness?—I first saw her conscious myself about half-past twelve.

At what hour did she make the first statement to you?—She complained of pain about half-past two.

Do you know whether she had regained consciousness prior to half-past twelve?—I had heard she had, but I cannot say from my own personal knowledge.

Having regained consciousness on Wednesday, 17th March, did she remain fully conscious, in your view, until she developed a delirium on Thursday, 25th March?—Yes.

So that there was a full period of a week during which a dying deposition could have been taken?—Yes, she was perfectly conscious.

Did you know from the condition you found the patient in on 17th March that there was a grave risk of a fatal termination?—Yes.

When you interviewed Constable Watt at the Infirmary on 19th March did you inform him that there was a grave risk of a fatal termination?—Yes.

Did he in your presence communicate with his official superiors?—He communicated with the lieutenant on duty.

On the 20th of March you had an interview with Inspector Fleming?—Yes.

You know, I suppose, that he represented the Criminal Investigation Department?—I knew that he was a big man, that he was an inspector.

Did you inform Inspector Fleming that Mrs. Merrett's condition was such that a fatal termination might be anticipated?—Yes, I said she was very ill.

Did he suggest to you the taking of a dying deposition?—No.

Did you regard that as a matter for his consideration as a responsible officer of the police?—Yes.

John Donald Merrett.

Dr R. S. Holcombe

Was any communication ever addressed to you by the Procurator-Fiscal as to whether Mrs. Merrett's condition admitted of a dying deposition being taken?—No.

Was any communication ever addressed to you by the Criminal Investigation Department as to whether a dying deposition should be taken?—No.

I understood you to say that Mrs. Merrett developed a condition of delirium on Thursday, the 25th?—Yes.

Prior to that delirium becoming apparent, must not there have been considerable mental disturbance?—I did not see it.

If not mental disturbance, must not there have been an inflammatory condition of the brain to produce delirium?—My lord, is not this more a question for experts?

I am putting it to you as a doctor—do you agree that if a delirium developed on the 25th of March there must have been a considerable period prior to that date during which some inflammatory process was going on in the brain?—I took that delirium as the first sign of an inflammation coming.

Is it your view that the symptom was coincident with the inflammation?—Yes.

Can you exclude the view that the inflammatory condition, in a more or less degree, may have been present for some considerable time prior to the delirium developing?—I do not know.

I think your first conversation with Mrs. Merrett was on the Wednesday?—I just used to go in and ask her how she was, and it was on the Wednesday night at seven o'clock she first spoke.

Had she been X-rayed by that time?—She had been X-rayed twice, and she wanted to know the result of the X-ray examination.

So far as the Wednesday is concerned, can you recollect clearly at all what she said?—I do not remember her exact words, but she complained of definite pain. She asked the result of the X-ray examination on the Thursday.

I want to get this so far as it is possible. So far as the Wednesday is concerned, can you really tell us anything definite at all as to what she said?—No.

Coming to the Thursday, did the conversation regarding the occurrences of the Wednesday morning open with a question from you?—Yes.

She did not voluntarily come away with a statement to you?—No.

What was the question you asked?—" Now, Mrs. Merrett, how did this accident happen? "

How did you come to put this question to her?—Because I received a report from Sister Grant that Mrs. Merrett——

Had made a statement?—No, she did not tell me what statement she had made.

You received a report from Sister Grant, and you went to make some inquiries?—Yes.

I want you to be very careful about this. In answer to your

108

Evidence for Prosecution.

Dr R. S. Holcombe

question, " How did this accident happen? " what exactly did she say?—She said, " I was sitting down writing letters, and Donald was standing beside me, and I said, ' Go away, Donald, and do not annoy me,' and the next thing I heard was a kind of explosion in my ear."

Did you write it down at the time?—No.

Then are we at the mercy of your recollection some ten months after the event?—Yes.

Have you never given at any time a different version as to what she said?—I do not remember ever giving anything different.

I quite accept that you are repeating to the best of your recollection, but you see my information is this: did you not say, " She said she was sitting at a table writing a letter, and her son Donald was standing in the room, and she heard an explosion "?—I do not remember giving that statement.

May you have given it?—It is possible.

You see there is an important distinction between the words " standing in the room " and the words " standing beside me." You appreciate the importance of that distinction?—I do.

Well, can you say, speaking at a distance of ten and a half months, that her words were not, " Donald was standing in the room "?—I cannot swear to that.

May she have said, " standing in the room " and not " standing beside me "?—It is possible.

You followed the matter up by putting a second question— " Who were you writing to "?—Yes.

And she replied, " I do not know "?—She said, " Oh, I do not know." [With a gesture.]

The gesture you made just now was a gesture of impatience?— Yes, it could be taken that way.

She did not want to be bothered with questions?—I do not know what she meant by that.

Did it strike you as odd when you asked her to whom she was writing that she should answer, " I do not know "?—Yes.

What was odd about it that struck you?—I do not know whether she was annoyed or whether she meant, " What has it got to do with the thing at all, who I was writing to? "

Was she not rather annoyed about you questioning her at all?—For the first part, she seemed only too willing to give the statement.

Having received a head injury which ultimately proved fatal, do you say that she was, on the Wednesday, fit to give a proper statement?—I consider she was conscious.

Is that all you can say?—Yes. These head injuries should be left entirely alone. They should be left perfectly quiet.

I agree. Is it in accordance with your experience of head injuries that the patient's mind may be a blank as to what happened at the time the injury was received?—Yes.

109

John Donald Merrett.

Dr R. S. Holcombe

And also a blank as to what happened a short time before the injury was received?—Yes.

Is that a very common feature of head injuries?—It is a well-recognised feature.

And is it in accordance with your experience that often, in the case of a patient who has done something to himself, his mind may be a blank as to what has actually happened?—That is quite possible.

Both as regards the time of its happening and the immediately prior time?—Yes.

You said to Mrs. Merrett, " How did this accident happen "?—Yes.

Did she ever repudiate the suggestion that it was an accident?—No, she never did to me.

One word about the accused: you did not see him, I think, until the Friday?—Yes.

Do you know he was there on the Wednesday and the Thursday?—I heard he had been up.

Is not it the case that the accused asked you whether he should send for his mother's relatives?—The accused did not ask me that.

Are you quite clear about that?—I am positive.

Do you know that the only relatives he has are relatives with whom he is not on good terms?—I don't know anything about that.

I thought you told us he said something about not being on the best of terms?—Yes.

To whom was he referring?—To his mother's sisters.

Mrs. Penn?—Yes, and the other—I don't know who she is.

But whether he was not on good terms with Mrs. Penn you cannot say?—I do not know.

Did you happen to see Mrs. Penn when she did come?—Yes.

Was not she fussing about a great deal?—She was very excited.

Was not she rather inclined to make suggestions as to how the thing had occurred?—She was.

And suggestions against the accused as to how it had occurred?—She never actually made it against the accused to me.

Not in terms?—No.

Not in terms; but can you say that Mrs. Penn was not pointing the finger at the accused and insinuating that he had something to do with it?—I cannot say she was actually insinuating against him.

Was she coming pretty near to insinuating that the accused had something to do with it?—You could take it that way.

Was that prior to Mrs. Merrett's death?—Yes.

In view of that insinuation of Mrs. Penn, did it not occur to you that it would be wise to communicate again with the police with the view of having a deposition taken?—I did not communicate again.

110

Evidence for Prosecution.

Dr R. S. Holcombe

Having done it once, you concluded they would look after all private interests?—Quite.

Re-examined by the LORD ADVOCATE—Did Mrs. Penn absolutely decline to believe that her sister could commit suicide?—She would not believe it at all.

On the Friday when the question of the relatives arose between you and the accused, was his statement to the effect that he was not on good terms with his mother's sister, or that his mother was not on good terms?—His mother.

The occasion on which you asked Mrs. Merrett how it had happened was on Thursday, the 18th?—Yes, the Thursday night.

At that time did you consider that Mrs. Merrett was perfectly fit to give an answer to your question?—I did.

She had been in your ward for a day and a half, nearly?—Yes.

You told us in examination-in-chief that Mrs. Merrett's reply to you as to what had happened was that Donald was standing beside her and she said, " Go away. Don't annoy me "?—" Go away, Donald, and don't annoy me "

Now, in cross-examination you said, in answer to my learned friend, you could not swear whether the words were " standing beside me " or " standing in the room "?—I never remember making that statement which was put to me.

Do the words that you have told us, " Go away. Don't annoy me," or " don't bother me," suggest to you whether what you really heard was " standing beside me " or " standing in the room "?—I believe she said " standing beside me," and I stick to that.

Was Sister Grant present when you had this conversation with the accused about the terms on which his mother was with her relatives?—Yes.

Did you sign the form for the death certificate?—[Shown production No. 185]—Yes.

And the cause of death as meningitis?—Meningitis, following a bullet wound in the cranium.

By the LORD JUSTICE-CLERK—How often do you suppose you saw Mrs. Merrett between the time when she was admitted first on the 17th and the evening of Thursday, the 18th, when she made a certain statement to you?—Eight times.

Did you have any conversation with her on all these occasions?—No, just the once.

Only on the Thursday?—Yes, except just to say, in the ordinary way, " How do you do? " and " How are you feeling? "

Did you discuss with her any other topics than simply her illness?—I do not remember.

Did you have much conversation with her regarding her condition?—No; I saw her just for about a minute every time.

You had no opportunity of judging, had you, whether she

111

John Donald Merrett.

Dr R. S. Holcombe

could talk sensibly about ordinary matters?—She never discussed those with me at all.

Did you think that at the time she made the statement to you she was in full possession of her faculties, or had you some doubt about it?—I thought she was perfectly conscious.

"Conscious" is one thing; but the question I put to you is whether you thought she was in full possession of her faculties?—Yes, I thought so.

ELIZABETH FRASER GRANT (37), examined by the LORD ADVOCATE—I am a sister attached to ward 3 in the Royal Infirmary. On the forenoon of Wednesday, 17th March, 1926, the late Mrs. Merrett was brought into that ward suffering from a bullet wound in the head. When brought in she seemed to be conscious of pain, but she did not speak to us.

How soon did she fully regain consciousness?—She asked to be attended to, I think, a little after twelve o'clock. I did not see the wound in her head on her admission. I understand the dressing of the wound was done up in No. 16 theatre before she was brought to us. Mrs. Merrett was in a room by herself in ward 3 nearly all the time; I think one afternoon there was another patient there, who was removed the same day.

Did Mrs. Merrett speak to you on the subject of what had happened?—The night after she was admitted, Thursday, the 18th, yes.

Tell us what passed?——

Mr. AITCHISON—As a matter of form, my lord, I should probably renew the objection in the case of this witness.

The LORD JUSTICE-CLERK—I think my ruling covers this.

Mr. AITCHISON—But I formally ask your lordship to give it in the case of this witness.

The LORD JUSTICE-CLERK—I refuse to give effect to the objection.

Examination continued—Tell us what passed?—Nurse Innes and I were attending to Mrs. Merrett, making her bed and changing her, and she said, "What has happened? It is so extraordinary." She could not understand it—or words to that effect. I said I did not know what had happened, could not she tell me, and she said she was sitting writing at the time, when suddenly a bang went off in her head like a pistol. I said, "Was there not a pistol there?" and she said, "No, was there?" in great surprise. I think it was here she asked me if the X-ray had not shown anything. I said I could not tell her that. So I continued then to ask her if she was quite sure she was writing at the time of the accident, and she said, "Yes, quite sure. Donald can tell you; he was standing beside me, waiting to post the letter."

Did Mrs. Merrett seem quite clear mentally at that time?—Yes, she seemed to me clear.

112

Evidence for Prosecution.

Elizabeth F. Grant

Did you thereafter report that to Dr. Holcombe that evening?
—Yes. Dr. Holcombe came to do his rounds somewhere about
seven, and I told him what had happened, and asked him if he
would see Mrs. Merrett on his visit, and he did.

Were you present at the conversation between Dr. Holcombe
and Mrs. Merrett?—Yes.

What passed then?—Dr. Holcombe opened the conversation,
and she said practically the same to Dr. Holcombe. The first visit
by the accused after his mother was admitted was in the forenoon
of Wednesday, between twelve and one. I saw him when he
arrived.

And did he ask to see his mother, or how she was?—He asked
me if his mother was still alive, and I said, " Yes, and she has
spoken to us." He asked me, if his mother got better, not to tell
her what had happened, as he did not wish her to know anything
about it.

Was Nurse Innes present at this conversation?—I do not think
she was actually in the room with me at that time.

Are you clear about that? I mean, if Nurse Innes says she
was there?—She may have been about the corridor. We were just
at the doorway. She may have been, but not actually beside me.
She may have been within hearing of the conversation; I could not
say.

Did the accused tell you as to how the accident had happened?
—He told me before his mother was admitted to the ward; he came
to give me notes about the case.

What passed then?—Nurse Innes and I were both present when
we were questioning him, and the usual card was filled in. I proceeded to ask him what had happened, and he said he had found
his mother in the drawing-room about 9.45 with a bullet wound—
or " shot in the face " were the words exactly. I said, " Had she
been worried about anything? " He said, " Yes, she had been
worried about money matters." Before he left I asked if his
mother was in a normal state that morning and the night before,
and he said, " Yes, she had been quite normal that morning and
the night before."

Come back now to the time between twelve and one when you
saw the accused. Did the question of what had happened come up
then again?—Yes, it did. I asked him what had actually happened, and he said he was sitting reading at the window and his
mother was writing at the table when it happened. I cannot
remember the exact wording.

Did the accused come back again that afternoon?—Yes. I
think it was on this occasion he was accompanied by a lady and a
gentleman. I cannot say how long he stayed; I was very busy at
the time.

On any of these occasions, and, if so, which, did a question
about relatives being communicated with come up?—I asked him,
I think, on that occasion in the afternoon if he had any relatives
and he said, " No." I said, " You have no brothers or sisters? "

John Donald Merrett.

Elizabeth F. Grant

and he said, " No."   I said, " Haven't you a soul in the world now but yourself? " and he said, " No."

Did the accused pay another visit that same evening, on the Wednesday?—Yes, and on this occasion he was accompanied by a lady only.

Was it the same lady as had been there in the afternoon?— Yes, I thought it was the same lady. He saw his mother on that occasion, and the accused and I then went to the doctor's room. While there I asked him if anything happened during the night or at any time he wanted him, would I send the police to Buckingham Terrace, and he said, " No; he was staying with friends." He hesitated, and I said, " What is the address, please? " and he said he was then staying at the County Hotel, Lothian Road. I said, " Will I find you there any time I want you? " and he said, " No," and he stepped out to the corridor, and, addressing the girl in the corridor, he said, " Betty, what is the number of the Dunedin Palais? " and he gave me " 766 " and told me to ring up to 1 a.m. any time I wanted him, and ask for Mr. Scott, and I would find him there. After the accused left I looked up a telephone directory to verify the number.

Did you hear about Mrs. Hill being wired for that day?— Yes, he told me that his mother had asked him to wire for Mrs. Hill that night, and he said she was a great friend of his mother. The next day, on the Thursday, a wire arrived in the afternoon from Mrs. Hill announcing that she was leaving King's Cross that night for the north, and when the accused called that evening I handed the wire to him in his mother's presence.

On Friday, the 19th, did Mrs. Hill come early in the morning to the Infirmary?—It was reported to me she did. I went on duty about a quarter to eight.

Did Mrs. Hill and the accused come to the Infirmary after you had gone on duty?—Yes, about half-past nine or ten o'clock. I saw them there.

Did the accused seem in a hurry that morning?—He told me he was in a hurry.

And did he go off, and Mrs. Hill stay in the Infirmary?—Yes. Before the accused left the ward I asked him to come up and see Dr. Holcombe. He went upstairs, but did not see the doctor. The doctor was not there.

That was to see the result of the X-rays?—Yes. He said he would come back again. Mrs. Hill arranged that he would come back for her at lunch time.

Did he return for Mrs. Hill?—Not until two o'clock. Mrs. Hill left at two o'clock to go to the hotel where the accused was staying in case he would be waiting for her. I did not see Mrs. Hill again; that evening I got a telephone message from Mrs. Hill between 6 and 6.30, before I went down to dinner. I told Mrs. Hill that Donald had not been back to the Royal Infirmary.

114

Evidence for Prosecution.

I left instructions with Nurse Innes to send him straight down to the hotel to see Mrs. Hill, because she wanted to see him.

On Friday evening was the accused in his mother's room when the doctor paid his evening visit?—Yes. I was there too. As we were coming out a conversation took place between the doctor and the accused with regard to his mother's prospects of health.

Tell us what passed?—What I heard was, " So it is on the cards that my mother will still recover." I am not quite sure of the doctor's reply. I asked the doctor if the boy should not send for his relatives, and the doctor said, " Yes, certainly, they should be sent for." I also think it was on this occasion that Donald said that he had been standing there when his mother was writing.

Did Donald say anything about the relatives?—He said he would send for them. He said that it would not be much use sending for them, because they were not on friendly terms.

Did you have any general talk with Mrs. Merrett?—Oh, we often spoke to her when we were attending to her; she used to converse with us.

Dr. Holcombe told us she first became subject to delirium on Thursday evening, the 25th?—Yes.

From about noon on the Wednesday when she fully recovered consciousness, until the delirium set in on Thursday evening, the 25th, what do you say as to Mrs. Merrett's mental condition and her capacity to talk and understand?—I felt her conversation was quite normal, the things she told me.

Do you know, from your own knowledge, whether she signed a cheque during that period?—On the morning of the 25th I think there was a cheque signed. I was not present when it was signed, but I went into the room. Mrs. Merrett required assistance.

What kind of assistance?—Well, when I went into the room Mrs. Penn was on the left-hand side of the bed holding the cheque for her, and Donald was on the right-hand side of the bed assisting her to hold her up a bit to let her sign a paper. The left arm was paralysed. She could not hold the cheque herself.

Are you able to say whether that was the only time she signed a cheque?—The only time, to my knowledge, a cheque was signed, and the only time I was asked about one being signed.

Do you remember the accused coming to see you in your room one evening?—Yes.

What passed on that occasion?—He came to my door and said that his mother was very anxious to see some one from outside, an outside doctor, Dr. Grant, I think. I explained to him she could not see Dr. Grant professionally; he could come as a friend, on a friendly visit. I then went on to tell Donald his mother could not understand what had happened, and that she had said that he could tell me, because he was standing beside her at the time she was writing, waiting to post the letter; and he said,

115

John Donald Merrett.

Elizabeth F. Grant

" Yes, I was standing beside her, and she said, ' Go away, Donald, don't worry me.' " Then the accused made some reference to her being removed away from the Royal Infirmary, and I said she could not possibly be removed from the Royal Infirmary, because at present she was lying under a charge of attempted suicide, and had to be handed to the police.

While you were on duty did the accused see his mother alone at any time?—Yes, he was in sometimes alone, but not for any length of time.

On Tuesday, the 23rd, did you get a wire from Mrs. Penn inquiring how her sister was?—Yes. After communicating with Dr. Holcombe, I wired that Mrs. Merrett was very ill, and advised Mrs. Penn to come on at once. I informed the accused about that when I saw him that evening.

When you came on duty on the Wednesday morning was it reported to you that Mr. and Mrs. Penn had arrived early that morning?—Yes. Mr. and Mrs. Penn and the accused came to the ward about ten o'clock that morning. I noticed the change first when I came on duty on the Friday morning. The accused came about seven o'clock on the Friday evening, and I told him that his mother was much worse.

And did you ask him to give any message to the relatives?— I asked him about his aunt and uncle. I told him to tell them that his mother was much worse.

Cross-examined by Mr. AITCHISON—When Mrs. Merrett came to your ward on the forenoon of Wednesday, the 17th, it was quite plain that she had received a very serious injury?—Yes.

And did she remain seriously ill right down to the time of her death?—No, I think there was a slight improvement in her condition.

Well, ups and downs, I suppose?—Ups and downs.

And she suffered a good deal of pain?—Yes, she complained of pain.

And she developed a delirium five or six days before her death?—Yes, on the Friday.

Was she a bit confused about things?—I did not find her so until that time.

Did she seem to be a bit confused as to what had happened on the Wednesday morning?—When she spoke to me on the Thursday evening she seemed to be quite decided that she was writing at the time. She was very plain on that point.

But, as regards what actually had happened, do you think her mind was more or less a blank?—No, she said she did not know what had happened, she could not understand it.

Was it on the Thursday evening that you said to her, " Are you sure there was no pistol "?—Yes.

And you say she said, " No, was there a pistol "?—She said, " No, was there?" in great surprise.

116

Evidence for Prosecution.

But just before that, according to you, she had said, " I was writing at a table when suddenly a bang went off like a pistol "?—" When a bang went off in my head like a pistol."

If she said that to you, why do you say she said, " Was there a pistol?" in great surprise?—Because she seemed very surprised.

Who mentioned " pistol " first of all?—She said, " like a pistol in my head."

Can you account for the idea of a pistol?—She said the bang was like a pistol.

Can you account for her describing the bang as being a bang like a pistol?—No, except that it was a noise like a pistol she heard.

But am I right that the idea of pistol came from her and not from you?—Oh, yes, she suggested the bang was like a pistol.

And yet you told us that, although the idea of a pistol was in her mind, when you said to her, " Are you sure there was no pistol?" she replied, " No, was there a pistol?" in great surprise?—Well, it was surprise.

In great surprise?—She simply said, " No, was there a pistol?" She seemed very much surprised, as far as I thought.

Have you treated many cases of attempted suicide by shooting?—No, I have not.

Can you say, from your professional experience, that attempted suicides, who have failed in their attempt, very frequently affect surprise as to what has happened?—No, I cannot.

Can you contradict the view that they do frequently feign surprise as to what has happened in attempted suicide?—I cannot say. I never heard them express surprise.

At any rate, do you agree with this view, that in cases of accident involving serious injury to the head, the mind of the victim may be either a blank or very much confused as to what has happened at the time?—That is in an ordinary accident.

Any accident involving injury to the head. You agree that the patient's mind may be a blank as to what has happened at the time?—Well, in my experience I have known patients who have met with an accident and who have not known anything about it; the mind has been an absolute blank.

That is quite common?—A patient meeting with an accident, concussion, or anything like that.

Is it in accordance with your experience, where a person meets with an accident resulting in unconsciousness, the mind of the person may afterwards be a blank as to what occurred at the time when the accident occurred?—In head injuries, if there is concussion, yes.

Can you explain unconsciousness if there was not concussion?— No, I am not prepared to explain.

Were you present when Mrs. Merrett made the statement to Dr. Holcombe?—I was at the bedside, yes.

John Donald Merrett.

Elizabeth F. Grant

Can you tell me, as nearly as you can recollect, was the statement this—did Mrs. Merrett say that she could not understand what had happened?—Yes.

Did she say, " I was sitting at a table writing a letter "?—Yes.

" And my son Donald was standing in the room "?—I think she said " beside me."

May it have been " in the room "?—" Beside me," I think it was. I thought it was " beside me."

But how can you be positive about a matter of that kind?—I am not positive. I said, " I think it was ' beside me.' "

You say you cannot be perfectly positive?—Not word for word.

But do you agree that what may have been said was that " Donald was standing in the room "?—I am not prepared to say, because I do not remember the exact words; it is some time ago.

I suppose you did not interrogate Mrs. Merrett in order to clear up any ambiguity there might be in what she said?—No. All I said is what I have already told you.

But was there any attempt made by you or by any one else, so far as you know, to explain anything that might be ambiguous in what she said?—No.

So that one is just left to conjecture as to what she meant?—Well, no one ever questioned Mrs. Merrett at all, to my knowledge.

Is it within your personal knowledge that an intimation was received from the police authorities that Mrs. Merrett was under arrest on a charge of attempted suicide?—I got that myself.

You got that intimation yourself on the day of her admission?—I think it was on the afternoon of admission I got it from the superintendent's office.

You told us about a conversation which you had with the accused in which he said, as I have got your words, that if his mother recovered you were not to tell her, as he did not wish her to know what had happened?—Yes, that is right.

Was he not referring to the intimation that she was under arrest on a charge of attempted suicide?—No, I do not think so. I thought he meant that he did not wish the mother to know that she had a wound.

But is it not just possible you may have taken him up wrongly in that respect?—I do not think so.

He did know, of course, that his mother was under arrest?—No, he did not know at the time.

How do you know what sources of information he had?—Well, he led me to understand, that evening when I spoke to him in my room, that he did not know his mother was under arrest.

How did he come to mention it?—I said to him his mother could not be removed, because she was a prisoner there under

Evidence for Prosecution.

Elizabeth F. Grant

arrest for attempted suicide, and he did not seem to realise that at the time I told him.

You see, it is a considerable distance of time. Is it not a possible view, having regard to your recollection, that what he was anxious about was that if his mother recovered she should not know anything about her ever having been put under arrest?—No, I thought he did not wish his mother to know that she had a wound in the head. That is the impression he gave me.

You told us that Mrs. Merrett in fact did not know what had happened?—She could not understand what had happened.

Did it strike you as a tactful thing that her son should not want her ever to remember what had happened?—No, I did not think it.

Do you think that, in the case of an attempted suicide recovering, the tactful thing is to remind the suicide of what he has done or attempted to do?—No, certainly not.

Is it not in accordance with your experience as a nurse that when an attempted suicide recovers and has forgotten the incident, it is medical policy not to remind him of the incident?—Well, in my experience, this is the first one who had forgotten it, if she had forgotten it.

Have you many of them?—We have several of them, not shooting themselves, but we have a great many suicides.

But, in any event, whether the would-be suicide remembered or not, would not it be a tactful thing not to refer to it?—Well, we do not usually do so.

And is not the reason why you do not do so just because it is bad for the patient?—Well, the patients usually refer to it themselves.

If they remember?—Well, I never had another occasion when they did not remember.

You cannot speak, from your own knowledge, of cases in which they did not remember?—That is so.

When did Mrs. Penn come on the scene?—On the Wednesday morning, a week after.

And you have seen her a good deal since?—I saw her at the time a good deal.

And since?—Yes.

And talked about the case a good deal with her?—Well, not a great deal.

She has pretty strong views about the case, I think?—In what way?

Don't you know?—Well, she has spoken rather kindly to me about the case any time she has spoken.

Very sympathetic to the accused?—She has been, on occasions, extremely sympathetic.

On occasions?—Nearly always.

Does she very much resent the suggestion of suicide?—Yes,

John Donald Merrett.

Elizabeth F. Grant

she resents the idea of her sister having been in the hospital under a charge of suicide; it upsets her.

And she prefers some other explanation, if she can get it?—She never said that to me.

Has she not conveyed the impression to you that, if she can manage it, she will get some other explanation than the explanation of suicide?—Not exactly; she has not.

What do you mean by " not exactly "? In substance, is that not the case?—Well, I think she was rather glad it was supposed to be an accident; she was very satisfied that it was an accident at the time.

She welcomes the accident theory?—At the time it was cleared up as an accident.

What exactly do you mean by that expression?—At the time of Mrs. Merrett's death or thereabouts; I can remember myself reading in the newspaper it was an accident.

You seem to have had a good many conversations with the accused at one time and another about the matter?—Well, never any length of time; simply when he came to the ward he asked for his mother, and I answered his questions.

I suppose, casual conversations?—I cannot remember the conversations; it is rather long ago.

You cannot pretend to tell us exactly what was said, either by himself or by you, with any accuracy?—Not unless it was anything directly in reference to the case.

Do you agree that when you, to use your own expression, questioned the accused, he told you that he had been sitting reading when his mother was at the writing-table?—Yes, that was the second time I saw him.

Generally, may we take that to be the gist of what he said to you regarding what he was doing at the time of the occurrence? —He said so, yes.

Did you ask him about his relatives?—Yes.

Did he say that he had not a soul in the world?—Yes, I asked him the question, " Have you not a soul in the world but yourself? " and he said, " No."

Do you know that that is the truth?—Well, I understand he has two aunts.

You refer to Mrs. Penn?—Mrs. Penn, at least.

Who is the other?—I think it is a Mrs. Chadwick I heard him speak of. I have not seen her.

Do you know that, with the exception of Mrs. Penn, he has not a soul in the world?—No, I did not know.

When he gave you an address, I think he gave you the address of the Dunedin Palais?—He gave me the County Hotel first.

Is it within your knowledge that he had taken rooms at the County Hotel instead of going back to the flat?—That is where he told me he was staying.

Evidence for Prosecution.

Elizabeth F. Grant

Do you know that the only friends he had in Edinburgh, apart from his mother, were an instructor and an instructress at the Dunedin Palais?—No, I know nothing about his outside life.

Do you know that the instructor's name is Scott?—Yes, I learned that.

When you asked him where you could find him, did he tell you to ask for Mr. Scott and he would find him?—Yes, till 1 a.m. in the morning.

I do not know what the point of this evidence was, and perhaps you cannot tell me. Is the suggestion that the accused was dancing while his mother was lying seriously ill?—Well, I could not swear to that. I had been told he had been seen dancing, but I am not prepared to say.

Can you contradict me if I tell you that in that suggestion there is not a particle of truth?—I am not in a position to do so.

As regards Mrs. Hill, am I right that it was the suggestion of the accused that Mrs. Hill should come?—It was the mother's suggestion.

Were you there at the time?—No; the accused told me that his mother had asked him.

By the LORD JUSTICE-CLERK—You have told us of certain conversations which you had, some important and some less important, with the deceased Mrs. Merrett. These were in March, nearly a year ago?—Yes.

Did you make notes at the time of everything she said to you?—Not at the time.

I want you just to think carefully before you answer this question. When did you first, after March, 1926, retail to any one the terms of the conversation which you have spoken of to-day?—I think it was on 7th April.

And did you either put in writing, or see put in writing, the details of the conversations which you have spoken of to-day, on the 7th April of last year?—My conversation was taken down.

And in that conversation did you give the terms of the conversation which you had with Mrs. Merrett as you have given them to us to-day?—I only gave the conversation that I had on the Thursday night on that occasion, I think.

JEAN INNES, examined by the LORD ADVOCATE—I am a nurse in the Royal Infirmary, Edinburgh. On the 17th of March, 1926, I was on duty in ward 3. I was not actually present in the ward when Mrs. Merrett was brought in; but I was there soon afterwards.

Was she unconscious when you first saw her?—No, she was conscious when I first saw her. That was one o'clock. I did not notice Mrs. Merrett's wound till the evening. There was no blood coming away from it at that time.

Were there any signs of blackening about the wound?—None at all.

121

John Donald Merrett.

Jean Innes

Were you present when a conversation took place between Mrs. Merrett and the last witness, Sister Grant?—Yes. I cannot remember just whether it was the Wednesday or the Thursday.

Tell us as nearly as you can remember what Mrs. Merrett said?—She said, "Whatever has happened; why am I here?" We asked her to try and remember just what she could and tell us what she could remember. She said she remembered distinctly her sitting writing letters, and she said, "Donald was standing beside me waiting to take them to the post, and suddenly something burst in my head, just like a pistol shot."

Did she say something further?—"Was it a pistol?" I was on duty at different hours from the day of Mrs. Merrett's admission until she died. When I was out Nurse Grant usually took my place.

Were you present when a cheque was signed by Mrs. Merrett? —No, never.

Was any cheque signed by her that you saw?—Not that I saw.

Cross-examined by Mr. AITCHISON—Was the wound in Mrs. Merrett's head bandaged?—Yes. I removed the bandage in the evening, with a view to dressing the wound.

Even at that time was there not a certain amount of blood coming from the wound?—No blood; a serum discharge.

A certain oozing out?—Yes, oozing from it.

Did you happen to notice that the edge of the wound was slightly brown in colour?—No, it was red in colour.

When you say there were no signs of blackening, did you look specially for signs of blackening?—I did not look specially, but there were no signs of blackening.

All you can say is that you did not observe any signs?—I did not observe any.

As regards what Mrs. Merrett said, of course it is a long time since the conversation took place. May I take it you cannot be sure what were the exact words used by Mrs. Merrett?—I can remember those words quite well.

I wish you would just remember a little more than those words. Do you pretend to be able to give us an exact account of the conversation that took place between Sister Grant and Mrs. Merrett?—On the occasion when she asked why she was there, do you mean?

Yes. Do you remember if Nurse Grant said, "Don't you know what happened"?—Yes.

What was the reply?—She said, "I don't know what has happened."

Are you speaking from your exact recollection, or are you just conjecturing what you think was the reply?—That is as well as I can remember.

Do you remember Sister Grant saying, "Are you sure there was no pistol"?—No, I do not remember.

Evidence for Prosecution.

Jean Innes

Do you remember Mrs. Merrett saying, " No, was there a pistol " ?—I remember Mrs. Merrett saying, " Was there a pistol ?"

But you cannot tell us whether that was in answer to a question or not?—No, I cannot remember.

So your recollection of the conversation is incomplete?—It is just as I can remember it.

Did Sister Grant say, " That is what we want to know " ?— Yes.

Would it be fair to describe Mrs. Merrett's condition of mind in this way, that she seemed confused as to what exactly had happened?—No, I think she was quite clear.

If she was quite clear, why was she asking questions about it?—I mean that she remembered what she had been doing.

What is your recollection of what she said regarding Donald? —She kept saying he was beside her.

Can you be certain whether she did not say that Donald was standing in the room at the time when the occurrence happened?—She said, " Donald was standing beside me."

I want to know why it is that you with the other witnesses are so positive about the words " beside me " ?—(No answer.)

How do you come to remember so clearly the words " beside me " when your recollection is so fogged as regards other details of the conversation?—I do not know, but I do remember that.

Have you discussed it with any of your sisters in the Infirmary?—Not at all.

Are you in the same ward as Sister Grant?—Not now.

Do you say you have never discussed the matter with Sister Grant?—We may have discussed it, but we never influenced one another in any way.

I am not talking about influencing one another. Have you discussed with Sister Grant the words which were used by Mrs. Merrett on the occasion of which you speak?—Yes.

Had you some difficulty in agreeing as to what the words were?—None at all.

Did your recollection correspond with hers in every detail as regards the words " beside me " ?—Yes.

Did you discuss with her whether the words " beside me " had been used or not?—No.

This, you know, is a very serious charge. Just answer me this question. Is it not the case that you have discussed with Sister Grant the precise words that Mrs. Merrett used on that occasion ?—Yes.

And accordingly the evidence as to what Mrs. Merrett said is evidence given by you after discussing the matter with Sister Grant?—My first evidence was given before I had discussed the matter with Sister Grant.

What do you mean by " first evidence was given " ?—The first time I was questioned about the case.

John Donald Merrett.

By whom?—I do not know.

At what date?—I cannot remember.

Was it taken down?—Yes.

Have you seen it since?—I have not seen my own statement.

You have not seen your own statement. Whose statement have you seen?—I saw Sister's.

The statement of evidence she was to give here?—Yes.

When?—I cannot just remember that.

Did that help your memory?—Not at all.

How did you happen to get Sister Grant's statement?—I did not see Sister Grant's statement until after I got my citation.

Till after you got your citation to come here as a witness?—Yes.

Who showed you Sister Grant's statement?—Sister.

Who was with you when you saw Sister Grant's statement?—Sister.

Where did you see it?—In hospital.

And you read it over?—Yes.

And did Sister Grant see your statement?—I do not know whether she did or not.

Had you it at that time?—I have never had a statement.

Speaking at this distance of time, from your recollection, is it not quite possible that you may be mistaken as to the precise words used by Mrs. Merrett?—I might be, but I am almost sure of them.

Do you remember the day following upon Mrs. Merrett's admission Donald suggesting that he might bring his mother's own clothing to the Infirmary for her to wear?—As well as I can remember, it was on the Thursday, the day after her admission.

Did you get the impression that he did not like to see her in hospital clothing and would rather see her in her own things?—He asked me if he could bring them, as he did not like to see her in hospital clothing.

Re-examined by the LORD ADVOCATE—This statement which Sister Grant had, you did not know where it had come from or who had made it up?—I did not know anything about it.

You did not know whether it was a statement made up by Miss Grant to be given to the defence or not?—No.

By the LORD JUSTICE-CLERK—Did you have a number of conversations with Mrs. Merrett?—Yes, quite often.

On general topics?—Yes.

I mean altogether apart from the events of the 17th March? —Yes.

Did she talk quite sensibly on these other topics?—Yes, quite sensibly.

Did you see her in particular on Thursday, the 18th, the day on which she made the statement which you attribute to her?—Yes.

Had you talked with her more than once on that day?—Yes, I think I would.

Evidence for Prosecution.

Jean Innes

Were you in charge of her for at least part of the day up to the time that she died?—Not actually in charge of her.

Did you speak to her every day?—Yes.

Up till the Thursday prior to her death did you see any traces of her mind wandering?—She became rather incoherent about 26th March.

Between the time when she recovered consciousness on the 17th and the time when she became incoherent on the 26th was her mind, so far as you could judge, clear?—Quite clear.

Mrs. BERTHA HILL, examined by the LORD ADVOCATE—At the present time I reside at 1 Devonshire Place, Brighton, and I am the wife of Lawrence Maye Hill, who lives at Oamaru, South Island, New Zealand. I have been in England for some two years. I first met Mrs. Bertha Merrett and her son, the accused, in New Zealand some seven or eight years ago. In or about May, 1924, I came to England. Mrs. Merrett and her son followed about a month later. I went to live near Reading, and a little later on Mrs. Merrett and her son came to see me there and stayed near me. I was friendly with Mrs. Merrett. I changed to Brighton later; I think it was in March, 1925. Mrs. Merrett paid visits to me there. About the end of November, 1925, Mrs. Merrett paid me a short visit before coming to Edinburgh with her son. After Mrs. Merrett came to Edinburgh she corresponded with me regularly. On the evening of Wednesday, 17th March, 1926, I got a telegram from Edinburgh from the accused, Donald Merrett, informing me that his mother was ill, and asking me to come at once, or words to that effect. I wired in reply that I was just going to Hampstead, but I would put it off and come immediately if I was really required. The following day, 18th March, I received a telegram from the accused in the morning asking me to come north at once. I accordingly went to London and came north that night, Friday, 19th March. I sent a wire to Donald Merrett saying I was coming. I addressed it to Buckingham Terrace. I got into Edinburgh on the Friday morning about six o'clock, and went straight to the Royal Infirmary. I saw Mrs. Merrett at that time, but I did not speak to her. She was sleeping. Having had the address given me by the sister of the Infirmary, I went to the hotel where Donald Merrett was staying.

Did the question of what had happened pass between you?—The sister had told me.

Will you kindly tell us what passed?—As near as I can remember, I told him I had been to the hospital, and that the sister had told me that the injury was caused from a bullet, and I think I asked him how it could have happened—could any one have got into the room, or what could have happened. He said, " No, because I was there," and as near as I can remember he gave me to understand that he was leaning over his mother, and

John Donald Merrett.

Mrs Bertha Hill

she said, " Go further back, I cannot write, you overlean my shoulder," and he went back and picked up some books. He heard a shot and saw his mother fall. I passed some remark, as nearly as I can remember, about having a revolver, and he told me he got it for shooting in France. I think I said something about it being loaded, but I do not remember his answer. I do not know that he did answer me. I then said, " But if she did it, what would be her reason for doing such a thing? " and he gave me to understand she was in money difficulties, having that day or quite recently received from her bank information that she had an overdraft of somewhere about £20. I think I then said, " Well, I shall see you later," and left him to go to my breakfast. That is what passed, as near as I can remember. After breakfast the accused and I went to the Infirmary together, and I went in to see Mrs. Merrett. Mrs. Merrett seemed pleased to see me.

Did she know you perfectly well?—He said, " Here is Mrs. Hill come to see you." She extended her hand and said, " Thank you, dear, I am so grateful."

Did you go later on in the same day to see Mrs. Merrett?—Yes.

And did you have a conversation with Mrs. Merrett about what had happened?—Yes.

Will you please tell us as nearly as you can what passed?—She said, " Why am I here? What has happened to me? " and, having been told by the sister that they wished to keep her as quiet as possible and not to allow her to know the extent of her injuries, I said, thinking it did not matter, " You have had a fall." " But," she said, " my left side is injured." I said, " Yes, you have had a fall on this side, and it has injured your leg." She said, " No, I have not had a fall. I was writing a letter." I said, " To whom? " and she said, " Mrs. Anderson, and a pistol went off under my ear." I said to her, " How could it? Did you see the pistol? " and she said, " No." I said, " Did you handle one? " and she said, " No." I said, " Was there one there? " She said, " No." Not wishing to excite her any more, I gave her something to drink and walked away.

Was that the last time you saw Mrs. Merrett?—No, I sat in her room for two hours, but we had no conversation.

This was the last time you had a talk with her?—Yes, about the subject.

You say you sat in her room for two hours. What time did you go to the Infirmary?—I sat and waited for her son from twelve to two, but he was engaged and unable to come to see me. He said he would come between twelve and two if he could, but he did not come. Mrs. Merrett asked me to go to her flat to see to things. I let her think I would. She also asked me to write to her sister Mary.

Is that Mrs. Penn?—No, Mrs. Chadwick. I went back to

126

Evidence for Prosecution.

Mrs Bertha Hill

London that night. I saw accused again before I went off, at the hotel somewhere about six o'clock, I think.

On 19th March, when you were with Mrs. Merrett, what was her condition mentally? Was she quite clear?—Yes, quite clear. She said, " You know my little purse." I said, " Yes." She said, " There is £6 in it; take what you want to go on with."

Was the purse with her at the Infirmary?—She said it was at her flat, but I did not go there.

You say you had constant correspondence with Mrs. Merrett? —Yes.

At any time during your friendship with Mrs. Merrett did she mention money difficulties to you?—Never difficulties.

What do you mean when you say, " Never difficulties "?—She discussed planning her money and making things pan out, like one might, but she never expressed any feeling of difficulty whatever.

You mean how she was going to spend it, but not the want of it?—Yes, to do the best for her son, herself, and every one else— to make her money go to the best advantage, but she never complained about any difficulties.

Did either her conversation or her conduct ever suggest to you that she was likely to try to take her own life?—Never.

Did it suggest the contrary?—It suggested the contrary.

You saw her often, and you corresponded with her often. I want to know what type of woman she was?—Highly strung, emotional, a keen grip of life and everything it contained, but never a suggestion of doing away with herself.

Was she a good business woman?—Very clever in everything.

Cross-examined by Mr. AITCHISON—You describe her as highly strung, emotional. Would you say nervous?—I remember of one occasion a tramp coming, and she was nervous then, but that was all—just little things like that.

Apart from a specific example of that kind, would you say she was a woman of nervous temperament?—No.

But highly strung. What do you mean by highly strung?— When little things happened they were apt to affect her before she thought over them for any length of time.

You mean easily upset?—She was upset a little easier than a good many people.

I think you were an intimate friend of hers?—Very.

Had you a good deal of her confidence?—A great deal.

You say she had come from New Zealand a year or two before?—About a year before, or perhaps a little less.

Is it within your knowledge that she was very fond of travel?— Yes.

And had been a good deal abroad?—Yes.

In Switzerland?—Yes.

And France?—Yes.

127

John Donald Merrett.

Mrs Bertha Hill

Is it within your knowledge that she was always anxious, if her means permitted, to spend holidays abroad?—Yes.

And particularly in France?—Yes.

Did she sometimes go abroad at Easter?—She had not been abroad, to my knowledge, while she was in England this time.

Do you know what school the accused, her son, was at before he came north to Edinburgh?—Malvern College.

Was that immediately before he came up to England with his mother?—Before the Christmas holidays.

So that he had practically just left school?—Yes.

And he had come north with his mother for his further education here?—Yes.

I do not want you to give me much detail, but did Mrs. Merrett ever talk to you about her husband?—Yes.

Did she ever express a fear to you that her husband was following her to England?—Where from?

That is what I want to know. Did she ever express to you any fear, after she came to England, that her husband was coming over to England?—No.

Is her husband alive or dead?—I was told the other day in London that he was in India.

Did Mrs. Merrett ever tell you anything about him?—Yes.

Did she tell you that she used to send him money?—No.

Did you know that they were living apart?—Yes.

Did you know that there was some vital disagreement about some matter or other?—No.

You cannot say that she ever said to you that she was being pressed by her husband to send money to him?—No.

The telegram that you received to come north came from the accused?—Yes.

We have not got the actual wire, but did it say, " Come at once," or something like that?—Yes.

And as an old friend of Mrs. Merrett you did come at once?—Yes.

On your arrival you had some conversation with Donald regarding the matter. Am I right that he would not hear anything of the suggestion that any one could have come into the room and shot his mother?—He gave me to understand that it was impossible.

So he gave no countenance at all to that idea. Is that right?—Quite so.

I suppose that in telling us what you have, you have given us merely the gist of the conversation between you and Donald?—All, I think.

What I mean is you do not pretend to be able at this distance of time to give the exact words that were used either by him or by you?—No.

As regards your conversation with Donald as to what had

The Bureau.

(From the original in the Editor's possession.)

Evidence for Prosecution.

happened on the morning of the 17th, did he tell you that he had gone over beside his mother while she was writing a letter ?—Yes.

Do you remember whether he said that he had pointed out to his mother that she had mis-addressed an envelope ?—No.

You cannot recall that ?—Not to me.

Do you remember him saying anything to the effect that his mother said, " Go away ; don't worry me " ?—Yes.

After that did he say that he walked over to the other side of the room ?—Yes.

And did you understand him to say that after he was there working with some papers or books he heard a shot ring out ?—Yes.

And did he say he saw his mother fall ?—Yes.

Can you recall whether he said anything as to a pistol falling from the hand of his mother ?—I suggested it. I said, " Did she fall like this [indicating a fall to the right-hand side] with the pistol under her hand ?" and he said, " Yes."

Did you understand him to say that he had seen the pistol falling at the time his mother was falling ?—I do not remember it.

But something was said about the pistol falling on the floor ?—At my suggestion.

Never mind whose suggestion, but something of that kind was said ?—Yes.

And if it was your suggestion he assented to it ?—Yes.

Am I right that the accused was rather disinclined to accuse his mother of having attempted her life ?—I do not remember.

At any rate, can you bear out this view, that the accused certainly at no time was insisting that his mother had attempted her life ?—I do not quite follow the question.

Let me put it this way : beyond the conversation which you had, and of which you have told us, had you really very much more talk with him at all regarding the matter ?—No, none.

Is it within your knowledge, as an intimate friend of Mrs. Merrett, that she and her son were on very good terms ?—Yes.

She was devoted to him ?—Yes.

And they got on well together ?—Yes.

Now, you visited his mother in the Infirmary on the morning of your arrival ?—Yes.

And Mrs. Merrett was very glad to see you ?—Yes.

Was Donald there at the time ?—Yes.

And did he kiss his mother when he went in ?—Yes.

Were they, so far as you saw on the morning of your visit to the Infirmary, on quite friendly terms ?—Yes.

Mrs. Merrett asked you to communicate with a sister, Mrs. Chadwick ?—Yes.

Did Mrs. Merrett ever ask you to communicate with her sister, Mrs. Penn ?—No.

Did you communicate with Mrs. Chadwick ?—Yes.

Was she abroad at that time ?—Yes.

John Donald Merrett.

Mrs Bertha Hill

Where was she?—The south of France, I think.

Do you remember whether Mrs. Merrett said to you that she had been looking forward to visiting her sister at Easter in the south of France?—She had told me previously that she was going to the south of France.

Did you come in contact with Mrs. Merrett and Donald much when they were staying in England before coming north?—Yes.

I think you had known them also in New Zealand?—Yes.

Do you remember Donald having a pistol in New Zealand?—No.

Or in England?—No.

You never happened to hear that?—No.

As regards the conversation which you had with Mrs. Merrett, was what she said in answer to questions put to her by you?—She said, " Why am I here? What has happened to me?"

Do you remember if any one else was present at the time of your conversation?—I do not think so. A sister or a nurse may have been moving about. I don't remember.

Did she say something about a pistol going off in her ear?—Yes.

You told us you said, " Did you handle one "?—I said, " Did you see one?"—" No." " Did you touch one?"—" No." " Was there one there?"—" No."

Did you use the word, " Did you handle one "?—I cannot remember whether I used the word " handle " or " touch."

You see that is just the trouble about this sort of thing. Pardon me putting it this way : did you ever until to-day in the witness-box, or to any one, say that you said to Mrs. Merrett " Did you handle a pistol " ?—I do not remember.

I put it to you that until to-day you have never suggested to any one that you put to Mrs. Merrett the question, " Did you handle a pistol?" Is not to-day the first time that the suggestion has been made?—I gave my evidence to the police a fortnight after the tragedy.

And was it taken down in writing?—Yes, I signed my name to every page.

Did you at the time make any note of your conversation with the accused?—No.

Or any written note of your conversation with Mrs. Merrett?—No.

Have you seen, since the date you gave your statement, a copy of it?—No.

And, accordingly, are you speaking purely at a distance of ten and a half months from your recollection of what the conversation was between you and Mrs. Merrett in the Infirmary?—Yes.

May I take it that you cannot be certain as to the exact words used either by you or by Mrs. Merrett?—Yes.

Did Mrs. Merrett ever use any expression connecting the injury which she had received with any one?—No.

130

Evidence for Prosecution.

You were on terms of intimacy with her?—Yes.

And friendship?—Yes.

And confidentiality?—Yes.

Did she ever at any time insinuate that her son had shot her?—No.

Re-examined by the LORD ADVOCATE—In the conversation to which you have spoken which you had with the accused on that occasion with reference to how it had happened, did the accused volunteer the information, or was it given in reply to questions put by you?—I questioned him.

Did you convey the information of Mrs. Merrett being in the Infirmary to Mrs. Penn?—I did, by wire.

Mrs. Penn was on the Riviera?—Yes.

And did you see Mr. and Mrs. Penn in London on their way north to Edinburgh to see Mrs. Merrett?—Yes.

Mrs. ANNIE ELIZA PENN (62), examined by the LORD ADVOCATE— I am the wife of Walter Penn, and we live at Bosham, near Chichester. The deceased, Mrs. Merrett, was my sister. She was married to John Alfred Merrett about twenty years ago in New Zealand. Mr. Merrett was an electrical engineer at the time of their marriage. After the marriage they went to live in St. Petersburg, but subsequently they separated and lived apart. Mr. Merrett is still alive, and I believe he is in India. It was a long time before the war that they separated. The accused was quite young at that time.

What was the reason of the separation?—He practically deserted them. It was soon after the desertion that Mrs. Merrett and her son went to New Zealand. They went to Verey, in Switzerland, first, and later on they went to New Zealand. Mrs. Merrett came home on a visit on one occasion from New Zealand and stayed with me. About a year and a half or two years ago she came with her son to live in this country, and they resided near me. The accused attended Malvern College for about a year, when Mrs. Merrett and the accused left the district and made their way to Scotland somewhere about December, 1925. They resided for about a fortnight in December, 1925, in the same village where I reside just before my husband and I went to the Riviera. We went to spend the winter on the Riviera. I corresponded with my sister regularly. The last letter I got from her was in the beginning of March. I was on very good and affectionate terms with my sister.

In the later letters, and particularly the last letter, were there any complaints about money matters, or money difficulties, by your sister?—None whatever.

Can you tell us, roughly, what your sister's income was?— £700 to £800 a year. She was an extremely careful person about money matters, and an excellent business woman. I know that she kept accounts; I have seen her account book. [Shown produc-

131

John Donald Merrett.

Mrs Annie Eliza Penn

tion No. 148]—That book is in my sister's handwriting. I heard
from Mrs. Hill that my sister was lying ill in the Infirmary in
Edinburgh, and in consequence of that information I left the
Riviera at once in order to go to Edinburgh. On my way through
London I saw Mrs. Hill, and learned from her what she had found
in Edinburgh. I went straight on to Edinburgh on the morning
of Wednesday, 24th March, and on my arrival, which would be
about six or seven in the morning, I went straight to the Infirmary.
I found my sister asleep. I returned later and saw her and spoke
with her. It would be between ten and eleven in the morning of
the 24th.

Will you tell us what passed between you that morning? Was
she pleased to see you?—Very. She thanked us; she was delighted
that we had come.

What else did she say?—She said several things.

Please tell us?—Is this in order, my lord? Am I to answer
this question?

The LORD JUSTICE-CLERK—Certainly.

The WITNESS—She first of all asked me if I would look after
Sister Grant; would I find her a present, &c., that she had been
so good to her. She asked if we would at once go to the flat and
look after Donald. She was perfectly clear, and asked us if we
would go to a certain church to hear certain music. She spoke
of the kindness she had received. She asked me if I would get an
ear specialist for her. She said that they had said that she had had
a fall.

Examination continued—She said they said she had had a
fall?—I understood that. She said she was in doubt about that
fall. She said she was sitting at the table writing when a sudden
explosion went off in her head. She asked me particularly if I
would look after Donald for her, mentioning that Edinburgh was a
particularly wicked city, &c.

Did she add anything further to what you have told us?—
May I be excused, my lord?

The LORD JUSTICE-CLERK—Answer the questions which the Lord
Advocate puts to you.

Examination continued—You have told us she said, " I was
writing when a sudden explosion went off in my head." What I
want to know is if she added anything further to these words, and,
if so, what?—Yes, " as if Donald had shot me."

Did you say anything to that, or what further passed between
you? I just want to know the whole truth, nothing more and
nothing less?—I replied that would be impossible.

Was that all that passed?—I was to go to the flat and take
her fur cloak. My husband was not present when this conversation passed between Mrs. Merrett and myself. I cannot remember whether Nurse Grant was present or not. She may have been
within earshot. On that same day I asked Sister Grant for the

132

Evidence for Prosecution.

Mrs Annie Eliza Penn

use of her room for the purpose of having a conversation with the accused. Besides myself and the accused there were also present my husband and Mr. Jenks.

What passed between you and the accused on that occasion?—I asked Donald if he could explain matters. He said he had not shot his mother.

Did he suggest who had shot his mother?—No.

Or whether she had done it herself?—No.

Was there any suggestion as to how it had happened at this interview?—An accident.

Who made the suggestion?—We all agreed on that point.

And what was the explanation?—I do not understand you.

I asked you if you and the accused made any suggestion between you at this conversation as to how it had happened, what had caused it?—No.

Was there any suggestion as to it being an accident?—Not then.

When was accident suggested?—At the flat, after we got there.

Who were present then?—Mr. Jenks, my husband, Donald, and myself.

What was the suggestion as to accident, and who made it at the flat?—I cannot remember. The suggestion was that the pistol was in the secretaire drawer, and that it might have been taken out in some papers and gone off accidentally. That is as far as I can remember.

You mean among some papers, or mixed up with some papers, and it had gone off accidentally?—Yes. I was present on Thursday, 25th March, when Mrs. Merrett, my sister, signed a cheque. It was in the morning, as far as I remember. I do not know whether my sister required to be held up while she was doing it, as I was not watching at the time. My husband gave the cheque to Mr. Jenks, who was her business man; I have not seen it again.

You have told us that accident was suggested when you got back to the flat. Was suicide ever suggested to you?—No.

By no one?—On our arrival it was.

By whom?—Donald.

Did you accept that explanation?—Indeed I did not.

Did you conceive it as possible that your sister would commit suicide?—I knew my sister intimately, and, of course, I could not think of such a thing.

So far as you know, was there any reason which could be suggested for her doing such a thing?—None whatever.

When you saw your sister that day what kind of condition was she in mentally? Was she quite clear?—Quite clear—suffering greatly. On the second day of our arrival she became delirious. My husband and I took up residence at the flat and remained there for some time, as I had promised I would do to my sister. We remained for about two months. [Shown production No. 159]—That is evidently an account book. I have not seen this before.

133

John Donald Merrett.

Mrs Annie Eliza Penn

I cannot say whether it is in the accused's handwriting; it is certainly not my sister's. [Shown production No. 176, being letter dated 12th March, 1926, signed " Bertha Merrett "]—The body of that letter is in Donald's handwriting. The postscript down at the bottom is also in his handwriting.

Cross-examined by Mr. AITCHISON—Did you refuse a precognition to the accused's advisers in this case?—I did not.

Did your husband, to your knowledge, write to the accused's law agents and say that he did not want to be bothered about the matter, and neither did you?—Yes, then.   He did not say so afterwards.

What do you mean by " then "?—At the precise moment when we received the letter I was ill.

Is it not the case that you had to be directed by the Procurator-Fiscal to give a statement to the law agents for the defence?—I suggested that myself.

Answer the question.   Is it not the case that you were directed by the Procurator-Fiscal to give a statement to the law agents for the defence?—No.

You say that is untrue?—That is untrue.   He did not direct me.

Did he ask you?—No.

I put it to you it is true?—It is not true.

Did you know that your nephew was on trial for his life?—No.

Did you know that he was under a charge of murder that was to involve a trial for his life?—No.

Do you know it now?—Yes.

And are we to take it from you that all through your attitude has been one of willingness to help him?—Certainly.

To the utmost of your power?—Certainly.

Did you go to the office of the law agents for the defence in this case at their request?—We went ourselves.

Willingly?—Yes.

And eagerly?—Yes.

And what happened when you got there?—We received insults. From Messrs. Norman Macpherson & Dunlop?—Yes.

They insulted you?—Well!

Is that your evidence?—Yes.

I want to know what happened?—We came away.

Just tell us about the insults you received from Messrs. Norman Macpherson & Dunlop?—They said that my husband was too good to live.

And did you agree with that?—Certainly not.

I want to know what insult you received from Norman Macpherson & Dunlop?—That my husband was too good to live.

And that is what you mean by insult?—Certainly.

And after that you left, did you, or did you not?—Mutually we agreed.   They did not ask a single question.

Evidence for Prosecution.

Mrs Annie Eliza Penn

You had gone there for the purpose of giving the law agents charged with the defence in this case information as to what you knew about it. Is that right?—Mr. Dunlop said we were of no use to him.

Please answer the question. You had gone there for the purpose of giving information to the law agents for the defence as to what you knew regarding this matter?—Should they require it.

And your evidence is, first, that you were insulted, and, secondly, that you mutually agreed to part. Is that your version of the matter?—They said we were of no use to them.

Is not it the fact that at your interview with the law agents for the defence you displayed such temper that the interview had to be brought to an end and you had to be told to leave the office?—That is utterly false.

A fabrication?—A fabrication.

A lie?—(No answer).

Do you say it is a lie?—I was not in a temper.

Were you just as composed as you are now?—Certainly.

Did you live for some time at the hotel at Rumbling Bridge?—We did.

Do you know whether on the 7th of this month your husband wrote solicitors in London who were dealing with the case, Messrs. Wood & Sons?—I do, yes.

Do you know that your husband wrote, " I will not be interviewed here by any one regarding this matter "?—Yes, *here*.

Was that your attitude?—No.

Was that his attitude?—There, at Rumbling Bridge.

Was it going to be an inconvenience for you to be interviewed at Rumbling Bridge?—Yes.

And inconvenient for your husband?—Yes.

In a matter affecting the life of your nephew?—We were coming to Edinburgh.

And you thought the matter could wait?—Yes.

It did not matter very much that the defence were cramped for time?—We did not know that fact.

Your sister, I think, lived with you for some time—I am referring to Mrs. Merrett—in Bosham?—She visited us there.

Did she live in your house?—In the village.

Why did she not live with you?—It suited her purpose. It suited both our purposes that she should have her own rooms. I was minus two maids.

Had you no rows?—None whatever.

Is not it the case you had a row and you turned her out of the house?—That is not true.

Do you say you had no row?—No row.

At no time?—No.

You were always good friends afterwards?—Indeed we were.

You told us that Mrs. Merrett was a good business woman?—She was excellent.

John Donald Merrett.

Mrs Annie Eliza Penn

And always very accurate about the entries she made in her books?—Certainly.

Did she always carry forward the bank balance shown by her bank book into the book which was kept showing her affairs?—I do not know that.

I show you a bank pass book of the London Joint City and Midland Bank (No. 11a of productions). Do you see that the bank balance at 31st December, 1925, is £453?—Yes.

I show you No. 148 of productions, which is a book kept by Mrs. Merrett. Do you see that her entry for 1st January, 1926, is £413?—Yes.

Is that what you call good, accurate business?—I cannot say.

Did you know anything about her methods of business?—They were always in order.

Had you ever had occasion to investigate them?—No.

Can you tell me what the age of the accused is at the present time?—Eighteen last August.

After you arrived in Edinburgh you went to see your sister at the Infirmary?—Yes, I did.

And you have told us regarding the conversation which you say you had with her. Was any one present at that conversation besides yourself?—I cannot remember.

It is important, you know. I wish you would try to remember. Can you say whether any one was present at that conversation?—It is quite possible that one of the nurses may have been around.

You have no recollection of seeing any nurse present at that conversation?—I cannot distinctly remember.

I think the next day your sister became delirious?—Yes.

Is not it the case that that day, the day of the conversation, she was suffering considerably?—No, she was very bright indeed.

Was she not complaining of pain?—Only in the ear, and she asked me to get a specialist.

Did not she want a specialist owing to the pain she was suffering?—She could not understand it.

Was it not owing to the pain she was suffering that she was anxious that somebody else should be brought in?—Regarding the ear trouble.

I put it to you that on the day of your interview, which was the day prior to her becoming delirious, she was confused in mind?—No.

You gave us certain details of a conversation which you say you had with Mrs. Merrett. Did you take any written note of that conversation at the time?—No.

So you are speaking purely from your recollection?—Her words were burnt into my mind.

Are you speaking purely from your recollection?—Yes.

I put it to you that what took place at the conversation was
136

Evidence for Prosecution.

Mrs Annie Eliza Penn

this, that Mrs. Merrett said to you that something had happened, and that she was not sure what ?—No.

Did she say that she knew what had happened ?—She said, " As if Donald had shot me."

What was the earlier part of the sentence ?—" An explosion went off in my head suddenly."

" A sudden explosion went off in my head." Was it not you who put the question to Mrs. Merrett ?—I deny it.

You deny what ?—That I put the question to her.

What question ?—The question you have just repeated.

Was not it you who put the question to Mrs. Merrett, " Did Donald do it " ?—No.

I put it to you that that is the truth of the matter ?—No.

And I further put it to you that her answer to you was, " That is impossible " ?—No.

I think you have been asked a good deal about this matter ?—No.

By the Procurator-Fiscal ?—Before we left in June we gave our evidence.

And last week also ?—Not on that subject.

As regards the conversation, have you not been asked about it more than once ?—No.

Is not it the case that when you came to give a statement regarding this matter you expressed yourself as being in considerable doubt as to what it was that Mrs. Merrett had said on the occasion of the conversation ?—No, I have never hesitated on the point.

Did you say at any time, " She made a remark something like this, either ' Donald hit me,' or it was put in the form of a question, ' Did Donald hit me ' " ?—No.

Do you say upon oath that you never at any time put it alternatively ?—No.

To no one ?—No.

Do you say that you have never varied your story from first to last ?—No.

Did not you say that you were not quite sure in what way the statement by Mrs. Merrett was put ?—I have always been sure.

Did you at any time say that you were not quite sure as to the form in which the statement was made by Mrs. Merrett ?—I cannot remember.

At some stage of this conversation you said that that was impossible ?—Yes.

Is that your evidence ?—Yes.

Did you think it impossible ?—Yes, I did, then.

Have you changed your mind ?—I do not know.

You expressed that opinion then. I would like if you would express an opinion now ?—I have nothing to say.

John Donald Merrett.

Mrs Annie Eliza Penn

And at the time when Mrs. Merrett was alive and able to tell her own story, if it had had been taken, you said that any suggestion that Donald had shot his mother was impossible?—I said it to her to hearten her.

Did not she agree with you?—No.

Did not she say it was impossible?—No, she did not.

I again put it to you that it was you who suggested to her that Donald had shot her, and that it was his mother who warmly repudiated the suggestion as being an impossible suggestion?—That is quite untrue.

I think your nephew Donald is heir to his grandfather, is he not?—Yes.

And, failing Donald, who is the heir?—My own son.

Have you never at any time expressed yourself strongly that Donald should not succeed to the estate?—No, never at any time.

Never since this case was started?—Never since this case was started.

Do you say that on oath?—Yes.

Did you never make such a remark to Mr. Jenks?—No.

Where is Mr. Jenks now?—In London.

Do you know his address?—(No answer).

Did you communicate to the Fiscal that you had had a conversation with the accused in the presence of Mr. Jenks following upon the conversation which you had with your sister?—No.

You thought it unimportant?—I beg your pardon?

Do you really tell us that you have never told the Fiscal that Mr. Jenks was present when you had a conversation with the accused in the Infirmary following upon your interview with Mrs. Merrett?—Please repeat that.

Following upon your interview with Mrs. Merrett, I understand you to say you had an interview with the accused?—Not that day.

What day? Was it the following day?—When we heard there was no hope of her recovery—the following day.

At that interview on the following day was Mr. Jenks present? —He was present.

Did you ever tell the Crown authorities that Mr. Jenks was present?—No.

Why not?—It was not necessary.

Did you ever tell the Crown authorities anything at all about this meeting at which Mr. Jenks was said to have been present? —I may have done.

Did you regard it as of importance?—No.

According to you, you asked the accused to explain. What was he to explain?—(No answer).

Please listen to the question. You have told us that at the interview in the Infirmary on the day following your interview with Mrs. Merrett you asked the accused to explain. What was he to explain?—How the accident happened.

138

Evidence for Prosecution.

Mrs Annie Eliza Penn

Did you call it " the accident "?—I believe I did.

At that interview did you suggest to the accused that it could not have been suicide?—No.

Was no mention made of suicide?—No.

At this inquiry you held in the presence of Mr. Jenks what view was put forward as to what had happened?—Accident.

Were you all agreed upon " accident " as the explanation?—I suggested that we should go straight to the flat, and that Donald should show how he thought it could have happened.

And you went to the flat?—We went at once to the flat.

Am I right in saying that you have always rather resented any suggestion of suicide in connection with your sister's death?—Indeed I have.

Do you really tell us that there is no circumstance in your mind that suggests suicide as a probable explanation of your sister's death?—None whatever.

Nothing occurs to you?—Nothing could possibly. She was a splendid woman.

Nothing in the family history?—Nothing.

Is not it the fact that at the present moment your brother, and your sister's brother, is an inmate of a lunatic asylum in Manchester?—Yes, but not inherited. I can give you an explanation of that.

Whatever be the explanation, do you mean to tell me that the mental disorder from which your brother suffers did not make it occur to you that something may have gone wrong with your sister's mind?—No, never.

Did you consider that matter?—Never. There is nothing inherited in my family whatsoever. He brought it on entirely himself.

Subsequent to this tragedy did you take up residence for some time in the flat at Buckingham Terrace?—Yes.

And had you there as a servant Mrs. Sutherland?—We had.

Did not you discuss the happenings of the morning of 17th March with Mrs. Sutherland?—Indeed no.

Had you no interest to find out from the maid, who had been in the house at the time, what she thought of the matter?—Oh, yes, I asked her, but we did not discuss it.

You asked her what had happened?—Yes.

After she came into your service?—Yes.

Did you tell her that in your view the suggestion of suicide was absurd?—I believe I did.

Was that your view?—Yes, distinctly.

Would it be right to say that you, quite naturally, talked to the maid about the matter on several occasions?—I said very little.

Would it not have been a natural thing to ask a good deal of the maid as to how your sister had come by her death?—No, I had considered her already. She had suffered enough.

John Donald Merrett.

Mrs Annie Eliza Penn

What do you mean by that?—Her position—being there at the time.

Did you know that, apart from the accused, Mrs. Sutherland was the only person present in the house on the morning of the 17th March?—I understood that.

And knowing that, is it your evidence that you only asked her once as to what had happened?—I cannot say.

Did you not discuss the matter with her a good deal?—No.

Did you not theorise with her as to how the thing could have happened?—No.

Did you never discuss the accident with her?—No.

Since the accident have you seen Sister Grant a good many times?—Several times.

Have you discussed with her how the thing could have happened?—In a light way.

Is it a light matter?—Not to me, certainly not.

Did you not discuss it with her in a serious way?—No.

At any time?—Before I left in the spring.

You mean about the 10th of June?—Yes, I may have.

Have you seen her since?—On my return here.

Have you seen her this week?—Yes.

Have you been with her?—I have been attending the hospital myself, and I have always called on her.

Have you talked about this case to her?—Not particularly, in general.

Was it just a trivial sort of side matter of conversation?—No.

Was it not the principal topic of conversation between you and Sister Grant?—No.

Just mentioned casually?—Yes.

Look at the letter, No. 176 of productions. You have identified the handwriting in the body of the letter and in the postscript as being the handwriting of the accused?—Yes.

In whose handwriting is the signature?—My sister's.

And that is a letter dated 12th March, 1926, signed by your sister and addressed to the manager of the Midland Bank, Ltd., Boscombe?—Yes.

Re-examined by the LORD ADVOCATE—My learned friend, for some reason, saw fit to ask you about a relative of yours who is in an asylum in Manchester?—In the Midlands.

It is only one person, a brother?—Yes.

Do you desire to make some explanation about that? Your reply was that that could not affect the present question?—Yes.

Why?—Because his whole state was brought on through his own self.

He brought it on himself?—Yes.

It is not connected with the family history?—No.

Adjourned.

140

Third Day—Thursday, 3rd February, 1927.

Mrs. Annie Eliza Penn (*recalled*), examined by the Lord Justice-Clerk—I want to ask you one or two questions. Who is Mr. Jenks?—Mrs. Merrett's private business agent.

Is he a solicitor?—No.

What is he; what is his profession?—Simply a business agent. Where does he reside?—At Catford, near London.

How did he come to be in Edinburgh?—My husband and I wired for him immediately.

Did he accompany you?—No, he came on our instructions.

Was he present at any interview with Mrs. Merrett?—He saw her, but no special interview—no.

No special what?—No special interview. He saw her. He came into the ward.

Was he with you during any conversations you had?—With Mrs. Merrett—no.

Why did you bring Mr. Jenks?—Because my brother-in-law and sister could not possibly come. My sister was seriously ill, and my brother-in-law could not leave his Easter services at Belmont, near Montreaux.

I understood you to say that you stayed for two months in the flat after your sister's death?—We went there thinking we should be a few days, say, a week, and we were kept there because my brother-in-law and the Public Trustee could not send money for her bills, and for everything, so I financed it, and we stayed until we could leave Donald comfortably settled. We could not possibly get away till then.

In point of fact, I did not ask you the reason, but you did stay for two months in the flat?—I think it was about that.

Did the accused live with you during that time?—Yes. We were there with the object of his being with us. I gave my promise to my sister.

Why did he live for a time in a hotel, do you know? Did he tell you?—He said, of course, that he could not go back to the flat after this accident had happened.

When you had the conversation with Mrs. Merrett at the Infirmary of which you spoke yesterday—consider this question before you answer it, carefully—was she at the time suffering greatly, or was she not, so far as your judgment went?—She was suffering greatly with the pain in her ear.

I think you said yesterday that at the flat, when you discussed the matter, after going from the Infirmary, you all agreed that it was an accident. That was your expression, I think?—Yes.

And you said it was suggested that the pistol had been taken out of the drawer along with some papers and went off accidentally.

141

John Donald Merrett.

Mrs Annie Eliza Penn

Who suggested that detailed explanation of the event?—That I cannot quite say.

Just try to remember. I should have thought that that would have impressed itself upon your memory?—It was either Donald, my husband, or Mr. Jenks.

You told us yesterday that Mrs. Merrett said that "there was an explosion as if Donald had shot me." She said that to you in the Infirmary?—Her words were these——

Never mind. I think we have got them. What I want to ask you is this. You said at the time that that was impossible?—Yes.

Was that in order to comfort Mrs. Merrett, or because you believed it?—Certainly to comfort my sister, to keep her perfectly quiet.

Was that the sole reason?—That was the sole reason.

Did you believe it at the time you said it?—I could not believe it.

Follow the question. You said it was impossible. Did that view which you expressed give effect to what you believed at the time?—Yes, it did.

The Lord Advocate—Will your lordship ask her when did Mr. Jenks arrive?

By the Lord Justice-Clerk—When did Mr. Jenks arrive in Edinburgh?—We wired at once, and he came the following night, the night after our arrival.

Did he come overnight?—Yes. We should see him, I think, on the Friday morning. My husband will be able to vertify that exactly.

Walter Penn,[2] examined by the Lord Advocate—I am the husband of the last witness. I travelled north on the night of Tuesday, 23rd March last, and arrived in Edinburgh on Wednesday morning, the 24th. I proceeded with my wife straight to the Infirmary, where I saw Mrs. Merrett. I had some conversation with her.

What was it?—Direct conversation was rather slight. At one time she said nothing, but at another, when we were very anxious about her, she remarked to me, "Walter, you have been awfully good, and I have been most unkind at times. You will forgive me, won't you?"

Did anything pass between you and Mrs. Merrett with reference to what had happened?—She seemed to be very much upset at not knowing what had happened to herself. She seemed at a very great loss, because she said she had very great pain in her ear, and, knowing that I had suffered all sorts of things with my own ears, I suppose she was hoping I could give her some explana-

---

[2] This witness, who was very deaf, gave his evidence with the aid of an ear-phone.—Ed.

Evidence for Prosecution.

Walter Penn

tion about it, and she mentioned the noises she experienced in her ear. I said, trying to soothe her, " That is nothing ; I have very great noises in my own ears sometimes." Then she said on another occasion that she could not move her arm.

I want to know whether she spoke of anything that had happened on the previous Wednesday ?—No. I can say nothing at all about that.

Did you hear any conversation about that between your wife and Mrs. Merrett ?—I do remember that Mrs. Merrett was speaking to me about it, and said she heard a deafening noise in her head, and I said, " That is nothing, that is imagination. You fell down." Apart from that I heard nothing further from Mrs. Merrett. I could not swear to anything she said.

On one of these visits to the Infirmary were you present in the sister's room along with your wife and the accused, Donald Merrett ?—Very likely. We had rather great freedom in that little room.

Do you remember a conversation taking place between your wife and the accused ?—After going into the ward, we met there several times to talk over things.

Did a question, as to how the occurrence had taken place or had happened, arise in these conversations ?—Sometimes we were in grave doubt ourselves. We could not understand it.

I do not want to suggest anything that passed. I want you to tell the jury what passed ?—Will you give me a hint as to what conversation you are driving at?

Did the question of how the accident had occurred to Mrs. Merrett on the 17th arise at these conversations ?—On one occasion we tried in the nurse's room to get it from Donald, and I think on this particular occasion we had received a rather distressing account from one of the doctors. We had been buoying up ourselves with some false hopes that she was going to get over it, and eventually the doctor came and told my wife very quietly that he was very much afraid there was no hope whatever. That very much distressed my wife, who was very much upset indeed, and I had almost to carry her into the nurse's room. When she was sitting down she looked across at Donald, who was on one of the settees, and she said, " Donald, didn't you do it ? " and Donald said, " No, auntie, I did not do it, but if you like I will confess." I said to him at once, " What a ridiculous thing, boy ! You cannot do a thing like that." I suppose that was the sum and substance of it. Afterwards we spoke of the matter, and Donald explained what had happened. I do not remember any further argument about it at the hospital.

Did he not explain what he meant by saying, " I will confess " ?—No. He seemed to appreciate the fact that my wife was very much upset indeed. It was a terrific blow to her from the very first time it was known that Mrs. Merrett was dangerously

John Donald Merrett.

Walter Penn

ill; according to the telegram to France, my wife thought it was pneumonia, and she was very much upset then.

Come now to an incident at the flat after you got back, whether the same day or later. Was the question of how it had happened discussed in the sitting-room itself?—Yes, because there it was with the actual atmosphere of the affair.

Tell us who was present on that occasion?—I suppose, on the first occasion, it was only a matter of myself, my wife, and Donald. I do not suppose anybody else was present.

Was Mr. Jenks not there?—No. I wired to him to come down, I think, the next morning.

The next morning after what?—This would be the Wednesday, and I think I must have wired him on the Thursday. I think Mr. Jenks was with us on the Friday.

He travelled by night?—Yes. Of course, we asked Donald to explain matters.

First of all, can you tell us the date of what you are going to speak about now?—I think that is very awkward. Our statements have all been taken. Do you think it is fair to bring this up again ten months after? We can tell you the salient facts without any doubt, because the terrible tragedy in our family will never be obliterated.

By the LORD JUSTICE-CLERK—Will you listen to me. You are here to answer questions, and you will please answer the questions which the Lord Advocate puts to you, and make no comments.

Examination continued—I only want to know what you remember now. You said Mr. Jenks arrived on the Friday morning, and you also said at this first discussion in the flat in the sitting-room you think Mr. Jenks had not yet arrived?—No. We had an explanation before Mr. Jenks arrived.

Then it must have been either on the Wednesday or the Thursday?—Without a doubt we must have had some explanation from Donald, because we were anxious, not only for our own sakes but for his as well.

You think it was Wednesday evening?—Yes.

Tell us what passed?—Donald said he was standing behind his mother while she was writing in the morning, and his mother turned round and said, " Don't lean over me, Donald. I cannot write while you are there." She said, " Go away." With that he went round—and this is a part I misunderstood at the time—but I understood him to say he went to a table on the other side of the room and stood there. Well, there were some books on the table, and this report went off, and he turned round and saw his mother falling on to the ground. Well, we could not make any more out of that. Whether he said she shot herself or not it made very little difference at the time, because there was the explanation. There were only two of them in the room, and there was his mother falling on to the ground. Afterwards the explanation I got from him was, when he was told not to stand behind his

144

Evidence for Prosecution.

Walter Penn

mother, he went to the other side of the room, and sat down in a chair by the fireplace with his books. Then, having heard the report, he looked up and saw his mother falling.

Did he make an explanation or statement as to where the pistol had been?—I do not know on what occasion it was, but in explaining the presence of the pistol he said that on the Saturday previous he was going out with it, and, as soon as his mother saw his pistol, she said, " Donald, you shall not go out with that. You will give me that pistol," and, according to his statement, she took it from him and put it into the second lower drawer on the left-hand side of the secretaire, and there the pistol was. With regard to a further explanation as to how it had occurred, of course, we were trying all sorts of things, and the first thing that struck me—because I had three or four alternatives to weed out—was that she might have leaned round in her chair and presumably got something out of that drawer and caught hold of this, forgetting what it was, and that her thumb had got into the guard, and just as she lifted it out it had gone off.

By accident?—Yes. Well, we tried that very seriously. We tried our very best. We both visited detectives, and when by ourselves tried very much to see how it could be done.

Did you find an empty cartridge case?—I found that.

Can you tell us which day that was?—I maintain it is a very difficult thing, and I would like to know whether it is not the part of the police to take a note when these things are first given to them?

I do not think we are going to have much trouble about that? —I went to the West End Police Station and I took that cartridge the very same day as I first found it. Now, I think I could not do any better.

Do not assume that I or anybody else is blaming you. All we want to know is yes or no?—I do not want to make a mistake.

If you do not remember, say so. We can get the date otherwise. But you do not remember which day it was?—No. It might have been three or four days after we got here.

Where did you find it?—Approximately it was about a foot from the outside angle of the bay window, on the left-hand side of the bay window.

On the floor?—Yes, there is a mark on the floor still, because I made it with a blunt instrument.

[Shown label No. 3]—Is that the empty cartridge case that you found?—It is like it.

Do you know Inspector Fleming?—Very well, indeed.

Was it to him you handed that cartridge case?—No, I cannot remember whether I took it to Inspector Fleming after taking it to the West End Police Station, or whether I left it with the officer in charge there.

Cross-examined by Mr. AITCHISON—What are you?—I am a poor devil artist.

L

John Donald Merrett.

Walter Penn

What sort of art do you go in for?—Pictorial, anything I feel inclined for at the moment.

I suppose at a distance of ten and a half months it is extremely difficult to recollect conversations?—No, it is not. It depends on what the conversations consist of.

I thought you were complaining about having to rely on your memory?—For dates. On salient matters I very often think conditions make a vast deal of difference; there are things we could never forget in this world.

How many people were present when the conversation with Donald took place in the Infirmary?—My wife, Mr. Jenks, Donald, and myself.

Did you sit round a table?—No, there was no table to sit round; we were sitting on easy chairs, and on the angle of the settee.

Where were you sitting?—Between Mr. Jenks and Donald.

How far was Donald from you?—My chair was as close as it could conveniently be to the end of the sofa on which Donald was sitting.

Who put that question to him?—My wife, I believe. You see my wife was very distressed, very upset indeed.

How did you happen to hear the answer?—When you are in a small room, and you are sitting fairly close together, in my case I have noticed when the conversation is fairly sharp you make a point of catching these things. I tried my best to hear, but in a larger room I should have very great difficulty in hearing a general conversation.

At the time Donald made the remarks you say he made, was he speaking into your ear instrument?—No, I did not use the instrument at all. I will do without it to give you an idea of what my normal hearing is like. [Taking away the instrument from his ear.]

At the moment is your hearing normal or abnormal?—No, I cannot hear that. I cannot even hear that you are saying anything.

[Counsel stepped back to the dock rail.] " I will confess, if you like "?—I can hear you talking; I can almost hear your articulation.

[Counsel came nearer to the witness.] " I will confess, if you like "?—It seems to me you are not trying to raise your voice at all.

[Coming still nearer to the witness, to the position he formerly occupied when speaking through the instrument.] " I will confess, if you like "?—You said, " I will confess, if you like."

Was Donald's head as near your head as mine is to yours at the time?—That I cannot be quite sure of.

Would your wife hear the words?—Hear what words?

Hear the words that Donald said. Would your wife hear the

146

Evidence for Prosecution.

Walter Penn

words, " I will confess, if you like " ?—Oh, I should think so. I feel quite sure she would.

And they would burn themselves into her mind ?—That I do not know. It depends on what came after it, or anything else.

And Jenks would hear, would not he ?—He must, certainly.

And Jenks is a lawyer ?—No.

What is he ?—He is a business man.

Did you make at the time any written note of what Donald said ?—No, not at all.

So you are speaking purely from recollection ?—That is quite right.

Have you discussed the matter with your wife repeatedly since ?—We have discussed various phases of it, certainly.

Including conversations which you had with Donald ?—No, we ignored that, because we did not put any importance upon it.

When Donald said—if he said—" I will confess, if you like," was it just a jocular remark ?—I consider it was just a childish way of brushing it on one side.

You did not take the suggestion that he had shot his mother seriously ?—No, certainly not.

Coming to the meeting at the flat when the demonstration was carried out as to how the thing might have happened, were there detectives present at the time ?—On various occasions.

But, on the occasion when the demonstration was made how Mrs. Merrett might have drawn the pistol out from the drawer and shot herself by accident, were detectives present ?—On one occasion there were four detectives there.

On that particular occasion of the demonstration were detectives present ?—Yes.

ELSPETH ELLIOT GRANT (24), examined by the LORD ADVOCATE —I am a nurse in the Royal Infirmary. I remember being on duty in ward 3 on the 17th March, 1926, when Mrs. Merrett was being brought in. She recovered consciousness that day. Q. Was she able, having recovered consciousness, to speak quite sensibly ?— A. Yes. I spoke to her, but not on any serious topic. I remember Mrs. Merrett's sister, Mrs. Penn, coming to see her, and I was present at a conversation which they had. Mrs. Merrett asked Mrs. Penn what had happened, and Mrs. Penn said, " Oh, you had a nasty fall," and Mrs. Merrett said, " Oh, no, I did not." She said it was a most extraordinary thing; " There was a sound like a pistol or gun shot in my head," and she added, " Did Donald not do it; he is such a naughty boy ? " and with that Mrs. Penn left the room; she was very upset. I left the room too. While I was attending Mrs. Merrett she always said she could not understand it at all, it was so extraordinary. That was all I can remember her saying.

Cross-examined by Mr. AITCHISON—I know Sister Grant. I have not talked with her recently about this case, because I have

John Donald Merrett.

Elspeth Elliot Grant

been away from the Infirmary. It must be a few months ago that I talked with her about it, because I left the ward shortly after that. I saw Mrs. Penn in the witness-room yesterday.

Did you talk to her about the case?—We did not discuss any details about the case; we just said it was rather an unfortunate affair.

Who said it was rather an unfortunate affair, you or she?—I did.

Did she agree with you?—Yes, she seemed to think it was rather a pity that we should all be brought into it; that was all. I never had any conversation with Mrs. Penn yesterday as regards what Mrs. Merrett said. At no time have I ever discussed the matter with her. The only one I spoke to about it was Sister Grant, and that was on the same day. Mrs. Merrett was at that date paralysed down one side and suffering a lot of pain. The conversation would take place about midday. It was the following Wednesday after Mrs. Merrett was brought in—the first day Mrs. Penn arrived—when the conversation took place. It was the day prior to Mrs. Merrett developing delirium. I knew Mrs. Merrett was having drugs injected into her to deaden the pain. She sometimes had morphine and sometimes powders.

Can you tell how long before the conversation to which you have spoken it was that she got an injection of morphine?—I have no idea.

When Mrs. Merrett said, " Did Donald do it? " had there been a general talk amongst the three of you as to what had happened?—No.

Was Mrs. Penn putting questions to her?—No, Mrs. Penn was not.

Your version of the matter is that Mrs. Merrett said, " Did Donald do it; he is such a naughty boy "?—Yes.

Was that not just said jocularly?—No, she said it quite seriously. Do you remember Mrs. Penn saying, " That is impossible "?—No, I do not remember that. I was standing at the opposite side of the bed. Mrs. Penn was at the one side and I was at the other.

Is not it the case it was Mrs. Penn who said, " Did not Donald do it? " and Mrs. Merrett said, " That is impossible "?—No, I remember quite distinctly it was Mrs. Merrett who asked Mrs. Penn. I did not make any note at the time, but I remember what was said.

So you are entirely at the mercy of your recollection?—Well, I immediately told sister.

Whoever you told, you are entirely at the mercy of your recollection at a distance of ten and a half months?—I remember it very distinctly.

Do you remember any words like this, " There was a bang like a pistol as if Donald had done it "?—Not like that. She said there was an explosion in her head. It was like a pistol shot.

148

Evidence for Prosecution.

Elspeth Elliot Grant

Mrs. Merrett did not say, " As if Donald had done it." If she had I would have remembered it.

If Mrs. Penn, in answer to Mrs. Merrett's suggestion, " Did Donald not do it ? " had said, " That is impossible," would you have remembered that ?—I think so, but I did not hear Mrs. Penn say anything like that.

Can you remember anything Mrs. Penn said at all ?—Mrs. Penn told her she had had a nasty fall when Mrs. Merrett asked her. Beyond that, Mrs. Penn did not say anything further that I heard. If she had said, " That is impossible," I would have remembered it.

ELIZABETH HELEN CHRISTIE, examined by the LORD ADVOCATE—I am a dance instructress at the Locarno Club, Glasgow, where I have been since about December last. Prior to that I was engaged at the Dunedin Palais de Danse, Picardy Place, Edinburgh, first of all in the office, and latterly as an instructress. I am known amongst my friends as " Betty." I became acquainted with the accused, I think, about the end of December, 1925. He danced with me at the Palais. He was there quite often during the succeeding weeks. I am not quite sure how often he was there, but I should think he would be there about four nights a week, and sometimes in the afternoon too, perhaps once or twice a week. He said he was a student at the University.

Did he give you presents ?—He gave me two rings, one costing £2 5s. and the other £2. I am not quite sure when that was, but it was before the 17th of March, perhaps three weeks before that. On occasions he " booked me off." By that I mean if a person chooses to pay enough to cover what an instructress might earn in the afternoon he can book her off and take her out. At sixpence a dance it works out at fifteen shillings for the whole afternoon, and for an early night it would amount to £1, but for a late night it would come to thirty shillings. He booked me out three times in the afternoon and twice in the evenings. On Wednesday, 17th of March, I met the accused outside the Dunedin Palais about two o'clock in the afternoon. Q. Did he say anything about his mother ?—A. Not when he first met me. Q. What did you do then, did you go with him or not ?—A. Yes, I went out with him. He booked me off for the afternoon. He had his motor cycle with him, and he took me on the pillion down to Queensferry. We returned about four o'clock, I think. Q. Was it while you were away that he told you about his mother ?—A. He did not tell me when I first met him, but a few minutes afterwards, before we left the Dunedin, as he was looking very white, I asked him what was wrong, and he said his mother had gone through an operation. A few minutes afterwards he told me his mother had shot herself. We then went down to Queensferry. He said he was not sure whether she shot herself or whether it was an accident. Q. Did he say anything about a pistol on that occasion ?—A. Yes,

John Donald Merrett.

Elizabeth Helen Christie

he said it was his own pistol. I knew he had one; he had shown it to me once. He told me he had been sitting writing in the room at the time, and that the maid was in the kitchen. When we came back from Queensferry we went to the flat at Buckingham Terrace first. We were joined by Mr. George Scott. The accused then got a taxi and I went up to the Royal Infirmary with him. I waited in the corridor while he went in to see his mother. I was appealed to as regards the telephone number of the Palais. We would be about twenty minutes or half an hour at the Infirmary, and I left along with the accused. We went back to the Dunedin first of all, and from there to Buckingham Terrace to get the accused's suitcase, because he was staying in the County Hotel in Lothian Road. I was booked off that evening by the accused. We then went to the Caley Picture House. I was at the Infirmary again that evening with the accused, but I am not quite certain whether it was before or after we went to the pictures. After we had been to the picture house he took me back to Picardy Place, where I stayed. I cannot say how long the accused had had the motor bicycle at that time, but he had had it for a little while. That was the only motor cycle I knew of his having. The following day, Thursday, 18th March, the accused booked me off again both afternoon and evening. I am not certain where we were that night, but I got home pretty early. I did not see the accused very often during the next few days. I was up again at the Infirmary on the Thursday with the accused, but I do not know the time. We would be there about a quarter of an hour on that occasion. I heard of the death of Mrs. Merrett on the 1st of April. The accused came down to the Palais that day between twelve and one o'clock. He was not inside the Dunedin that day. I cannot quite remember when I next saw him. I did not see him for a day or two after that. I had tea with him on the Saturday afternoon, the 3rd of April, at the Dunedin, but he did not dance. I never saw Mrs. Merrett. Q. Did the accused always seem to have plenty of money?—A. He never seemed to be in want of it.

Cross-examined by Mr. AITCHISON—I met the accused in December, 1925, and we became what one might call "good pals." He sometimes booked me out for the afternoon. I was once down at Queensferry for tea with him, and I have also been down to the Marine Gardens with him.

On the 17th of March, when he came to see you at the Dunedin Palais, did you notice that he was upset?—Yes, he was very upset.

Did he tell you of the mishap that had befallen his mother?— Yes.

So far as you recollect, did he say to you that his mother had shot herself?—Yes.

And immediately afterwards did he add, " It may have been an accident; I do not know "?—Yes.

150

Evidence for Prosecution.

Elizabeth Helen Christie

When he said that to you was he in very great distress?—Yes, he was very upset.

Can you remember whether it was your suggestion that he should run you down to Queensferry to take his mind off the matter?—Yes, it was my suggestion. We went to Queensferry and had tea together there. He was greatly upset at tea-time, and I do not think he ate anything.

You saw him from time to time after that. Can you say that during that time he was frequently going to the Infirmary to inquire for his mother?—Yes.

Several times a day?—Yes.

And did you sometimes go up with him to the Infirmary?—Yes.

Did he always seem anxious to find out how she was getting on?—Yes. I knew before meeting with him on the 17th of March that he had a pistol. He said something about going shooting in France with it, but I cannot remember when he said he was going. He said his mother was going with him.

Prior to the 17th of March had the accused danced a great deal?—He danced quite often.

After the 17th of March, and up to the time of his mother's death, do you remember his dancing at all?—He was in the Dunedin, but more as a spectator.

Can you say, as far as you recollect, that during that period in which his mother was lying critically ill he did not dance?—I cannot remember him doing it.

Did you just regard him as a big romping boy?—Yes.

CHARLES NICHOL STOTT, examined by the LORD ADVOCATE—I am an assistant with Messrs. Hardy Brothers, 101 Princes Street, Edinburgh. I remember the accused calling at our premises wanting to buy a pistol, when I suggested to him that he must apply for a certificate first. He came back on 13th February, 1926, with the necessary certificate, and purchased a .25 automatic pistol, the price of the pistol being £1 17s. 6d. He also bought fifty rounds of ammunition, which cost 7s. 6d., making a total of £2 5s., which was paid in cash. Q. Did the accused indicate to you the purpose for which he required the pistol?—A. As far as I recollect, he merely said he purposed going abroad. The pistol in question has a safety catch, which is quite an effective safety catch as far as I know. The cartridge, when fired, is automatically ejected from the pistol. Q. Might the empty and ejected cartridge case spring some yards away?—A. Yes. Q. Is there any certainty as to what direction it will spring relative to the position of the pistol?—A. If the pistol is held tightly and properly it usually goes to the right. Q. And forwards or backwards or sideways?—A. I have ejected them as a rule a little to the back, and I have also picked them up forward, but the action tends to throw it to the right.

[The witness identified labels Nos. 4 and 5 as similar cart-

John Donald Merrett.

ridges to those he supplied to the accused. Also label No. 3, an
empty cartridge case, precisely similar to the others referred to.]

Cross-examined by Mr. AITCHISON—The pistol I sold to the
accused was a cheap pistol in comparison with the English makes.
It was made in Spain.

Is not it within your knowledge that these cheap makes of
pistols are often erratic?—No, some of those cheap makes are
better than some of the English makes.

But is not it the case that with those cheap makes of pistols
you can never be very sure where you are?—£2 or £1 17s. 6d.
for a small pistol like that is not considered cheap.

If the safety catch is on it won't go off?—No.

But if the safety catch is off, are they not very easy to discharge by accident?—Something would need to come in contact
with the trigger with a fair amount of power behind it.

You said something about the direction in which the cartridge
would be ejected on firing. I suppose it is quite impossible to
draw any sure inference as to the direction from which the shot
has been fired from the position in which the cartridge is found?—
If it comes in contact with nothing.

Do you agree that you can never be certain as to how the
cartridge will fly out or what course it will take?—You are never
absolutely certain. I am unable to say whether the cartridges I
supplied to Professor Littlejohn came from the same consignment
as those supplied to the accused.

ALAN MACNAUGHTON, examined by the LORD ADVOCATE—I am
a gun maker, carrying on business at Hanover Street, Edinburgh.
Label No. 1 is what is known as a .25 automatic pistol, the
magazine of which holds six cartridges. The recoil of a shot
automatically ejects the empty cartridge and brings another one
into the breach, but for the first shot the breach has to be drawn
back and released so that the cartridge will come into the chamber
and the pistol is then ready for firing. It has got a safety catch
on the left-hand side, which is operated by the pressure of the
thumb or finger. The opening through which the empty cartridge
is automatically ejected is on the right-hand side of the barrel,
and that tends to throw the empty cartridge when ejected out to
the right of the pistol. Q. May the empty cartridge be propelled
some yards?—A. In most cases a considerable distance. I tested
the pull of the trigger of label No. 1, and I found it was 5 lbs.
9 ozs. That is a fairly heavy pull for such a small pistol. Q. Is
that the type of pull that is likely to go off with an accidental
touch?—A. No. I was supplied with one cartridge from each of
labels Nos. 4 and 5, and I took out the bullets and ascertained the
explosive inside. I found a small charge of smokeless powder in
each exactly similar. Q. One often hears the expression " smokeless powder." Is there such a thing as an absolutely smokeless
powder?—A. Not that I know of. Q. When firing cartridges of

152

Evidence for Prosecution.

Alan Macnaughton

the type you have just spoken of in such a pistol as that, would there be a certain amount of smoke?—A. Very little.   Q. But still some?—A. I have carried out no tests.   Q. If such a pistol were fired at close quarters would it cause blackening on the object?—A. I have not been asked to make any tests for that, but I should say only at a very short distance.   The blackening is caused by the heat of the burning powder and partly the consumed powder blown from the barrel.   It is the want of complete consumption of the powder that causes the blackening.   Q. And would it be right to say the shorter the barrel the less chance of complete consumption of the powder?—A. Almost certainly.   Q. That is to say, the longer barrel you have, the longer area you have for consumption of the powder?—A. Yes.   Q. And this pistol has an exceptionally short barrel?—A. Very short.   Q. If such a pistol were fired almost up against human hair, say, at a distance of one inch, would you expect to find it singed?—A. Yes, I would, but I would require to make an experiment in order to ascertain precisely the border line between the distance in which you would find singeing and the distance in which you would not. Q. For what purposes are pistols such as label No. 1 useful?—A. For self-defence chiefly.   They are not useful for rabbit shooting or for killing any game.   They are also not useful for target practice on account of the shortness of the barrel.   It is very difficult to take a steady aim with them.

Cross-examined by Mr. AITCHISON—Is it your evidence that all the people who purchase pistols of that type purchase them for self-defence?—Some people purchase pistols without really having any great idea of using them for anything.

Is it your view that the majority of people who purchase pistols of that kind do it for self-defence?—Yes.   I should say that there have been very few sold in this country since the passing of the Firearms Act.

Is it your view that in determining a question of accidental discharge it is immaterial to ascertain whether or not there are imperfections in manufacture?—If the pistol is working all right, and the pull sufficiently heavy, I think it is immaterial.

Is it not your experience of firearms that accidental discharges occur which you often cannot account for?—Yes, sometimes.

Am I right that the explosive in this type of cartridge is not gunpowder but cordite?—A modified type of cordite called smokeless powder.

Do you agree when you get discoloration from cordite it is a different kind of discoloration from what you get from gunpowder?—It would be.

I mean a gunpowder cartridge, if discharged on close range, may give you a real blackening?—Yes.

On the other hand, with cordite, can you be sure whether you would get blackening, or to what extent you would get

John Donald Merrett.

Alan Macnaughton

blackening?—I have carried out no experiments with that small cartridge with that in view.

I understood you to say that the blackening was caused, if you got it, by unconsumed powder?—And by the heat from the burning of the powder.

I put it to you that is wrong, and the correct view is that what causes the blackening is the burnt powder, whatever the powder may be; do you agree?—No.

Have you ever considered whether the blackening is caused by the consumed powder or by the unconsumed powder?—So far as I have considered it, I consider the blackening to be caused by both.

You say you may get singeing of hair if you fire a pistol of that kind near the hair. Do you mean that if you hold a pistol of that kind over a person's hair that you would singe it if you were close enough?—I should think so.

What you mean is if you are holding it directly over the hair at the time?—Very close.

But can you express any view whether you get singeing horizontally from the line of discharge?—I can—very close on the line—I would expect it there also.

Do you mean half an inch from the centre line of discharge?—Yes.

Again that is a theory?—Without having tried it.

Professor HARVEY LITTLEJOHN, examined by the LORD ADVO-CATE—I am an M.B., B.Sc., F.R.C.S.(Edin.), and Professor of Forsenic Medicine in the University of Edinburgh. On 1st April, 1926, in the mortuary at the Infirmary, Edinburgh, I examined the body of the late Mrs. Bertha Milner or Merrett. Dr. Kerr was also present. The body was identified by Dr. Holcombe. No. 1 of the productions is my report on the post-mortem examina-tion, and it is a true report. [Reads report.[3]] I extracted the bullet from the skull and handed it over to Detective Fleming. Label No. 2 is the bullet in question. At a later time, in January, 1927, I gave another report, which is production No. 1a. It is also a true report. [Reads report.[4]] Production No. 169 is a cardboard sheet upon which I carried out a series of experiments in August last. On 8th December, 1926, I also conducted a number of experiments, along with Professor Glaister, on cards, using cartridges which were bought from Messrs. Hardy, to show the effects of firing at different ranges, and these cards are pro-duced, and are productions Nos. 163 to 168. I probed the direc-tion of the bullet, and I found that, having entered the skull at the concha, it proceeded directly to the spot where I found it. Q. We know that the symptoms of meningitis started late on

---

[3] See Appendix I.

[4] See Appendix II.

Evidence for Prosecution.

Professor Harvey Littlejohn

Thursday, 25th March. Is there any reason, from what you saw at the post-mortem examination of Mrs. Merrett, why her mental condition should have been affected before that?—A. No, I saw nothing. The brain, as I say, was to all appearances uninjured. I was also present at some further experiments which were carried out on Sunday last, 30th of January, 1927. These experiments were carried out in my premises at the University by the representatives of the defence, Sir Bernard Spilsbury and Mr. Churchill. Q. Tell me first of all, generally, how the results of these experiments compare with your previous experiments?—A. The results of the experiments which I witnessed last Sunday were strictly comparable with the experiments done first of all by me in August, and, secondly, by me and Professor Glaister in December. It was with the pistol which is label No. 1 that the experiments were conducted on Sunday last, and the cartridges used were taken from the box I bought from Mr. Stott (label No. 5), from the box of cartridges which was found in a drawer in Buckingham Terrace (label No. 4), and one cartridge which was attached to the pistol (label No. 1). Thirteen shots were fired, and the whole of the thirteen experiments that I saw were directly comparable with the ones I had already done. The experiments were carried out at ranges varying from point blank to 6 inches. At 6 inches the experiments show practically nothing, and correspond exactly with the experiments carried out by Professor Glaister and myself, and also with my own experiments. Sir Bernard was good enough, when I was with him on Sunday, to show me the cards of experiments which he had conducted in London. They differed essentially from those he conducted in my presence at the University, and also from our experiments conducted here. The main difference was that it was not so much blackening but more yellowness, and evidently a different kind of powder had been used. That is my explanation. The passage of the bullet within the lady's skull I describe as being rather forward at an angle of 120 degrees, and slightly upwards. Q. Of course, that might have happened even with the pistol being held on the level, by whoever was firing it, whether she or anybody else?—A. Yes. Q. For instance, if the lady had been bending forward writing, the pistol might have been fired on the level?—A. Yes, and the tendency would be for the shot to pass slightly upwards. It depends on the position of the figure. Q. You have had a long experience. Have you ever had a case of a woman shooting herself before?—A. Yes. Q. Often?—A. Not often, but I have had cases of women who have shot themselves. One case comes to my mind which happened here where a woman committed suicide by shooting herself in the temple, but they are not common in women; they do not use firearms as a rule. Q. Was the case to which you referred that of a type of woman at all similar to the type of Mrs. Merrett?—A. No; she was a woman who was arrested for getting lodgings by

155

John Donald Merrett.

Professor Harvey Littlejohn

false pretences. Q. What the newspapers call an adventuress?—A. Yes.

[At this stage the witness demonstrated what he described as "the awkwardness of the angle at which the pistol would require to be held," assuming a case of suicide, holding the pistol at a distance of 3 inches from the point of entrance of the bullet, which brought the muzzle of the pistol about the lobe of the ear, with the arm in a strained backward position.]

Q. We have been dealing with possible suicide. What about accident?—A. The suggestion has been made that the lady while writing put her hand into the bureau, took the pistol out of the drawer when getting out some papers, and that it went off by accident. Well, in order to have an accidental wound like that she would have to put her hand into the drawer and take the pistol with the butt in her palm, and in taking it out of the drawer she must not only do that, but turn her hand so that the muzzle points towards herself, otherwise accidental discharge is impossible. The muzzle must be pointing towards herself, and in addition she must put her thumb or her finger on the trigger and give it a pull of not less than 5 lbs. Q. And in the event of the safety catch being on, there must be accidental shifting of the safety catch?—A. An accidental shifting of the safety catch, which is not an easy matter; it has got to be done deliberately. Q. Will you tell us what you have to say of the possibility of blackening or tattooing being removed by rubbing or washing?—A. That occurred to me, in the first place, when I did my own experiments, and afterwards with Professor Glaister, and we tried by means of a sponge to wash away by rubbing the blackening produced at a distance of 1 inch, which was a very marked blackening, as all the experiments show, and the result of that washing is shown in figure No. 2 on my piece of cardboard (production No. 169). That is the result of washing with the sponge to get away the blackening. Some of the surrounding blackening is less, but the central zone of blackening, which in all these experiments is always the darkest part, was quite unaffected, and is to be seen on a radius of about three-quarters of an inch of intense blackening still after washing. Professor Glaister and I also did experiments on a piece of skin, and when we tried to wash away the blackening produced at a distance of 3 inches we found the same result, that we could not get rid of the main evidence of blackening. Q. I suppose that in the course of a certain lapse of time and a certain number of washings it would tend to disappear?—A. In a living person, but there you have living tissue, and living tissue acts differently in a living person. You have a constant change going on, and it would be got rid of at the end of a fortnight or so. Q. Then what about dead tissue?—A. Then it remains. I have had a piece of skin shot at at distances of 1 inch and 3 inches, and have had it soaking in water for about two months or seven weeks, and there is absolutely no change. I have

Evidence for Prosecution.

Professor Harvey Littlejohn

brought it with me, and it is available if desired. Q. I would like if you could tell us accurately the difference between what is called blackening and what is called tattooing?—A. When a pistol is discharged, more especially if black powder were taken as a typical test, you get the zone of blackening immediately surrounding where the bullet enters—very deep blackening—which consists very largely of unconsumed particles of powder driven into the skin. That cannot be washed away. Besides all that there is a varying zone of blackening which is due to the smoke, and which is not difficult to wash away. With a modern revolver, such as the pistol produced to-day, you evidently get the blackening such as I mentioned. You have a very deep zone of blackening in all these, immediately surrounding where the bullet enters, with it more or less diffused round about. The one is more easily removed than the other. The central blackening, in my opinion, cannot be easily removed. Q. In your opinion, if existing, was it bound to be observable by Dr. Holcombe and Dr. Bell on 17th March?—A. Yes. Q. Is tattooing something different from what you have been telling us of?—A. There is always a certain amount of unconsumed powder or carbon which is driven into the skin. Tattooing is merely like putting carbon into the skin with a needle, and it always remains as a black mark.

Cross-examined by Mr. AITCHISON—Before you can draw any confident conclusion as to whether a wound is homicidal, suicidal, or accidental, do you agree that you must be very sure of your data?—I agree that, before you can form an opinion, you ought to know all the available data.

If your data are incorrect, or incomplete in any material respect, do you agree that it would vitiate your conclusion?—It might modify; I do not say vitiate.

Or vitiate?—It might, if it was a serious difference; then it might vitiate.

Am I right that the conclusion which you reach in the present case is a conclusion relating to probabilities only?—No. The conclusion I have arrived at is more than a probability, in my opinion.

I see from the second of your reports that you say this in the second last paragraph, " From these considerations I am of opinion that suicide was in the highest degree improbable "?—Yes.

Does that represent your view?—Well, if you put it to me, I am stronger than that still; I say it is inconceivable, in 'my opinion.

I just want to know how far you will go?—Well, I put it at that definitely, that to my mind suicide is inconceivable from the facts that I know.

By " inconceivable " do you mean impossible?—Nothing is humanly impossible, but it is inconceivable.

You do not like the word " impossible "?—Nobody likes the word impossible.

John Donald Merrett.

Professor Harvey Littlejohn

Do you say that accident is inconceivable?—I think so.

Not impossible?—I must put in a word there—unless it was a near or close discharge. If it can be proved to be a close discharge then either suicide or accident was possible.

If there is a doubt as to whether or not it was a close discharge, could you exclude suicide?—I have no doubt—and therefore I give my opinion, based upon my own experiments and observations—I have no doubt that it was not a close discharge.

That is not an answer to the question. You are accustomed answering hypothetical questions. I will put it to you again. If there is a doubt as to whether this discharge was, or was not, a near discharge, would you agree that suicide cannot be excluded—if there is a doubt?—What do you mean by " a near discharge "?

I am using the term in the sense in which you have used it?—I used the term " near discharge " as within 3 inches. If you accept that, then I can answer your question.

If there be a doubt as to whether the weapon was discharged within a range of 3 inches, do you agree that suicide cannot be excluded?—I agree.

Similarly, if there is a doubt as to whether the weapon was within 3 inches, do you agree that accident cannot be excluded?—I agree.

I understand that you base your conclusion mainly upon two factors—first, the unusual site and direction of the wound, and, secondly, the absence of blackening around the wound?—The evidence of the discharge being at a distance of over 3 inches.

Am I right that you base your conclusion upon the concurrence of these factors?—I do.

And would you agree that if I can succeed in displacing either of your factors your conclusion would go?—Oh, no. If you will allow me, you must displace the chief factor, namely, the distance of discharge. The other two are both possible in both suicide and accident if it was a close discharge.

Would you concede me this, that if I can succeed in displacing your main factor, which is closeness of discharge, your conclusion goes?—Well, it will be shaken very much.

Before we come to the close discharge, I just want to ask you one or two questions about the direction of the wound. How could you say that the wound made by the bullet was straight?—Do you mean to say, " How could I say that the line between where the bullet entered the skull and where it was found is a straight line?" By passing a probe along.

What kind of probe did you use?—A thing like a needle.

Did the probe go in easily?—Yes, fairly easily.

Had not there been a suppurative condition of that wound for a period of some ten days?—There was no visible evidence of suppuration at all.

If you had meningitis resulting from a wound of that kind, was not there bound to be a certain amount of swelling

158

Evidence for Prosecution.

Professor Harvey Littlejohn

of the tissue surrounding the wound?—No. I think you are mistaken. The wound itself was to all appearances perfectly healthy, but organisms had entered and set up the suppuration inside the skull, and that is where I found evidence of suppuration.

In using a steel probe in order to ascertain the direction of a wound, don't you agree that it is extremely easy when a probe is in the fleshy part of the wound to be really deflecting the direction without being aware of it?—Oh, no. I am afraid you do not understand.

I understand perfectly. Your answer is no?—No, I do not think you quite understand the situation.

If you want to add something, do so?—I was only going to add this, that the wound was like a pencil hole—no bigger and no less.

I quite follow that?—And this pencil hole passed from the external wound to where the bullet was found. There was no fracturing of bone visible on either side. It was apparently a direct line.

I agree when you come to the length of the bone you get a direct line, but before you get the length of the bone is it not very easy when you are inserting a probe to deflect the flesh through which you are putting the probe without being aware of it?— No, and you have only to put your finger on your ear and find that there is a cartilage there, and there is nothing to deflect it.

Look at No. 2. Do you observe the point of the bullet?—Yes.

My information is that the point of that bullet points unmistakably to deflection having occurred?—No.

Do you not agree with that?—No, I wholly disagree. There are simply two dents in the point of the bullet which would be produced by the bone through which it passed.

On this question of the direction of the wound, and the conclusion you can draw from it, I want to put a passage from Professor Dickson-Mann's book, the second edition, page 307. The passage is this, " It is quite clear that the direction of a wound often enables a correct opinion to be formed as to its suicidal or homicidal origin. Still, should the direction not agree with that which is held to be characteristic of suicidal wounds, suicide is not therefore to be excluded from consideration, unless the position and direction are such as to make it impossible for the wounds to have been self-inflicted." Do you agree with that as a general proposition?—But that is acknowledged by everybody.

Well, you agree with it?—I do, certainly.

And do you agree with the further sentence, " Experience teaches the necessity of great caution in applying general rules to special cases "?—There is no question about that.

And, further, you agree with this, I take it, " In all doubtful cases allowance must be made for exceptional occurrences "?—And for special experiments to see if your conclusions are correct. And

John Donald Merrett.

Professor Harvey Littlejohn

I must add to that—you have read that from your Dickson-Mann —he has referred to cases of shooting where there is no doubt at all—but you will find further he says, " Any suicide case should show evidence of a near discharge."

I know what you have said in your own book. I am coming to that. You describe the direction of the wound as making an angle of 120 degrees with a longitudinal line drawn through the centre of the skull?—I say " about."

Take it at your own figure. Do you say you can conclude from that that the weapon must have been held at an angle of 120 degrees to your longitudinal line?—*About.*

The LORD ADVOCATE—You mean the barrel.

Cross-examination continued—Of course, when I say the weapon, I mean the barrel of the weapon?—Quite.

Have you considered this view that the weapon might have been held at 90 degrees to your longitudinal line, that is, at right angles?—Yes.

And that at the very moment the trigger was pulled the person may instinctively have averted her head so as to increase the angle from 90 to 120?—No.

Is not that a very material matter to be taken into consideration?—I do not think it is possible.

Have you formed your conclusion upon the view that there was no alteration of the head between the moment the weapon was put in position until the weapon was actually fired?—I do not quite follow—that after the person had presumably pointed the weapon the position of the head was altered?

Yes. I mean the thing can be put quite plainly. Supposing that pen I am holding is the weapon, and supposing I put it at right angles to the head——?—Yes.

Supposing at the very moment of pulling the trigger I instinctively turn the head away from the weapon, am not I altering the angle?—Yes.

And, if that be so, is not it quite plain that you might have the weapon held in a perfectly natural position at an angle of 90 degrees and the angle altering not through an alteration of the hand, but through an alteration of the head?—No.

But try it?—I beg your pardon—if you will allow me—not to the extent of 45 degrees. And, further, the bullet won't go straight in. It was not a person holding a revolver at right angles——

The assumption I am asking you to take is, that the weapon was held at right angles to what you call the longitudinal line?—Yes.

I am putting it to you, would not it account for a greater angle to the longitudinal line if at the moment of discharge the head was instinctively averted away from the shot?—It would—a greater extent.

So that you might get a wound actually passing from behind

160

The Automatic Pistol (Actual Size).

(From the original in the Justiciary Office, Edinburgh.)

Evidence for Prosecution.

Professor Harvey Littlejohn

forwards without putting the hand into a strained position at all?
—You might if——

I am coming to a near discharge in a minute. Do you really think there is any difficulty in holding that weapon behind the ear without putting the arm into a strained position?—None at all—no difficulty at all.

At a near distance?—No difficulty at all. Anybody can do it.

And is it not simpler if, instead of holding the weapon what you might call vertically, you turn it horizontally? If you turn the weapon so that it is lying in what you might call a horizontal position, you can get the arm further back with comparatively little difficulty?—So long as you are keeping it close to the skull there is no difficulty to a certain extent.

Of course, do you agree that the range of movement of a shoulder joint varies very considerably from individual to individual?—Oh, yes.

Do you agree that in the case of a woman you very often get very great extension of the shoulder joint?—Yes.

And is not the reason of that, at one time at any rate, women used to put up their hair?—Quite true.

I see that in your first report—that is the report of 5th April, 1926—you say this—I am reading from the last paragraph of the report—" So far as the position of the wound is concerned, the case is consistent with suicide." Do you still adhere to that?—I still say that.

And then you say, " There is some difficulty in attributing it to accident, although such a view cannot be wholly excluded "?—Yes.

And do you still adhere to it?—Yes.

And, accordingly, may we now take it that you base your conclusion against suicide or accident really upon the one factor, namely, the absence of blackening?—The distance at which the discharge must have taken place.

Your inference as to distance is an inference which you draw from the absence of blackening?—That is so.

Very well now, I just want you to concede the matter of the blackening. Do you agree that the blackening you would get would depend upon the material at which you fire?—Yes, that is so—it naturally would—if you were firing crosswise, and so on, but, firing at a cardboard or any white substance, I think the burning would be more or less the same.

Do you agree when you fire at skin, as regards blackening, you get a very different result from the result which you get when you are firing at cardboard?—No, we get exactly the same result.

Well, have you seen the experiments which have been made by Sir Bernard Spilsbury in this case?—No, except these cardboard ones.

Have you seen the experiments which he made upon skin?—No.

M

161

John Donald Merrett.

Professor Harvey Littlejohn

If I tell you in the case of experiments upon skin you get very much less blackening than in the case of experiments upon cardboard, can you challenge that?—Yes, I do challenge it. May I ask this question? Did Sir Bernard Spilsbury do these experiments on skin in London or here?

I am told the experiments were made in London and also here, but, whether they were made in London or here, what I want to put to you is this, that if you make comparative experiments on cardboard and on skin, you will find that the degree of blackening is very much less on skin than it is on cardboard?—Oh, no.

Have you made any experiments to test that?—I have.

Where did you get the skin?—I got the skin from a case of amputation.

How old was it?—Quite fresh.

I want to know how old?—A day, twenty-four hours, twelve hours—not more. I could show you my experiments; they are here.

They are not produced?—I say they are here, if you want them.

You are familiar, I know, with the medico-legal literature on this subject?—Yes, I think I may say so.

Do you agree that the textbooks all emphasise the danger of drawing inferences as to the distance of discharge from the absence of blackening?—No, I do not agree. If you name some I will be very pleased.

I will put one or two to you as bearing on this matter. First of all, I think you know Professor Sydney Smith's book?—Yes.

You wrote the introduction to it?—I did.

It was published in 1925; and I put to you a passage on page 132 of that book, and I want to know whether you agree with it. That is dealing with automatic pistols, and the author says this, " Except for this the wounds are similar to those described under revolver, but the student must remember that automatic ammunition is always charged with smokeless powder, and absence of burning and blackening in close discharges, such as is found in suicides is relatively common." Do you agree with that?—(Witness hesitated to reply.)

If you like I will read the passage again?—Oh, no. I know the passage. I do not agree with it in this respect, that my experience—and I have had very considerable experience of injuries by automatic pistols—is that there has always been a certain amount of blackening. When absolute cordite has been used, I admit—as I have seen in many cases of firearms—where the cartridge has consisted of cordite pure and simple, you do not get blackening; with the so-called smokeless powder you still get blackening, although you get no singeing.

I see from your introduction to Professor Sydney Smith's book that you say this—" A perusal of Professor Sydney Smith's

Evidence for Prosecution.

Professor Harvey Littlejohn

book shows an expert knowledge and original study on many of the subjects contained in it." Let me put the question to you this way. Are you in a position to challenge the view expressed by Professor Smith that the student must remember that automatic ammunition is always charged with smokeless powder, and the absence of burning and blackening in close discharges, such as is found in suicides, is relatively common?—From my experience, I say yes, although I am not prepared to say that sometimes you do not get it; but further on in the book you will see that in doubtful cases you ought to make experiments with the alleged pistol and ammunition and see the results. We have done that. I hesitated to give an opinion in this case until I had seen what happened with the cartridge and with the pistol.

But don't you agree that the great objection to experiments is this, that you can never be sure that your conditions are the same as the conditions that actually prevailed at the time?—In what way?

Let me give you one way——?—Temperature?

Temperature, and as regards the degree of moisture of the skin. How can you be certain that your experiment coincides with the actual condition that prevailed at the time?—I think they correspond. You take a piece of skin, you fire at that, and you get a certain result. The temperature of the air, and so on, I think, do not make any difference.

I would like to know this. In carrying out your experiments upon skin was the skin dry or wet?—It was dry and wet. We had several.

Did you wet the skin for the purpose?—It was taken from a wet place where I had kept it. It was moist, not wet.

Were you careful to carry out experiments with skin in different states of moisture?—No, not altogether different states of moisture. We carried out experiments upon moist skin and experiments on dry skin.

May I put it to you—because this is an important point upon which I am leading expert evidence—that the degree of moisture in skin makes a very material difference to the degree of discoloration which you will get. Can you challenge that?—I do not challenge it.

The actual composition of the explosive in this case was cordite?—No, I think it was smokeless powder, popularly called cordite, but not really cordite.

Have you analysed it to find out?—No, I did not analyse it.

Assume from me that there was a very large percentage of cordite. Is not it the case that with the use of cordite, or an explosive containing a large percentage of cordite, on skin, you practically get no blackening at all?—Well, I really cannot say definitely on that point, except in this, that we used the same cartridges and the same pistol on several occasions, and we did get blackening, and blackening which corresponded very closely

John Donald Merrett.

Professor Harvey Littlejohn

with the patterns we got upon the cardboard. I cannot say any more than that.

I would like to put to you what you yourself have written upon this topic in your book published in 1925, at page 120, where you say this, " With cordite a fine brown grey powdery dust around the skin is all that may be seen in place of blackening as a result of the explosion "?—Quite so. I have already said that, but it is cordite, not smokeless powder. I base that opinion on certain cases of suicide and accidental deaths by rifles, the cartridges of which were filled with cordite pure and simple. The result was you got no blackening. You merely got this brownish grey powder, and not blackening.

Do you agree, or do you not, that the powder in this case answers the description of a grey powdery dust?—No, it did not. It is little discs, not actual powder.

Never mind whether they are discs or not?—They are little discs—not powder.

Very well, we will call them discs. Do you agree that the powder answers a description of scales of rectangular shape and steel grey colour?—I agree generally that it is quite a good description.

Of course, as regards the impression that material of a steel grey colour would make when discharged, would you agree it would be different from the impression gunpowder would make on discharge?—There is still a certain amount as the result of the explosion and combustion of that powder you are talking about; you get a certain amount of carbon evolved, and that carbon causes the blackening. You cannot have that composition without combustion.

I want to put to you another passage from Dickson-Mann, the same edition, page 314, bearing upon this matter which says—" Blackening of the wound being evidence of close proximity of the muzzle of the firearm to the body at the moment of discharge, is the absence of blackening, ordinary gunpowder being used, proof to the contrary? " Now, that is the question. " When a firearm is used on the body within 1 or 2 feet some amount of blackening is almost invariably produced, but exceptional cases are recorded where no blackening of the wound was present although the firearm was held in the hand of the victim." He is there dealing with gunpowder which would blacken more readily than the cordite composition. Do you agree that there are exceptional cases where no blackening of the wound was present although the firearm was held in the hand of the victim?—Well, I can only say that I have seen, off and on, very nearly 500 cases of wounds from firearms, and I do not agree with that statement—that is, with common black powder.

Let me put to you one other passage from a textbook. I am referring to Taylor, the seventh edition, volume i., page 539, and I first put to you the passage at page 539, which is to this effect—

164

Evidence for Prosecution.

Professor Harvey Littlejohn

the passage occurs in a chapter on gunshot wounds—" At what distance fired ? " He says, " The following conclusions are drawn from these experiments :—(1) Marks upon the skin; blackening produced by smokeless powder is much less distinct and definite than those caused by black powder." Do you agree with that ?—Yes.

Do you agree with this further conclusion, which he states on the same page, conclusion (3)—" At a distance of 3 inches or less powder marks may be present, but they will also be faint, and may in many instances be wiped away from the skin with a wet or dry cloth " ?—May I see the book ?

Yes [handing up book] ?—[Consulting book.] Yes, I see that these are experiments by Dr. Mackintosh.

What about them ?—I never heard of them before, except seeing them there. I have made experiments, and I put my experiments against his.

If experts differ, what are we to do in the matter ?—I do not know.

Let me put just one final passage upon this matter, also from Taylor, page 540. I want to know if you agree. " The matter may be summed up thus : if there are marks of powder or burning the weapon was not more than 1 foot away when fired. If there are no marks it is impossible to tell how far off it was, for one negative upsets any number of positives in this instance." Do you agree with that passage ?—I agree with that passage with this proviso, if I may be allowed to say so, that I think in all cases where the question arises of the distance of discharge of a weapon there ought to be experiments with that weapon and with the same cartridges to see what are the results produced by that weapon. Different weapons vary, and therefore I think it is only right, before giving an opinion, that one ought to satisfy oneself that the particular weapon does produce certain results. That we did in this case.

Am I right that the textbooks to which I have referred are recognised textbooks on this subject ?—Excellent textbooks.

Do you know any better ?—Than my own book ?

I was taking that for granted—apart from your own book ?—They are all recognised and good textbooks.

One other matter I want to put to you. Do you say that washing the skin in the neighbourhood of where the wound has been received has no effect in removing blackening or tattooing ?—I did not say that. I said the opposite. I said that washing with a sponge did take away some of the blackening, but the major portion remains unaltered.

I want to put to you two productions of experiments made by Sir Bernard Spilsbury. I put to you first of all the production which is numbered 18c, a portion of skin showing blackening at a range of 1 inch ?—Yes.

John Donald Merrett.

Professor Harvey Littlejohn

You notice that you get a certain amount of not very well-defined blackening round about the entrance to the wound?—Well, I must open this.

Well, so long as you do not destroy it?—I won't destroy it, but I must open it. I want to look at the skin. I think there has been some formalin used—yes, it is a hard piece of skin.

Well, what about it?—It shows very distinct blackening.

Do you have to use your glass to find it?—No, I can see it distinctly, but I was looking to see the individual particles of powder. There is a very distinct zone of blackening, half an inch, I see, and then surrounding that for a radius of 1 inch there is what I would call slight blackening. It is all very marked.

I am quite willing to accept that explanation. Look for a moment at No. 18g, which is also a portion of skin, at a range of 1 inch. Do you notice that you only get blackening on one side?—Yes, I notice that.

Do you know that the blackening on the other side was removed by a single movement of a piece of wet cloth over the area? —No, I do not know. I have never seen this before, and I know nothing about it. But I would like to know whether this was produced by cartridges which were fired in London, which gives a totally different appearance from cartridges such as were used on Sunday last.

I am not putting this to you for the purpose of the degree of blackening. The point is this, assuming what I am putting to you to be correct, that the cloth was moved once over the left side, does that not point to this, that it takes very little indeed to remove blackening from skin?—To remove *this* blackening from the skin.

I am told both these were made in London?—Then they are totally different. I can show you a specimen made here with the same cartridges, and it is totally different from these.

But we can only deal with the productions we have got?— Well, first of all, this is not the blackening you get from the cartridges I have been accustomed to, and which we have used here. Where you have gone over it with something wet the blackening has disappeared, but there are still very marked little particles of unconsumed powder driven into the skin and remaining there still.

As a general proposition, do you agree that the application of any wet cloth will at once remove the blackening?—No, except in so far as I have already told you. I suppose we are only dealing here with the cartridges and the pistol in question in this case. I told you that I washed, and Professor Glaister did the same, and we could not wash away the blackening. Some of it did come away, but not by any means the major portion.

As regards the particles which you get from cartridges such as we are dealing with here, is not it the case that the flat scales of the powder do not become embedded in the skin as is the case

Evidence for Prosecution.

Professor Harvey Littlejohn

with black powder?—The scales do, but we are not talking of
scales. I am talking of particles of blackness. That is all
powder, and you can see in the last specimen you showed me a
little black particle embedded in the skin.

Let us get away from blackening, for the moment, to the
tattooing. In the case of tattooing, with cartridges such as you
have here, do you agree that the particles do not get embedded,
that they merely penetrate by their edge the skin or cardboard
as the case may be?—I cannot say anything about the cartridges
you have used in London.

Stick to the cartridges that were used here. Can you contradict the view that with the cartridges that were used here scales
of the powder do not become embedded at all, but that they merely
penetrate with their edges?—I admit that the scales of the powder
do not become embedded, because the powder has undergone combustion, and it cannot be scales of powder—it cannot be the product
of combustion.

May I put it generally? My information is that, dealing
with the kind of cartridges which you have here, not only the
blackening but the tattooing upon the skin can be removed with
the utmost ease with a mere passing of a wet piece of material
over the surface. Do you agree with that or not?—I do not.
Professor Glaister and I tried it, and we could not remove the
blackening caused by the cartridges used in this case.

I would like to remind you again of what you say in your
book at page 120. You are dealing with a case of a near discharge, and what you say is this—" We thus have unmistakable
signs of a near discharge. With a sponge the blackening of the
smoke and any blood could be wiped off." Do you adhere to that?
—Certainly, and if you look at the diagram you will see what I
mean.

What do you mean?—I was referring to figures 82 and 83, a
case of a man who had committed suicide by shooting in the temple.
I took a photograph as I found him and after I had washed away
all I could wash away. I found I could get rid of blood and smoke,
but I could not get rid of blackening caused by tattooing.

Do you see that your figure 83 shows no blackening at all?—
You have referred to the diagrams. I see it in the unwashed one,
but where is the blackening in the washed one?—If you will take
my lens——

What you are pointing to as blackening in figure 83 is at
the entrance to the wound. It is not blackening at all?—Not at
all. If you take the lens you will see the entrance to the wound
and around that a zone of blackening. The two are quite distinct.

Will you concede this, that figures 82 and 83 illustrate the
effect of the use of a sponge upon a wound?—Yes.

Am I right that when you compare figures 82 and 83 in your
book they show a very, very marked difference as a result of the

167

John Donald Merrett.

Professor Harvey Littlejohn

use of a sponge on a wound?—In taking away blood and some of the smoke.

In the present case is it your evidence that there was a very considerable amount of coagulated blood over both wounds in the ear, over the antehelix and the wound in the concha?—Yes.

We had it from Dr. Holcombe that the removal of that blood necessitated the use of a wet swab?—Yes.

Would not it be sufficient to remove any blackening or adherent particles of powder there may be about the wound?—As I have already said, I think a wet swab, or, as we used, a sponge, will remove some of the blackening, but by no means all.

If the evidence of Dr. Holcombe be right, that he had to cleanse this wound thoroughly, apply pressure for the removal of coagulated blood, could you be certain that he would not remove entirely any blackening and tattooing, if there was blackening and tattooing there?—My experience enables me to say that in my opinion it would not remove the blackening from a close discharge.

Could you be so certain of that, that in a case of this gravity you can draw any certain conclusion?—Yes. If you will tell me that this weapon was discharged within 2 inches of that woman's head, then, taking your own experiments (that is, those of Sir Bernard Spilsbury) and those conducted by myself and Professor Glaister, I say it is impossible from using a swab to get rid of all the blackening.

Your evidence is that, if there was coagulated blood and a wet swab had to be used by a surgeon who had to thoroughly clean the wound in order to prevent it becoming septic, you would get evidence of smoke about the wound?—No, I do not say smoke. You are confounding two things. If there was any smoke due to blackening, nothing is easier than to remove that. But there is other blackening besides that in this case—and that is what your evidence here is, that in all these experiments there is blackening due to smoke, a diffused blackening which may be got rid of with anything—but there is also a zone surrounding where the bullet went in that is not easily removed.

In order to ascertain whether blackening has been removed or not, in a case where a wound has been washed with a swab, would not the proper course be to use a magnifying glass?—By a surgeon?

By any one who wanted to ascertain the presence or absence of blackening?—No. I think the blackening must have been evident or not. I do not say that the little particles of powder driven into the skull would be so very neutral, but any blackening would require no lens.

I understand you to concede that washing, at any rate, would remove some of the blackening?—Yes, I think it would.

If it be the fact that washing would remove some of the blackening, would it not be a wise precaution to examine with a hand lens in order to ascertain whether any blackening remained?

168

Evidence for Prosecution.

Professor Harvey Littlejohn

—I do not think I would do that, even if my sight was not what it used to be, if I saw any blackening when I was dressing the wound.

When you wrote your first report you said that what you found was consistent with suicide——

The LORD ADVOCATE—The direction of the wound.

Cross-examination continued—Is that so?—Oh, yes. I am quite willing to admit that as regards the direction and position of the wound, if it was a close discharge, I have nothing to say against that.

There was only one wound here?—Two wounds, or, rather, three wounds.

But only one bullet?—Only one bullet, but three different wounds.

Does not that suggest suicide, rather than homicide, or accident?—No, I do not think so. I do not know about homicide; he might fire two or three times. Even a suicide fires twice sometimes.

As a general rule, is it not recognised by medical men and jurists that, in cases of suicide and accident, you only get one discharge?—Yes. One is sufficient in suicide in most cases. They generally fire on the temple, and do not choose the ear.

You said something about the unusual site of the wound?—Yes.

Do you agree that in cases of suicides you sometimes get extraordinary sites?—Yes. I only go the length of saying it was unusual. I do not say it was at all impossible, but very, very rare.

Do you concede that sometimes, in cases of suicide, you get wounds in the back of the neck?—Not at the back of the neck, but at the back of the head, and there they hold it with two hands, and it must be a short revolver. Of course, they cannot hold a long revolver like that.

Then you attach importance to the near site?—Yes, the near site. I cannot draw any conclusion from that.

I see you say in your second report that the suicide as a rule leaves nothing to chance?—As a rule.

But there are such things as attempted suicide?—Yes. Then it is not a case of leaving anything to chance, but because some accident occurred. The gas turned on has petered out, or the water that he tried to drown himself in was too shallow, or something, but he did not mean to give himself a chance.

Do you agree that there is a popular idea that behind the ear is a very vital part?—I never knew of that.

Have you never heard of it?—I never heard of it. Do you mean in gunshot instances?

Is there not a popular idea that an injury behind the ear is likely to prove fatal?—I do not think I know of that.

Coming for a moment to the question of accident, can you really be certain that you can exclude accident in a case of this kind?—I would like to say this, that I cannot conceive how an

169

John Donald Merrett.

Professor Harvey Littlejohn

accident took place. If you can put it before me how you think it took place, I will answer you.

I put, quite shortly, two views of accident before you, either of which on my information is quite feasible. First of all, take this. Supposing Mrs. Merrett was sitting on a chair at the table and turned round towards the bureau, which lay on her right hand?—Yes.

Supposing she withdrew the pistol which was lying in one of the pigeon holes?—Yes.

Supposing also that as she turned round she had pulled up her chair in order to reach it?—Yes.

Supposing, further, that she overbalanced and was going to fall, would not she instinctively put out her right hand to protect her head?—I think so.

If she had the pistol in her right hand at the moment of falling, is there any impossibility at all in the wound having been inflicted on her head just where it was?—I think so.

Why?—Because it would have to be turned pointing from behind forwards, and, again, I must say at a distance over 3 inches. [Demonstrating with his hand towards his head.]

Never mind that?—But I must say that. If you say a near discharge, I have already said I cannot exclude either accident or suicide.

Do you agree that in the case of accidental discharge of fire-arms it is always extremely difficult to reconstruct what has happened?—I think so.

Especially if the person is dead and cannot give an account of it?—Yes. There are generally the surrounding circumstances, that he is examining or cleaning a weapon, or something like that.

Is it not consistent with your experience that there are a great many accidental discharges of firearms of which you can never get any satisfactory account?—I think there are a great many where you begin to doubt whether it was really a case of accident, and was not rather one of suicide.

Let me put to you one other view of accident. Supposing that Mrs. Merrett turned round towards the bureau, the pistol lying in one of the pigeon holes, and had to lean over towards the bureau in order to reach something in the pigeon hole; of course, if she had to lean over, that would incline her head towards the bureau?—She is sitting at the table, and she turns round?

Yes, and she has to tilt her chair and lean over in order to take something out?—Yes, as I am doing now [demonstrating].

Supposing the pistol was lying in the bureau and in such a position that the muzzle was pointing out towards her, is there any improbability in her touching the pistol and sending it off accidentally?—Yes, I think there are several things very much against such a theory. First of all, you ask me to visualise that she took the pistol with the muzzle pointing towards her.

I am asking you to assume that the pistol had been put into

170

Evidence for Prosecution.

Professor Harvey Littlejohn

one of the pigeon holes of the bureau pointing towards her?—Yes, and that she took it out still pointing towards her?

Yes?—And then she has got to put her finger upon the trigger.

What do you mean by having got to put her finger upon the trigger?—It won't go off unless you do.

I am not so sure of that. Supposing she put her hand out, is there any possibility at all, as she gripped it, of just gripping it with her thumb inside the trigger-guard?—I suppose it is possible.

Well, if a thing like that happened, and she happened to lose her balance at the moment, is there any impossibility in the pistol going off?—I presume it is possible, as you put it.

There is just one other matter that I want to put to you. I understand, from your post-mortem examination, that the bullet had not penetrated the brain?—No.

It is in evidence that following upon the wound Mrs. Merrett was suffering from a hemiplegia?—Yes.

How do you account for it?—I am not an expert physician. On account of the accident—shock, perhaps, or there might have been some microscopic injury to some of the tissues.

As I am calling expert evidence on this, I put it to you?—Do you want me to explain why she was paralysed on the left side?

The view of our experts is this, that in the absence of injury to the brain itself you would get a hemiplegia due to pressure on the carotid artery. Do you agree to that view?—On the carotid artery of the opposite side? This was her right side, and I understand it was the left arm that had the hemiplegia.

The view I have is this, that the bullet would be pressing in some way on the carotid artery?—It was not pressing on the carotid artery.

Then, how can you account for it?—If you ask me, I say I am not an expert physician, but I have no doubt the brain received a shock when the pistol fired, and the result was that for several hours she was unconscious—concussion, I think you call it. She recovered from that unconsciousness, but I do not know that the brain completely recovered, and I believe hemiplegia was due to some minute injury to the brain not visible to the naked eye.

Can you get a hemiplegia without a grave disturbance of the brain?—You can get a passing one. I do not think this was a permanent hemiplegia, but it was a thing that would wear off.

If there was a hemiplegia continuous from admission to the Infirmary right down to death, do you agree that there must have been very considerable disturbance to the brain?—Yes. I think there must have been considerable disturbance to the brain.

If there was disturbance to the brain extending for a period of nearly a fortnight between the wound and death, can you be at all certain that there was not also disturbance of the mind?—

John Donald Merrett.

Professor Harvey Littlejohn

The two things are totally different. Many a man who has had a shock, a stroke of apoplexy, goes throughout the rest of his life a hemiplegiac, and yet his mind is perfectly clear.

You mean that his mind clears up after a time?—He recovers in every respect, except that he is paralysed in his leg and arm, but his intellectual powers are very often unaffected.

I am quite prepared to concede that you may have a brain disturbance without a corresponding mental disturbance?—Intellectual disturbance.

But if you have a brain disturbance that ultimately results in death, can you be at all certain that there was not a mental disturbance there also at the same time?—It was not a brain disturbance which resulted in death. It was the direct infection of the brain, and was due to septic poisoning. The entrance of the organism was through the course of the bullet.

But there must have been brain disturbance?—Yes.

And, there being brain disturbance, can you be certain that there was not mental disturbance, even although not apparent?—Listening to the evidence of Mrs. Hill, I was very much struck with the fact that when Mrs. Hill went to her that morning after she arrived and asked her what she was doing she said, " I was writing a letter." Mrs. Hill said, " Do you remember to whom you were writing? "—and even that she remembered. With a person who had no intellectual balance, mental balance, it was an extraordinary thing that she not only remembered something which happened, that writing of a letter, but she actually remembered to whom she was writing.

I want to put this to you, because I am calling very eminent medical testimony. I am told that, in the case of a serious head injury, you may get a condition of what is called altered consciousness, that is to say, that the mental condition of the patient may not be quite sound, although it may not be apparent to an observer. Do you agree with that?—You have put a very wide question, and asked for a definite answer. I agree that, if a person has received a severe head injury, his mind when he recovers consciousness may be a blank. That is point 1. Secondly, that he may remember a good many things, but still have some confusion. I agree with that. About this question of altered consciousness, I cannot tell you, but I do know that there are cases of severe head injury in which apparently a person can remember everything up to the time when the injury was received.

I want to know if you can exclude this view, because I am calling expert testimony that in the case of an attempted suicide a suicide may remember everything up to within a minute of the act, and may completely forget both the act of attempted suicide and also the impulse towards suicide. Can you contradict that view?—You have said suicide in a wide sense, and you mean, I suppose, by firearms.

Quite?—That comes to the same question of a head injury. I

172

Evidence for Prosecution.

Professor Harvey Littlejohn

am afraid I have not seen many cases of suicidal injury by fire-arms in which recovery has taken place, because, as I say, they always make certain and choose the temple or some vital part, but I can say this, that I have never seen a suicide—I do not say by shooting—who did not remember when he recovered, even if he became unconscious, what he did at the time. He was conscious that he made the attempt.

I have very definite information on the point, and I put it to you that it is a common feature in cases of attempted suicide by some form of injury to the head that the patient may remember up to within a minute of the act, and completely forget both the act of attempted suicide and also the impulse that moved him to it. Can you contradict that?—I am not prepared to contradict it.

Just one other point and I am done. We know that within twenty-four hours of certain statements alleged to have been made by Mrs. Merrett she developed an acute delirium?—Within twenty-four hours of what?

Of of the time when certain statements were alleged to have been made by her, she developed acute delirium. Do you say that you can place any reliance whatever upon statements made by a person within twenty-four hours of an acute delirium?—Most un-doubtedly.

But can you do it?—Certainly, why not? A person shows no signs of any abnormality, and then suddenly begins to wander in the mind and becomes delirious, but surely up to the time she shows signs of wandering she is apparently normal.

Of course, a delirium does not just arise suddenly, does it?—In this case her temperature was up, and then there was a wander-ing mind, and it was then called delirium, but I was not there.

Supposing delirium manifested itself late on the Thursday night, must there not have been a condition of very grave brain disturbance going on during the Thursday?—That is to say, twenty-four hours before?

Yes?—I do not think so.

But can you contradict the view that there may have been a very grave brain disturbance for twenty-four hours before the delirium became apparent?—I would not think of contradicting that view if the nurses and the doctor would corroborate what you say, that there was a marked change in the patient and that she showed signs of mental confusion, but without the evidence of the doctors and nurses, who are the best judges, I cannot give an opinion.

My information is that if you got an acute delirium on the Thursday night there must have been a very grave brain condition throughout Thursday, and that in these circumstances you can place no reliance whatsoever upon what a person in that condition might say. Do you agree?—I do not agree, for the reasons I have given.

John Donald Merrett.

Professor Harvey Littlejohn

I see from your first report that you say this, " On removing the skull cap the brain membranes were found to be inflamed and infiltrated with purulent matter." Is that a grave disturbance?— That is a disturbance which we call meningitis, which is a serious matter, but that was on 1st April.

Do you know what is the period of development of meningitis? —It may develop within a very short time, twelve to twenty-four hours.

Accordingly, if the condition of meningitis became definitely apparent on the Thursday night or Friday morning, must there not have been a condition of development going on on the Thursday? —I am not prepared to say that.

Can you exclude that view?—I cannot say. The evidence of the doctors and the persons in close attendance on the patient is best; they are the people best able to speak as to that.

Do you not agree that it would be extremely hazardous to base any conclusion, in a serious case such as this, upon statements alleged to have been made by a person within twenty-four hours of an acute delirium?—Who appeared to those attending her to be normal?

So taking it?—Then, I should rely upon her statements.

I put it to you that it would be hazardous in the extreme, especially in a case of life or death like this?—I do not agree.

Re-examined by the LORD ADVOCATE—And would you hold that opinion if these statements, made by the lady in these conditions, were statements similar to those made on previous days in the Infirmary?—Yes. May I say this, because I do not want to be misunderstood. I would not give an opinion in such a case unless corroborated by the evidence of those in close attendance upon the patient. If they told me she was not normal, then I would certainly agree with counsel for the defence.

My learned friend put a series of passages to you from text-books. Does that citation of passages suggest to you how essential it is, in a case of this kind, to rely on experiments made with the particular weapon and the particular powder in this particular case?—All medical jurists have laid that down, from Taylor onwards.

It is practically impossible to dogmatise generally?—Unless you made experiments and saw what particular effects that particular weapon and that particular charge would have, certainly not.

I am not quite sure how far I was able to follow it, but there were two suggestions made to you of a possible case of accidental discharge of the pistol in the right hand of Mrs. Merrett.? —Yes.

I show you production No. 4 for the defence. Take it as a general illustration. There is the chair on which the lady was sitting, writing; and my learned friend asked you to assume that

174

Evidence for Prosecution.

Professor Harvey Littlejohn

she leans across towards the bureau, stretching her hand towards the pigeon hole at the left-hand end of the bureau, and tilting her chair. If her chair was tilted, what direction would it be tilted in, towards the bureau, or away from it?—Towards the bureau. It must be towards it. If the drawer she was trying to get at was in the left-hand side of the bureau, it is near her right hand.

If she loses her balance because the chair is tilting towards the bureau, what direction is her body propelled in?—Backwards. She must fall backwards towards the door.

Towards the other end of the bureau?—Towards the other end of the bureau, and that is towards the door.

Assuming that sketch to be approximately correct, part of her back would be falling against one corner of the bureau, would it not?—Yes.

And would she not almost necessarily come in contact with the bureau?—Apparently she would, from this drawing.

Assuming that she did come in contact with the bureau, can you suggest how her hand could get back to behind her right ear?—I cannot.

Whichever way the pistol was pointing?—Whichever way it was pointing.

By the COURT—I want to be quite certain if I appreciate your attitude. In your first report dated 5th April, 1926, you decline to rule out either suicide or accident as the cause of Mrs. Merrett's death?—That is so.

In your second report of 13th January, 1927, you in effect rule out both these theories?—I did.

May I take it that the sole reason why you reached a different conclusion on the second occasion was the absence of blackening as revealed by your experiments?—That is so.

Involving that the wound could not have been a near wound?—It could not have been a near wound.

And, not being a near wound, could not have been self-inflicted, or accidentally inflicted?—Self-inflicted, either suicidal or accidental.

And, therefore, your conclusion is that it must have been inflicted by an outside agency?—By an outside agency.

You got a pistol and cartridges and experimented with them on 6th August, 1926. How came it that you wrote your report in January, 1927?—After I had done the experiments I informed the Procurator-Fiscal of the result, and that I was now fortified in the opinion which I had expressed before that I doubted very much whether it was accident or suicide, and now could only believe that a third party had inflicted the injury. That was represented, I presume, to the Crown, and then I got a note from the Crown asking me for my views upon various questions. I wrote out these views, and only this year I got a note from the

John Donald Merrett.

Professor Harvey Littlejohn

Crown saying they would prefer that what I said in the precognition should be put in the form of a soul and conscience report.

It struck me as unusual that, having made certain experiments in August, you should not have written with regard to the results of them in the way of a report until January of the following year?—I was not asked for a report.

Mr. AITCHISON—Before the next witness is examined I ask leave of your lordship to add the name of another witness to the list of witnesses for the defence, Professor Robertson. I regret to make this motion late in the day, but it is in view of certain information which we did not anticipate, and we thought it right to bring in another doctor, and have intimated that to the Crown.

The COURT—You do not object, Lord Advocate?

The LORD ADVOCATE—I do not think I can object. I would place no obstacle in the way.

The COURT—That being the attitude of the Crown, I should not dream of excluding it.

Professor JOHN GLAISTER, examined by the LORD ADVOCATE—I am a Doctor of Medicine and Professor of Forensic Medicine in the University of Glasgow. I have had a very long experience of forty-six years in medico-legal work. On the instructions of the Crown I prepared No. 2 of process, being a report on the present case. That report is dated 10th December, 1926, and is the production No. 2. [Reads report.[5]] That is a true report. [Shown Nos. 163 to 168]—These are the productions which I sent to the Procurator-Fiscal as part of my report. They show my shooting experiments, and they are all duly labelled, giving the distances. [Shown No. 169]—That is a record of the previous experiments by Professor Littlejohn which he showed to me in his department at the University. They correspond very closely in results with our joint experiments. We took steps to test the question of the effect of rubbing or washing on the blackening or tattooing. Professor Littlejohn took a piece of sponge and wetted it, and I saw him rub one of the blackened marks round the bullet wound.

Was that on the cardboard or skin, or both?—On the skin. We never touched the cardboard experiments we made that day. And while a part of it was washed off there was more than sufficient left to indicate that blackening had taken place.

Was it real hard rubbing?—Good hard rubbing with a sponge.

Assuming that there had been blackening or tattooing, in your opinion, could that have been entirely taken away by the first dressing which Dr. Holcombe gave the wound?—I do not think so.

And that is apart altogether from whether prior to the dressing there were places on which he could have seen the blacken-

---

[5] See Appendix III.

Evidence for Prosecution.

Professor John Glaister

ing free from blood?—Whether or not he saw clear pieces of skin, the dressing would not have removed the blackening.

Do you regard it as of the greatest importance—the tests which have been taken in this case—to prove the results of the actual pistol used and the actual ammunition used?—Yes. We had the pistol, which I am informed was the pistol in question, and also these .25 Eley cartridges. We measured the distance from the cardboard to the muzzle of the weapon in each case by means of a measured instrument. The shot was fired when the muzzle was exactly at the distance recorded, and then the record left and signed by us. Label No. 1 is the pistol. [Shown label No. 5]—That is the box of cartridges. I have initialed this box of cartridges, " 8/12/26, J. G." That was the box from which the cartridges were taken.

Cross-examined by Mr. AITCHISON—In your report which you read is the main thing on which you rely the absence of blackening round about the wound?—With regard to what?

With regard to the conclusion which you draw as to the probabilities of the wound being homicidal, suicidal, or accidental? —That is one of the factors. The other factor being the direction of the wound, which is a very important one. The blackening is only indicative of the distance from the head at the moment of firing.

It would be fair to say that you rely upon the conjunction or concurrence of the two factors?—In order to answer that question —self-inflicted or otherwise.

In your view, is the more important factor the absence of blackening or the direction of the wound?—I take them both together. You cannot exclude the one or the other; both are equally important.

Let me test it this way : supposing conditions were such that you could not say whether there had been blackening or not, could you draw any sure conclusion from the direction of the wound itself?—Oh, yes, particularly in a case where the bullet goes through the solid bone of the base of the skull. Where a bullet goes through a skull bone, which is a plate, you cannot be quite sure after that, but if it is through the solid bony part of the skull you can get it perfectly accurately.

I think you misunderstand me. Assume the direction as found by Professor Littlejohn is correct. Supposing there was a doubt as to whether there was or was not blackening, can you from the mere direction of the wound draw any conclusion at all as to whether the wound was self-inflicted or homicidal?—If one knew the relationship of the person struck with the manner of firing the weapon one could give an opinion, but not readily without some knowledge of the facts of the shooting.

I think you would rather assent to the view that if all you had to go on was the direction of the wound it would be very

John Donald Merrett.

Professor John Glaister

dangerous to draw any sure conclusion?—That is why I said at the end of my report that one would require to know more of these factors, and I suppose that is why I am here to hear the evidence.

I suppose you will agree with what Professor Littlejohn says at the end of his report, which is this, " So far as the position of the wound is concerned, the case is consistent with suicide "?—Yes, I would say it is barely possibly consistent with suicide, for the reasons I give in my report.

And do you further agree when he says, " There is some difficulty in attributing it to accident, although such a view cannot be wholly excluded "?—I think you never can exclude any question as to suicide or accident so long as you do not know the facts and circumstances.

And does not that just point to the danger of theorising unless you are absolutely certain of what your facts are?—Of course, we can only help you so far as we know the facts. It is for the Court to decide on hearing the whole facts what the issue is.

Would you agree that you may get a wound that has all the appearance of a homicidal wound and that yet may be a suicidal wound?—You cannot tell a homicidal wound from a suicidal wound unless you are dealing with the actual weapon in your hand and see the wound produced. There is nothing written on the wound to say, " This is suicidal " or " This is homicidal."

Confine yourself for the moment to the site of the wound and the direction of the wound—leaving the blackening out of account. May you get a wound in such a position as suggests homicide, while in reality it is suicidal?—Suicides as well as homicides usually attack a vital part of the body with the intention of killing, consequently the head is the site of both homicidal and suicidal gunshot wounds.

I refer you to Taylor, seventh edition, page 546. " In the following case of admitted suicide the characters of the wound somewhat resemble those which are commonly imputed to homicide." And then he gives a case in 1844 of a man who was brought to Guy's Hospital with a large ragged gunshot wound on the right side of the head behind the right angle of the jaw and between it and the ear?—That means that that is evidently the course of the traject of the bullet.

The direction was from behind forwards and from above downwards?—It might be so.

Accordingly, that was a case of undoubted suicide?—I do not know.

It is stated in the book. " From behind forwards and from above downwards, and above the angle of the jaw." The first impression is that that would be a homicidal wound?—I would not be inclined to form any impression until I knew more about the facts, and I think that writer had to wait for his facts before he could state what he did.

Evidence for Prosecution.

Professor John Glaister

I see in your report you say this under question 2—" While the main direction of the wound in the skull was horizontal, it also showed a slight upward inclination from the point of entrance into the skull to the point where it was found embedded "?—Yes.

" The slight upward inclination was probably due to the position of the head of deceased at the moment that the bullet entered the skull." Is not that a pure conjecture?—No; it shows that there must have been some relation to the point of entrance to the bullet landing where it did and the direction horizontal and slightly upwards.

I am not challenging the direction, but you say, " The slight upward inclination was probably due to the position of the head of the deceased." How can you say that? Can you say that the upward inclination was probably due to the inclination of the head of the deceased?—I did not say that.

You did?—Where? What I said was the slight upward inclination was probably due to the position of the head of the deceased at the moment the bullet entered the skull.

What is the force of the word " probably " in this connection? —Probably in this sense, because the wound was a little higher at its termination than at its commencement, that the head would probably be in that position when the bullet struck the skull.

If it was a suicidal wound with the weapon held about the ear or behind the ear, would not you expect a slight upward inclination of the wound?—No. It depends entirely on the relation of the muzzle of the weapon to the head at the moment.

Would not a slight upward inclination of the wound be more likely than a downward inclination?—It would depend entirely on the position of the two things.

Do you agree the whole thing is in the region of conjecture?— I used the word " probably."

That is what I am complaining of. Don't you agree the whole thing is in the region of conjecture, unless you were an eye-witness to what actually happened?—That is true of the whole facts of the case. It is problematical.

I understand you made some experiments on skins?—We did.

Where did you get the skins?—There was an unfortunate man who had met with a railway accident and whose lower limb had to be amputated, and we were able to use that amputated limb to make the experiments.

Was it a recently amputated limb?—Yes, and it was the whole limb, not merely the skin. You have brought out a fact that I did not think it was necessary to bring out to the Court.

I just wanted to know where you got it. Now I want to ask you this: you made some experiments of washing the skin after you had fired certain shots?—Yes.

Do you agree that the effect of the washing was to remove the blackening to some extent?—Oh, yes. It was in some measure

John Donald Merrett.

Professor John Glaister

removed, but there was sufficient blackening left to have enabled anybody to see that blackening had been originally there.

Did you make any experiments on a wound over which blood had flowed for half an hour, and on which blood had coagulated? —I do not know any circumstances where we would be permitted legally to do any such experiment.

Accordingly, may I take it in making your experiment it was quite impossible for you to reproduce the actual condition with which we have to deal in this case?—As a matter of fact, with regard to the washability of this blackening, we kept that piece of skin in water from the date of the experiment until to-day, and the blackening is as fresh to-day as it was at the moment of production. It has been kept in water all that time from the 8th of December until the present moment.

Have you been rubbing it all that time too?—Oh, no, we have not. You cannot rub it very well if it is in water.

You don't think very much of that experiment?—What experiment?

That one which is under water now?—Why do you say that?

Why did not you produce it here?—It could be produced if the Court will allow it. It is in the Court building now.

As a medical jurist of experience, you know the time when the Crown can produce things, don't you?—Yes, I know, but sometimes they don't, even like the defence, produce them at the time they might.

Tell me this. It is in evidence in this case that from the ear wound there must have been a very considerable flow of blood extending over a period of at least half an hour; it is further in evidence that that blood had coagulated over the wound; it is further in evidence that in order to remove that blood a wet swab had to be used and applied with pressure. These being the facts, can you say with any certainty that the blackening would remain? —I was not present when these measures were taken. I cannot tell you the amount of scrubbing that was done, but I know this from what I heard in Court, that this poor woman fell on her left side, that the blood therefore would run down by the action of gravity towards the lower part of her neck, and would tend to run away from the wound rather than otherwise. But I cannot tell you what the doctor at the Infirmary did. He is the person to speak to that.

We have had his view already, but let me ask you this. If it is the fact that pressure had to be applied in order to remove the coagulated blood, would it be safe to draw any large conclusion from the absence of blackening in these circumstances?—If the blackening had been present originally, I say it would not have been completely removed by any such application.

Can you be quite certain of that?—I am only speaking from

180

Evidence for Prosecution.

Professor John Glaister

experience, and from the fact that we made these experiments in this particular case.

You did not make experiments where the blackening had been covered with blood which had been congealed?—That would not make any difference in the blackening. The blackening is due to the driving into the substance of the skin of minute particles of the unconsumed powder from the pistol.

Is it your evidence, in a case of this kind, that it does not matter in the least whether the blood flowed away or was congealed on the blackening?—I do not think it makes very much difference so far as the blackening is concerned.

I suggest to you it makes all the difference in the world?—Perhaps you know better than I do, but that is my view.

Re-examined by the LORD ADVOCATE—If the Infirmary doctor who first saw the body says that there were patches of the edge of the wound which were free from the accumulation of bleeding, and that he saw no signs of blackening or tattooing, would that confirm what you have said?—It would simply confirm what I have been trying to get at.

There is only one other thing I want to put to you, and that is with regard to that quotation from Taylor. In that passage he refers to a case of a man brought into Guy's Hospital with a long, torn wound which proceeded from behind forwards. That is cited by Taylor immediately under this statement—" Again, unless elaborate preparations for suicide (strings, sticks, &c., attached to the trigger) have been made it is very rare indeed, if not absolutely impossible, for the suicide to shoot himself from behind," and then he cites this case to show that it is not absolutely impossible?—That is why I put the point that it was not absolutely impossible. I did not know the facts in detail.

That is quite consistent with what you have said?—Quite consistent.

Adjourned.

Fourth Day—Friday, 4th February, 1927.

GERALD FRANCIS GURRIN, examined by the LORD ADVOCATE—I am a handwriting specialist, and I practise at Bath House, Holborn Viaduct, London. I am a Fellow of the Royal Microscopical Society of England, and have made a special study of the subject of handwriting, and everything pertaining to disputed and forged documents, for a period of over twenty-two years. In my professional work I have been consulted by most of the Government Departments, including the Criminal Investigation Department, Scotland Yard, London, and other Police Forces, and also by a number of the principal banks, including the Bank of England. I had submitted to me by the Crown authorities a number of documents in this case for examination. As instructed, I made the necessary examination and report,[6] which is No. 4 of the Crown productions. The documents submitted to me fell into three classes. Class 1 consisted of documents bearing the signature "Bertha Merrett," which I understand were in dispute; class 2 consisted of documents which bore the undoubted signatures or were in the handwriting of the late Mrs. Bertha Merrett; and class 3 consisted of documents which I was instructed were in the handwriting of, or bore the signatures of, John Donald Merrett, the accused. I have with my own hand taken photographs of the material documents appearing in each of those three classes, and I have made up a book of prints of them. That book is arranged in six sections. Section 1 contains the whole of the 56 cheques in class 1, known to me as the questioned documents, and include 29 which are the subject of the charges in the present case. My instructions were contained in the form of questions, but generally they amounted to this—to examine the documents in class 1—that is the 56 questioned documents—and to ascertain whether or not, in my opinion, the signatures of those documents or any of them were or were not written by Mrs. Bertha Merrett. If I found any of the signatures in class 1 were not written by the deceased Mrs. Merrett, in my opinion, I was to report whether or not there was anything to connect them with the handwriting in class 3, which is submitted as the handwriting of the accused.

Will you describe how you proceeded with your examination of the questioned documents and the other documents?—The first step in an examination of this kind where the genuineness of the signatures has to be reported upon is to study the undoubted signatures of the person whose signature is in question, in order thoroughly to familiarise oneself with the characteristics of that person's handwriting.

---

[6] See Appendix IV.

182

Evidence for Prosecution.

Gerald Francis Gurrin

What struck you about the documents in class 2 from your point of view when you had studied them?—The particular features of those documents were the cleanness and the speed with which they were executed. Those were the outstanding features. Then, in addition to that, of course, one familiarised oneself with the method of construction in detail.

Did you find any frequent signs of hesitation or patching up? —No, perfectly clean and straightforward from beginning to end— unusually so, in fact.

Could you tell whether they were normally blotted quickly or allowed to dry?—They were blotted quickly.

What is the result in blotting quickly?—The result is that you get on the paper a transparent film of ink enabling you to see the paper quite clearly below.

Did you next turn to the documents in class 1, consisting of the 56 cheques?—I did.

When you examined them, did you have the whole of them in front of you, or how did your examination proceed?—Before I started to examine the questioned documents they had been arranged in such fashion that I could see nothing but the signatures of those documents; the bodies were covered up, and the dates were covered up, and there was nothing but the signatures.

What did you find?—Two points struck me with regard to the signatures when I came to examine them. I found that a number of them were heavy and unnatural, and that others of them were suspiciously like each other. That was the result of my first examination of the 56. That led me to make a further examination. As both of these features themselves were suspicious, I proceeded microscopically to examine each and every one of the 56, and I found that 29 out of those 56 were solid so far as the ink strokes were concerned, and that appearance of solidity was caused by the fact that two signatures existed. The first signature, that is to say, what had first been placed upon the cheque, was a violet outline, either of a carbon impression or a pencil. It was a little difficult to determine whether it was violet or blue, because ink had passed over it subsequently. On the top of that violet outline there was a blue-black ink outline which practically covered it from beginning to end. That applies to the signature itself, " Bertha Merrett," in each of those 29 cases. In the case of the underline of the signatures it only applied in one case. In quite a number of cases there were protruding portions of the violet outline. With a view to illustrating what I found, I made the enlargements which I have already referred to as being contained in section 4.

[At this stage certain of the enlargements were exhibited to the jury, and the witness pointed out what he had described as the double signature.]

In every one of the 29 there is a violet outline which is repre- sented by the dark line on the photograph. It is quite unmis-

John Donald Merrett.

Gerald Francis Gurrin

takable on every one of the 29, both as to density and as to colour. That second line, the dark line, is completely absent in any of the signatures which were submitted to me as the undoubted signatures of Mrs. Merrett. In my opinion, the presence of an outline of that kind in the signature is not consistent with a genuine signature. I have never come across or heard of a case where the genuine writer of a signature used a model of this kind and duplicated the signature.

What is the method by which such a model is produced or used?—There are two methods, by one of which it must have been produced. First of all, the first method is to take the cheque— we are dealing with cheques in this case, and I shall say cheque— which would be a blank cheque, put it on the table, place over it a piece of carbon paper, and them upon the top of the carbon paper place the document bearing the genuine signature, and take a point of any kind, a fine pencil or a knitting needle, and go over the genuine signature so that a reproduction is made by the carbon upon the cheque form below; then to take a pen and very carefully go over the outline so produced and make a signature which will have the correct outline of the genuine signature. Of course, it is only when one comes carefully to examine it that one can find anything wrong with it. The second method is to take the genuine signature and shade it with a light behind it, say, for instance, place it on a window pane, then to take the cheque form upon which the signature is to be produced and with a blue pencil go over the outline which you can see by the transmitted light coming through the window, and then subsequently to ink over that pencil outline. In this case either of these methods might have been used.

You have told us a feature that struck you about the signatures submitted to you as genuine was the speed and cleanliness and want of hesitation or patching up. Do you find a similar feature in these 29 cheques?—No, you do not. On the contrary, you find that the signatures are heavy, and have been very slowly executed so far as the pen strokes are concerned. That would necessarily be the case when one was carefully going over the outline.

Was there another feature that struck you in the course of your examination of these 29 cheques?—Yes, the second general feature which struck me was, as I have said, the similarity between a number of the questioned cheques themselves. In order to test that I made a tracing of a signature taken at random, and I placed that tracing over each of the 56 questioned documents in turn. I found that in the case of 16 of the cheques out of the 56 it corresponded almost exactly with the outline of the signatures. When they were superimposed you could barely tell the difference between them. So that, with the one I took and the other 16, made 17 signatures which were almost exactly alike.

And were these 17, one and all, included in the 29 on which

184

Evidence for Prosecution.

Gerald Francis Gurrin

you have found the double line?—Yes, all those 17 had the outline as well.

Did you take, in order to test it, another cheque, No. 44 of the productions?—I did. I superimposed a tracing of that signature also upon the whole of the 56 signatures in turn, and I found that this outline corresponded in 10 other cases; so that there were 11 signatures made exactly in that form.

And, again, did the whole of those 11 have a double line and form part of what you have spoken of?—Yes.

What have you to say about this feature of those cheques, so many of them corresponding so nearly to the same model, from the point of view of genuineness?—Ought I not to say that I put those impressions over every one of the undoubted signatures as well, and over every one of these signatures there was nothing approaching coincidence in any case?

Will you tell us now what you have to say about that feature being consistent with the genuineness of the signatures?—Wholly inconsistent. I have never known a case of a genuine signature to which you could apply to it the tracing of another signature and find correspondence in the position of the letters and the total length of the signatures.

In your opinion, so far as the 17 and the 11 are concerned, is the agreement far too close to be genuine?—Far too close. I possibly ought to mention, in connection with the tracings, that, although the signatures do coincide, the underline does not, and also it has no violet in it, so that that was taken with the pen independent of any tracing operation.

Come now to the questions that you were asked. The first question was whether, in your opinion, any of the Clydesdale Bank cheques bore signatures which were not the genuine signatures of the deceased Mrs. Merrett, and, if so, which of them? And the answer is what?—In my opinion, 12 of the cheques on the Clydesdale Bank do not bear the genuine signatures of the deceased Mrs. Merrett.

Then question two, whether, in your opinion, any of the Midland Bank cheques bore signatures which were not the genuine signatures of Mrs. Merrett, and if so, which?—In my opinion, 17 cheques on the Midland Bank do not bear the genuine signatures of Mrs. Merrett.

The third question was, assuming you were of opinion that some of the signatures to the cheques were written by some one other than Mrs. Merrett, were you able to form any opinion on the handwriting of J. D. Merrett as to whether the signatures were written by J. D. Merrett?—The answer is that in cases of freehand copying of a genuine signature it is possible, in spite of the close adherence to a model, for some features of the writer's own peculiarities to appear in the signature produced. In cases of traced forgery, such as appear in the 29 signatures in this case, which I do not believe to have been written by Mrs. Merrett,

185

John Donald Merrett.

Gerald Francis Gurrin

the models have been accurately traced, and there is practically no possibility of the writer's peculiarities becoming manifest. My reply to the third question, therefore, must be that there is nothing to enable me to form an opinion as to whether the 29 signatures, which I do not believe to have been written by Mrs. Merrett, were written by J. D. Merrett.

Did you examine the cheques for any other feature which might throw light upon the matter?—In summarised form, yes.

Tell us what you noticed?—I noticed that the 29 signatures all showed clear indications of carbon outline; secondly, that 28 of the 29 signatures are clearly reproduced from two models; thirdly, that all the 29 cheques are payable to J. D. Merrett; fourthly, that not in the case of any of the 29 cheques was the body written by Mrs. Merrett; and, fifthly, that in the remainder of the cheques, that is to say those which I believe to be genuine, there is no instance, with the exception of two cheques payable to the University of Edinburgh, of the body having been written by any other hand than that of Mrs. Merrett. The bodies of these two cheques were, I believe, written by J. D. Merrett.

Among all the cheques submitted to you for examination, are there any cheques, except the 29, in which J. D. Merrett is the payee?—I think not, certainly none in the 56.

Did you examine the bodies of the 29 cheques to see if you could express an opinion as to the identity of the writer?—I did. I compared the handwriting in the bodies of the 29 cheques, both with specimens of the handwriting of Mrs. Merrett and with specimens of the handwriting given to me as that of J. D. Merrett. I came to the conclusion that the bodies were not in the handwriting of Mrs. Merrett, and were written by the person who wrote the specimens of J. D. Merrett.

[Shown No. 176]—That is a letter dated 12th March, 1926, signed " Bertha Merrett," and addressed to the manager of the Midland Bank at Boscombe. Was that letter submitted to you for examination?—It was.

First of all, there is no question about the signature, I understand, but in fact you did examine it?—I was not told anything about it, but told to report generally on it, and I reported that it was genuine.

There is no trace of the double line?—None at all. It is perfectly clean.

What about the body of the letter and a postscript which there is in the left-hand corner?—That I compared with the specimens in class 3, which I understood to be those of J. D. Merrett, and I found agreement, and my opinion is that they were written by the same person.

Namely, the accused?—Yes.

Take the writing in the postscript and the writing in the body of the letter, can you say whether they were written continuously?

186

Evidence for Prosecution.

Gerald Francis Gurrin

—There is this about it, that the writing in the body is sloping well to the right, as the class 3 writing does in some of the documents, and the postscript is practically upright, as it is in others of his documents, notably the account book. It is a distinctly different slope in the postscript to that seen in the letter.

The postscript is rather cramped for room?—The postscript is cramped for room. It fills up the whole of the available space.

Cross-examined by Mr. MACGREGOR MITCHELL—In the letter of 12th March there is no doubt that that is the genuine signature of Mrs. Merrett?—In my view, none at all.

And, in your view, is there any suggestion, because the postscript of the letter is in a different slope from the body of the letter, that there was any attempt to disguise the hand of the writer?—No, I have not suggested anything of the kind.

So I may take it generally from you that in your examination of that letter there is nothing at all which you could report as suspicious?—Nothing which suggests that they were not straightforwardly written by the person who is supposed to have written them. The only question with regard to the postscript is whether or not it was written continuously with the letter, and this seems to me to be a thing that can best be judged by the facts contained in the letter. I cannot form an opinion.

Coming to the question of the questioned signatures, I suppose you will agree that your art or science is to direct the attention of his lordship and the jury to the features in the letters so that they may form their own view of them?—Absolutely.

And your evidence is based upon your opinion, certainly strengthened by your experience?—It is based upon the facts which I discovered in my examination.

That is to say, things which you take to be facts; perhaps there might be some difference of opinion about them?—Well, no. We are all influenced by the evidence of our own eyes, and here there are facts which are available to anybody's eyes who examines them.

Therefore, it is for the examiner's eyes to state whether all the things you have said exist or do not exist?—Oh, yes.

Am I putting it fairly if I say that your opinion is based upon two points—first, what you would call the extraordinary close similarity between the signatures; and, secondly, the fact that you say they have been written by tracing—or is there any other element?—I should only amend that to this extent, that I would say not extraordinary close similarity but coincidence, which is a very different thing.

I suppose you will admit that the signature of the deceased lady in this case was one of character?—Yes.

In the case of a signature of character, is not there more coincidence than when a signature is ordinarily loosely made?—There is no coincidence at all between her genuine signatures.

John Donald Merrett.

Gerald Francis Gurrin

Well, then, correspondence?—Where you get the greatest resemblance between signatures is in the signatures of business people who are constantly signing, but never coincidence.

I am quite willing to take it that way, but you get a close correspondence?—Yes.

Is not that also markedly so in the case of signatures to things like cheques?—Yes, so long as we still exclude the word " coincidence " altogether.

I thought I had departed from that?—They are two entirely different things.

Take your own words, " Almost corresponding "?—Then I disagree with you if you are using these words. I say in the case of signatures of character, as you put it, there is not always correspondence.

Does it make a difference to a signature, first of all, the paper on which it is written?—Yes, it may make a difference, certainly.

Well, if you get signatures written on cheques, that eliminates to a certain extent differences in the signatures?—No, particularly not in this case, because I had specimens of exactly the same kind of cheques as the questioned signatures.

Does the ink make a difference?—The ink may make a difference, but the same applies there. I had the same class of document to compare it with.

Does the pen make a difference?—It may make a difference, but there I had the same pen so far as I could see.

Can you say, or do you not say, that certain of the signatures show that they were written by what you would call a new pen, and others by a scratchy pen?—So far as the large majority of the cheque signatures are concerned in class 2, the undoubted signatures of Mrs. Merrett, I should say that the type of pen used was either a fountain pen or a relief pen, or some type of pen which did not score the paper in any way. There were, of course, her pay-in slips which may have been written in any bank where a different pen was used.

Is it the case that some 50 odd cheques were submitted to you under what you would call questioned cheques, and that of these you found 27 genuine?—That is so.

Is it also the case that in all the material you have got you cannot find anything in the writing to connect the accused with the alleged forgeries?—Yes, I cannot find anything, and I should not be likely to find anything, to connect anybody with them, because that type of signature leaves no trace.

You commented more than once on the appearance of solidity or heaviness in what you call the questioned documents?—In some of them, and that occurred only in the 29.

I want now to turn to the point about " they almost exactly coincided." You tested that, and you directed the Court's attention to the fact that you had superimposed one signature over another. First of all, for the purpose of comparison, is it fair,

188

Evidence for Prosecution.

Gerald Francis Gurrin

or is it not fair, to take the enlargements of those very signatures?
—For the purpose of distinct coincidence do you mean?

Yes?—I have not done it. I tested that first of all on the
original documents themselves, when I originally reported and did
nothing else, and then subsequently by photographic films accurately reproduced by the camera, not by hand at all.

You have not compared the enlargements?—There was no
necessity, because if the enlargements of the questioned signatures
and the enlargements of the undoubted signatures were accurately
made in each case they would be bound to be in the same proportion as the original, and there was therefore no necessity.

Assuming that you were comparing or overlapping two
genuine signatures, what variations, if any, would you expect to
find?—You would find variations in the length of strokes, in the
spaces between the letters, and the total lengths of the signatures.

In the joining of the letters?—The height of the letters and
the position of the connecting strokes. It is best illustrated if
one takes one of the photographic films which I have reproduced
and applied it on top of a series of undoubted signatures; you then
see what an enormous variation there is in the genuine signatures.

You would probably also expect to find a difference in the
slope of the letters?—You might, but that depends on the particular case. I do not think you could consider that as a
generality.

Suppose you found, in a comparison of signatures, that is,
by putting one above the other, slight discrepancies in the formation of the letters, in the spaces between the letters, in the align-
ment of the letters themselves, the stroking of the letters, the joining of the letters and the slope, would you say then that they corresponded exactly?—It is all a question of degree in each one of
the features you have put to me. If there was close correspondence
—and close correspondence is correspondence which is obvious to
the man in the street, or anybody who may examine them—then I
should say they were not genuine. If there was no such close correspondence, then the test fails, and you have to resort to other
things.

Roughly speaking, in the signature of Bertha Merrett, which
is comparatively short, how many such variations would you expect
to find in a comparison of two genuine signatures?—I should not
expect to find any particular number at all. One makes the test
and applies the tracing or film as the case may be over the original,
and one can see at once whether they coincide or not.

[After dealing at length with the details of various signatures,
Mr. Mitchell proceeded in his cross-examination of the witness as
follows:—]

Of course, you have given evidence, having made enlargements and drawn deductions from them, but do you say the deductions which we wish to draw when we point to differences are not

189

John Donald Merrett.

Gerald Francis Gurrin

accurately shown in the original?—To start with, in making this particular test, I have neither used a microscope nor made enlargements. I have simply taken tracings of one signature and put them over the other, and found that they corresponded.

Do you still say that these correspond very closely?—I say so, undoubtedly. There are bound to be human variations, because it is a humanly performed operation.

How many variations would you expect to find?—It depends on how much you enlarge them. There might be hundreds of thousands, if you enlarge them sufficiently.

Now, we have got the signatures of thirteen letters. I have shown you something in the region of two dozen variations. Do you still say that these are not just the natural variations which you would find in genuine signatures?—I say most certainly they are not.

What other variations than those I have pointed out would you expect to find?—I would expect to find different distances, greater divergence, and greater length of signature.

You are just stating these generalities. It all depends on where, when, and how the signature was signed?—No.

If I take a small tracing, then, all the divergencies probably are covered up to a certain extent, but when we get to the enlargement, and see the natural divergencies, I put it to you that these are the natural divergencies one would expect in genuine cases?—No, they are not anything of the kind. They are completely different.

You have spoken about tracing?—Yes, that was in the original tests I made.

You said in your report, if I recollect aright, it was done either by carbon paper or by a soft pencil?—The method of reproduction is a method of tracing.

Have you made up your mind in this case what it was?—No.

You are not prepared to speak to one or the other?—No. There are two slightly varying methods either of which might have been employed.

You said you found evidence of tracing in all the 29 signatures?—I do not know that I stopped to see how many I could see with the naked eye. What would happen would be that in going through the signatures I found some which by experience one gets to recognise are muddy. You would at once put a microscope on them to see what the cause was.

Is the answer you cannot tell me how many you detected?—I cannot tell you.

In regard to tracing, are you a chemist?—No.

Did you subject the ink of any of the signatures to chemical analysis?—No.

So that all you are giving us evidence on is an examination by the eye and by the microscope?—And the coincidence test.

190

Evidence for Prosecution.

Gerald Francis Gurrin

Re-examined by the Lord Advocate—A business man is constantly signing his name to cheques and other documents. If you took a number of those cheques you would expect to find them, on looking at them, very similar?—Yes, quite similar.

Would that be mainly because the same characteristics would be present in each of them?—Yes.

If you come to the question of mechanical measurement of each of the specimens, you might find some very great variations? —In genuine signatures you undoubtedly would.

And that is a normal thing to find in genuine signatures, mechanical variations, while individual characteristics are present? —Yes.

Is what strikes you in the 29 cheques here in question the great similarity of what I may call the mechanical formation of the letters?—Yes, the position of the letters mainly.

As I understand your evidence, it is that the genuine signature has been copied by a violet medium, in the first instance, and then that violet copy has been inked over in ordinary ink?— Yes.

You would expect that there would be some very slight divergencies in the copy?—Yes.

As regards the inking over of the violet copy, you would expect to find greater divergencies?—Yes, you would.

And, in fact, that is what you found?—Exactly.

By the Lord Justice-Clerk—May I take it that in your opinion, whether rightly or wrongly entertained, you think it is beyond reasonable doubt that Mrs. Merrett's signature has been forged by some one on the cheques which are included in this indictment?—Yes, my lord, beyond all reasonable doubt.

But on your examination of these cheques you are unable to connect the accused with the forgery?—I am unable.

Have you had experience in other cases of signatures imposed upon tracing?—Yes, quite frequently—one only last month.

Have you any doubt that by some one that was done here?— Not the faintest doubt; there can be no doubt whatsoever about it.

William Morrison Smith, examined by the Lord Advocate— I am an engraver at Forth Street, Edinburgh, and I have given considerable attention to disputed handwriting for over thirty years. I was requested by the Crown authorities in the present case to make an examination of four groups of cheques. Assuming that the third and fourth groups are the genuine signatures of Bertha Merrett, I am of opinion that the first and second groups were not written by the same person. There is a slower movement in pen-writing, if one might call it so, while in the others I find fluent and spontaneous writing. One of the first points that attracted my attention with regard to the latter group was the presence of a foreign marking or colour which had no part of the

John Donald Merrett.

writing fluid on it, and on careful examination with a magnifying glass I found that that was more or less visible throughout the whole series of the two latter groups. Q. How has that been arrived at, or made, in your opinion?—A. We can only assume a method; without seeing the operation we cannot give any direct evidence, but there are various methods by which it can be effected. A very common and very crude method of transferring a drawing from one source to another is by placing it up against a window, but, of course, in this case to me it is something better than that. In fact, I am convinced that a tracing has been laid in position upon the cheque to be written upon, interposed between the tracing and the cheque was a film of some nature containing a colouring matter, in all probability an ordinary carbon tissue used in typewriting, of a bluish tint. Thereafter it was traced over by some rounded point, leaving a blue outline marking which has been overwritten by ink fluid. I found that definitely in each of the 29 cheques. In two cases—I think it was the first and the last—I had to use a microscope to be satisfied that it existed throughout the signature, and I found that it did so, but, as regards the others, it is quite apparent to the naked eye.

Cross-examined by Mr. MACGREGOR MITCHELL—I measured the signatures by tracing. I put the compass on a few of them, but not them all. I did not measure the size of the letters, or the spaces between the letters, or the spaces between the " Bertha " and the " Merrett."

You cannot say by measurement whether there was any remarkable coincidence?—Well, I took the tracing to be a measurement in effect, and as accurate as any hand placing of a compass could be, or the applying of any foot rule.

You are relying upon the photographic transparency?—Most assuredly.

If you take photographic reproductions of two signatures, say of one that is in dispute and of another which is genuine, and superimpose them, what I understand your point to be is that there is a marked similarity, so marked that it points to it not being genuine?—Along with the fact of a blue outline.

Take the superimposition, do you say that that is an exact fit, to put it in popular language?—Not an absolute fit.

Are there any variations in the formation of the letters?—To an extent.

Are there any variations in the way in which the letters are joined?—To an extent.

Are there any variations in the slope of the letters?—Certainly.

Assuming that you find all these variations in the two signatures, what more would you expect to find if they were genuine signatures?—I would not expect the total length of the signatures to remain the same, or anything approximating the same.

Tell me the variations that you would expect to find in genuine

192

Model A.

Model B.

Model C.

Tracings of the three model signatures of Mrs. Merrett used in the production of the forged cheques.

Evidence for Prosecution.

signatures?—I would expect to find the total length varying, and the spaces between the letters and the forms of the letters.

If you find variations in spacing, variations in letters, and difference in length, does that point to the genuineness of the signature?—But you have to take it in conjunction with it being traced over or written over a tracing.

You always come back to the tracing?—Yes.

Which is easier, copying over tracing or copying through the light?—I would certainly say that to produce the most perfect result would be by tracing, transferring the tracing to the paper and overwriting it. That is the practical method adopted by all draftsmen.

Supposing one can point to over two dozen differences between the forged and the original signature on this method, would that have some effect on your opinion and influence you to think it was a genuine one?—I do not know that that would influence me for two reasons—first, the fact of the tracing which no genuine signature ever is done by, and, secondly, the fact that the pen has been lifted repeatedly in forming the signature. That is not the fluent writing of what I would term a genuine signature.

Involved in this charge are 12 Clydesdale cheques and 17 Midland cheques. In how many do you say the tracing went right through?—You wish to know in how many of them do I see complete tracing? Only in about two is the tracing absolutely complete.

In the rest you pick out what you think is tracing?—From its relative position it is self-evident that it is tracing.

May I put it to you that in evidence such as you are giving there is necessity for great caution?—Most assuredly.

Have you known cases where serious injustice has been done on experts' opinions on handwriting?—I have heard of such things, but I am not familiar with them.

Is there not a famous one? Do you know the famous and classic instance of it?—No, I do not.

Re-examined by the LORD ADVOCATE—The case that one best knows about is the case of Adolf Beck, and that was a case of comparison with the normal handwriting of the accused, quite a different thing from the present case, which is mechanical copying? —Yes.

WILLIAM BETHUNE FERGUSON, securities clerk with the Clydesdale Bank, Ltd., George Street, Edinburgh, was examined with reference to the late Mrs. Merrett's account with that bank. He stated that her account was overdrawn on two occasions, on 13th March and 16th March. The bank manager wrote two letters to Mrs. Merrett calling attention to the overdraft, and on each of these occasions the overdraft was put right by a credit.

HENRY JAMES MERCER KERR, teller in the Clydesdale Bank, George Street, Edinburgh, spoke to knowing the late Mrs. Merrett

John Donald Merrett.

Henry J. M. Kerr

and her son, the accused, by their coming to the office of the bank. He said he was familiar with their signatures and handwriting. During January, February, and March, 1926, they were frequently at the bank, sometimes alone. and sometimes together, but latterly the accused usually came alone.

[The witness was shown a number of the cheques in question, payable to J. D. Merrett, and said they were cashed by him, believing that the signatures of the drawer were the genuine signatures of Mrs. Merrett.]

Cross-examined by Mr. AITCHISON—[Witness was asked to examine the signature of Mrs. Merrett on one of the cheques]— We are told by experts that that is a forgery. As a banker of experience, do you see anything about it at all to suggest forgery? —No.

[On being asked to examine the signature with the aid of a magnifying glass, witness gave the same answer to the question.]

Would you have any hesitation in passing that signature?— No hesitation.

Have you been able, after a careful examination of these questioned signatures, to pick out a single one that, as a banker, you are prepared to say is a forgery?—No.

Re-examined by the LORD ADVOCATE—If you were informed that on close examination the signature showed that it was really two signatures, one on the top of the other—a tracing and then copied over—would you be ready to cash the cheque without further inquiries?—I would make further inquiries.

By the LORD JUSTICE-CLERK—Have you had any experience of forged cheques?—No.

HUGH SUTHERLAND RICH, teller in the Clydesdale Bank, gave evidence as to the cheques dealt with by him, and said he had honoured them in the belief that they bore the genuine signature of Mrs. Merrett.

Adjourned.

Fifth Day—Saturday, 5th February, 1927.

CECIL GEORGE MINTO HARROWER, JOHN ANDERSON, and ROBERT SMITH HENDERSON, bank clerks, engaged in the offices of the Clydesdale Bank, George Street, Edinburgh, and ROBERT JAMES LEE HENDRY, manager of the George Street branch, gave evidence relating to the passing of cheques drawn on Mrs. Merrett's account. In one of the cheque books produced three counterfoils were missing. There was a credit arrangement between the Clydesdale Bank and the Midland Bank by which £30 could be transferred from the latter at any time. On two occasions, on the 13th and 16th March, letters were sent to Mrs. Merrett drawing her attention to the fact that her account was overdrawn. Mrs. Merrett never questioned the state of the bank account, nor raised any points about it. As the result of the letters of the 13th and 16th March, the account was on each occasion squared by the credit arrangement.

CHARLES ARTHUR RIDGE, accountant at the Boscombe branch of the Midland Bank, stated that Mrs. Merrett had an account with his branch during 1925 and part of 1926, until the account was closed by her trustees. The bank received a letter from Mrs. Merrett on the 4th of March giving instructions for her bank pass book to be made up and sent to her at Palmerston Place, Edinburgh. She stated that she had to pay out rather, for her, large cheques, and was anxious to know what amount stood to her credit at the bank. The pass book was duly forwarded to her at Palmerston Place. The book showed at that time a credit balance of £286 2s. 4d. A letter was received from Mrs. Merrett from 31 Buckingham Terrace dated 12th March, asking for a new cheque book of thirty cheques, payable to order, and not crossed. She explained that her old cheque book had been destroyed by accident during their removal from Palmerston Place. In the same letter she acknowledged receipt of her pass book, sent on from Palmerston Place. In response to her request for another cheque book, they sent one to Buckingham Terrace on the 15th of March, the book containing thirty cheques.

Cross-examined by Mr. AITCHISON, witness read the following extract from a letter, dated 26th February, 1926, from Mrs. Merrett, written when returning her bank book :—" Donald has taken to life at the 'Varsity. I have heard from Malvern the other day he had taken Honours in Higher Mathematics, the last examination he took before he left there ; but it is satisfactory, as he left a good record as regards his school work while he has been at college." In a letter dated 4th March, 1926, Mrs. Merrett

John Donald Merrett.

wrote to Mr. Rooker, the manager of the Boscombe Bank, " Donald has done well at the University, and has quite settled down to the life here."

ROBERT ANDERSON (47), examined by the LORD ADVOCATE—I am a house agent, carrying on business at 7 Drumsheugh Place, Edinburgh. I let the flat at 31 Buckingham Terrace to the late Mrs. Merrett, who got entry on the 10th of March. The agreement at first was not quite definite as to the amount to be paid per month, but it was ultimately fixed at £50 for the term, until the end of June. The rent was paid in two portions, the first payment being made on 2nd March. The payment was made by a cheque on the Midland Bank for £25. [Production No. 75]—On the 12th of March, two days after Mrs. Merrett got entry, she paid the balance of £25 to me. [Production No. 59]—That payment was made by a cheque on the Clydesdale Bank. The first transaction took place in my shop, but the second one took place in her house in Buckingham Terrace, and on both occasions Mrs. Merrett handed me the cheques herself.

Mrs. AGNES MARY ANDERSON, examined by the LORD ADVOCATE —I am the wife of and live with William Eddie Anderson at 64 Murray Place, Stirling. I knew the late Mrs. Bertha Merrett for some thirty years.

You had kept up your friendship with her, I suppose, mainly by correspondence?—Mainly. Mrs. Merrett was abroad for a considerable period of that time.

Have you kept any of the letters you received from her?—No, I destroyed all the letters, but one turned up later, after I saw the Procurator-Fiscal, a letter dated April, 1925.

About the beginning of March, 1926, did you meet Mrs. Merrett in Edinburgh by appointment and have tea together?— Yes.

And a general conversation?—Yes. She told me she had got a flat in Buckingham Terrace, and hoped to get into it shortly. It was just before she got into Buckingham Terrace.

While having tea with Mrs. Merrett, did the accused John Donald Merrett come in?—Yes.

Apparently on his way to his University classes?—Yes.

Was that the only occasion on which you had seen the accused since he was some nine years of age?—Yes. I saw him again the day after his mother's death.

Was Mrs. Merrett apparently in good spirits?—Very.

Can you give us, approximately, the date when you last got a letter from her?—About a week before the occurrence. It was soon after I had tea with her in Edinburgh.

Was she at Buckingham Terrace when she wrote you that letter?—I cannot be quite sure.

Evidence for Prosecution.

The day following Mrs. Merrett's death I think the accused came to visit you?—Yes.

Mrs. JOAN SHARP (39), residing at 33 and 35 Palmerston Place, Edinburgh, said that the late Mrs. Merrett and her son came to reside in her boarding-house. She paid weekly for her board, and all the payments, so far as she could remember, were paid by cheque. Mrs. Merrett was very cheerful and bright, and was a person of very methodical habits.

Cross-examined by Mr. AITCHISON, witness said that Mrs. Merrett was not excitable at any time in her presence.

I am not suggesting mental peculiarities, but was not she at times a little bit excitable?—No, never.

EMSLIE MARK LEE (41), examined by the LORD ADVOCATE—I am a trust officer with the Public Trustee, Kingsway, London. It has fallen to the Public Trustee to administer the estate of Mrs. Merrett. The income of her estate at the time of her death would be about £100 a year. That is Mrs. Merrett's own estate. In addition to that, she had an interest in her father's will to the extent of about £600 a year, making a total of about £700 a year. The interest in the whole of the mother's estate came to the accused. The interest under his grandfather's estate did not pass to him to the same extent, but to a smaller amount.

Cross-examined by Mr. AITCHISON—Under Mrs. Merrett's will the Public Trustee is guardian of her son, John Donald Merrett, and he has been present throughout these proceedings until yesterday, when he had to return to London.

JAMES DUNDAS PATON (36), examined by the LORD ADVOCATE—I am a salesman with the Rossleigh Motor Company, Shandwick Place, Edinburgh. The accused on the 22nd of March, 1926, gave an order for an " H.R.D." motor racing cycle and side car, at the same time asking what he would be allowed on an " A.J.S." motor cycle which he had. The " H.R.D." was to cost £133 8s., and, with accessories, £139. The accused was to be allowed £30 for the " A.J.S." cycle. The accused told me he wanted a cycle for general use, and, occasionally, racing. Thereafter the company received sums paid on account of the price of the cycle as follows:—23rd March, £20; 24th March, £15; 26th March, £20; and 27th March, £15—a total of £70. The payments were all made in cash. In the middle of April we got a wire from the accused in London asking us to send the cycle at once to London. We did not do so. Three days later we got another wire from him asking if the cycle had not been sent, and we replied that we must have payment before we could send it. Later, the Public Trustee intervened and gave authority for the sale of the cycle.

197

John Donald Merrett.

William Davidson

WILLIAM DAVIDSON (35), constable attached to the firearms
department of the Edinburgh City Police, said that on 12th
February, 1926, while on duty at the West End Police Station, he
received a form of application from the accused, and went that day
to 35 Palmerston Place. The accused stated that he intended
going to France during the University holidays with friends, and
that he wanted the pistol to use in the woods there for shooting
small game and birds, and at trees. Witness forwarded the application, along with his report of the interview, to the Central
Police Station.

GEORGE ARMSTRONG SCOTT (19), examined by the LORD
ADVOCATE—The Dunedin Palais de Danse opened in 1922, and
from that time until near the end of March, 1926, I was clerk and
dance instructor there. Since the latter date I have been working
as a motor driver. I first came to know the accused about the
beginning of January, 1926, at the Dunedin Palais. He was there
twice or three times a week, I should say. I had a motor bicycle
about that time. I remember going a run with the accused on the
16th of March; we each had our own motor cycles. The accused
had a slight accident while riding my motor bicycle, and sustained
some cuts which required dressing. I knew the accused had an
automatic pistol, but I never saw it. He told me himself that he
had it. I remember on Wednesday, 17th March, the accused
coming to me and telling me he had been at the Infirmary with
his mother, that she had either met with an accident or had shot
herself. He told me he was in the room sitting by the fire when
he heard the shot and saw his mother falling, and he 'phoned for
the police, and she was taken to the Infirmary.

Did he mention the pistol at all?—He said she was shot with
the pistol.

Did he mention the maid?—Yes. He said he had gone
through and told the maid about it.

Did he say where he had gone through to?—To the kitchen. I
went with the accused to the Infirmary on several occasions. Later
that day, the 17th, in reply to a telephone message, I went along
to the flat at Buckingham Terrace. From there I went to the
Infirmary, and at the Infirmary it was arranged that I should go
and book a room for the accused at the County Hotel.

Was the accused at the Dunedin that evening?—I am not sure,
but I think so.

Did you know that your name had been given as a reference
to be rung up by the Infirmary, if necessary?—Yes, I did.

Was it the accused who told you that?—No, he was not at the
Dunedin on the Wednesday.

Was he there the following evening?—I think it was the following evening. He was there one evening when he told them to
ring up to the Dunedin, but I am not sure which it was.

198

Evidence for Prosecution.

Do you remember later in the week than the 17th of March the accused coming back to the subject of how his mother's injury had been caused—the question as to whether she could have shot herself or not?—I do not remember.

Or subsequently?—We talked about it. He said it was an accident, or a possible suicide.

That is what I want to know. What did he say on that occasion?—That was all, that it was probably an accident or suicide, but he could not say which.

JAMES PEARSON CAIRNS (38), examined by the LORD ADVOCATE —I am manager with John Adam Porter, motor agent, Greenside Place, Edinburgh. In the beginning of March, 1926, the accused came to the shop wanting a second-hand motor cycle. At that time I had a customer who wanted to get rid of an "A.J.S." motor cycle, and I effected a sale of the cycle to the accused. I cannot recollect the price, as it was a matter of arrangement between the customer and the accused, but it was approximately £28. The transaction was fixed up on 6th March, and as he could not cash the cheque that day I agreed to take it as a deposit. He came back on the Monday morning, 8th March, took the cheque away, and came back with the cash. The cheque was made payable to Mr. Merrett, and he said as it was made out to him he could only cash it himself.

JOHN LAWSON (18), examined by the LORD ADVOCATE—I am now a private in the Cameron Highlanders at the Inverness depot. Before I joined the Army I took my father's place as motor car attendant at the Dunedin Palais de Danse while my father was off for three months in hospital. I remember about six weeks after I went there finding the bank book (production No. 14) lying on the second top step inside the boiler-room door, which opens off the stair leading to the cloakroom, one stair down from the street level. The door of the boiler-room was not locked. It was usually left open for the staff to go through, as there is a garage at the back. I could not say how long it had been there; it would not lie long there without somebody seeing it. I handed the book to Thomas Ritchie.

EVELYN PEARCE (29), examined by the LORD ADVOCATE—For some time past I have been employed in the office of the Dunedin Palais de Danse, Picardy Place, Edinburgh, as cash-keeper. I remember the accused coming to the Palais on occasions. I just heard through the papers of the death of Mrs. Merrett. I had handed to me the Clydesdale bank book, which is production No. 14, but I have no idea when it was handed to me. I do not even know the month. I cannot remember whether it was after the death of Mrs. Merrett. I took charge of it, thinking that Mr.

199

John Donald Merrett.

Evelyn Pearce

Merrett would be in the Dunedin some time and I would give it to him, but the opportunity did not occur. Towards the end of the year I learned of the arrest of the accused, and it recalled the book to my mind. I spoke to the manager about it, and handed it over to Mr. Fairley, with the result that the book was given to the police.

DONALD ROSE, examined by the LORD ADVOCATE—I am an inspector in the Edinburgh City Police. Early on the morning of the 3rd December, 1926, while I was acting as lieutenant in the charge office at the Central Police Station, Edinburgh, the accused was brought in under arrest. I read over the charge in the warrant to the accused, and duly cautioned him. I asked him if he had anything to say to the charge, and he replied, " No." He paused a moment and then said, " I have nothing to say."

JOHN MICHAEL GEOGHEGAN, examined by the LORD ADVOCATE— I am a member of the Society of Accountants in Edinburgh, a member of the General Examining Board of the Chartered Accountants in Scotland, and I practise in Edinburgh as an accountant. I was asked by the Crown to examine certain productions in the present case with the view to a report. My report is dated 28th December, 1926, and is production No. 7.[7] Mrs. Merrett kept accounts with the Midland Bank at its Boscombe branch and at the Clydesdale Bank at its George Street branch in Edinburgh. The Midland Bank account was her principal bank account, and from this account the Clydesdale Bank took in credit from time to time. [Shown production 148, being an account book kept by Mrs. Merrett for her personal expenditure] —That is a very carefully kept book. It shows the operations on each bank account, sums put in and sums withdrawn, with a statement of the balance remaining to her credit from time to time.

Do the transactions, as recorded by Mrs. Merrett in that account book, agree with the transactions shown in the copy of the Midland Bank account?—They do not, in this respect, that in the bank pass book there appear cheques drawn from the bank, and in the case of the Clydesdale Bank sums paid into the bank, which do not appear in the record which Mrs. Merrett kept of her bank transactions. On the 4th of March there was entered in Mrs. Merrett's personal book as paid into the Clydesdale Bank the sum of £25. On the same date in the bank pass book the amount of £20 was entered as paid in, the pay-in slip being signed by the accused.

Are there certain cheques which appear in the bank account which do not appear in Mrs. Merrett's own account book, and are all those cheques in favour of the accused, J. D. Merrett?—Yes.

---

[7] See Appendix V.

Evidence for Prosecution.

John Michael Geoghegan

The total amount of the cheques drawn on the Midland Bank account, and not recorded by Mrs. Merrett in her book, is £370 9s., and adding 5s. for the cheque book it came to £370 14s. If that amount is taken from the amount which Mrs. Merrett shows in her book as her credit at the Midland Bank, you are left with £4 3s. 4d., which is the balance brought out in the copy bank account lodged among the productions. That means that, while Mrs. Merrett, according to her account book, thought she had over £370 in the Midland Bank, there was not £5 in it. The sums paid in to the Clydesdale Bank which are not recorded in Mrs. Merrett's book were all paid in on the same dates as the cheques not recorded in Mrs. Merrett's book, but drawn from the Midland Bank. The cheques drawn from the Midland Bank on these dates are in each case larger sums than paid into the Clydesdale Bank. In the case of the last five cheques there was no payment into the Clydesdale Bank at all to the credit of the account of the Clydesdale Bank. The last payment to the Clydesdale Bank was on 18th March, being the Midland Bank cheque for £30, of which £17 was paid in. Mrs. Merrett recorded in her book her own personal expenditure under various headings, and the record is very accurate. From January to March, 1926, under the various headings, the record of Mrs. Merrett's personal expenditure as entered in her personal account book was £200 9s. 9d., the details being set forth in my report.

Has Mrs. Merrett left no record in her account book of the application of the cheques drawn from the bank in favour of the accused?—None whatever.

Or any record which shows that such cheques were actually drawn by her?—None whatever. The cheques drawn on the Midland Bank in favour of the accused amount to £370 9s., and on the Clydesdale Bank £87 4s. 6d., making a total of £457 13s. 6d. The cheques which are not recorded in Mrs. Merrett's book are the 29 cheques in respect of which the charges are made in the present case, and these 29 cheques are, every one of them, in favour of " J. D. Merrett " as drawee. There is no other cheque produced in this case on which the name of J. D. Merrett appears as drawee against Mrs. Merrett's account from January to March. The whole of the 29 cheques in dispute are endorsed by the accused. [Shown Clydesdale Bank pass book]—That pass book shows that the account was overdrawn to the extent of £21 6s. on 13th March, when, according to Mrs. Merrett's account book on that date it showed £10 9s. to her credit. Similarly, on 17th March, according to the bank account and the letter sent by the bank, there was an overdraft on her Clydesdale Bank account of £6 11s. 3d., whereas again, according to her own account, she had £10 9s. to her credit with the bank. If Mrs. Merrett had seen her Midland Bank pass book written up to the 5th of March by the bank it would have shown her that she had a balance at her credit of

John Donald Merrett.

John Michael Geoghegan

£286 2s. 4d., whereas if she had looked at her own account book, and the balances she kept there, she would have found at that date £374 17s. 4d., showing a difference of £88 15s., made up by the cheques in dispute drawn on the Midland Bank up to 5th March in favour of J. D. Merrett, which are not recorded in his mother's account book up to that date.

Looking at the operations on the Clydesdale account by means of those 29 cheques, and the amounts paid in from the Midland Bank cheques, and the credit of the account in the Clydesdale Bank from those cheques, was the result, generally speaking, to keep the Clydesdale Bank in credit?—It was. Generally speaking, it was to keep the balance in the Clydesdale Bank in agreement with what she was showing in her account book.

Evidence for the prosecution closed.

Adjourned.

Sixth Day—Monday, 7th February, 1927.

Evidence for the Defence.

CHARLES A. MACPHERSON (53), examined by Mr. AITCHISON—I am a member of the bar, and I am Public Prosecutor for the City of Edinburgh. On 18th March, 1926, I received information concerning a shooting occurrence that had taken place at 31 Buckingham Terrace on the 17th.

Following upon that, is it within your knowledge that a charge sheet was made out against Mrs. Bertha Merrett, now deceased?—No, a charge sheet was not made out.

What exactly happened?—What happens in these cases is that the police information which is prepared lies in the charge office against the recovery of the person who is in the Infirmary, for the purpose of notifying the surgeon of police, Professor Littlejohn. It was brought to my office on the 18th, and I have no doubt, although I have not a clear recollection, that I passed it on to him either personally or through an officer of the Court. Thereafter the paper was returned to the charge office, and I did not see it again until 2nd April.

Is it within your knowledge that Mrs. Merrett was put under arrest?—The police technically arrested her.

The LORD ADVOCATE—Detention.

Examination continued—Was it arrest or detention?—Detention.

What is your proper term for it? Don't you call it arrest?—Yes.

Was intimation made, to your knowledge, by the authorities to the Royal Infirmary?—I understand so.

And, in terms of that intimation, were the authorities at the Royal Infirmary bound to intimate to the criminal authorities before they discharged Mrs. Merrett from the Infirmary?—That is so.

With the view, if thought advisable, of her being taken into custody?—Yes.

Cross-examined by the LORD ADVOCATE—Would it be correct to say that it was detention by the police pending inquiry?—Yes.

Colonel G. ST. C. THOM (56), examined by Mr. AITCHISON—I am superintendent of the Royal Infirmary, Edinburgh. On the 17th of March I received a communication from the criminal authorities with reference to Mrs. Merrett. The document is in these terms—" Police Station, West End, Edinburgh, 17th March, 1926. I have the honour to inform you that Bertha Milner or

John Donald Merrett.

Colonel G. St. C. Thom

Merrett, now detained in No. 3 ward, Royal Infirmary, is a prisoner charged with attempted suicide, and I am directed by the Chief Constable to ask you to be good enough to inform the lieutenant on duty at the High Street, Edinburgh, the date and hour on which it is proposed to discharge the accused, in order that arrangements may be made for taking her into custody.—Your obedient servant, Hugh Ross, Sergeant.''

Dr. LEWIS GEORGE ROSA (28), examined by Mr. AITCHISON—I am a medical practitioner residing at 28 Pitt Street, Edinburgh. I practise there in partnership with my father. On the evening of 17th March, 1926, I received a call from Mrs. Rita Sutherland, 107 Broughton Road, who is on my father's list of panel patients. She was complaining of feeling unwell. I prescribed for her. In the course of my interview with her she made certain statements regarding an occurrence that had happened that morning. In the month of December of last year I read that the accused, John Donald Merrett, had been arrested on a charge of murder, and, in view of statements which had been made to me on 17th March by Mrs. Sutherland, I was in doubt as to what my duty in the matter was—whether I should disclose what she said, having regard to the duty of confidentiality which is imposed upon a doctor. Accordingly, I consulted my law agents, Messrs. Buchan & Buchan, as to the course I ought to pursue. It is within my knowledge that they took the advice of counsel on the matter. I was advised that I was bound to disclose the information in my possession, and I have done so to the agents for the defence, and also to the Crown.

Coming back to the evening of 17th March, 1926, what did Mrs. Sutherland say to you regarding the events of that morning? —She said that she was employed by a lady in Buckingham Terrace, and that that morning she had been in a room in the house where her mistress was sitting at a table writing, and that the son of her mistress was at the other side of the room reading. She said that whilst she was in the room she observed her mistress remove her false teeth, and that struck her as a strange thing. Later she proceeded to leave the room and turned her back (she emphasised that) on her mistress, and as she was leaving the room her mistress shot herself.

Did she say anything further as to what she saw?—That is all I can swear to as regards definite statements she made.

I appreciate that at this distance of time you cannot be positive as to the exact words used, but can you say whether she conveyed any impression to your mind as to having seen anything after the shot rang out?—I took it that she saw Mrs. Merrett falling.

After the shot?—Yes.

Although you cannot remember the exact words which she used, did she leave that very definite impression upon your mind?—Yes.

Evidence for Defence.

Dr Lewis George Rosa

And was it in consequence of that that you thought it right to communicate with your law agents when you heard of the arrest of the accused on a charge of murder?—Yes.

Cross-examined by the LORD ADVOCATE—You stated that you communicated this information to the Crown authorities. To whom and where—as my information is that the Crown authorities were never communicated with?—I was asked two questions at once. I was asked if I communicated with counsel for the defence and the Crown authorities.

Then did you not communicate with the Crown authorities?—I was not precognosced.

And you did not communicate?—No.

But you did communicate it to the agents for the defence?—Yes. That was what I was advised to do.

Was it not very important that the Crown authorities, at the very early stages particularly, should have all the information available?—I followed the advice that I had received to do the right thing.

Mrs. Sutherland was consulting you as a patient, I understand?—Yes.

Was she not very well that night?—That concerns the subject of the consultation. My obligation as to secrecy prevents me from making statements as to that.

I do not want to know the cause of the illness, but surely, if you say that she made so important a communication, you are bound to tell us as to the condition she was in when she made the statement?—She looked tired, and as if the events of the morning had worried her somewhat. She was not nervous, not unduly so.

Did she mention the accused at all?—Yes.

Did she say where he was?—She said he was at the other side of the room reading.

At the time the shot went off?—While she was in the room.

Did you gather from the statement, or did you understand, that she was still actually in the room when the shot went off?—That she was leaving the room at the time.

And still in it, at the door, do you mean?—Yes.

Can you give us her exact words?—No, I cannot.

You are merely reproducing what you recollect as the sense of what she said at the time?—Yes, the particular facts that she went over.

Did Mrs. Sutherland explain why it was strange that a person should take her false teeth out?—No.

Did it strike you as strange?—In connection with the whole story, it did.

But it is not a strange thing for people to take their false teeth out, is it?—It depends upon the person and the teeth.

That is quite a fair answer—and the circumstances?—Yes.

Re-examined by Mr. AITCHISON—Of course, there is nothing strange in taking your false teeth out, if you have got them, but

John Donald Merrett.

Dr Lewis George Rosa

did Mrs. Sutherland comment on Mrs. Merrett having done so as being something strange?—Yes. She said she thought it was strange.

Did you gather from her that it struck her at the time as peculiar?—Yes.

By the LORD JUSTICE-CLERK—Did you make any note of this conversation at the time?—No.

Did you give a thought to the matter between March and December?—Possibly I did.

You do not remember?—No.

Are you quite clear about the statement which you attribute to Mrs. Sutherland regarding Mrs. Merrett's teeth?—Quite clear.

Let me read to you what Mrs. Sutherland said on this matter. Mrs. Sutherland was asked this, " I put it to you that you said to Dr. Rosa that you noticed your mistress taking out her false teeth a few seconds before the shot occurred, and that that struck you at the time as strange." Her answer was, " That is a downright lie, for I never said that." The next question was, " Is it your evidence that if Dr. Rosa tells us that you mentioned some incident about Mrs. Merrett's false teeth, and you being struck with it as being strange, that that is a falsehood on Dr. Rosa's part?" and the answer was, " Yes." Now, being referred to these definite statements made by Mrs. Sutherland, do you still adhere to the evidence that you have given to-day?—Certainly. I can recall that fact as clearly as if it had been told me a fortnight ago.

WILLIAM HENDERSON (47), examined by Mr. MACGREGOR MITCHELL—I am a detective-sergeant in the Edinburgh City Police. On the morning of 17th March I accompanied Inspector Fleming to 31 Buckingham Terrace. Mrs. Sutherland was alone in the house at the time we called. It would be about 10 a.m. when we called. We had a conversation with Mrs. Sutherland in the hall near to the door leading to the room where the occurrence took place.

Will you tell us in your own words your recollection of what Mrs. Sutherland said?—Inspector Fleming asked her what had happened. She stated that she on that morning had been in the kitchen, heard a report of a revolver, or something like that, and looked out and saw Mrs. Merrett falling from the chair to the floor, and a revolver falling from her hand.

Did she say anything about the door of the room being open? —It was.

Do you recollect her saying anything about being in the room before the occurrence?—Some little time before that she had been in the room doing something, tidying up.

Did she say what the position of the occupants of the room was at that time?—She stated that Mrs. Merrett was sitting at a table writing letters, or a letter, and the accused, " Donald," as

Evidence for Defence.

she termed him, was sitting beside the fireplace in a chair, reading a book.

Was the impression which the statement made upon you at the time that she had been practically an eye-witness of what had occurred?—That is so.

In consequence of the statement which she made was Mrs. Merrett taken to the Infirmary on a charge of attempted suicide? —I did not know about that at the time.

Had you any conversation at all with the accused, Donald Merrett?—No.

Cross-examined by the LORD ADVOCATE—Did you hear Detective Fleming having a conversation with the accused?—No.

By the LORD JUSTICE-CLERK—Was the statement which you attribute to Mrs. Sutherland volunteered by her, or was it elicited by way of questions?—Volunteered by her.

What sort of condition was she in at the time? Was she agitated?—A little bit.

Had you any reason to doubt the accuracy of her statement at the time?—No.

Tell me this, were the other constables who had visited the flat that morning gone before you arrived?—Yes.

ELIZABETH HARDIE, examined by Mr. AITCHISON—I live at 7 Mayfield Road, Edinburgh. In January last the now deceased, Mrs. Merrett, and the accused, John Donald Merrett, came to live at my house. They arrived on the 4th of January, 1926, and remained with me for a period of three weeks. I saw a great deal of them during the time they were living in my house.

Did they get on well together?—Quite well.

Did you ever see any difference or disagreement between them?—None whatever.

How would you describe the attitude of the accused towards his mother?—Quite as a son ought to behave towards his mother.

Was he attached to her?—Quite.

Did he seem devoted to her?—Yes, he went about with her always.

Did he sometimes take her to dances?—Yes, once or twice.

Was there anything at all to suggest any difference or disagreement between them?—Nothing.

On the contrary, would you say that they were on intimate and affectionate terms?—I would say that.

I think they left on the 25th of January?—They were with me exactly three weeks.

After they left you on 25th January, did you see them again? —No.

During the time they lived with you what would you say about Mrs. Merrett—about her temperament? How did she strike you?—She struck me as a very loving mother.

John Donald Merrett.

Elizabeth Hardie

I don't want to put any words into your mouth. Did she strike you in any particular way as regards temperament?—No, not at all. She was devoted to the boy in every way. That was what struck me.

And he was devoted to her?—Quite.

Did she speak to herself a lot?—Occasionally you would hear her, but most people speak.

I mean it did not strike you as being out of the ordinary?—Not at all.

Was she a nervous woman?—No, I would not say that.

Excitable?—No.

Impulsive?—Yes, as far as her boy was concerned. She did things perhaps on the spur of the moment so far as he was concerned.

Did she strike you as an impulsive woman?—Not exactly.

THOMAS BOWHILL GIBSON, examined by Mr. CLYDE—I am an architect, and I carry on business at 3 Rutland Square, Edinburgh. I received instructions to prepare certain plans for the defence, in consequence of which I went to 31 Buckingham Terrace and measured the house and the rooms. I also measured certain articles of furniture. I saw Mrs. Sutherland, and she gave me a description of where the furniture was placed in the rooms on the 17th of March. Defence production No. 4 is a plan prepared by me, showing a pictorial representation of the room in which the occurrence took place. [See illustration.] Defence production No. 5 is a plan showing the measurements which I took of the furniture, and defence production No. 6 is another representation of the room as seen from above, and shows the position of the furniture as indicated to me by Mrs. Sutherland. Defence production No. 7 is a ground plan of the flat at Buckingham Terrace. All these plans are accurate representations based on the information which I received.

Cross-examined by the LORD ADVOCATE—And executed according to scale?—Well, the half-inch plan is according to scale, the perspective is a picture, and it is drawn according to proportion and in scale.

You saw the actual furniture?—Yes.

Professor GEORGE M. ROBERTSON, examined by Mr. AITCHISON—I am a Doctor of Medicine of the University of Edinburgh, President of the Royal College of Physicians, Professor of Mental Diseases in the University of Edinburgh, and physician consultant to the Royal Infirmary. I am also physician superintendent of the Royal Asylum at Morningside, Maudsley lecturer to the Royal Medico-Psychological Association, and president of the Section for Mental Diseases of the British Medical Association. I was in charge of the Craiglea Home for Officers suffering from shell shock

208

Enlargement of forged signature (model B) showing broad ink strokes underneath which are thin dark strokes constituting an outline of this signature. (Arrows show points at which outline is not covered by ink.)

Enlargement of forged signature (model A) showing dark outline beneath ink of signature in some places and protruding from ink strokes in others.

Evidence for Defence.

Professor G. M. Robertson

during the war. I have read the newspaper reports of this case, and have been kept informed of the medical facts. The temperature chart shows that during the first three or four days that Mrs. Merrett was in hospital her temperature was subnormal; and this indicates that she was suffering from a degree of physical shock to the whole body. Then I see that on the fifth day after admission the temperature rose, apparently rather suddenly, to over 101 degrees; she became very feverish, and this lasted over a couple of days. This indicates that there was some infection of the wound. Then the temperature subsided a little, but never came absolutely down to the normal again. Practically on every day there was a state of feverishness, which is best shown on the special chart in which the temperature was recorded every four hours. This temperature gradually became higher again, although there were variations, and ultimately she died with a temperature of 103. This shows that an infective process, due to the entrance of some organism into her cranial cavity, was going on, and producing a state of inflammation, which ultimately caused the death of the patient.

As regards shock, you base your conclusion upon, first, the nature of the injury she received, and, secondly, the subnormal temperature, as shown by the chart?—Yes. The nature of the injury she received was of such a serious character that this of itself would suggest that she would suffer from bodily shock. But, in addition to that, the fact that her temperature was subnormal and her pulse on the whole rather slow is definite proof that she was suffering from physical, apart from mental, shock.

Assuming it to be in evidence that there was some discharge of a watery fluid from the ear, what does that indicate to your mind?—That there must have been a perforation of the coverings of the brain, and the liberation of the cerebral spinal fluid which surrounds the brain.

Assuming again, as established in evidence, that she suffered during the whole period in the Infirmary from a hemiplegia affecting her left side, what does that point to?—It means that she was paralysed on one side of her body, and, of course, no one can be paralysed on the one side of the body without having sustained very serious damage to the brain or the nervous system. Taking the history of the illness as I found it from the temperature chart, it is plain that during her whole period in the Infirmary Mrs. Merrett was in a very grave condition. In the early stage she was suffering from the effects of the shock, and after that had passed off she was suffering from the effects of an inflammation surrounding the brain. I examined the temperature chart with the view to ascertaining what doses of morphia she was receiving. The doses of morphia which she received are very properly recorded on the temperature chart, and I find that on the first day she received an injection of one-sixth of a grain of morphia, and on the second

P

John Donald Merrett.

Professor G. M. Robertson

day she received two injections of a quarter of a grain, which I consider a very full dose of morphia in a case with mental symptoms. No doubt it was required under the circumstances.

But are you satisfied from your examination of that chart that she was being dosed with morphia up to the maximum amounts? —I may say, excepting the cases of those persons who have been under my treatment for recovery from the morphia habit, who were accustomed to large doses, I have not ordered in mental cases more than a quarter grain for the last twenty years in one dose. On the second day when she received the quarter of a grain of morphia, no doubt it was on account of the pain she was suffering.

Does the size of the dose indicate to you that she must have been suffering acutely?—She must have been suffering severe pain, and in order to deaden the pain a full dose of morphia was given. These morphia doses were given off and on throughout the whole period of her illness. On the 25th there was no morphia given, but I think, with the exception of the 25th, she had some morphia every day, and after that the amount of morphia she received was very greatly increased.

Are injuries such as were sustained by Mrs. Merrett in this case calculated to produce very serious mental changes?—Undoubtedly.

And have the mental changes produced by injuries such as Mrs. Merrett sustained been carefully studied by specialists in recent years?—Unfortunately, owing to the war, we have had many opportunities of studying these conditions. The war afforded unrivalled opportunities for studying the effects of brain injuries upon the mentality of the patient.

What effect have injuries such as Mrs. Merrett sustained upon the mentality of the person who sustained them—or rather what effect are they calculated to produce upon a person who sustained them?—Well, it is obvious they must produce some disturbing effect. In this case we know that paralysis was produced, and we know that mental changes such as emotion are more easily effected than nervous disturbances. Mental disturbances are produced by an injury of this kind.

When injuries such as were sustained here are produced, do you sometimes get a condition known as " altered consciousness "? —Yes, that is so.

I think there are various terms expressive of that condition? —Yes.

Such as dissociation?—Dissociation is probably the more correct term from a scientific point of view.

By the LORD ADVOCATE—They are alternative expressions?— Yes.

Examination continued—And is dissociation a well-marked feature of mental change produced by severe physical head injuries?

210

Evidence for Defence.

Professor G. M. Robertson

—It is. When Mrs. Merrett regained consciousness in the Infirmary on the afternoon of 17th March, in my view there were present the conditions which usually accompany altered consciousness. The conditions were that she had sustained a very severe injury to her skull, which had produced a condition of unconsciousness which had lasted for some time, and she was labouring under physical shock, suffering also severe pain, and probably in a disturbed emotional condition.

Can you say from your experience that these conditions are usually the inducing causes of altered consciousness?—These are the commonest conditions which produce a state of altered consciousness. At a later stage in her illness when her temperature rose for four days, and there was a condition of septic meningitis, she developed a toxæmia, which is a poisoning of the brain and nervous system. That condition, either in its full development or during the process of development, conduces to a condition of altered consciousness. It probably conduces more to a condition of altered consciousness than any other single cause. I have had in my experience as a specialist in these matters a good many instances of altered consciousness following upon head injuries.

Before I come to illustrations, let me take this from you. May there exist in a patient who has sustained severe head injuries a condition of altered consciousness without it being apparent to the ordinary observer?—Yes, and also very often without it being apparent to the expert observer who did not previously know the patient.

Might the person in a condition of altered consciousness due to head injuries be apparently quite normal, apparently quite able to recollect comparatively recent things, apparently able to ask questions and to give instructions, and at the same time be in a condition of altered consciousness?—That is so.

And has your experience furnished you with some very striking illustrations of that?—Yes, it has. In particular I have a record of an instance where a person apparently normal had mistaken the person who had been the cause of the injury from which he suffered.

I wonder if you could just tell us, using popular language, what altered consciousness is?—Well, as the term suggests, in a state of altered consciousness, or altered personality, the person certainly has a state of consciousness and a personality, but it is not his own real personality, it is a different personality. There are slight changes which may be noticed by those who know the patient well; the patient may look at subjects from a different angle from that which he would do in his normal condition, and his prevailing mood may be slightly different. A confident person might be shy, or *vice versa;* or a courteous person might be inclined to be rude. There is a change in character and disposition, but any one not knowing the person previously might not be able to note that there was any difference.

John Donald Merrett.

Professor G. M. Robertson

Might there be all the appearance of normality co-existing with the presence of abnormality?—There might be the complete appearance of perfect normality, and the test, or the dramatic proof of the fact that there was a state of altered consciousness, would be this, that afterwards the patient would suddenly come to himself and would have absolutely no recollection of what had taken place in the interval.

Supposing—of course, this is hypothetical, but I want to take it in this way—supposing Mrs. Merrett had recovered from her injuries, having regard to the nature of the injuries which she sustained, and to the history of her illness, do you think it is probable that she would have been able to remember what had occurred during the time she was in the Infirmary?—I think that probably she would have remembered most of the things that took place in the Infirmary, but it is quite possible she might have been in such a state of altered consciousness that she would have no recollection at all of anything that happened in the Infirmary. I can give as an illustration the case of a patient who came under my care who had been somewhat depressed, and who had attempted to commit suicide. He had gone upstairs to go to bed, and while in his dressing-room he hanged himself with the cords of his dressing-gown. His wife went up some minutes afterwards and found him completely unconscious, cut him down, and saved his life. I was particularly anxious to find out from this patient— who I may say was a medical man—exactly what had passed through his mind and his state of consciousness as he was en- deavouring to hang himself. He told me he had absolutely no recollection whatsoever of ever having attempted to commit suicide. The whole thing was blotted completely out of his memory, and he could not tell me anything about it at all.

Is it consistent with your experience that a person who attempts to take his own life, or her own life, may have no recol- lection whatsoever of the act of attempt?—That is so. This was a case in point.

Is it further consistent with your experience that a person making such an attempt may have no recollection of the impulse which induced the attempt?—That is so.

Is it further consistent with your experience that a person failing to recollect the act, and failing also to recollect the impulse, may none the less recollect incidents almost bordering as regards time upon the act and upon the impulse?—Yes, he may. There is, however, almost invariably a failure of memory before uncon- sciousness takes place. The amount of it varies greatly in dif- ferent cases, and it is also curious that, as regards incidents that may have happened, some incidents may be recalled and others forgotten.

Assuming it to be the fact that Mrs. Merrett recollected accurately being seated writing a few minutes before the occurrence happened, is that quite consistent with a failure to recollect the

212

Evidence for Defence.

Professor G. M. Robertson

act of attempted suicide, or an impulse towards it, if that were present?—Yes.

Have you any hesitation in saying yes?—From my experience, such an incident might take place. I can give another illustration showing how a patient who has sustained a head injury may be very confused as to the person who inflicted the injury. This was a case that was reported to me by the doctor himself. There were two motor cyclists who came into collision, and one of these was rendered unconscious. The doctor was at once sent for. He lived about a mile away, and he arrived in his motor car while the patient was still unconscious. He ultimately regained consciousness and went home, and after he was at home he told his parents that the person who had caused the accident to him was the doctor. Matters became very strained between the doctor and this patient's parents, because it was assumed by them that he had caused this injury; and, had it not been for the cyclist who caused the collision coming forward and stating that it was he who was the real cause of the accident, it would have gone very badly with the doctor. This patient was not confused. He was perfectly clear that it was the doctor who caused the accident.

Is it your experience that people who have sustained head injuries are suggestible?—That is so. That is my own experience during the war.

Are they suggestible to a very marked degree?—Yes. There is undoubtedly a lowering of the intelligence, a lowering of the efficiency with which the brain performs its functions, and the result is that they are more easily persuaded.

So that, having regard to your experience in these matters, do you say that, although Mrs. Merrett may outwardly have given an appearance of normality, it would not be safe to exclude a state of altered consciousness?—No, that is so.

And, in particular, would it be unsafe to exclude a state of altered consciousness in a case which subsequently developed into acute delirium?—That is so. I have been " taken in " myself frequently. In my own experience I have met with people who have sustained serious injuries who have given all the signs of normality, and afterwards they have had no recollection of what they told me. My commonest experience has been in patients suffering from delirium, and coming out of delirium. I have sometimes come to the conclusion that they were perfectly normal, because they talked so rationally about themselves, and then suddenly one day, when they have really come to themselves, I have found that they had no recollection of what they had said to me during the previous few days or weeks, thus showing that they were not in a condition of ordinary or normal personality, but of altered consciousness.

Would that apply to a period prior to going into delirium and equally to a period subsequent to delirium?—Yes.

John Donald Merrett.

Professor G. M. Robertson

Do you regard it as a point of some importance in this case that, so far as we know, there was no examination made of Mrs. Merrett's mental condition during the period that she was in the Infirmary?—There was no proper examination made of her mental condition.

We do not blame any one, but doctors and Infirmary surgeons would naturally have their attention directed to the physical trouble?—There was a very serious physical injury, and their whole attention was very properly being directed to the physical condition. Accordingly, no examination would be made in order to test how far her condition, although apparently normal, was really normal. I think that, as regards these mental and subjective states, very little attention was paid to them. For instance, the fact that she was suffering from noises in the ear is not in the charts, which is very important from the mental point of view, but not from the physical point of view. With a serious head injury, such as Mrs. Merrett had, the aim of the treatment would be to keep the patient as quiet as possible.

I just want you finally to concentrate upon the features in Mrs. Merrett's illness. First the brain injury as evidenced by the hemiplegia. Having regard to that, do you think it would be safe to place reliance upon statements made by her, if made, with reference to the occurrences of the morning of the 17th March?—I think that any statements she made should be received with the very greatest hesitation.

Further, having regard to the condition of acute delirium which she developed, do you hold the same view as regards the weight to be attached to statements made by her?—I do.

Does the temperature chart show that she must have been developing an inflammatory brain condition for some days prior to the delirium becoming acute?—It must have been developing for some time before the conditions became so severe that delirium was obvious to any person.

I think it was suggested by one of the doctors for the Crown that the statements of Mrs. Merrett might be accepted as quite reliable up to the moment when the delirium became manifest. Do you agree with that view?—I most certainly do not agree with that view. A state of delirium does not develop suddenly. It is a gradual process, and, if careful observations are made, symptoms are discovered long before the actual delirium is obvious to every one. That is recognised particularly as regards the delirium of delirium tremens. One knows that there is a gradual process in the majority of cases.

In both cases you have an acute inflammatory condition of the brain?—In this case there was an acute inflammatory condition of the brain.

In your view, in a case of this gravity, can any reliance whatsoever be placed upon statements made by Mrs. Merrett during the period in which she was developing an inflammatory condition

Evidence for Defence.

Professor G. M. Robertson

of the brain resulting ultimately in acute delirium?—I would not go so far as to say that no reliance should be placed, but I would say that it would be hazardous to accept anything she then said as being strictly accurate.

Might it be accurate, in your view, and on the other hand, might it be entirely inaccurate?—That is so.

Cross-examined by the LORD ADVOCATE—By what means were you informed of the medical facts in this case?—Like every person else in Edinburgh, I have been reading the newspapers, and I have also met Sir Bernard Spilsbury.

Did you see the post-mortem report?—No, but I have seen the chart kept in the Infirmary.

But it would have been of advantage to you to see the post-mortem report?—I do not think it would have affected my opinion very much.

The morphia doses, I understand, were for pain from the wound in the ear. Is the effect of morphia, first, to stimulate, and then to dull the intellectual part?—Yes. There is a very slight amount of stimulation.

If anything, to stimulate first and then to dull?—The main symptom is the dulling.

It does not follow necessarily because a person has a hemiplegia affecting the left side, that they are mentally troubled—I think " intellectually affected " is the correct phrase?—No, it does not necessarily follow. Sir William Hamilton had hemiplegia for many years. It depends on the nature of the injury.

While you say that Mrs. Merrett's condition was consistent with altered consciousness, you do not profess to say whether it was in fact so, or not?—No.

For the reason that she did not live long enough to test it in the way you suggest?—Yes; neither was she properly examined, nor did she live long enough to be able to tell. Their attention would be mainly directed to saving the life of the patient.

They were on the look-out for the effect from the physical point of view, but would not the physical effect be intellectual?—They were directing their attention to the physical treatment of the patient.

Do you ever find this dissociated personality without the physical condition of the brain being affected first?—You may have this with comparatively slight disturbance of the physical condition of the brain, provided the person has been rendered unconscious.

We are all familiar with ordinary cases of concussion, where the person having received the concussion may go on apparently normal until the serious effects begin to develop, but this is not a case of that kind?—Well, one cannot tell, because the woman died before the ultimate effects could develop.

The type of case I am putting to you is of concussion where the person does not become unconscious, and goes on apparently

John Donald Merrett.

Professor G. M. Robertson

quite well, and then develops serious effects later on?—Yes, that has happened.   It is quite common, but this is not that kind of case.

Then there are cases, are there not, where there is loss of memory, or complete oblivion as to what happens between the time when the impact actually happens and the recovery?—Yes.

This is not a case of that kind?—Yes, this might be a case of that kind.

What we are most concerned with in this case is what happened before the pistol shot, and that is what I am trying to get your attention narrowed down to—that is what is most important here? —Well, what I have been referring to is this, that after a person becomes unconscious and then regains consciousness, people very often regard this condition of consciousness as a perfectly normal one, but it may not be normal.   A person may be in this abnormal condition for hours.

It is not necessarily normal?—Nor necessarily very abnormal. For example, as an illustration, a man has a collision in a football match, he becomes unconscious and lies on the ground for a minute or two, then gets up and plays on.   He plays out the game just as he does ordinarily.   He goes home to his dinner, goes out in the evening, and suddenly comes to himself and says, " Where am I; what has happened? "   During all that time people have regarded him as being normal, and he has never seemed abnormal, but still his mental state has been entirely dissociated from the rest of his personality.

What we are interested in here is what Mrs. Merrett said about what happened before the pistol shot went off.   Now, in your football illustration you were giving us what the man forgot for the six hours during which he went on apparently normal?—Well, but you are referring just now to what Mrs. Merrett said after she regained consciousness.   You are not referring to what happened before she became unconscious.   You are referring to a statement made by her after she had been unconscious in the Infirmary, and that is the period I am dealing with, when there might exist a variety of altered consciousness.

Let us come next to the dressing-gown case.   Why was he committing suicide, or trying it?—He was depressed, and most depressed people are suicidal.

You mean he was not in good health at the time?—He was not in perfect mental health at the time; he was suffering from depression.

But that is a very material factor, is it not, in comparing cases?—I do not think so, because a person suffering from mild depression may be perfectly clear and rational although depressed. It is an emotional condition.

Why was he depressed?—I cannot tell you exactly in this case why he was depressed.   I don't know why he was depressed.   He was suffering from a mild degree of melancholia.

216

Evidence for Defence.

Professor G. M. Robertson

I understand he remembered everything in connection with the attempt to hang himself?—He remembered everything up to a point, but he could not recall anything that took place after that, neither his suicidal impulse nor the preliminaries, nor the attempt itself. I was particularly anxious to know.

But there was in that case a reason for suicide, or an explanation for suicide?—I should say there was an explanation, for being depressed he would naturally be suicidal.

Come now to the motor bicycle case. Was it in the daytime or at night?—Well, I do not know.

Is it one of your own cases, or merely one you have read about?—The case occurred to a doctor living not many miles from Edinburgh, and he could tell you all the details. It was he who told me all about it.

As I understand, the collision occurred between two motor cyclists, and by the time the other motor cyclist had disappeared a doctor had come on the scene with a motor car. Is that right?—A doctor had come on the scene, but I don't know whether the other man had disappeared or not. He may have.

But that is very important?—Well, he may have.

Would you not infer that necessarily?—I would not necessarily infer that. I should fancy the other motor cyclist went for the doctor and brought the doctor to the scene.

Does not it look very much as if the injured man woke up, knowing he had suffered from a motor accident, and found a doctor there beside him with a motor car?—Yes.

And at once charged him with having done the damage?—He did not do it at once; he told his parents about it afterwards. But the important point is that the man had really no knowledge whatever of what took place. It is obvious he had no knowledge, because he did not remember the other motor bicycle, but he goes on to concoct a story which he believes to be true.

You would agree, I suppose, that if corroboration is found to a material extent of what Mrs. Merrett had said, it is of value as evidence?—That is so.

As I understand you—and, if I may say so, I agree with you—what you are doing is throwing out a note of warning that there should be careful consideration of the circumstances in which she made the statement, and the true circumstances as otherwise known, and then to test what she has said?—That is my position.

Re-examined by Mr. AITCHISON—You did not see the post-mortem report of Professor Littlejohn, but, on referring to that report, I find—" On removing the skull cap the brain membranes were found to be inflamed and infiltrated with purulent matter." Does that corroborate your view as to the danger of drawing conclusions in a case where statements are made by a person with an illness which after death shows signs of that kind?—That is a very serious cerebral condition, and the mental functions would probably be deranged in those conditions.

John Donald Merrett.

Professor G. M. Robertson

No doubt he says, " the brain was uninjured," but by that I suppose he means no more than this, that there was no laceration of the brain?—The brain must have been injured for a person to be half-paralysed, but apparently there was no obvious macroscopic, no large lesion, which they could put their finger on, but there must have been damage.

Can you get brain injuries of the utmost gravity apart from laceration of the brain altogether?—You can have injuries which cannot even be discovered by microscopic examination, and you may have disturbances, what we call commotion, without laceration.

As regards the point whether or not there was a watery discharge from the wound, did you obtain your information from the Infirmary report?—I did, the doctor's report. It was on the 24th—" Clear fluid discharge from right ear."

Is that a different thing from serum?—It is a different thing from serum. I should have fancied if it were serum the doctor would have used the words " serous discharge."

Does it happen by cerebral spinal fluid coming away from the ear?—That exactly describes it.

If there was cerebral spinal fluid coming from the ear, there may have been a puncture of the dura mater, which is the membrane covering the brain?—Yes.

If Mrs. Merrett was suffering from a puncture of the dura mater, with cerebral spinal fluid coming away from it, does not that confirm your view that the utmost care should be exercised before coming to conclusions upon any statement alleged to have been made?—It adds to the seriousness of the condition if the membranes of the brain had been punctured.

Of course, I suppose there are many cases of suicide in which you get a previous history of abnormality?—Yes.

And in which you get something that may be termed motive?—Yes.

But, on the other hand, do cases of suicide occur in which you cannot get a history of abnormality?—Where you do not get a history of abnormality, that is so.

Do you get cases of suicide where the first intimation of abnormality is the suicidal act?—Well, it would be difficult to say. Of course, the question has been discussed frequently whether a sane person may commit suicide or not; if so, there is usually a motive for committing suicide. But the point is, from my experience—and I have investigated many cases of distress in patients—that the most serious motives are usually unknown, they are not talked about, they are kept private.

So you would agree with the view that you might have a person with a suicidal tendency which ultimately passed into an impulse without there being any disclosure made by that person to any other person of the existence of the tendency or impulse?—I think so. I think that many of the most disturbing worries are kept secret and private.

Evidence for Defence.

Professor G. M. Robertson

Am I right, in uttering your caution against hasty conclusions in this matter, you have kept clearly before your mind that the doctor and the nurses and friends who saw Mrs. Merrett in the Infirmary observed no sign of abnormality?—Yes, that is so.

And does that in any way affect the conclusion which you have drawn as to the need for utmost caution?—No, because these people pay very little attention to mental symptoms. It is pointed out in the Report of the Royal Commission how defective the training is on these subjects, and I know from experience how little attention they do pay.

Can you say that disregard of mental symptoms by a good many physicians has been so marked that the Royal Commission drew attention to it?—It did.

And in the present case, when you go to the temperature chart of this lady, do you find there is reference made to the acute delirium which she had?—I have not observed any.

Does that suggest to your mind that attention had been directed to the effect which the brain injury had on the mental condition of this lady, or does it suggest to the contrary?—It suggests the contrary.

Is it your evidence that, where a person meets with a serious head injury, the memory does not, as a rule, come right up to the moment of unconsciousness?—No, that is the usual condition.

Take the typical case of a street motor accident; is it in accordance with your experience that a person who is knocked down when crossing the street, and becomes unconscious, may remember nothing after leaving the pavement?—Well, unfortunately, I have not had experience of that particular type of case, but I have had experience of many other cases of unconsciousness, and I know that the recollection does not come up to the period of the accident.

I want you to assume—and I am putting it as high against myself as I can—that Mrs. Merrett remembered being seated writing at the table to within half a minute of the occurrence; and I want you to assume that she remembered a moment when her son was at her side. Is her recollection up to that point of time consistent with an absence of recollection of an act of attempted suicide, and also consistent with absence of recollection of any impulse towards suicide?—Yes.

By the COURT—Assume that, in addition to what Mr. Aitchison has put to you, there is evidence to the effect that Mrs. Merrett not only described her position in the room, the position of her son in the room, what she was doing, but also the explosion which occurred, would you still say that that was consistent with the view that she might completely forget the suicidal act?—Well, I think it is quite possible that she might, but, putting it in that strong way, it is not quite so clear as it would be if she did not have these recollections. I would make this suggestion, that it is quite possible that the interval of time that elapsed between the

219

John Donald Merrett.

Professor G. M. Robertson

moment when Mrs. Merrett found her son beside her and when the explosion actually took place was very much longer than is suspected, because the sense of time is one of those mental processes which is very apt to be disturbed in these unconscious cases, and there may have been a considerable lapse of time; and also, a person may remember certain incidents, and others that were taking place at the same time may be blotted out altogether.

In the circumstances I have put to you, is your evidence that it is conceivable, but not probable, that Mrs. Merrett would forget a suicidal act?—That is my opinion.

Does " altered consciousness," in substance, involve an interchange of personality?—It does.

Does it necessarily destroy and upset judgment?—Not necessarily.

Assume that on Wednesday, the 24th of March, Mrs. Merrett welcomed two friends to the Infirmary, Mr. and Mrs. Penn, talked to them rationally, discussed ordinary topics with her nurses, and that all these people thought from what they observed at the time, including the nurses and the doctor, that Mrs. Merrett was in a perfectly normal mental state, do you still say it is consistent with all this that she may have been in a state of altered consciousness?—Yes, it is.

But, on the information before you, you are unable to affirm or to deny which it was?—That is so.

And does your evidence, therefore, really come to this, that it is necessary to proceed with caution in accepting statements made by Mrs. Merrett at such a time in respect that they may be accurate or may be inaccurate?—That is so.

ROBERT CHURCHILL (41), examined by Mr. AITCHISON—I am a gunmaker, and I carry on business at 39-42 Leicester Square, London. I have had a lifelong experience of firearms of all kinds. During the past sixteen years I have been frequently called upon to give expert evidence by the Public Prosecutor and the police in England. I have also on some occasions been called in to see gunshot wounds in Charing Cross Hospital, London. I conducted in London a series of experiments along with Sir Bernard Spilsbury, and the results of some of these experiments are produced in this case. The experiments were conducted with an automatic pistol of .25 calibre, firing at different ranges, and upon different substances, in particular upon cardboard and skin.

I do not propose to take you in detail over these London experiments, but, generally, can you tell us what difference you find, as regards marking, between experiments upon skin and experiments upon cardboard?—The cardboard certainly shows more blackening than the skin. Some subsequent experiments were made in Edinburgh by Sir Bernard Spilsbury at which I was present, and, as regards the relative sensitiveness of skin and cardboard, they confirmed the experiments which I made

220

Evidence for Defence.

Robert Churchill

in London. The experiments carried out in Edinburgh were carried out with ammunition similar to the ammunition with which the automatic pistol was loaded when the shooting incident occurred. I obtained the ammunition from Hardy's in Princes Street. The Edinburgh ammunition produced a greater degree of blackening than the ammunition which had been used in the London experiments. A .25 automatic cartridge contains 2 grains of flake smokeless powder. There is no powder entirely smokeless, but it is relatively smokeless in comparison, say, with gunpowder. Two grains being a very small amount, you do not get much of an unburnt residue when the shot is fired.

And what effect has that upon the degree of tattooing which you get at close discharge?—As powder charges increase, naturally the tattooing increases.

But with a pistol of small bore, such as the pistol in question here, do you get tattooing to any material extent?—No.

What form does the tattooing take where you use a flake powder?—It is very slight indeed.

But do you find that instead of getting particles embedded, say, in the skin, they just penetrate the skin, and adhere?—It is only a flake, and therefore it has very little penetration at all.

And is tattooing of that kind on that account much more easily removed than the tattooing you get where ordinary black gunpowder is used?—Yes.

Would it be correct to say that where you are using this flake powder the flakes just stick into the skin by one edge?—They have hardly any penetration at all. The granular powder, naturally, would penetrate.

What would you say as regards blackening upon skin; I mean, how would you describe it as regards its depth or indelibility?—Purely superficial.

Does it indelibly mark the skin?—No, not to the extent that it indelibly marks paper.

Is it in accordance with your experience and experiments that blackening upon skin is easily removed?—It is easily removed. I, along with Sir Bernard Spilsbury, carried out an experiment in London for the purpose of testing whether blackening upon skin could be easily removed.

I show you production No. 18g. Is that a portion of skin showing a bullet wound from a pistol at a range of 1 inch?—Yes. On the right side of the wound in that portion of skin there is a certain amount of blackening, and originally on the left-hand side of the wound there was also a certain amount of blackening, I should say an equal amount of blackening to what you have now on the right side. The blackening upon the left side of the wound is not now shown. I saw Sir Bernard Spilsbury lightly wipe this left portion with a little damp piece of cloth, or something that he had.

John Donald Merrett.

Robert Churchill

Did he seem to put any pressure on it?—No, very lightly.

And has the effect been really practically to obliterate any mark of blackening on the skin at all on the left-hand side of the wound?—Yes. That experiment was carried out in London. An experiment was carried out down here with a similar cartridge, and with similar results.

Do these experiments, to which you have spoken, confirm what you would have anticipated from your knowledge of the powder which is used with automatic pistols of this kind?—Yes.

In your view, do experiments upon paper carry you any length at all in a case of this kind?—Not in this particular case, as the wound had been washed.

I want you to assume that the wound bled for a considerable time, that the wound became surrounded with blood, that right over the wound there was congealed or coagulated blood, and that a wet swab had to be applied by the surgeon who dressed the wound, with considerable pressure, to remove the blood—assuming these conditions, would you expect to find any blackening at all?—No, with those conditions it would be impossible to determine any blackness.

Would the application of a wet swab, and the pressure required to remove it, remove any blackening, if blackening was there?—Yes.

Have you any doubt about that?—Not a bit. Our experiments on skin were easily washed off, but, of course, we had no blood; we never used blood at all there.

Assuming it to be the case that no blackening was found upon the wound after the blood had been removed, in your view, can any inference as to distance be drawn in these circumstances from the absence of blackening?—No.

Now, are you quite clear upon that?—Yes.

Have you considered, with reference to the question of whether the wound could have been suicidally inflicted or accidentally inflicted, the direction of the wound?—Both are possible.

Have you in your experience had a case of a suicidal wound behind the right ear?—Yes.

Was that the case of a man or woman?—The case of a woman.

Who shot herself behind the right ear?—Yes.

Was the weapon directed forwards or backwards?—Forwards.

Did it roughly correspond to the direction of the wound in this case?—Yes, roughly.

And was that an undoubted case of suicide?—It was brought in as suicide.

It has been suggested, but I do not think persisted in, that in order to get the weapon into such a position as to produce a wound of the kind we have here, the hand would need to be put into a strained position. What do you say to that?—I say that it is quite possible to reproduce that wound without any movement of the arm at all—just a movement of the head. I teach shooting,

222

Evidence for Defence.

Robert Churchill

and I find women flinch from the discharge at first, by closing their eyes and by turning the head away from the discharge, instinctively.

Does it come to this, that supposing the weapon were pointed at the side of the temple, an instinctive movement of the head, without any movement of the arm, might get the pistol into the position that would give you the direction we have in this case?—You could reproduce this wound exactly by doing that.

In your view, can the angle be easily accounted for on the view that the pistol was pointed at the temple, but there was an instinctive aversion of the head at the moment the trigger was pulled?—It is possible to absolutely reproduce this wound in that way.

And, if this was a case of suicide, would you, from your experience of instinctive movements of the head when firearms are fired, think it a likely thing to occur?—I think it is quite likely.

That is if it is suicide?—Yes. I have also considered the wound from the point of view of accident.

In your view, could a wound of this kind, having regard to all the facts, direction and so on, have been accidentally caused?—I could reproduce that wound by holding the pistol with the thumb on the trigger guard and the fingers of the hand at the butt of the pistol.

Assume that Mrs. Merrett—she seeing the pistol in the bureau—had picked it up in that position, and assuming that she over-balanced and fell, is there any difficulty at all in getting an accidental discharge that would produce a wound in the head such as you find here?—No.

[Witness demonstrated his theory by putting his thumb on the trigger, with the butt of the pistol in the palm of the hand, and jarring the back of the hand on the ledge of the witness-box, the muzzle being pointed towards the head, and the face averted from the pistol.]

Accordingly, are the facts in your view consistent with accident?—Accident is possible.

Similarly, supposing that, having lost her balance at the moment the pistol was in her hand, she instinctively raised her hand to her head to protect her head in the fall, is there any difficulty in getting the pistol into a position that is consistent with accident?—There is no difficulty in getting the pistol into position, but I should not expect it to happen that way. I think I have given the two most likely ways that this could happen. I think the most likely way is to pick the pistol up with the thumb on the trigger guard and to fall on it.

Which might happen if Mrs. Merrett had her chair tilted up at the time?—It is possible to reproduce the wound in that way.

Is it in accordance with your knowledge and experience of firearms that accidents occur which it is sometimes impossible to explain?—It is impossible to explain some of them.

223

John Donald Merrett.

Robert Churchill

In the case of gunshot wounds where you are using a gun—I mean suicidal wounds where you are using a gun—where do you usually find them, or where do you often find them?—Usually in the mouth.

Where you have a suicidal wound from a long-barrelled revolver, where do you frequently find them?—Usually in the temple. I am saying usually, because sometimes they are in the mouth.

But where you find a wound inflicted with a short-barrelled firearm, such as the automatic pistol you hold in your hand, where do you usually find them?—Usually in the side of the head. A shot gun, on account of its very long barrel, naturally can only be placed in the mouth. A long-barrelled revolver can be placed in the mouth, because there is something you can put in; and also it can be put, on account of its length, at the side of the head. But with an automatic pistol, such as I have in my hand, it is natural to do it at the side.

Taking all the facts as you have them in this case, do you find anything in the position or the direction of the wound to exclude either suicide or accident?—No.

Cross-examined by the LORD ADVOCATE—Take first of all your suggested possible method, that of suicide, which you have demonstrated, you are assuming a woman who is not skilled in firing pistols?—A woman who is nervous of firearms, and I find that every woman is nervous at first.

Is it a very uncommon thing for a woman to commit suicide with a pistol?—I have had a few cases. Naturally, it is not common.

And still more uncommon for women who are ignorant of the use of such weapons?—I would say that.

Among these few cases, was there any one of a woman committing suicide with a pistol in the presence of a near relative, such as a son?—In one case—the case I mentioned investigating for the Home Office—that was a case of a woman who committed suicide for no apparent reason. The shot was behind the ear, and no action was taken against the husband, who was asleep in a chair alongside. That is the only case that I can cite near to this.

Assuming that sitting in the chair Mrs. Merrett put her elbow at the angle you have suggested, it would come in contact, or risk coming in contact, with the bureau. Does not that exclude the possibility of your theory?—No.

If it did come in contact, it would upset it. If there was a risk it would render it doubtful?—Yes.

Come now to your suggestion of accident. The only suggestion you make, as I understand, is that the thumb goes into the trigger guard with the hand grasping the butt of the pistol?—Yes.

But, surely, the person so grasping it must have known the pistol was there?—That is right.

224

Case — before returning
to Edinburg. The [crossed out]
Xmas vacation I believe ends
on Jan 12th when I will
be returning to Edinburgh with
would come to see you as soon
as possible after that date —
that we could arrange any
further matters personally
I am sure I shall like
the little Flat — & very boy of
be most comfortable there while
here — & much appreciate
the allowing me to use your piano
& it will be a great joy to me
to be able to play once again —
on so good an instrument —
with kind regards
    Yrs sincerely
    B. R. D. Merrett

Genuine Handwriting and Signature of Mrs. Merrett.

(From the original MS. in the Editor's possession.)

Evidence for Defence.

Robert Churchill

You could not put any papers between, or the thumb would not go into the trigger guard, would it ?—No.

Were you assuming that the pistol was picked up off the bureau ?—I am simply assuming that the lady was sitting in the chair and was stretching out.

You do not know whether she needed to tip the chair or not, in order to reach the pigeon holes ?—No.

Or whether it would be possible for her to tilt the chair ?—I expect that in the case of accident she would have to tip the chair to fall.

Are you assuming that she is sitting at an angle to the bureau, with her back half towards it ?—Yes, falling back on the right hand against the bureau.

The effect of that would be to jerk the pistol out of her hand, probably, would it not ?—The way I am assuming is that she falls on to the pistol.

You are assuming that she stretched towards the pigeon hole to get the pistol out of it ?—Yes.

Are you aware that there are some 20 inches between the pigeon hole and the edge of the writing slab on the bureau ?—No, I do not know.

So that the pit of her arm would be touching the writing slab as she reached for the pistol ?—I do not know that.

That would rather affect the theory that you are putting forward ?—It would, if the body were stopped by this bureau.

You made certain experiments in London. It was you who actually did the firing ?—Yes.

Were those experiments made with a different pistol and different cartridges and gunpowder to those which we know were used in this case ?—Yes, a pistol of similar make, of Spanish manufacture, and the ammunition supposedly of similar but of later make.

It was a different maker, was it not ?—It was Nobel's ammunition. They are all one combine.

Do I understand that you experimented on both skin and cardboard in London and in Edinburgh ?—Yes.

Did the powder used in London produce more of a yellowish colour and not so black as in Edinburgh ?—The powder used in London produced more tattooing.

But was not the colour more of a yellowish tinge ?—Slightly flame.

You would agree, in view of your experience, that the advisable thing in every case is to carry out tests with the actual weapon, and with as identical powder and ammunition as you can get ?—Yes.

On the Sunday, 30th January, eight days ago, was it you who actually fired the pistol ?—Yes.

Was the pistol in good working order ?—Yes.

Re-examined by Mr. AITCHISON—Is it in accordance with your experience that pistols in good working order, especially if they

John Donald Merrett.

Robert Churchill

are of cheap makes, sometimes go off unexpectedly?—There is no reliance to be placed on them.

I think the automatic pistol in this case was a cheap Spanish make?—Yes.

Although you get a difference in density between the Edinburgh and the London experiments, does it make any difference at all to the conclusion which you drew as to the probability of any blackening being removed if the wound were washed?—No. As the wound was washed, it is impossible for me to determine any distance.

You say that in London you carried out experiments with what was regarded as the same kind of ammunition?—Yes.

Are these makers, Eley and Kynoch, really the same people?—They are all in the Nobel combine.

Were your London experiments carried out with the same stuff, but was there a difference as regards the age of the stuff with the experiments which you carried out in Edinburgh?—The powder is apparently similar, but gives different results. The London ammunition gives more tattooing, and the Edinburgh ammunition gives more smoke blackening. One is the powder unconsumed and the other is it consumed.

In any particular box of cartridges may there be differences as to the degree of ignition you get on firing?—Yes.

And would that affect the degree of blackening?—Yes. I noticed differences between Professor Littlejohn's and Professor Glaister's tests.

As I understand your evidence, your view of accident was that, in falling backwards, the hand holding the pistol came in contact with something and so caused the discharge?—Yes.

Do you see any impossibility in that view?—No. I could reproduce the wound in that way.

You were asked whether you knew of any case in which a mother had shot herself in the presence of her son. You do recollect a case in which a wife shot herself in the presence of her husband?—Yes.

And was there a Home Office investigation?—Yes.

Was that established as a case of suicide?—Yes.

And did the investigations reveal any motive of any kind?—No motive.

Sir BERNARD SPILSBURY, examined by Mr. AITCHISON—I am a Bachelor of Medicine and Surgery of the University of Oxford, a Member of the Royal College of Physicians in London, Lecturer on Special Pathology at St. Bartholomew's Hospital, London, and Lecturer on Medical Jurisprudence at the London School of Medicine for Women. I hold the position of Honorary Pathologist to the Home Office, and have had a very large experience, extending now to a period of twenty years, in the investigation of crime on its medico-legal side. I have been present in Court during

226

Evidence for Defence.

the greater part of this trial, excepting the time when the medical and scientific evidence was being led. From what I have heard and otherwise, I have been put in possession of the medical facts relating to the case, and I am familiar with them, including amongst these facts the history of Mrs. Merrett's illness as disclosed by the Infirmary records from the date of her admission to the Infirmary, 17th March, down to the date of her death. I have applied my mind to the question of whether it is possible to draw any certain conclusion as to whether the wound which resulted in Mrs. Merrett's death was homicidal, suicidal, or accidental. Wounds which are suicidally inflicted may have all the appearance of homicidal wounds; I mean any suicidal wound may be imitated by a homicidal wound. Accordingly, the fact that a wound may present the characteristics of a homicidal wound does not really carry you very far when the question to be investigated is whether the wound is homicidal, suicidal, or accidental. Of course, the converse proposition is not necessarily true, that any homicidal wound may be a suicidal wound. I have considered the site and direction of the wound in this case as bearing upon the question whether the wound can have been accidentally inflicted or suicidally inflicted. First, as regards the site of the wound as distinct from the direction of the wound, there is nothing in the site of the wound which in my view is inconsistent either with suicide or with accident. This position of the wound in the back of the ear (antihelix) is by no means inconsistent with either. I have had experience of suicidal wounds inflicted on the side of the head. In particular, I have had an example of a suicidal wound inflicted behind the ear and in a forward direction. It was a case of a man who shot himself, the bullet entering half an inch behind the right ear and passing out on the other side of the head immediately above the left ear, and in that case the weapon was found grasped in his hand. Death must have been instantaneous. There was no question of its being suicide. So far as my experience goes, there is nothing in the site of the wound in the case of Mrs. Merrett inconsistent with suicide.

Coming now to the direction of the wound, is there anything in your view in the direction of the wound that is inconsistent with its having been self-inflicted with suicidal intent?—Not with such a weapon as the one used in this case—there is nothing inconsistent.

Would you explain to the jury what you mean by that. [Handed pistol]?—The weapon is an automatic pistol which is light in weight and has a very short barrel, so that, as Professor Littlejohn pointed out, the muzzle projects only one and a quarter inches beyond the finger on the trigger, thus rendering it much easier to hold in a position against the side of the head. Owing to its light weight it would throw no great tax on the person wielding it, and it would be easy with this weapon to hold it up against the side of the head in such a position as this (indicating a position

227

John Donald Merrett.

Sir Bernard Spilsbury

with the nozzle just behind the ear and pointing slightly forwards), not necessarily pointing upwards, but more easily in a sidewards position. If held in that position, and fired perhaps in the most comfortable position for the arm, the bullet would tend to go forwards rather than downwards.

Is that position, while not so common as the position where the weapon is held nearer the temple, quite consistent with suicide?— Yes, quite, using such a weapon as this. In order to get the weapon into the position I have described there is no difficulty or strain upon the hand or arm. Even one, I think, unaccustomed to firing such a weapon would hold it quite easily and naturally in such a position. In the position I am indicating the trigger guard is more in a horizontal than a vertical position, and in such a position there would be no real difficulty in getting the hand a reasonable distance back from the head; it would be easy to hold the weapon 1 inch or even 2 inches away from the head without any strain. I could hold it even a greater distance—3 or 4 inches —without much strain, but I am not sure that all persons would be able to do it. It would depend upon the range of movement of the particular arm and of the particular shoulder joint. I agree with the proposition Professor Littlejohn assented to, that in the case of a woman you often find very considerable range of movement of the shoulder joint owing to the habit of putting up the hair.

It appears that the direction of the wound was not only from behind forwards, but that it had a slight upwards tendency. Is that again quite consistent with suicide?—Yes, quite. A slight inclination of the head would just make all the difference to upward or downward direction.

Supposing that the pistol had been held by Mrs. Merrett at an angle of 90 degrees to the line of the head—I mean taking Professor Littlejohn's idea of a longitudinal line through the skull, what do you say as to the possibility of an instinctive movement averting the head at the moment the trigger was fired?—Such a movement might well be made by a person who was about to discharge a weapon, especially dreading the explosion. A movement of the head towards the left shoulder would cause the direction of the bullet to be a forward one and not a transverse one, and would, of course, bring the point of entrance further back in the head. The movement of the head might alter the angle of 90 degrees to 120 degrees; it could easily turn 30 degrees, and even more, to produce such an angle. A movement of the head would be quite a likely thing to expect unless one were dealing with a very determined suicide. I agree with Professor Littlejohn's view in his first report, the post mortem report, dated 5th April, 1926, where he says, " So far as the position of the wound is concerned, the case is consistent with suicide." I also agree with his view that, " There is some difficulty in attributing it to accident, although such a view cannot be wholly excluded."

228

Evidence for Defence.

Sir Bernard Spilsbury

The doctors for the Crown in this case have laid the main stress on the absence of blackening round about the wound in the ear. I want to ask you one or two questions regarding that. In your view, having regard to the facts in this case, is there any evidence, and, in particular, having regard to the fact that there was considerable bleeding from the ear, that the blood congealed and that it had to be removed by pressure with a wet swab, can any sure inference be drawn from the absence of blackening as to the range at which the weapon was fired?—With the explosive that was used in this case I do not think it is safe under those circumstances to drawn any sure conclusion as to the distance. I mean, of course, there might have been at the time of the infliction of the injuries indications of near discharge which might have been removed, or almost completely removed by the washing from the surface of the blood, and the consequent cleansing of the ear when examined. When I say, " With the explosive that was used here," I mean the cartridges which I have been shown as being similar to the actual cartridge which was fired. With a view to ascertaining how far reliance should be placed upon the absence of blackening about the wound, I carried out certain experiments in London and also in Edinburgh.

Let me first take the experiments in London. Will you just summarise what these experiments were, and what results you deduce from them?—The experiments were made with Mr. Churchill, using an automatic pistol as nearly as possible like the one which was used in this case. We had a description of the pistol and we picked one having exactly the same length of barrel and the same bore. We also selected cartridges which corresponded as closely as possible to the description we received of those which were used in this case. We fired first of all at white cardboard at different lengths, and then, using the same type of cartridges, we fired at pieces of fresh human skin. In the experiments with the cardboard I tested the weapon at ranges from contact to a distance of 6 inches from the cardboard. When the weapon was in contact with the cardboard we obtained only an aperture where the bullet passed through the card, with considerable destruction of the aperture of the card all round, but very little disturbance of the card round about. Apart from the aperture, we found from the experiments on contact that we got very little blackening round the aperture.

Is it the case that where the weapon is placed close against the skin you may get less blackening than where the weapon is held at a range of 1 or 2 inches?—Yes, if kept firmly pressed there may be no change at all round the surface of the opening. As regards our further experiments, the next range was a range of half an inch, and the surface of the card was damaged to some extent round the orifice produced by the bullet, and there was an area of blackening around, extending altogether to about 1 inch around

229

John Donald Merrett.

the opening. [Exhibiting card.] That circular blackening is about 1 inch in diameter. I repeated the experiment at the same range, having previously damped the surface of the card with water, and I found as the result that the deposit of powder on the surface extended over a larger area and there was a more considerable deposit in consequence. I then attempted to remove the smoke by wiping it over with a damp cloth, and I removed a good deal of that on the left side of the card. [Exhibiting card.] The difference between the white and the unwhite portion on this card is quite apparent to the eye. The next experiment was at a distance of 1 inch, and from the card produced it will be noticed that the area of blackening increases and is rather more than 1 inch in diameter, but the depth of the colour is less intense. At a range of 2 inches my experiment showed only slight blackening around the entrance of the bullet, but the pitting of the paper by the remains of the powder shows very distinctly over a larger area.

When you say, " Pitting of the paper," by that do you mean tattooing?—It is not in fact tattooing, but it is produced by the fact of powder hitting the cardboard and producing a split on its surface without becoming deposited on it. My next experiment was at a range of 6 inches. At that distance there was no blackening round the paper at all, but only the pitting produced by the scales of the powder. In addition to those experiments which I carried out upon cardboard, I also made similar experiments upon skin. I could summarise the effect by saying that, when compared at the same range with the experiments on cards, I found that the appearance of blackening was less distinct in the shorter ranges than on the corresponding white cards. That difference is partly due to the difference in the nature of the surface, and, at the shorter ranges, up to, I think, 1 inch, it was due also to the fact that the paper surface was burned by the flame, whilst the same effect is not produced on the skin. In addition to those changes, the scales of the powder, when the weapon was discharged on the skin, lodged on the surface of the skin and were adherent to it to some extent, and these formed distinct projections, in the shorter ranges at any rate, round the entrance wound. [Witness at this stage referred to production No. 18b for the pannel.]

As to the scales to which you refer, which you have shown in exhibit No. 18b, are they scales of a rectangular shape?—Yes. They are of a steel-grey colour. They are not so readily seen without the aid of a hand lens, but you can see the general effect.

Are they easily removed?—Yes, by any wiping over the scales. At a range of 1 inch, when fired at the skin, the area of blackening was less marked than in the case of the paper, but the scales of powder could still be seen projecting from the surface. In another skin experiment which I repeated later I fired at the skin at the same range, and afterwards wiped over one half of the skin to remove as far as possible the deposit upon the surface. [Referring to production No. 18g.]

230

Evidence for Defence.

Sir Bernard Spilsbury

Taking No. 18g, in which the skin was wiped on one side of the wound, did the wiping remove the blackening which was present?—Practically completely so. There is just a little trace to be made out with the hand lens, but on inspection with the eye alone it appears to be quite clean.

And is the difference between the wiping off and the unwiping shown quite clearly in No. 18g?—Quite clearly. In wiping the portion of No. 18g I used a piece of cotton wool which I dipped into water and wrung out, but squeezed most of the water out, and I rubbed it over the surface between thumb and finger.

Did you bring much pressure to bear?—I rubbed it fairly well, just as I would rub ordinary skin, backwards and forwards.

Would you use less pressure than that to remove coagulated blood round a wound?—No, I tried to rub it in the same way.

And was the result to remove practically all the blackening?—Yes, to remove also most of the scales of powder projecting in that area.

From these experiments which you made, what general conclusion do you draw, first, as regards the sensitiveness of skin to take on blackening as compared with cardboard, and, secondly, as regards the ease with which blackening can be removed from skin?—In all the experiments with cardboard as compared with skin, at the same range, I found the pattern on the skin as regards blackening less distinct than it was in the cardboard experiments. The pitting produced by the powder grains was very similar in each case.

As regards the ease with which the stain could be removed, was it greater in the case of the skin than in the case of cardboard?—Yes. In the case of cardboard it is difficult to try and wash away the blackening without removing the surface of the paper with it.

You mean that you destroy the surface of the paper?—Yes. You can only wipe lightly, but in the case of the skin I had no difficulty in these experiments in removing practically the whole of the blackening. [Referring to production No. 18g for the pannel.] It was not easy to remove the whole, because the fine blackening tended to stick in the crevices where the skin was folded, but in the smoother part it came away quite easily. No. 17 of the productions for the pannel is a portion of the powder removed from one of the cartridges we used in the London experiments, in which the scales of a steel-grey colour to which I have referred can be seen. I have since compared these with the contents of one of the cartridges used in the experiments in Edinburgh, and I found that they were practically identical.

In carrying out the London experiments, did you find that the degree of blackening was affected by the state of moisture of the material upon which you were making the experiments?—Yes. In the case of the paper experiments, wetting the paper caused powder to be deposited over a larger area.

John Donald Merrett.

Sir Bernard Spilsbury

Would you say that generally the same held true as regards the experiments on skin?—Yes. The degree of moisture of the skin, or greasiness of the skin, would no doubt affect the pattern produced at a given range, and that emphasises the difficulty of reproducing in experiments conditions that were actually present at the time. The condition of the skin as regards smoothness or roughness would be a factor. Where the skin was smooth it would be more easy to remove than where the skin showed creases or folds.

If the skin is smooth, there is not the same lodgment for particles of powder, or what you call the scales?—Yes.

Taking the actual wound in the present case, what would you say as regards the skin, or in relation to its sensitiveness to powder or blackening?—The skin in the part of the ear through which the bullet passed is fairly smooth. [Pointing to the antihelix and concha of the ear.]

Accordingly, would the skin of the antihelix and the concha be less receptive to blackening than the skin of the back of the hand?—Not so much less receptive as more easily removed, owing to its smoothness. My remark applies to blackening and not to tattooing. I have considered also whether one would be likely to find blackening, having regard to the angle at which the weapon was at the moment of discharge. If the weapon was discharged within such a range as to produce blackening, the blackening would be most marked immediately around the wound in the antihelix, and probably behind that wound rather than in front of it; that is to say, on the outer edge of the antihelix; but blackening would extend further forward if the weapon was pointed forward, and would produce some blackening on the edge of the ear, but probably for not any great distance.

If there was considerable hæmorrhage from the ear as the result of the wound, was it a very easy matter to fail to observe blackening that may have been present?—Yes. The hæmorrhage would certainly have flowed over all this part of the ear, if we consider the different positions in which the lady must have been lying after the injury was inflicted, and during the period of removal to the hospital.

Do you say that, in order to say with any certainty whether there was or was not blackening after the wound was cleaned, that it would have been necessary to use the hand lens for that purpose? —Yes. I think perhaps the hand lens might have detected blackening where there were any breaks of the surface of the skin, such as might have been produced by the scales of powder which had lodged in it, but, as those were wiped away, the powder may have been taken off the surface.

It is in evidence that there was considerable bleeding from the wound. Taking the direction of the wound, must the bullet have passed through a very vascular part?—It passed through the organ

232

Evidence for Defence.

Sir Bernard Spilsbury

of hearing, and there is a fairly good blood supply to the interior of the bone, and that would certainly bleed quite freely for some little time.

Would the free bleeding over the wound, in conjunction with the rubbing required to remove the coagulated blood, easily remove any blackening that might have been there?—Yes; it might well have done so. In addition to the experiments which I made in London, I also made experiments in Edinburgh with ammunition similar to the ammunition used in the pistol on the day of the occurrence. Professor Littlejohn was present when these experiments were made. I got every facility from the Crown Authorities to make these experiments.

Without taking these experiments in detail, how far do they confirm the results at which you arrived from your London experiments?—The appearances on the cards at which we fired in the Edinburgh experiments differed from those in the London experiments, firstly, in that the depth and degree of blackening in the Edinburgh experiments was much greater at shorter ranges than in the London experiments, but the pitting produced by the powder grains in Edinburgh was much less marked than in the London ones.

As regards the ease with which blackening could be removed, was there any difference between the London experiments and the Edinburgh experiments?—I should say not. The blackening would be very much the same in character, although greater in amount, and, again, it would depend largely on the nature of the surface for the degree to which it could be removed.

Would you, therefore, say that your Edinburgh experiments were confirmative of the conclusions which you drew from your London ones?—They did not modify my conclusions.

On this matter generally, are you in agreement with the passages which I will read to you from Taylor, seventh edition, page 539, and at page 540? The passage at page 539, which is a passage quoted from the *British Medical Journal*, says this—" The following conclusions are drawn from these experiments "—that is, experiments of the discharge of pistols loaded with smokeless powder against skin, and so on—" (1) Markings upon the skin produced by smokeless powder are much less distinct and definite than those caused with black powder "?—I agree.

Then it says—" Conclusion (3). At a distance of 3 inches or less powder marks may be present, but they will always be faint, and may in many instances be wiped away from the skin with a wet or dry cloth "?—Yes, my own experiments showed that.

Finally, do you agree with this summation of the matter on page 540, " The matter may be summed up thus—If there are marks of powder or burning, the weapon was not more than a foot away on firing. If there are no marks, it is impossible to tell how far off it was, for one negative upsets any number of

John Donald Merrett.

Sir Bernard Spilsbury

positives in this instance.'' Do you agree with that?—I do, generally.

Would it be right to say that that conclusion is in accordance with the views expressed in various textbooks of medical jurisprudence by eminent authorities?—Yes, some of these conclusions are expressed in different books. They vary in expression in different textbooks.

Taking the matter generally, taking all the facts into account, do you find anything in the conditions as we have them here, to exclude suicide as a possible explanation of what occurred?—No, I do not.

I want you for a minute or two to consider the alternative view, the view of accident. I understand you agree with the view of Professor Littlejohn that accident cannot be wholly excluded?—Yes.

Do you see any difficulty in attributing what occurred to accident, looking at it from the medico-legal point of view?—No. It is always difficult to attribute accident in a case in which the circumstances are not known, but from my own experience of accidental shooting one knows of extraordinary positions sometimes resulting from the accidental discharge of weapons under various circumstances, and in such a position as this an accidental discharge, I think, could never be entirely excluded; and might even be at a range greater than that which would produce local marks round the wound.

Is it consistent with your experience that when accidents occur it is often extremely difficult to reconstruct them and to ascertain what the precise conditions were?—It may be quite impossible to do so in some cases.

May there be some factor present which has quite escaped the investigator, but which if known would point very strongly to accident?—Yes.

And is that particularly the case where at the time of the occurrence there is only a superficial examination made of the conditions prevailing?—Yes, that would make it rather more difficult. I am familiar with the history of Mrs. Merrett's illness from the 17th of March down to the date of her death. I have examined the chart, and I am familiar with the fluctuations of temperature from, first, subnormal to above normal.

You know that she was receiving throughout that period very considerable injections of morphia?—Yes, medicinal doses, of course.

But pretty well up to the maximum?—Yes. I also know that she developed on the night of the 25th of March an acute delirium. I agree that an acute delirium could not develop without there having been some pre-delirious period, some preparatory period in which an inflammatory process must have been going on in the brain. The post-mortem examination in this case revealed that the brain membranes were inflamed and infiltrated with purulent

Evidence for Defence.

Sir Bernard Spilsbury

matter. That makes it quite plain to me that there must have been a very acute inflammatory condition of the brain, and that it would take some time to develop. It must have been developing, I think, from the time when the temperature first showed a rise. The date of that rise was 22nd March.

With a brain condition such as must have existed here, in your view would it be safe to place reliance upon statements made by the patient within a comparatively short period—say twenty-four hours—of an acute delirium developing?—I think any such statements must be accepted with great caution.

Might such statements appear to be made by a person of normal mentality while in reality they were made by a person whose mentality was abnormal owing to physical illness?—Yes, that might be so.

And especially do you agree that they should be accepted with very great caution in a case of such gravity?—Yes.

Would you say that it is consistent with your experience that where people sustain serious head injuries the memory may be fairly good up to within a very short time of when the actual injury is received?—I have heard of such cases, but I have very little experience of those who survived such injuries for any length of time.

But, at any rate, you are quite clear that in the case of severe head injuries, which ultimately result in death, the utmost precaution must be shown in considering the weight to be attached to statements made by persons who have received them?—Yes.

Cross-examined by the LORD ADVOCATE—You first of all dealt with the possibility of suicide in this case. May I take it that the side of the head is not one of the more normal points at which a suicide puts the weapon?—It is not one of the more usual points.

But, of course, such cases occur?—Yes.

Secondly, may I take it that the suicide who intends to kill would naturally make sure of the aim by holding the weapon against the head?—Yes, against or very close to it.

If the suicide who intends to kill, and still keeps on intending to kill, turns his head, the natural thing is for the hand to keep the weapon against the head, or quite close to it?—I do not feel so sure of that. After the hand is placed in position the head may be turned instinctively at the time the trigger is pulled. They hold it close to, and turning the head like that [demonstrating a turn to the left], the position may be so altered as not only to bring the direction of the bullet wound through the head in a different angle, but it will also bring the head further away from the weapon to a certain extent.

But you would agree, would you not, that the more natural, the more probable, course would be, in order to make sure of its happening, even then, for the weapon to be kept in contact with the head?—Not if the head moves, I think. If the head is kept in that position, I agree, yes.

John Donald Merrett.

Sir Bernard Spilsbury

Of course we are merely discussing at the moment really physical possibilities?—Yes.

Every case must depend on the circumstances of the case?—Yes, quite.

And also, of course, as to what the other possibilities are?—Yes.

I will follow the same order as my learned friend did. Have you seen the results which Professor Littlejohn got from his experiments?—Yes, I have examined these.

Would you agree that the results of your Edinburgh experiments corresponded very closely indeed with Professor Littlejohn's? —Yes, in general they correspond quite accurately.

And that they both of them differ from your London experiments?—Yes.

Do you agree that the important thing in each case, if possible, is to make your test with the actual weapon and as near the actual powder as you can get?—Yes, of course.

And you would, therefore, in the present case prefer Professor Littlejohn's experiments and your Edinburgh ones?—Yes, in judging of the effect in the actual case I should, of course.

Your experiments on skin were made with the London powder, and Professor Littlejohn's were made with Edinburgh powder?—Yes.

And if Professor Littlejohn found that the Edinburgh powder on skin could not be so easily washed away as in the case of your London experiments, again I ask you would you not prefer to take Professor Littlejohn's experiments?—No, I think a good deal depends on the degree and the extent of the rubbing, as well as on the condition of the skin at the time the weapon was fired.

Assuming the conditions of rubbing and the conditions of skin being the same, you would agree that the Edinburgh experiments would be perfect?—I think we ought to judge by the combined effects of both in such a case as that.

You do not challenge, I suppose, Dr. Bell's evidence when he says he looked—I am paraphrasing it fairly, I hope—and found parts of the ear on which he would have expected to find blackening, and found none?—I do not in the least.

But we have direct evidence in this case on the point before any washing took place?—I do not know that we are entitled to draw a conclusion that there was no blood on that part of the ear.

That would depend upon whether Dr. Bell was right when he said that those parts of the ear were free from blood?—No, I do not think it would. The mere fact of moving the woman from the place where she was shot to the Infirmary would almost certainly lead to the escape of some of the blood which had formed on the surface of the ear, and it is almost certain that some blood would be wiped off in the removal, and probably there would be bare patches on the skin even although the blood had flowed over the whole of the ear at some time or other.

Evidence for Defence.

Sir **Bernard** Spilsbury

You are speculating on what may have happened; you do not know?—I think it is almost certain what would have happened.

That depends on which way the blood was flowing and the volume of the blood?—Yes, it does, of course.

Coming to the experiments in London, I want to ask you one question about them. As regards the first one you spoke of, where the muzzle of the pistol was in contact with the cardboard, you said there was considerable destruction of the cardboard round the orifice, and the edge that was left had very little blackening on it. Is that fair?—Yes.

You know that in the case of Mrs. Merrett's wound there was very little destruction of tissue round the wound?—Yes. Dr. Holcombe told us so.

Does that suggest, at any rate, the muzzle of the pistol was not hard up against the skin?—Yes, I am quite sure that in this case it is quite impossible that the muzzle could have been pressed against the skin.

Therefore, it is a question of either what may be fairly called a near discharge, as Professor Littlejohn described it, or a discharge further away, and not a discharge in contact?—Yes, that is so, certainly not a discharge in contact.

Now, deal just with the question of the suggestion of accident. Do you agree with the way Professor Littlejohn puts it in the last sentence of his report which was read to you?—Yes, I do.

We had better get the exact phrase from you, because my learned friend put it in his own language. " There is some difficulty in attributing it to accident, although such a view cannot be wholly excluded." Does that express your view?—Yes, I think it does.

And do you further agree that as it may be found that the point of the pistol may be held further away the less likely is it to be an accident?—I do not think I can go as far as that. I think an accidental discharge might well have occurred with the weapon at such a distance from the head as to leave no indication of near distance—at a distance of more than 3 inches.

Is it not fair to say it was less probable?—Yes, in the case of an accident it is all a matter of degrees of improbability, and it is very difficult to say whether a near or far discharge is more likely to have occurred.

I do not want to go through the whole length of categories, but does your idea of a possible accident assume the arm being out at full length?—Not necessarily at full length.

Stretched out?—No. I am rather picturing the condition in which a person falls with a weapon, and the finger on the trigger with the weapon in the hand ready to go off, and if the weapon strikes a particular object the weapon might be discharged some distance from the head.

You are assuming they have got the weapon in the hand in a position to shoot?—Yes.

John Donald Merrett.

Sir Bernard Spilsbury

Do you regard that as an accidental probability?—Oh, yes.

Here, again, the position of the furniture, for instance, is a very important element in considering that possibility?—Yes; then, again, anything which the arm might strike in falling is a matter to be taken into consideration.

If Mrs. Merrett was falling backwards and mostly towards the bureau behind her, and she had got the pistol into her hand—we will say by accident—out of one of the pigeon-holes, her shoulder would come against the bureau?—Yes.

You have seen the plan?—Yes.

The probabilities are that it would?—I am not sure she was sufficiently near to say that the shoulder would catch, or the outstretched arm would catch.

Whether it was the shoulder or the outstretched arm, if she was falling backwards, would you not expect that the contact with the bureau would cause the arm to be thrown outwards?—Yes.

How in that way would you get the impact which is necessary to press the thumb against the trigger which was described by Mr. Churchill?—By its being delivered by a jerk from the elbow. [Illustrating.]

Where does the elbow hit?—I am speaking of the edge of the bureau, or the top of the bureau, on which she fell.

Do you mean right on the top?—I do not mean the back but the projecting edge.

Isn't it that very projecting edge that we are assuming has caught either the shoulder or the upper part of the arms?—Yes, quite so.

How could it catch the hand as well?—I did not say the hand; I said the elbow.

Is it not essential to the pressing of the thumb against the trigger to get a blow or contact with something on the back of the hand, the way Mr. Churchill demonstrated?—I do not think I was picturing quite the same type of accident. I was picturing a weapon held in the hand like that [demonstrating], and a fall on the elbow.

And in order to get that blow on the elbow would you assume that Mrs. Merrett was standing, or something like standing, so as to be at the necessary height?—No, I was rather picturing her as falling backwards in the chair when she was originally in the sitting position.

Will you look at No. 4 of the productions for the defence? Are you assuming that the proceedings began with Mrs. Merrett sitting in the chair beside the bureau?—Yes, I am.

And that she never actually rose from the chair, but only tilted it?—Some such position as that.

Do you still suggest that if she was falling off the chair, having lost her balance, she could get the point of her elbow on

238

Evidence for Defence.

Sir Bernard Spilsbury

to the flat top of the writing portion of the bureau?—I am not sure that she would with the chair just in this position, if you assume that was the accurate position. If it was a little further round I rather think she might do so.

Would that elbow not be too low for any such possibility?—No, I do not think so. If she had stretched over the bureau to get something out, the arm would presumably be over that part.

Mr. AITCHISON—No further questions.

By the COURT—Is it your opinion that all traces of blackening around a wound, assuming them to have existed, may be obliterated by wiping or rubbing, or both?—Yes, my lord, I think all traces might, or such a slight trace remain as would be difficult to detect without minute examination.

In your opinion, if there was no blackening, is that necessarily conclusive of a near wound?—Do you mean originally?

Yes?—If there was no blackening originally I think one must conclude that the weapon must have been at least 3 inches from the head—the muzzle of the weapon, of course.

Mr. AITCHISON—My lord, that is the case for the defence.

The Lord Advocate's Address to the Jury.

The LORD ADVOCATE—May it please your lordship, members of the jury, it is now my duty to address you on behalf of the Crown in this case, which has reached the sixth day, and while much of it may have been tedious to you—where it has been necessary to go through the formal proving of documents which were not explained to you at the time—it was all essential, as doubtless you will accept, for the purpose of establishing the case. I do not spend time in reminding you what the duty of a jury is in such a case as this, nor need I remind you of what the duty and position of the Crown is. In this case, as in all other cases of Crown prosecution, the Crown undertake to prove the case against the accused. And when I say " prove the case," that means to such an extent that shall satisfy the jury beyond reasonable doubt.

In the present case you have to deal with two charges in the indictment. They are two quite separate charges, but I need hardly say that the second charge has a very important bearing on the first one. I shall ask you, when I have concluded my remarks, to return a verdict against the prisoner on each and both of these two charges.

The second charge is that the accused, on the dates set out in the schedule, and in the office of the Clydesdale Bank, did utter as genuine the cheques set out in the schedule, which were in his favour and had Mrs. Bertha Merrett's name on them, and uttered them as genuine by presenting them for payment to the persons

John Donald Merrett.

whose names are set out in the schedule. The Crown undertakes to prove that he uttered these cheques as genuine, knowing them not to be genuine. On the other hand, it is not essential to the Crown to prove, in order that conviction should follow, that he was the actual fabricator or maker of the non-genuine signatures. It is enough that he knew. And it may well be that, in a particular case, the circumstances prove beyond doubt that the person who presents or utters the false writings was the fabricator, or at least must have been a party to the fabrication. But the crime, according to our law, is not the fabrication, the forging of the signature, but the uttering or presentation of the signature as a genuine signature to the teller of the bank, and that is the crime with which the accused is here charged.

There is no dispute that the late Mrs. Merrett sustained a wound in her head from a pistol, and there is no doubt that it was from the pistol here, on 17th March, 1926, somewhere about half-past nine in the morning, and that later she died from the result of that wound. There is equally no doubt that the occurrence took place in the sitting-room of the flat at No. 31 Buckingham Terrace, and that when the shooting occurred there were alone present in that sitting-room Mrs. Merrett and the accused. I wish first to direct your attention to what were the circumstances of Mrs. Merrett and the accused on the morning of the 17th day of March last. I wish next to deal with what happened on the 17th of March, as we know it from the evidence before the Court, and the subsequent actings and expert inquiries. Finally, I shall suggest the conclusions at which I am to ask you to arrive.

Ladies and gentlemen, what were the circumstances of these two parties prior to 17th March? Mrs. Merrett and her son lived together happily, so far as we know, the only members of the family living together, the husband having many years ago deserted Mrs. Merrett; and, although certain suggestions were made in cross-examination, there is no evidence to show that the husband was in communication with Mrs. Merrett or pestering her with demands for money, or that she was in any way worried about him. He disappeared from the scene many years ago, and so far as the evidence of this case is concerned he does not seem to come back into it at all. Mrs. Merrett enjoyed an income of about £700 a year, and we know her character fairly well from some of the witnesses. Mrs. Hill, who was perhaps her oldest friend, described her in a phrase I think you will remember : " Highly strung, emotional. A keen grip of life and everything it contained, but never a suggestion of doing away with herself." Then I asked her, " Was she a good business woman?—A. Very clever in everything." Then my learned friend asked in cross-examination : " You described her as highly strung, emotional. Would you say she was a woman of nervous temperament?—A. No." And at least five other witnesses who spoke to her character all agreed that, while she may have been a little emotional or

240

The Lord Advocate.

(The Right Hon. William Watson, K.C.)

Addresses to the Jury.

high spirited at times, she was not nervous in any sense of the word, and was a good business woman who was very methodical in her habits and in her account keeping. There is just one point to mention in fairness to the accused, that Mrs. Sutherland, in answer to my friend, said that Mrs. Merrett, two or three days before, spoke of having had a hard life. But that was all. There was nothing beyond that phrase, and we do not know what significance it may have had. Again, there is another suggestion made in cross-examination, to which I refer to get rid of it, the suggestion of a lunatic brother; but it was at once explained that he brought that condition on himself, and there was no question of any heredity, or any family connotation. Therefore you may disregard that suggestion altogether. Then, what about the accused? We know that he had spent a year at Malvern, and that he took honours in higher mathematics. We know that he was a student at Edinburgh University, and we know further, from the evidence, that he amused himself very often in another direction.

I want to consider more closely the financial position : what happened with regard to the cheques, the mother's bank account, and the cheques in respect of which these charges are made. Mrs. Merrett had two bank accounts. Her main bank account was with the Midland Bank at Boscombe. After she came to Edinburgh, in the beginning of January, she opened an account with the Clydesdale Bank, George Street branch. That was an account on which she could only operate to the extent of £30 at one time, and which she kept fed by cheques drawn on her main account at Boscombe. We know, because we have her account book, that Mrs. Merrett kept most careful personal accounts, not only containing her expenditure, but containing in the same book her bank balances as she went along, an account for each bank. If she paid a sum to her credit in the Clydesdale Bank, she put it down in the last balance and added the two together; and if she drew a cheque on the Clydesdale Bank, the next day she put it down and deducted it, and so she had a consistent record of her actual banking operations. Unfortunately—there may have been good or bad reasons for it—we have only been able to find the counterfoils of one of the cheque books, that of the Clydesdale Bank. On examination of that cheque book it shows that she followed exactly the same method on the counterfoils of her cheques; the balance carried over from the previous counterfoil, and then, if there is a pay-in, she puts the two together on the same counterfoil, and on the left-hand corner is put the amount of the cheque which she draws, and when she turns over to the next cheque it carries that amount, less the cheque just drawn. And so throughout in the counterfoils she really is reproducing the same balances as she had in her account book.

The accused, according to his statement to Detective Fleming, had a pocket-money allowance of 10s. a week. We find that he

John Donald Merrett.

spent some £27 or £28 on the 8th March on a motor cycle. There is no evidence that his mother knew of that or paid for it. There is no trace of it in her accounts or his accounts. He kept an account book also. In that account, while we find tickets for the Palais, 5s. ticket (only one entry), there is no trace of the 15s. or the 30s. for booking out the girl Betty Christie, or of this expenditure of £27 or £28 on the bicycle, or any other expenditure which will account for the sums to which I am going to refer you. That he always had plenty of money was the evidence of the girl Betty Christie. I am going to undertake to satisfy you that from 2nd February onwards the accused was operating on his mother's bank accounts by means of cheques which were not genuine cheques of his mother. There are 29 cheques, the subject of the charges, 12 of them being Clydesdale Bank cheques and 17 of them Midland Bank cheques. Prior to 17th March all the 12 Clydesdale Bank cheques had been presented and cashed, or credit given on them, and 11 of the Midland Bank cheques. There are thus 23 cheques out of 29 which were presented before 17th March. The other 6 were presented on subsequent dates. There can be no doubt on the evidence before you that in the case of each one of these 29 cheques the body of the cheque and the endorsation is written by the accused, and I submit that there is equally no doubt that the signature was not written by Mrs. Merrett, although it bears to be her signature.

As you will remember, there was what I might call an expert examination of cheques, and I would particularly draw your attention to the way in which these documents were submitted for examination. Mr. Gurrin, who first made the examination, had submitted to him the whole of Mrs. Merrett's Clydesdale Bank cheques, every cheque on her account from the time it was opened on the 12th of January until the close of the account, and, secondly, all the Midland Bank cheques for the year 1926, making three months, the same period. There was no choice of them. The whole of the cheques from that date onwards were submitted to him, and for comparison we sent to him some 61 illustrations of undoubted writings by Mrs. Merrett. Along with them we sent 60 cheques of the Midland Bank of the previous year, about which there could be no dispute at all. Mr. Gurrin's evidence—and it is corroborated by Mr. Smith—is to this effect, that there is on 29 of the cheques a double signature. If that is established, that of itself is sufficient to remove any suggestion of genuineness, because nobody ever suggested that on a whole series of cheques like that a person wrote their own signature twice over in two different colours. And when you add what he and Mr. Smith also observed that, whereas the other signatures were fluent and free, although the thickness or the nib used may have varied, each went on without any breaks or halts. In the case of all these 29 it was more halting and hesitating, which is just what you expect when you are copying over a specimen signature. That is never done by the true owner of the signature.

242

Addresses to the Jury.

These two points are sufficient to establish that these are not Mrs. Merrett's signature, and, as I said to you, it is not necessary to the Crown's case to prove who in fact actually did the tracing. We do not need that in any way; but there can be no doubt that the accused either did it himself or got somebody else to do it in collaboration with him. Why do I say that? He was the party in whose favour every one of these cheques was drawn. He was the party, as is clearly proved by each of the accountants, who presented the cheques and got cash or credit to himself, and who endorsed each one of them.

Again, that of itself is sufficient to establish the crime of uttering false writings. We are not concerned, except in so far as it may help to prove my contention, as to what was done with the money. That is not a necessary part of the crime. The essence of the crime is the presentation, or the uttering of the writings as genuine, knowing them to be false.

You will remember that Mr. Smith made an independent examination, and that there was another interesting thing brought out: the extraordinary similarity which struck them both independently as regards certain numbers of these 29 signatures, with the result that they classified them identically into three classes, Mr. Gurrin's model A, model B, and model C. Model C, which comes last in the alphabetical order, was the first one. It was the trial cheque, and its form was never repeated. It was the one used on 2nd February, 1926, and it is the only one in which there is a double underline, where the underline forms part of the tracing. The remaining 28 fell into two classes, 17 in class A practically identical, and in class B 11 practically identical. There was a good deal of cross-examination on this point, but one has only to remember the method by which it is suggested that this copying was done to realise that you would expect, first of all, in the original copying, to get a little variation in each case, and, secondly, that when inking over the copy, it is not surprising to find a little difference, a junction here and there which varies. But the point is that in the actual spacing, except between the two names, they are almost identically correct, so like each other that you could never imagine them to be genuine signatures. And when you couple that with what has been said about the duplication of the signature and the halting nature of the writing, contrasted with the free handwriting on the other documents, I think you can come only to one conclusion, namely, that these are not the signatures of Mrs. Merrett.

There are some other facts of intense interest, in addition to the expert evidence on this point. We have in this case between 120 and 130 cheques, with Mrs. Merrett's signature on them in some form or another; and the only ones on which the name of the accused appears as drawee are those 29 cheques in question. There is no other case in which his name is entered as drawee. Another thing which is very striking about these cheques is that, except for one trifling exception, the mother uses the cheques strictly in

John Donald Merrett.

numerical order. The forged cheques, on the other hand, come, not only out of order as regards the cheque books that are current, but even if you extract the handful, that handful is not used in the same order until the mother is in the Infirmary, and then the later cheques are used in the same order. I want to deal with this, because it has a very great bearing on this question. Take first the Clydesdale Bank account. There were four cheque books sold. From the first cheque book there are 3 among the forged cheques, No. 2011, No. 2015, and No. 2016. The rest of that book, the other 9 cheques, were used by Mrs. Merrett strictly in their numerical order, and the last of them used by Mrs. Merrett, which was No. 2014, was used on 15th February. The next cheque book was sold on 11th February, and again 3 forged cheques are out of that book. That is the one the counterfoils of which we have recovered, and you will remember that these three counterfoils have disappeared altogether. They have been torn off the missing numbers, namely, Nos. 2329, 2330, and 2340, the first two and the last one in the book. Mrs. Merrett again used her cheques in numerical order, and the last one, which was No. 2330, was used by her on 13th March. Note that date. That is the last cheque used by Mrs. Merrett in the second book. But on 22nd February another book has been got, the third book, and we are not aware of any genuine cheque being used out of that third book by Mrs. Merrett. We have got 6 forged cheques used out of it, Nos. 3602, 3605, 3606, 3607, 3608, and 3609, inclusive. The last one used out of that third cheque book is dated 11th March. And you will remember what I asked you to observe: that the last cheque used by Mrs. Merrett out of the second cheque book was on 13th March; so that was two days before. It seems quite obvious that Mrs. Merrett never knew anything about this third cheque book. She was still using the other cheque book. And then, having finished the cheques left to her in the second cheque book, she wanted another one; and a fourth one is got on 13th March, when the second one was finished. But the fact is that she only needed it because she never knew of the third one and had finished the second one. As to that fourth cheque book, we have no trace of any of the cheques being used, and the book itself has disappeared. As to the amount of the forged cheques in each of those books, in the first one, the 3 cheques there were £13 3s., in the second book the 3 cheques came to £25 10s., and in the third book to £48 11s. 6d.; making the total drawn by means of the forged cheques in under six weeks out of the Clydesdale Bank £87 4s. 6d. That is prior to 17th March. These were all the operations on the Clydesdale Bank. The counterfoil No. 17, which we did recover in this case, was found by Inspector Fleming in the bureau in the sitting-room on 30th March. None of these forged cheques are entered in Mrs. Merrett's account book, either in the case of the Clydesdale Bank balance or of the Midland Bank balance.

Let me turn now to the Midland Bank, where we have only

Addresses to the Jury.

two cheque books to deal with, because they are much larger ones. The first cheque book, which was for 30 cheques, the numbers of which were 73931 to 73960, was sent on 24th December. Mrs. Merrett's last cheque out of that book was 73948, on 4th March. It was on 4th March that Mrs. Merrett asked for her bank book to be made up. On the 5th it was sent off made up, and then there is a letter by Mrs. Merrett on the 12th in which she asks for a new cheque book to be sent, because the old one has been destroyed in moving. In fact, a good many of those cheques out of that old book were used by the accused after that book was said to be destroyed. Now, there was another cheque book, which was sent in reply to that request for a new one on 12th March, and that was 76541 to 76570, and they were used consecutively in order by the accused from the 24th to 27th March, just shortly before Mrs. Merrett's death. They are the last 3 of the forged cheques.

The only suggestion of the defence—it was made by the accused to Detective Fleming—was that Mrs. Merrett gave blank cheques to the accused; and the phrase " customary " was used. Well, that is not impossible. But if they were blank cheques, that was no reason for the counterfoils being torn out. It cannot explain the number of cheques in this case, that 29 out of the 62 cheques drawn on the Clydesdale Bank were actually given in blank by this lady with a fixed income of £700, who was so careful about her expenditure, trying to make it fit her income, especially when you find the amounts that these cheques were being used for. The first 3 Clydesdale forged cheques were on 2nd, 3rd, and 5th February, and the first Midland cheque was on the 8th of February. Up to 17th March the forged cheques used on the Midland Bank amounted to £196 19s. 6d. ; but of that—they had all been cashed at the Clydesdale Bank—£79 1s. was paid in to the credit of Mrs. Merrett's account there, which means that in the case of these Midland cheques there was received, at the Clydesdale Bank £117 18s. 6d. Now, the Clydesdale Bank cheques cashed up to that date amounted to £87 4s. 6d. ; and, if you add it to the sum I have just mentioned, it means that, in less than six weeks, by means of these cheques, a sum of £205 3s. had been secured by the accused.

There were disturbing factors that arose, which suggested possible trouble to the accused, before the 17th of March. You remember he bought this pistol on 13th February, eleven days after the first forged cheque was used—a pistol the primary use of which, however much people may want to suggest sporting purposes, is a totally different one. What about the pass books, because that has a great bearing on the question? First, as to the Clydesdale Bank pass book. If that pass book was made up, and Mrs. Merrett had been looking at it, she would see these cheques, and if they were her own she would not have minded. If they were not her own, undoubtedly there would be trouble. What happened? The Clydesdale Bank book was made up to

245

John Donald Merrett.

The Lord Advocate

13th March, and at that date would have shown a very considerable number of the forged cheques. It was not in the bank's possession after 13th March. Where was it? Who had it? Did Mrs. Merrett see it? That is the book found in the boiler room some weeks afterwards at the Dunedin Palais de Danse, which we know the accused frequented both before and after the occurrence. It is right I should explain that the evidence of the teller was that the 13th was the last time it was in the bank's possession, but it had obviously been taken back on the Tuesday following, the 16th, because the credit then got by means of a forged cheque for £25, a Midland Bank cheque, which squared the £22 overdraft, is entered in the book itself. It must have been taken back for that purpose and taken away again. There is no doubt whatever that that pay-in was made by the accused, and I think you will readily assume that his mother was not anywhere near the bank at the time that was done.

What about the Midland Bank pass book? It had been left at first at Boscombe; Mrs. Merrett wrote for it on 22nd January, and on the 23rd of January it was sent to her. On 21st February Mrs. Merrett sent it back to the bank and asked them to keep it meantime. Then, on 4th March, Mrs. Merrett writes asking for the bank book to be made up to date. You will remember the expression used—"As I have drawn one or two, for me, rather large cheques lately." One or two! There was not only one or two, there were several more that she did not know of at that time. But there were at least two, if not three, genuine cheques of considerable amount which fully corresponded to her description. She drew a cheque to herself for £30, £20 of which she put into the bank, and there was a cheque to Robert Anderson two days before for £25, and a cheque to herself for £20 also two days before, making a total of £75 in three days. That was heavier than her usual withdrawals, and these are admittedly genuine cheques. She writes for her bank book on 4th March, and it is sent off on 5th March. They were then at Palmerston Place, and did not remove until 10th March.

We come next to a most significant item in this history. Did Mrs. Merrett, or did she not, ever see that bank book again? We know of no reason why, if not intercepted, Mrs. Merrett should not have got that bank book either on the Saturday or the Monday following; and yet on the following Friday we find a letter by Mrs. Merrett, dated 12th March, the body of which is in the handwriting of the accused: "Would you kindly send me a new cheque book of 30 cheques, payable to order uncrossed? Owing to our removing, the old cheque book I had was destroyed by accident, so I cannot send the usual form. I wrote and asked for my pass book some few days ago, but as yet I have not received it. Could you kindly forward it to my new address at your earliest convenience, made up to date?" Now, if that letter had gone to the bank there was trouble in the wind for the accused, for the cheques

Addresses to the Jury.

he had been drawing; because it would have meant a reply that the book had been sent off on the 5th, and very possibly a copy of what was the balance of the account. When that account came it would have shown a very great difference in the balance from what Mrs. Merrett thought, according to her account book, she had in the Midland Bank at that time. Therefore it is interesting to find, pushed into the corner of the letter, a postscript which prevents that eventuality occurring; and what you have to ask yourselves is whether Mrs. Merrett ever saw that postscript to her letter. That postscript admittedly is in the accused's handwriting, and it is to this effect : " My pass book has just arrived from my old address, where they have had it some few days. It is quite in order."

Ladies and gentlemen, I submit that that is a most significant letter ; and that was on the Friday before the occurrence on the 17th, namely, on the 12th of March. Now, that book was found, with the envelope and the letter inside it, lying in a drawer in the accused's bedroom by Detective Fleming. It was still in the envelope, and there was no sign of re-direction. And this was the book that was sent off on the 5th of March. It was found in the accused's bedroom. You will remember that Mrs. Sutherland in her evidence refers to having heard on the Saturday Mrs. Merrett talking about a cheque book being lost, and asking the accused to write for another one. But the cheque book was not lost or destroyed, because, in spite of the letter written on the 12th of March containing the statement that it had been destroyed, the accused had used a cheque out of it on 8th March, and he used another on 13th March—out of this book that was lost or destroyed ! And subsequent to the 12th of March he used six cheques out of this very book.

Now, the pass book which was made up to 5th March, if Mrs. Merrett had got it on Saturday, 6th March, or Monday, 8th March, would have shown a balance of £286 as due to her. Mrs. Merrett's account book, with trifling adjustments of error in summation, showed £374 as what she thought she had. The difference in the two sums, £88 15s., is precisely the amount of the forged cheques on the Midland Bank up to that date. Can it be suggested that Mrs. Merrett knew or suspected anything about those cheques? And is it not equally clear that the moment she saw the difference in her credit at the Midland Bank she would be perplexed and alarmed? And bear this in mind, ladies and gentlemen, the debit on the balance on the Clydesdale Bank was really immaterial, because it merely meant another cheque from the Midland Bank. The important thing to her would be what she had at the Midland Bank, because that is where she accumulated her income; and there is a difference of £88 in what she had at the Midland Bank, and £88 is a big slice out of an income of £700. Undoubtedly, that would have alarmed her, and would have led to an inquiry which might have been exceedingly awkward to the accused. I think, therefore, it is clear that he was at any

247

John Donald Merrett.

rate busy taking some steps to prevent that discovery so far as he could.

Come, now, to the next question—the overdraft on the Clydesdale Bank. Here again is a most significant fact, in view of what happened on the 17th of March. There were two letters from the Clydesdale Bank addressed to Mrs. Merrett, intimating that her account was overdrawn. The first one was written on Saturday, 13th March, and, while the accused had been very careful and clever in keeping the Clydesdale Bank account balanced up to that moment, I suspect he did not know of the cheque that had been issued to Robert Anderson, and the result was that he drew too heavily by the forged cheques on the Clydesdale Bank, and an overdraft of £21 11s. occurred. This was intimated on the Saturday by a letter which, in the ordinary course, would have reached Mrs. Merrett either on the Saturday afternoon or the Monday morning at latest. What happened to that letter? I don't know what the suggestion of the defence is. It was found, eventually, arranged with the other letter on the bureau, by Detective Fleming on the 17th, but the evidence is that there was only one letter seen before the occurrence of that morning, and that was the second letter.

What is the suggestion? Is it that the first letter was delayed and did not arrive until the 17th, or is it that the mother had seen the first letter on Monday, the 15th? The second letter was only intimating an overdraft of £6 10s.; but the interesting thing is that in between, on the Tuesday, the debit on the Clydesdale Bank account had been cured by a forged cheque. Therefore, whoever went—and it was the accused—to rectify the balance by means of a forged cheque, knew of the letter intimating the overdraft, and knew that the bank said the account was overdrawn. There was a Midland Bank cheque presented on Tuesday, the 16th, for £30, of which £25 was paid into the account and £5 was taken in cash. That £25 did put the account slightly in credit. I submit that that is a most significant fact—that rectification of this balance, intimated by the letter of the Saturday, by the accused; and I shall have something to say later on as to its effect on any suggestion of any motive on Mrs. Merrett's part for suicide on account of monetary worries. With regard to the second letter, the letter of 16th March was an intimation that the account was overdrawn by a much smaller sum—£6 10s. I do not think there can be much doubt, in view of the evidence, that that letter did arrive in the ordinary course on the morning of the 17th, that it had been opened and was lying on the bureau when Mrs. Sutherland went in the first time. That is her evidence. Whether the mother had seen it and had been, to use his own expression, " quarrelling " the accused about it, is a matter that falls more naturally into the next part of my case, and with his lordship's leave I would suggest adjourning now.

Adjourned.

Seventh Day—Tuesday, 8th February, 1927.

The Lord Advocate's Address to the Jury—continued.

The LORD ADVOCATE—Members of the jury, I had brought you yesterday up to the 17th of March, the day of the tragedy with which we are here concerned, and if you have followed the evidence I have been dealing with, you will realise that when that morning opened the accused had already had two, if not three, alarming warnings in regard to the course of forgery which he was at that time pursuing. He had been alarmed with regard to the Midland Bank book, the one which had been written for, which had come, and with regard to which he had to write at his mother's dictation a letter on 12th March, a week after it had been sent off from Bournemouth, asking why it had not come; and it is in that letter that you find the postscript in the corner, saying that since writing the above the book has turned up. He was also alarmed by his mother missing her cheque book and trying to find it, which also is dealt with in that letter, where it is stated that it was destroyed in the course of moving. And, thirdly, there was the alarming letter from the Clydesdale Bank, written on the Saturday, which certainly arrived on the Monday, intimating an overdraft for the first time on Mrs. Merrett's account of £22. On the Tuesday he had put that right by a forged cheque for £30. of which £25 was paid into the credit of the account. But it is interesting to note that on the Monday, two days before the events we are coming to, he had also cashed a forged Midland cheque for £22 10s. 6d.

So far as Mrs. Merrett is concerned, the evidence is that she was not in any way alarmed, financially or otherwise, up to this stage. The accused's statement was that they had a lady in the previous evening, and that his mother was " all right," normal. Another statement was that after coming to Buckingham Terrace " everything was quite cheerful." What happens on Wednesday, the 17th, to cause this tragedy? We know that the previous day there had been written a second letter from the Clydesdale Bank, intimating a small overdraft of £6 10s., and it seems quite certain that letter did arrive at that flat that morning in due course of post. More than one witness speaks to it; the letter was open, seen on the bureau.

We have the evidence of Mrs. Sutherland; the evidence as to what Mrs. Merrett said in the Infirmary; and evidence as to statements made by the accused. What I wish particularly that you, members of the jury, should fix your attention on in considering this evidence is, first of all, what we hear about what Mrs. Merrett

249

John Donald Merrett.

was doing, and what could possibly have caused her to be so upset that she committed suicide, as suggested—and on that question the shortness of time of the occurrence spoken to by Mrs. Sutherland will be of importance; and, lastly, one of the most vital points in the case: did Mrs. Merrett ever know or hear of this pistol at all? The only evidence—if it be evidence—we have to the effect that she did know is the statement of the accused himself. Mrs. Sutherland did not know anything about the pistol. Did Mrs. Merrett? I shall draw attention to Mrs. Merrett's statements as bearing on that point, as clearly indicating she knew nothing about the pistol; and then intimately connected with that will be the question—not quite clear, I agree, upon the evidence—as to where the pistol was lying when it was found, and what happened to it on the 17th. These are the four points which are of importance in this matter.

Let me take, first of all, Mrs. Sutherland. She arrived at nine o'clock in the morning, and she was twice in the sitting-room before the tragedy happened. The first time she went in was to clear the breakfast table. Mrs. Merrett at that time was standing at the bureau, putting away some things from the breakfast table. The accused was there at that time; he was also there on the second occasion. Mrs. Sutherland goes away, cleans up her dishes, and comes back to do the sitting-room fire, which was not yet lit. She sees Mrs. Merrett busily and quite placidly writing at the table, and the accused is still in the room, in the corner of the recess, with his books. Then Mrs. Sutherland goes back to the kitchen, goes for her ashbucket, goes again to the kitchen, and is in fact in the act of bending down to start her work on the kitchen fire when she hears a shot. Ladies and gentlemen of the jury, I propose to read to you what she says about that, and I will read it as shortly as I can. She said she just got started when she heard the shot. [Reads from Mrs. Sutherland's evidence, pp. 62-64. " I was just making to bend down . . . scattered on the floor."]

I asked her in re-examination, " Q. Was there anything out of the ordinary about Mrs. Merrett at any time? Was she an ordinary healthy woman?—A. Yes, as far as I thought. Q. An active woman?—A. Yes, very active. . . . Q. On the morning of the 17th did she appear her ordinary self?—A. Yes, but she seemed as if she was in a great hurry. Q. As you told us, you said to the accused immediately after the occurrence, ' She seemed quite all right this morning.' That was how it had struck you?—A. Yes." I asked her if she could put an estimate on the lapse of time between the various things she heard. We all know how difficult it is to put a precise estimate, but you can get a rough idea as to the relative periods. " Q. You heard a shot, and a thud, as of a body falling?—A. Yes. Q. How soon after the thud would you hear the books falling in the lobby?—A. It was a few seconds. Q. And how soon after you heard the

Addresses to the Jury.

books falling did the accused appear in the kitchen?—A. Just immediately after. Q. It fitted in with his having dropped the books as he came along?—A. Yes. Q. Were you able to judge whether the accused had come straight to the kitchen as quickly as he could immediately after the thud you heard, or whether there had been some few seconds elapse?—A. Oh, there was a little delay."

The importance of that is this, if the accused was sitting reading in his chair and heard the shot, and came straight to the kitchen to Mrs. Sutherland, I could understand him having a handful of books; but if there is a delay—and his own statement is that he went across to the body and picked up the pistol—how did he come, if it was accident or suicide, to have picked up books in order to go to the kitchen to tell Mrs. Sutherland about what had happened? It seems to me clear that that was part of the arrangements which the accused made after the happening.

Mrs. Sutherland's accuracy is attacked on the ground of an undoubtedly faulty statement which she made to Detective Fleming. I would like to read her answer to that. I will read her answers to the Court. His lordship asked her this—[Reads from Mrs. Sutherland's evidence, p. 76. "I understand it is suggested . . . what I did say."]

Now, this is essentially a matter for you, members of the jury, to judge. You saw Mrs. Sutherland in the witness-box, and it is for you to say whether you believe the story which she has, with that exception and a statement to Dr. Rosa to which I shall refer, told throughout. The variation in her story is the one point. She told Detective Fleming that she heard the shot and moved out of the kitchen, and when in the passage saw Mrs. Merrett tumbling backwards, with the pistol falling out of her hand. Whether that is physically possible, whether she had time to move across the kitchen from the grate, is for you to judge. Then the story told to Dr. Rosa was a different one. It was that she had not left the room; but just as she was going out she heard a shot, turned round, and saw Mrs. Merrett falling, which is quite inconsistent with every other bit of evidence we have in the case. But I wish you to observe this : the statement that Mrs. Sutherland made in the witness-box she made, before she saw Fleming, to Middlemiss, the first person to whom she made any statement. She repeated it to Constables Watt and Gibson on the 21st March, the following Sunday; and when Fleming himself came on 30th March, she gives the story that she says now, while admitting, in a somewhat similar fashion as she has to his lordship, that she was mixed up, and may have given Fleming on the 17th that other story. There is another interesting thing : her story—I mean the story she tells in the box— is confirmed by the accused himself. This is his statement to Betty Christie. " Q. Did he say (that is the accused) what he was doing in the room?—A. Yes, he was sitting reading at the fireside. Q. Had he said where the maid was?—A. He told me

John Donald Merrett.

she had been in the kitchen." And to the witness Scott : " Q. Did he mention the pistol at all ?—A. He said she was shot with the pistol. Q. Did he mention the maid ?—A. Yes, he said he had gone through and told the maid about it. Q. Did he say where he had gone through to ?—A. To the kitchen." Now, that was his statement, made either the same day or within the next two or three days, and that is corroborative exactly of the story which Mrs. Sutherland told to Constable Middlemiss the very first time, and, with the exception of what she said later to Fleming and to Dr. Rosa, it has been adhered to by her on every occasion.

I suggest this to you. The only people in the flat when this occurrence took place were the accused and the maid, who only came in for the day. I think such an occurrence would upset a maid so situated. While she has the accused there, while the policemen are there, and they are all busy helping Mrs. Merrett, she may well have kept her wits about her. But they go off, the accused and the policemen, with Mrs. Merrett in the ambulance, and the maid is left alone in the flat; and it is then that Inspector Fleming comes with his colleague. Surely that is just the time you would expect a reaction—just the time when you would expect Mrs. Sutherland to be somewhat " mixed." It is for you to judge whether the story now told by her is correct.

The next person I have to deal with is Mrs. Merrett. I agree at once that anything Mrs. Merrett may have said must be approached with caution, and you must consider whether it is sufficiently natural, and corroborated by the other circumstances that we know, to be accepted as having been said with full mental consciousness by her. I do not trouble to take you through the evidence that the doctors and nurses, the friends and relatives who saw her, gave in the box—they were all fully convinced that she was quite clear and quite normal, and some of them referred to the kind of things she was talking about as evidence of that.

But then we have the evidence of experts, in particular Professor Robertson, whom you heard yesterday with regard to the possibilities in such cases. I do not think I could do better than remind you of what Professor Robertson said, first, in answer to a question from me, and, secondly, in answer to a question by the Court. I asked him, " You would agree, I suppose, that if corroboration is found to a material extent of what Mrs. Merrett had said otherwise, that it is of value as evidence ?—A. That is so. Q. As I understand you, and if I may say so, I agree with you, what you are doing is throwing out a note of warning that there should be careful consideration of the circumstances in which she made the statement, and the true circumstances as otherwise known, and then to test what she has said ?—A. That is my position." And then in answer to the Court, when his lordship asked the question, " Q. And does your evidence therefore really come to this, that it is necessary to proceed with caution in accepting

252

Addresses to the Jury.

statements made by Mrs. Merrett at such time in respect that they may be accurate or inaccurate?—A. That is so.''

In reference to the illustrations that Dr. Robertson gave, what struck me about them was this, that some of them are quite familiar to many of you; they are cases where a bit is cut out of a man's or a woman's memory by an accident. But that is not the question here. What we are considering is whether the account that Mrs. Merrett gave, up to the time of the pistol shot, was correct or not; and the only case that came near it, and that very remotely, was the case of the cyclist who was in the collision, because he imagined something had happened which did not happen.

If Mrs. Merrett's evidence is not correct, then she has imagined something to have happened which did not happen. But it is for you to judge. This is a matter for a jury. It is quite right to suggest possibilities; but, when you come to consider the statements made by Mrs. Merrett, I submit that there should be no difficulty whatever in accepting them, because she made five different statements, and, while the fifth was a very brief one, they are all consistent, and four of them are practically identical. They are identical, in fact, in the version of the happenings which she gave. The first statement was made to Sister Grant on the Thursday evening about seven o'clock. She was brought to the Infirmary on the Wednesday, and undoubtedly she required rest. There was some talk about an accident, but no statement that really has any bearing on the matter; the doctor put her off to keep her quiet. But on Thursday evening she makes a very important remark to Sister Grant. You will observe that all these statements of hers are her own statements; they are not in any way suggested by questions put to her. It is very important that the statement should be a voluntary one. Now, these statements are vital to the case, because, as I say, one of the most important things is, whether the mother knew anything about the pistol at all. If she did not know about the pistol, then it was neither suicide nor accident, and the pistol was never in that bureau drawer. And, as I shall point out to you later on, if homicide was in fact what happened—if the shot was discharged by the accused, and the lady was sitting writing peacefully this half-finished letter, which had nothing to do with money troubles—then the place and the direction of the shot is exactly the place and direction in which you would expect to find it: that is to say, fired by a person standing behind with a pistol in his right hand, and the lady slightly bending forward, writing her letter.

Let us examine Mrs. Merrett's statements. This is the evidence of Sister Grant : '' We were attending to Mrs. Merrett, making her bed and changing her, and she said, ' What has happened? It is so extraordinary.' She could not understand it—or words to that effect. I said I didn't know what had happened, couldn't she tell me; and she said she was sitting writing at the time, when a bang went off in her head like a pistol ''—not *a* pistol, but *like*

John Donald Merrett.

a pistol. " I said, ' Was there not a pistol there?' and she said, ' No, was there?' in great surprise. And I think it was here she asked me if the X-ray had not shown anything—did the X-ray examination not show anything? And I said I could not tell her that. So I continued then to ask her if she was quite sure she was writing at the time of the accident, and she said, ' Yes, quite sure. Donald can tell you; he was standing beside me, waiting to post the letter.' " This was on the Thursday evening, and it is confirmed by Nurse Innes. Sister Grant reported that to Dr. Halcombe, and he goes in on his evening visit and has a conversation with Mrs. Merrett. I asked him, " Q. Tell us what passed between you?"—that is, between the doctor and Mrs. Merrett. " A. I said, ' Now, Mrs. Merrett, how did this accident happen?' And she said, ' I was sitting down writing letters and my son, Donald, was standing beside me. I said, " Go away, Donald, and don't annoy me," and the next I heard was a kind of explosion, and I don't remember any more.' " Sister Grant was present and corroborates this. " Q. Was that all that was said by Mrs. Merrett that night?—A. No. I said, ' Mrs. Merrett, who were you actually writing to at the time of the accident?' And she said (making a gesture of impatience), ' Oh, I do not know.' " And, of course, you will bear in mind that the " Go away, Donald, don't annoy me," appears in the accused's statement, and that he corroborates it, and there is also no doubt about the writing of the letter. These were the two statements on Thursday, the 18th.

The next day, Friday, the 19th, her oldest friend, Mrs. Hill, arrived, and you get a very striking conversation between her and Mrs. Hill. " Q. Will you please tell us as nearly as you can what passed?—A. She said, ' Why am I here, what has happened to me?' and having been told by the sister that they wished to keep her as quiet as possible and not to allow her to know the extent of her injuries, I said, thinking it did not matter, ' You have had a fall.' But she said, ' My left side is injured.' I said, ' Yes, you have had a fall on this side, and it has injured your leg.' She said, ' No, I have not had a fall. I was writing a letter.' I said, ' To whom?' And she said, ' Mrs. Anderson, and a pistol went off under my ear.' I said to her, ' How could it? Did you see the pistol?' and she said ' No.' Not wishing to excite her any more I gave her something to drink and walked away." You will notice the importance of that statement. It is a consecutive account, as the previous one was, of what had happened up to the time the pistol went off, and, not only that, this one gives the name of the lady she is writing to. " Mrs. Anderson " is correct.

The following week, on Wednesday, the 24th, Mr. and Mrs. Penn having arrived, and about noon, she has a conversation with Mrs. Penn, the main part of which is corroborated by Sister Grant. There is no doubt that on the following evening symptoms of

Addresses to the Jury.

delirium commenced, and she had become actually delirious on the Friday; but this was at midday on the Wednesday. The importance of this statement is that in its essence it is similar to the statement she made on previous occasions, and that it is a vital thing to notice about these five statements. " She first of all asked me if I would look after Sister Grant, would I find her a present, &c., that she had been so good to her. She asked if we would at once go to the flat and look after Donald. She was perfectly clear, and asked us if we would go to a certain church and hear certain music." Surely all that is a person with an active intellectuality at the time, who is thinking about things. " She asked if I would get an ear specialist to her. Q. She said they had said she had had a fall?—A. I understood that. She said she was in doubt about that. She said she was sitting at the table writing, when a sudden explosion went off in her head." Now, that is exactly what she said on the three previous occasions. " She asked me particularly if I would look after Donald for her, mentioning that Edinburgh was a particularly wicked city," &c. I asked her if there was anything more, and she appealed to the judge as to whether she should answer or not, and she was told she must. " Q. You have told us she said, ' I was writing, when a sudden explosion went off in my head.' What I want to know is, if she added anything further to these words, and, if so, what?—A. Yes—' as if Donald had shot me.' " Now, I do not consider these words in any sense as indicating that Mrs. Merrett imagined for a moment that Donald had shot her; she is merely giving an illustration. But the importance is, that it confirms the fact that the shot had come from beside her, and that she was surprised about it. She is sitting there quietly writing when an explosion like a pistol goes off. The last phrase—" as if Donald had shot me "—was not heard by Sister Grant, but the rest was.

Then the final statement is that made to Mr. Penn : " I do remember that Mrs. Merrett was speaking to me about it, and said she heard a deafening noise in her head, and I said, ' That is nothing, that is imagination. You fell down.' Apart from that I heard nothing further from Mrs. Merrett. I could not swear to anything she said." Of course, that is not so material as the other statements, though it is on the same lines; but there are four quite clear statements which I submit are totally inconsistent, in the first place, with any knowledge on her part of the accused having a pistol anywhere about, and, secondly, if that be so, with the possibility of suicide or accident—or of her having handled the pistol at all. Of course, suicide or accident necessarily involves that. She was not stretching her hand up to the bureau. I agree with the possibilities, but I will deal with them later.

I come next to the accused's story. I do not propose to deal at length with this, but there are some points to which I think it

John Donald Merrett.

The Lord Advocate

necessary to draw your attention. He gave versions of what happened to twelve different people, and the first person he gave any version to was Mrs. Sutherland. " Q. Did you say to him " —that is, did Mrs. Sutherland say to the accused—" ' Surely she will come all right? '—A. Before that I said, ' She seemed quite all right this morning—whatever has happened to her? ' " A very natural question to ask. " Q. Did he agree with you?—A. He did not say. He just said he had been wasting her money, and she had quarrelled him about it." Then to Middlemiss he gives an account next, almost immediately after that, and in cross-examination Middlemiss says that he did not give it freely, and he used the phrase, in answer to Middlemiss, that his mother had been troubled with money matters. Izatt, who was the other constable there and who heard the statement, gives a slightly different version. The main statement is the one before which he was cautioned and which he gave to Detective Fleming. You will remember that Mr. and Mrs. Penn, Mr. Jenks, and the accused went back to the flat, and that day, and on some subsequent occasions, were busy trying to reconstruct the scene, and to suggest a possible accident. I do not propose to say anything about the interview in the sister's room between Mrs. Penn, who was evidently very much upset at the time, because she had been told there was no chance of the recovery of her sister. The accused was supposed to have said, " I will confess." Mr. Penn said he regarded that as a childish remark. It is quite evident they were all very much upset, and my own view is that nothing really of value can be got out of that.

But what I wanted to come to at this moment is this : it is true that on the day of the accident, or immediately afterwards, the expressions he used to Miss Betty Christie, and to the witness Scott, did give the alternative of accident; but it is not until after these experiments at the flat had been made in the following week that his statement to everybody else, or to any of the police, suggest that the pistol was in the bureau and that there was an accident. You see it is necessary, in order to support the theory of accident, that the pistol should get in the way of Mrs. Merrett's hand when she is trying to do something else. Nobody suggests that she would willingly handle a pistol, and therefore it has to get into her hand by accident; and as she was sitting writing at the table, it was necessary to get the pistol into the bureau.

The next thing we hear about the pistol was when it was suggested that his mother stopped him going to the Braids to shoot rabbits the previous Saturday. That was the statement to Detective Fleming on 30th March, after they had been evolving these experiments, after this reconstruction of the scene down at the flat ; and you will remember that apparently he had used six cartridges already. He bought fifty, and there were only thirty-eight found in the flat. That leaves twelve. Of these twelve one was the shot that was fired, and other five were in the magazine,

256

Addresses to the Jury.

so that there are other six unaccounted for. His statement to
Fleming was made on 30th March, the first time Fleming saw him.
He told Fleming that his mother allowed him 10s. a week, sometimes extra for outside meals. Not a word about getting other
sums. " I also purchased a motor cycle three weeks ago for
£27. After coming to the flat at 31 Buckingham Terrace everything was in good spirits and getting on all right. When in
Palmerston Place she got on to me for spending too much money.
She also got on to me for going out too much and neglecting my
lessons. This was when we came to Edinburgh first. On the 16th
March, 1926, we had a Miss Macglashan, 7 Ann Street, visiting
us, there just being the three of us. Mother went to bed, I
having retired before her. About 8.30 a.m. on the 17th March I
got up and dressed and had breakfast. Some letters arrived in
the morning, and one was an intimation from the Clydesdale
Bank in George Street to the effect that she had overdrawn her
account." What about the other one, the £22 one, that had been
written the previous Saturday from the bank? There is no
mention of it. " After breakfast I went into my room, which
adjoins the dining-room, and mother got the dishes removed.
When I returned to the dining-room mother was sitting at the
table writing, when I saw an envelope my mother had addressed
to Mrs. Anderson, 64 Murray Place, Edinburgh. I pointed out
the mistake, and she said, ' Go away, you worry me.' " That
exactly confirms what his mother said. " I went to the other side
of the room to get my books, when I heard a report and saw my
mother in the act of falling on to the floor. I rushed over to my
mother and saw the maid in the hall, when I said, ' Mother has
hurt herself.' She fell on the left side, and the revolver was
lying beside her right hand. I telephoned for the police, and
they removed the body to the Royal Infirmary, where she was
detained." I wonder why they did not telephone for a doctor.
" Q. Have you not missed a sentence? Do you not say something
about lifting the pistol?—A. No, I have nothing here. He mentioned to me afterwards that he had lifted the pistol. Q. Please
go on?—A. In the dining-room there is a writing bureau with
three drawers. About noon on Saturday, 13th March, I had the
pistol and loaded it with six cartridges, one being in the breach,
and the safety catch on. I was going to the Braids to shoot
rabbits. I wanted to take it on the Sunday morning, but she
took it from me and put it in the small drawer in the writing
bureau. I think I told my mother to be careful, that it was
loaded. I never again saw the pistol. Q. Did he say something
about lifting the pistol?—A. He said he lifted the pistol off the
floor and put it on to the corner of the bureau. Q. Did he say
at what stage he had done that?—A. Shortly after his mother had
fallen on the floor. Q. Did he say whether he had tried to lift
his mother?—A. He said he had tried to lift his mother, but
could not. Q. Did he say whether that was before or after he

John Donald Merrett.

The Lord Advocate

had seen the maid and the maid had come into the room?—A. Before he had seen the maid.'' This explains the delay. '' Q. Did he say anything about his mother having worries over money? —A. He said his mother had been worrying herself over money matters.' That, of course, is quite inconsistent with the evidence in every respect. Then there is a very striking passage; I confess that it does seem to me that Inspector Fleming was far too much wedded to this theory of suicide, and did not seem to realise what might be the import of the next statement. He cannot have taken it seriously, and I do not know that you should either. This was on a later occasion; he saw him on one or two occasions after the 30th. '' Q. And on one of these occasions did you ask the accused about the pistol and ammunition?—A. I did. I asked him where he got them. Q. And what did he tell you?—A. He told me he had purchased it from Hardy Brothers in Princes Street, along with fifty cartridges. Q. Did he tell you whether his mother had known whether he had the pistol?—A. He did not think his mother knew he had the pistol.'' Now, surely if that were true, it had the most vital bearing on the question of suicide or not. Then, in order to make quite sure, the same question was put in cross-examination by my learned friend. '' Q. At one of your interviews with the accused you asked him some questions regarding the pistol he had?—A. I did. Q. Did not he tell you that his mother had given him the money to purchase it?—A. Not that I can remember. Q. May he have said that?—A. He may have said it. Q. So far as I can see from your note book, you have made no note of any conversation regarding the pistol?—A. No, no note.'' And then in re-examination I put this to him in order to clear the matter up, '' Q. I want to get a little more clearly, if I can, what the accused said to you about the pistol in question. Can you tell us what he said about whether his mother knew of his having the pistol or not?—A. I think he told me he did not think his mother knew about the pistol. Q. Well, did he suggest, or tell you anything to suggest, that his mother in any way provided the money for the pistol?—A. No.''

There is just one statement to another witness that I want to quote, and that is to Mrs. Hill, whose evidence is as follows:— '' I then said, ' But if she did it, what would be her reason for doing such a thing?' and he gave me to understand she was in money difficulties, having that day or quite recently received from her bank information that she had an overdraft of somewhere about £20.'' That was the first letter, the Saturday letter, not the one that arrived at the flat that morning, and that was the one which had been put right by one of the forged cheques on the Tuesday morning by the accused himself.

There are one or two points I want to clear up before dealing with the expert evidence. As to the position of the pistol, I have read you what Mrs. Sutherland says, and the accused's statement to Fleming that he himself lifted it up and put it on the bureau.

Addresses to the Jury.

The Lord Advocate

You remember the two constables who first went to the flat—Middlemiss, the man who picked up the pistol, but who could not say whether he picked it up from the bureau or off the floor; and Izatt, who said he saw Middlemiss bending down to the floor and picking up the pistol. Whether it had found its way back there, or what the true explanation of that is, I do not know; but I think, from the evidence of Mrs. Sutherland and the statement which the accused made to Detective Fleming, that clearly it was, at one time subsequent to the happening, on the corner of the bureau, and on the corner which was not within reach of Mrs. Merrett's hand.

Next is the question of the unfinished letter. It is unfortunate that Detective Fleming did not put that letter in his pocket when he found it, and let us have it produced; but he did read it, and he gives the sense of it. He says, " Mrs. Merrett was writing to some friend in Stirling mentioning the fact that she had got a flat at last, and that she had some trouble in getting a maid, but that she had got a maid who was coming there daily. Q. Was there anything about money troubles in it?—A. Nothing." That letter disappeared. The next time Fleming is in the flat he asks the accused what has become of it; the accused's answer is that it had blood on it, and he had thrown it away.

Then I asked Detective Fleming about the Clydesdale Bank letters, which he had found in the flat. [Reads from Detective Fleming's evidence, p. 88. " Q. On the same occasion . . . on the writing bureau."] It is perfectly obvious that that first Clydesdale Bank letter, with regard to the £22 overdraft, had been seen by the accused before the Tuesday morning, because it is on the Tuesday that the £22 overdraft is put right, to a credit of £5.

With regard to the expert inquiry, doctors and gunmakers, you have the medical evidence, you have the shooting tests, and the question of blackening or tattooing. If Mrs. Merrett never knew about the pistol, this evidence is of no value at all, and the alternative of suicide or accident is excluded. The medical evidence may be put very shortly. There is no doubt as to what was the direction of the shot. It was through the ear, slightly forward, on a line drawn straight between the ears, and slightly upward. There is a question as to whether a person could easily shoot himself suicidally in that way. Nothing is impossible in this world—doctors' evidence always shows that; but what you have got to judge of are all the circumstances, not only the medical possibilities or physical possibilities; and it is perfectly clear on the evidence that if a person did shoot himself that way it is not a usual form of shooting. This lady was in the room with her only child, and, even if she had any motive for committing suicide, is it likely that she would do so in these circumstances—sitting writing quietly a letter to her friend that had nothing to do with money matters, when it is alleged she suddenly leant over to the bureau, took out the pistol, and shot herself

259

John Donald Merrett.

The Lord Advocate

in the presence of her only child? It is possible; all things are possible. But the purpose of having juries is to deal with such matters on reasonable grounds; and the question is whether that is a reasonable possibility.

Further, there is the question of a near, or not a near discharge. What about the shooting tests? Here there really is agreement, except on one point, between the medical and shooting experts on both sides. There is no dispute that the tests in London were carried out with different cartridges and a different weapon. They might have produced identical results; but it is certain that the experiments in London produced results which differ materially from the results of the experiments carried out in Edinburgh by both sides with the actual pistol, with cartridges actually found in the accused's room, and with cartridges bought from the same shop in Princes Street, and supposed to be from the same consignment. I am going to show you the results of both experiments. [Exhibits four cards, two in each hand.] Is that sufficient to convince you that the London experiments differ in some way, either because of the pistol or the ammunition used? Therefore any conclusions drawn from the London experiments are not worth bothering about; you can discard them.

What is the conclusion about the tests in Edinburgh? Professor Littlejohn and Sir Bernard Spilsbury agree that the Edinburgh tests are practically the same. What do they show? The conclusion clearly is that, with what we know as a near discharge—something within 3 or 4 inches of the head—there would be a substantial amount of blackening. And really the issue comes to be whether that blackening might have been washed away before the wound was inspected by the doctors in the Infirmary. As to the possibility of washing the blackening or tattooing from the wound, you are in no difficulty, because, despite the suggested possibilities by Sir Bernard or by the contention of the defence that blood might have covered this wound entirely so as to leave no portion of the surface of the ear free from blood, that cannot weigh against the perfectly specific evidence of Dr. Bell. That very point was put to Dr. Bell by my learned friend. Dr. Bell was the doctor in the casualty ward, the place where they took Mrs. Merrett first to settle which ward she was going into, and Dr. Bell examined her and passed her on to the theatre first and then to ward 3. No washing was done in Dr. Bell's ward. It was simply an examination, before any washing had been done, and he said that he saw no signs of blackening or tattooing, that he actually examined the wound for that purpose, and that there was no smell of any explosive. Therefore he was fully alive to it and was looking for this very thing. [Reads from cross-examination of Dr. Bell, p. 101. " Q. Was it quite plain . . . I could not find any. I looked for it."]

You will remember Sir Bernard, when he was explaining how the blackening would be left, said that he expected to find most

260

Addresses to the Jury.

of the blackening on the upper part of the ear, that is to say, behind the actual shot, and less of it in front. But that is the very place Dr. Bell was examining to see, and the very place he would have found it. So all these theories that somebody wiped it off you can disregard, because there you have the evidence of the man who looks for it and cannot find it. That is confirmed, too, after washing—after the wound has been swabbed by Dr. Halcombe, and also by the nurse that evening at seven o'clock when she dressed it; and therefore you get into a realm of dispute as to whether such blackening can be washed off in that way. Here, again, you are in difficulty, because undoubtedly any experiment ought to be conducted on skin, so as nearly as you can to reproduce the same conditions. But the only washing that Sir Bernard and Mr. Churchill did was in London, on the results of the powder that produced different effects, and therefore that is of no value at all when set against what Professors Littlejohn and Glaister told you was the result of their hard rubbing, namely, that while a good deal of the blackening went, the major portion, Professor Littlejohn said, and a substantial portion, Professor Glaister said, remained. Therefore, if it was there, it must have been seen by Dr. Halcombe and by Nurse Innes. They corroborate Dr. Bell, and therefore this was not a near discharge. Now, while, as we learned yesterday, practically no position in an accident is impossible, you have to consider whether the circumstances in this case render any such alternative reasonably possible.

Before I deal with this matter in conclusion, I will revert for a moment to the second charge, that is to say, what the accused did with regard to the forged cheque after the 17th March. His mother is taken to the Infirmary, unconscious, on the morning of Wednesday, the 17th. There is this letter with the £6 10s. overdraft at the Clydesdale Bank. On Thursday morning, the 18th, one of the forged cheques, a Midland cheque, for £30 is cashed, and £17 of it is paid into the Clydesdale Bank account, which put it in credit again, and £13 is retained as cash in his pocket. The mother cannot have known anything about that. And subsequently five more cheques are drawn and presented, which are paid to him in cash. That is the last payment, £17 into the credit of the Clydesdale account, which was left lying dormant, but cheques were drawn on the Midland Bank and cash taken in turn. Now, he got £13 in cash out of the first cheque, the balance of the £30, and the five later cheques amount to £143 9s. 6d., which added together amounts to £156 9s. 6d., and the last cheque is dated 27th March. If you add that £156 9s. 6d. to the £205 hard cash that he received before the 17th, it comes to £361 9s. 6d. that he got in a period of under eight weeks out of the moneys of a lady who had only £700 a year of income to keep them both. £361 in under two months! We know nothing about what happened to that money, with the exception of a sum of £70 which was paid to account of another racing cycle combination,

John Donald Merrett.

which he had ordered from the Rossleigh Company, the net price of which was going to be some £109, and that order was not given until 22nd March, the beginning of the second week that his mother was in the Infirmary. He ordered it on the Tuesday, and on the Monday he pays £20, on the Wednesday £15, on the Friday, the day his mother is delirious, £20, and on the 27th, the Saturday, £15, making a total of £70. He cashed a cheque on the Saturday for £25, and during the following week he cashed cheques for £30 on Tuesday, Wednesday, and Friday, and on the Saturday, £28 9s. 6d. We know that the mother did sign one cheque while she was in the Infirmary, that was on the 25th of March, the Thursday, the day before she became delirious. That cheque has never been presented, and we do not know anything about it. All we know is that it was given to Mr. Jenks, and we have not been able to get hold of it.

What are the conclusions that you, as reasonable men and women, are to come to in this case? I submit you can come only to one conclusion on both charges, and that is a verdict of guilty. I have tried to put before you as clearly and fairly as I can the issue on the first charge; also on the second charge regarding the uttering of these cheques. I submit there can be no doubt whatever as to your conclusion on that charge, and I ask you for your verdict. The much more important and more vital charge is the first one, and what you have got to ask yourselves is, whether the Crown have established beyond all reasonable doubt that Mrs. Merrett was shot by the accused on the morning of 17th March. If there is reasonable doubt, if there is a reasonable possibility of either suicide or accident, then you must give the accused the benefit of that doubt; but I submit there is none.

There are one or two vital points about the occurrences of 17th March. In the first place, with regard to the question of the two alternatives—murder or suicide—what were the motives? Had Mrs. Merrett any motive sufficient to account for suicide? I submit none that could at all suggest the probability of that. You know what her character was, what her habits were, and whether she ever saw the pistol. As regards the Clydesdale Bank letter which arrived that morning, whether that was what precipitated the occurrence I cannot deliberately submit to you. I think the probabilities are that she did see that letter with the £6 10s. overdraft intimated, because you will remember Mrs. Sutherland's evidence is that the first time she was in the room that letter was lying open with the envelope on the top of the bureau. That suggests that Mrs. Merrett knew what was in it, and she may have been a little worried about it. But was this lady going to commit suicide because she was £6 10s. down on the Clydesdale Bank account which was only her channel of pay? The important account for her was the Midland Bank account.

A startling thing about the occurrences of that morning is the rapidity with which they happened. I have indicated the

Addresses to the Jury.

accused's position on the morning of the 17th—£200 of his mother's money in his pocket, ever getting nearer the risk of discovery and trouble. He had been alarmed by the question of the Midland Bank pass book; he had been alarmed by, but had staved off, the first overdraft of the Clydesdale Bank. He had been alarmed about the loss of the cheque book, but he had managed to get a letter written for another one. And he had—it was found in his possession—the Midland Bank book which had been sent north, made up, on the 5th of March. He had a cheque book of the Midland Bank in his possession with certain cheques missing, and when Detective Fleming asks him as to these missing cheques he knows nothing about them. He had used one of them the day before! There were five missing. He had used three of them—on the 24th, 26th, and 27th. Then a day or two later he tells Fleming, who had asked him to search for them, that he had searched and he had discovered two. The two are blank, not used yet. He did not produce the other three, because he had used them already, and they are the last three of the forged cheques. Did that frighten him from using any more before his mother's death? There was not much time, because she died two days afterwards, on the 1st of April. The fright he gets on the 30th accounts for the cessation of his actings.

To return to the 17th : the mother had no motive for suicide; the circumstances were all against it, sitting quietly writing a letter to her oldest friend with her son in the room. She had seen the letter about the overdraft before that. If there was any trouble in her mind, it was over, and she was placidly sitting writing. She had recovered herself if there had been any trouble; Donald was leaning over her and she says, " Go away, don't worry me "—both she and the accused are agreed about that—and the accused's story is that he went back to the chair. The next thing that Mrs. Merrett knows is a thing like an explosion of a pistol in her ear. I submit it is clear that that is how it happened. She says, " Don't worry me, go away." Donald is standing there with a pistol in his hand, and, whether the fear of detection and the impulse is too much for him or not, he is exactly in the position to inflict the wound which was in fact found in Mrs. Merrett's head.

As to the vital question, which, as I have said more than once, is whether Mrs. Merrett knew of the existence of the pistol. The only person who has ever said she knew was the accused himself. It is for you to say whether any value attaches to that statement. It is his explanation of what had happened. It is perfectly plain that, assuming that he himself had shot his mother, when questioned by the police it was the most obvious thing to say, to account for her using the pistol on herself; and so, on the theory of accident, after they had experimented, you find the suggestion that he had been going to shoot rabbits on the Braids with this pistol, and that his mother had stopped him,

John Donald Merrett.

and had herself put the pistol away in the bureau drawer. It is for you to say whether you can accept that statement.

Then the time is so short. Is it conceivable that Mrs. Merrett would suddenly commit suicide on an impulse, and nothing said; and after the shot a scream, and after the scream a thud, and then some delay until the accused appears in the kitchen? What is happening during that delay? On his own statement, he picks up the pistol and puts it on the corner of the bureau. Did he do that, or did it not go from his hand on to the corner of the bureau, which is the natural thing to happen? Observe, if he is standing behind his mother and shoots her, the corner of the bureau on which the pistol is seen after the event by Mrs. Sutherland is exactly on his right hand! And an important point in this connection is his coming down the passage. Is he running excitedly because his mother has shot herself? No. He has been over to the body, on his own admission. He has been handling the body. He comes down the passage with books in his hand, which must have been picked up from the table in the recess, and he drops them on the way. What is that for? Is that consistent? I suggest that the whole of this was an attempt—a hurried attempt —to try and stage a scene.

Ladies and gentlemen, my submission to you on this first charge is, that when you look at the evidence, and when you look at the facts, it is beyond all reasonable doubt clear that the accused was guilty of the first, as well as the second charge, and I ask your verdict accordingly.

Mr. Aitchison's Address to the Jury.

Mr. AITCHISON—May it please your lordship, members of the jury, since this trial opened a week ago I have shared with my learned colleagues, Mr. Macgregor Mitchell and Mr. Clyde, the anxious and responsible duty of conducting the case for the defence, and it now falls to me to discharge what I confidently believe will be my last duty in this case—the duty of presenting to you the grounds upon which we feel justified—and more than justified— in inviting you to find a verdict for the accused upon both the charges upon which he stands indicted. Members of the jury, there are two charges in this indictment—a charge of murder and a charge of uttering. I shall have something to say upon that topic before I conclude. Meanwhile let me say this: I hold a very strong view indeed that when a man is on trial for his life he ought to be on trial for his life, that no prisoner should ever be put in the position of having to fight a charge of murder with his right hand and a charge of uttering with his left hand. Yet that is the situation in which the accused is now placed. I do not dispute that it was competent for the Crown to place two charges

264

Addresses to the Jury.

Mr Aitchison

in the one indictment, but there are bigger things than competency, and there are bigger things than legality; there is fair play. As I say, I shall have something to say upon that topic before I end.

I propose to take the charges in the order in which they appear in the indictment. For my part, I do not believe in a case of this kind in postponing consideration of the major charge to the later part of one's speech. I shall deal first with the charge of murder. I shall then deal with the charge of uttering. Then I shall come back, in conclusion, to the charge of murder, which is the supreme issue in this case. But before I come to deal with the evidence upon the charge of murder I would like, if I may, to make one or two very brief preliminary observations. They may be familiar to you; I have no doubt they are, but let the gravity of this charge be my excuse for bringing them once more to your recollection. Let me first remind you that it is for the Crown to prove their case. That is an elementary and indeed an axiomatic rule of our criminal law. And it follows, in necessary sequence from it, that wherever there is a doubt regarding any matter either as affecting a particular matter in evidence, or as affecting the general conclusion to be drawn—wherever such a doubt exists, the accused, as we put it, is entitled to the benefit of the doubt. What we call the presumption of innocence is not now, and it never has been, a fiction in the law of Scotland; the presumption of innocence is the cardinal principle of the criminal jurisprudence of Scotland. And it also follows from what I have said to you—I need scarcely remind you of it—that suspicion is not proof, and conjecture is not proof, and probability is not proof. These indeed are elementary propositions, but vital to be remembered in a case such as this. There is one other thing of a preliminary nature I would like to say to you. There is a great tradition in the Criminal Courts of Scotland—a tradition of which we who are engaged in the administration of the criminal law in any capacity are justly proud. It is a tradition that has grown up with the growth and development of our criminal law, a tradition that has come to a rich maturity, and the tradition is this; wherever you are dealing with a question affecting the life or the liberty of a fellow-man, the angle from which you approach that question is not the angle of trying how many points you can get against the prisoner, but rather the angle of trying how many points you can get in his favour. That is the spirit of our justice. It is a great tradition, a splendid tradition of the Criminal Courts in Scotland, and you members of the jury, I am sure, will worthily maintain that tradition to-day.

There is perhaps one further observation I ought to make. This is a stale prosecution. The trial is taking place some ten months after the occurrence of the events which are being investigated, at a time when every circumstance that might have exonerated the accused has been obliterated. I do not hesitate to tell

265

John Donald Merrett.

you that we, who have been responsible during these anxious days
for the conduct of the defence, have felt ourselves very gravely
handicapped by the absence of proper investigation made at the
time by the police who were charged with the duty of inquiry.
It is all very well for the Lord Advocate to come before you and
suggest that if the police had made fuller inquiry at the time they
might have discovered something that would have been conclusive
against the accused. I can tell you that our view for the defence
is a very clear and a very definite view, that if there had been
proper investigation at the time these charges would never have
been brought, and the accused would never have been put on trial.
And when you are dealing, as you are dealing here, with a stale
prosecution there is an imperative duty upon you which I am
certain you will not forget—a very imperative duty indeed—to
see that the utmost fair play is shown to the accused.

Now, members of the jury, I come to the first charge, which
is the charge of murder. I rather demur, if I may say so with
respect, to the way in which the Lord Advocate stated the question which you have to decide upon the first charge. Subject to
what his lordship may tell you, the question which you have to
decide is not whether Mrs. Merrett died from a homicidal wound,
or a suicidal wound, or an accidental wound. It may be—I do
not say that it will be—it may be that at the end of the day you
will be quite unable to affirm with any certainty whether the
wound was homicidal or suicidal or accidental, and I think it is
very important that you should keep that clearly in view, because
some expressions which were used by the Lord Advocate in the
course of his speech rather seemed to indicate that you had to
make up your minds as to which of three possible and conflicting
theories was the true theory. Now, with great respect, that is
not the question which you have to judge at all. The question
which you have to determine is a different question, and the
question is this : have the Crown, by the evidence which has been
put before you during the last seven days, proved that Mrs. Merrett
died of a homicidal wound inflicted by her son ? In other words,
have the Crown proved that the accused murdered his mother ?
And I submit to you—and this being matter of law, you will
follow the direction which his lordship gives you upon it—that
unless you are able to say upon the whole evidence that the Crown
have excluded accident and suicide as hypotheses reasonably consistent with the facts—unless you are able to say that the Crown
have excluded these things—the accused is entitled to your verdict,
and entitled to it, not as a matter of concession or generosity,
but as a matter of legal right, according to the law of Scotland.
Now, as this matter is put with so great clearness and accuracy
in a book of great authority in England, I would like just to
read a single sentence from it. His lordship will tell you whether
it accurately represents the law of Scotland. I am reading from
" Wills on Circumstantial Evidence," edition 6, page 343. What

Addresses to the Jury.

the learned author says is this—" In the proof of criminal homicide the true cause of death must be clearly established; and the possibility of accounting for the event by self-inflicted violence, accident, or natural cause, excluded; and only when it has been proved that no other hypothesis will explain all the conditions of the case can it be safely and justly concluded that it has been caused by intentional injury or criminal negligence." Well, of course, criminal negligence is out of the question here. " Only when it is proved "—that means proved by the Crown—" that no other hypothesis will explain all the conditions of the case can it be safely and justly concluded that it has been caused by intentional injury." Now, subject to what his lordship may tell you, that is the question to which you must apply your minds. Is it proved that the accused murdered his mother? Not can you affirm, was it murder, or suicide, or accident. But is it proved that the accused murdered his mother?

Members of the jury, I am going to ask you to examine with me briefly—because I do not think this is a case in which it is necessary to go into a long, detailed, and minute examination of the evidence; it is a case which you must judge on broad considerations and upon a broad view of the facts—I am going to ask you to consider with me very briefly what are the grounds upon which the Crown invite you to find a verdict of murder against the accused. And I venture to say this to you, that if you take the evidence and analyse it fairly, you will find that your analysis brings you to this and nothing more : the Crown ask you to find the accused guilty of murder. Why? Because he was present in the room at the time his mother received the wound of which she died. Analysed, that is the Crown case, and there is nothing more in it. When I come, as I am coming now, to ask your consideration of the evidence, I think you will agree with me that the Crown case rests there—begins there and ends there.

Now, in dealing with the evidence for the Crown, I propose first of all to take the evidence of Mrs. Sutherland. I will next say something about the statements made by Mrs. Merrett in the Infirmary. I will then ask you to consider whether you can draw any adverse inferences from the conduct of the accused, including the statements made by him. I will ask you to consider the evidence so far as relating to motive; and, lastly, I will ask you to consider the medico-legal aspects of the case. Upon the whole matter I will invite your verdict.

Members of the jury, take first of all the evidence of Mrs. Sutherland, the " help " who was in the house at the time. We have two versions from Mrs. Sutherland. That is an odd feature of this case. It is not confined to the witnesses to fact; when you come to the evidence of Professor Littlejohn you will find two versions there also. Now, we got two versions from Mrs. Sutherland. First of all, we got the version given by her at the time when the facts were fresh in her mind. I should have

John Donald Merrett.

thought, speaking for myself, that the Crown would have attached very great importance to what Mrs. Sutherland said at the time. If Mrs. Sutherland had said at the time, " I saw the accused, Donald Merrett, shoot his mother," and had then gone back on that story, what do you think the Lord Advocate would have said to you? The Lord Advocate would have said to you, " Oh, she has been tampered with. The best evidence is what Mrs. Sutherland said at the time." And the Lord Advocate would have been right. Then, in addition to what she said at the time, we have got her revised version. How she came to revise it nobody knows. She does not pretend to know herself. There has been much controvery in this case as to which is the true version, and in one sense I think that is unfortunate, because it is apt to create a wrong impression in your mind. In one sense, members of the jury, I do not care which you accept as the true version, because either version is favourable to the accused. Let us take first the revised version. The revised version is that upon the morning of 17th March Mrs. Sutherland in the ordinary course of her duty went into the dining-room, and she found Mrs. Merrett seated at a table, writing. She found the accused seated on the other side of the room, reading at a table somewhere near the fire-place. I do not think I need trouble you with plans. Just keep in view that the bureau and the writing-table at which Mrs. Merrett was seated were on one side of the room, and the table at which the accused, Donald Merrett, was seated was on the other side of the room. Now, Mrs. Sutherland sees them there; she goes out and leaves the door open, she hears no quarrel, and the door is never closed; then a shot rings out, and the accused comes through— whether into the lobby or the kitchen does not matter much—he comes through in very great distress. Is not that far more consistent with innocence than with guilt? I would like to know what the Crown theory about it is. Does the Lord Advocate suggest that the accused on the morning of 17th March deliberately shot his mother at a time when there was a maid in the house, at a time when the dining-room door was open, in a room into which the maid could see, and into which at any moment she might enter? That won't do. It won't fit the facts. But you might say, " Well, it may not have been a deliberate act of murder; it may have been an impulsive act of murder." That, I think, must be the Crown view of it. But it is a very dangerous theory for the Crown to say that the accused in a moment of impulse might take the life of his mother; is not it equally probable that his mother in a moment of impulse might take her own life? Impulse is a dangerous theory for the Crown in this case. The accused is bone of her bone and flesh of her flesh; if he could impulsively take her life, could not she impulsively take her own life? But, taking the revised version of Mrs. Sutherland, there is one thing in it that to my mind absolutely clinches the case, on that version, in favour of the accused. Mrs. Sutherland described in her evidence

Addresses to the Jury.

Mr Aitchison

how, having heard the shot ring out and the scream, and the thud of the body falling, she then heard Donald coming towards the kitchen (I am taking the revised version), and, as he came, she heard the noise of falling books. Members of the jury, how does the Lord Advocate explain that away? How can you explain that away? Is not it the strongest possible corroboration of Mrs. Sutherland's evidence that Donald was sitting when she last saw him, or standing on the other side of the room, working with his books? The incident as to the falling books is very strong evidence indeed—evidence that does show that Donald was engaged in his work up to the very moment when the thing occurred. What is the alternative to that? The alternative suggested by the Lord Advocate was that this was some device on the part of the accused to create an impression that he had been working and that he had had nothing to do with the shooting. Well, if that be true, all I have to say is that the accused is a consummate actor. Can you really accept an explanation of that kind for a moment? The Lord Advocate founds upon this, that Mrs. Sutherland said that there was a little delay between the shot and the scream, and Donald's coming from the room. Well, with great respect, I do not think the Lord Advocate is entitled to found upon that. It was put by the Lord Advocate, not in examination-in-chief, but it was put by him in re-examination at the time when I had no opportunity of cross-examining upon it. But, after all, it carries him no distance at all. A second might well seem a minute to Mrs. Sutherland in the circumstances that prevailed at the time. And, therefore, members of the jury, I put it to you—and I put it to you with confidence—that even if you accept Mrs. Sutherland's revised version of what occurred on the morning of the 17th March it is no evidence against the accused. On the contrary, it is evidence that is far more consistent with innocence than with guilt.

But then, fortunately for the ends of justice, there is another version, and that is the version given by Mrs. Sutherland at the time. And if you believe that at the time Mrs. Sutherland said to Inspector Fleming and to Sergeant Henderson, and the same evening to Dr. Rosa, what these witnesses say she said, that is an end of the Crown case. Now, members of the jury, the Lord Advocate has never faced up to this, that Mrs. Sutherland said at the time that, hearing a shot ring out, she ran out and saw Mrs. Merrett falling from the chair and the pistol falling from her hand. If she said that at the time, is the Lord Advocate really going to ask you to find a verdict of murder against the accused? It is fatal to the Crown case. And, if there is even a doubt as to whether she said it at the time or not, it is fatal to the Crown case. I have never heard a more extravagant or a more monstrous proposition than to ask a jury to find a verdict of guilty of murder in a case where the only witness said at the time, " I was an eyewitness, and I saw the weapon falling from the hand of the woman after the shot rang out." Now, that she did say that there is no

269

John Donald Merrett.

question at all. I am not going to read the evidence to you on that matter. You have heard the evidence of Inspector Fleming, the evidence of Detective-Sergeant Henderson, and the evidence of Dr. Rosa. Dr. Rosa is not absolutely clear as to what Mrs. Sutherland did state, but the evidence of Dr. Rosa is entitled to very great weight, and I will tell you why. He was consulted by Mrs. Sutherland on the evening of 17th March regarding some ailment. He remembered what she said, but he did not think much more about it. And then in the month of December Dr. Rosa reads that the accused is arrested on a charge of murder, and he at once says, " Well, that is very odd, after what Mrs. Sutherland told me on the 17th of March," and, being a doctor, Dr. Rosa was unwilling to divulge anything which might have been said to him in his capacity as a doctor. He felt that there was an obligation on him of confidentiality, and he went to his law agents and took the advice of counsel; and he was advised— and I think properly advised—that, in the circumstances, it was his bounden duty to divulge to the advisers of the accused what Mrs. Sutherland said to him on the night of 17th March. I am not going to read Dr. Rosa's evidence. It is quite fair comment for the Crown to make that he did not pretend to recollect with precise accuracy what was said—I wish some of the witnesses for the Crown had been as fair as Dr. Rosa in that matter. But he is perfectly clear on this, that on the night of 17th March Mrs. Sutherland conveyed to his mind the impression that she had just left the room, or was on the point of leaving the room, when a shot rang out, and that she saw Mrs. Merrett falling from her chair to the ground at a time when Donald was seated on the other side of the room. Now, members of the jury, if you accept the view—and I humbly think you must accept the view—that these statements were made by Mrs. Sutherland to Inspector Fleming and Detective-Sergeant Henderson, and to Dr. Rosa, that is an end of the Crown case. For my part I have the greatest difficulty in understanding how the Lord Advocate can come before you in a case of this kind and say, " Fling over Inspector Fleming "— that is in effect what you are asked to do—" fling over an experienced officer of police like Inspector Fleming, fling over Detective-Sergeant Henderson, fling over Dr. Rosa, and accept the revised version which Mrs. Sutherland now gives us."

Now, there is one other matter as to what occurred in that house on the morning of 17th March. We have heard a great deal regarding what the accused said about the pistol. The Lord Advocate said truly that he had given twelve statements; there were certainly twelve interrogations. I do not care very much what may have been said by the accused about the pistol, or what witnesses may have thought he said about the pistol. But I take the evidence of Constable Izatt; and Constable Izatt said this, that he saw Constable Middlemiss lift the pistol from the floor and put it on the bureau. I do not want to give you long passages

270

Addresses to the Jury.

of the evidence, but this is what Constable Izatt said : " Q. A pistol was lying at her side on the floor ?—A. Yes, on the floor. Q. Did you handle the pistol at all—touch it ?—A. No, I never did. Q. Did Middlemiss take it ?—A. Yes, he took it. Q. Did he take it up from the floor, or where ?—A. Well, I believe he did. Q. I want to know what you remember, and not what you believe ?— A. He bent down on the floor and picked it up, as far as I noticed. Q. And not from the top of the bureau against the wall ?—A. No. Q. Are you sure about that ?—A. Oh, yes, I am sure. You see, when I went first I saw him bending down, and he got a piece of paper and rolled up the revolver in a piece of paper and put it in his pocket." Now, members of the jury, how can you get round that ? There, again, it won't do for the Crown to come and say, " But Mrs. Sutherland, or somebody else, says the pistol was lying on the bureau." There you have the evidence of Constable Izatt. And he is not my witness ; he is a Crown witness, called by the Crown to throw light on the case ; and the evidence of Constable Izatt is this, " I saw Constable Middlemiss pick the pistol up from the floor, from beside where the body was lying." And that, of course, is corroboration, and remarkable corroboration, of the statement made by Mrs. Sutherland at the time, that she saw Mrs. Merrett falling to the floor and the pistol falling from her hand. If that be true, I should have expected to find the pistol lying on the floor, and in fact the pistol *was* lying on the floor, because, as I have just read to you, Constable Izatt saw Constable Middlemiss pick it up. Now, members of the jury, that is all I have to say regarding what occurred at the house on the morning of the 17th of March.

Let me come now, as briefly as I can, to the statements alleged to have been made by Mrs. Merrett during the period she was in the Infirmary. Members of the jury, when that evidence was tendered I felt bound to take objection to its admissibility. That objection was overruled, and the evidence is in the case, and, of course, I am bound to take the case with the evidence as it stands. I need scarcely say I loyally accept the ruling which his lordship gave upon that matter ; but although the evidence of these alleged statements was admitted, I am in no way precluded from making comment upon the evidence. Indeed it is my duty to comment upon the evidence, and to ask you to consider what the quality of the evidence is, and what weight you can attach to it. I am not going into it in any detail, for it seems to me that that evidence is open, as regards its quality and weight, to three vital comments. First of all, do not forget that it depends upon the recollection of witnesses ten and a half months after the event. I think that is important. In an English case, in which the question arose as to the weight to be attached to a statement said to have been made after an interval of time, I find that the learned judge who tried that case said this : " Words are transient and fleeting as the

John Donald Merrett.

Mr Aitchison

wind; they are easily misunderstood and easily forgotten "—and I think that is a true comment. The danger of proceeding upon the recollection of witnesses as to statements made in their hearing some ten months before was very well illustrated by a question I put to Dr. Holcombe. According to Dr. Holcombe's recollection, Mrs. Merrett said that Donald had been standing beside her. He was not quite clear whether she meant beside her before the thing happened or when it happened; and I put it to Dr. Holcombe in cross-examination, " Can you be certain that she did not say Donald was standing in the room?" Now, there is a big difference between standing in the room and standing beside her. When I put it to Dr. Holcombe, he admitted it was quite possible she might have said " in the room " and not " beside her." His impression was that the words she used were " beside me," but still he admitted that the words might have been " in the room." Now, that is just one illustration.

Members of the jury, why should an accused person be at the mercy of the recollection of witnesses as to what was said ten and a half months after the words were spoken? But then there is a second comment to make upon that evidence. The words founded upon by the Crown as spoken by Mrs. Merrett were words spoken by her when she was suffering from a very grave condition of shock, when indeed she was dangerously and critically ill. Upon this matter of the reliability of statements made in such conditions, I think you will attach great weight to the evidence of Professor Robertson, which we put before you yesterday. The medical facts are not in any way in dispute. Mrs. Merrett had sustained a severe head injury; she was suffering severely from shock; she was in great pain; she had received, and was receiving, doses of morphia up to the maxima of the British Pharmacopœia; she was paralysed on her left side, there being a hemiplegia resulting from the head wound, and that necessarily indicated a brain injury. And yet in the face of these uncontroverted facts you have Crown doctors who come and tell you that you can take her statements as if they were the statements of a perfectly normal woman. Members of the jury, I do not care in the least what the Crown doctors say in these matters. In these matters a layman is as good as any doctor. Do you think it right, in a case of this gravity, involving an issue of life or death, to place any reliance whatsoever upon the statements made by Mrs. Merrett in the physical and mental condition in which she was? It may be true that Dr. Holcombe, and the nurses and the friends who saw her, regarded her condition as normal, but there might be, as Professor Robertson has told us—and there is no more eminent authority on this matter than Professor Robertson—there might be an apparent normality co-existing with a very real and active abnormality not observable by the ordinary eye—what Dr. Robertson described as a condition of altered consciousness. Now, I cannot help making this observation—the fact that the Crown have relied upon the

Mr. Craigie Aitchison, K.C.

Addresses to the Jury.

statements said to have been made by Mrs. Merrett in the condition of illness in which she was shows that the Crown case is bankrupt of any real substance against the accused. Has justice come to this pass that you as a jury are to convict of murder upon the recollection of witnesses as to the import of statements made by Mrs. Merrett when her mental condition was one bordering on delirium? And yet that is what the Crown ask you to do. You will deal with it.

Before I pass from this aspect of the case I have a further comment to make. I am not sure of the exact date, but you will remember, that when Dr. Holcombe first heard of certain statements having been made, he at once got into communication with the police. He thought, and properly thought, they might be important; and a constable of the police went up to the Infirmary and interviewed Dr. Holcombe, and asked him whether a dying deposition should be taken. And then, having learned that Mrs. Merrett was dangerously ill, that there was a grave risk of a fatal termination to her illness, the officer communicated with the Criminal Investigation Department, and was told not to take a dying deposition, that a superior officer would go up and attend to the matter. A superior officer went up the following day—I think on 20th March—and what happened we do not know; but we do know this, that although the superior officer was again informed by Dr. Holcombe that Mrs. Merrett was critically ill, and that there was a danger of a fatal termination to her illness, no deposition was taken. Members of the jury, I want in this case to speak with moderation, but I am bound to say that the failure to take a dying deposition in this case, in the circumstances which were brought to the knowledge of the Criminal Investigation Department, was in my judgment not only gross neglect on the part of the responsible authority, but almost criminal neglect of an obvious and imperative duty. If a dying deposition had been taken, I suppose the Crown would say it might have implicated the accused. We hold a different view. In the opinion of those of us who are charged with the conduct of the defence in this case, we think, whatever the Crown may, that, if a dying deposition had been taken in the presence of a magistrate, the accused would never have been put on his trial upon either of these charges. Members of the jury, while the evidence as to statements is before you, and while you must anxiously consider that evidence now that it is here, I am quite confident that you will have no hesitation at all in reaching the conclusion that in a case of this gravity you cannot proceed upon evidence of that kind.

Now, before I leave the matter of the statements, I should just like to make one other comment. I think you will agree that in this case there is good ground for thinking that behind some of these statements we have the active and suspicious mind of

T

John Donald Merrett.

Mrs. Penn. I do not want to say anything harsh about Mrs. Penn, and I do not want to say anything unjust about Mrs. Penn. You saw Mrs. Penn in the witness-box, and you will form your own conclusion. It may very well be that Mrs. Penn was greatly upset by the illness and death of her sister; I should be sorry to think it would be otherwise. But, speaking for myself, I cannot say I was impressed by her apparent hesitancy in the witness-box, and her apparent reluctance to answer questions. I do not want to make any harsh comment, but it struck me as play-acting, and bad play-acting at that. And when you come to consider what weight to attach to the statements made by Mrs. Merrett, and what part Mrs. Penn played in these statements, you cannot leave out of account what Professor Robertson told you, and that is that a patient in the condition of Mrs. Merrett is very suggestible —very apt to be receptive of anything hinted or suggested to her. Now, when you consider the part played by Mrs. Penn you will bear in mind the evidence of Dr. Holcombe. This is what Dr. Holcombe says : " Q. Was not she fussing about a great deal?—A. She was very excited. Q. Was not she rather inclined to make suggestions as to how the thing had occurred?—A. She was. Q. And suggestions against the accused as to how it had occurred?— A. She never actually made it against the accused to me. Q. Not in terms?—A. No. Q. Not in terms; but can you say that Mrs. Penn was not pointing the finger at the accused and insinuating that he had something to do with it?—A. I cannot say she was actually insinuating against him. Q. Was she coming pretty near to insinuating that the accused had something to do with it?—A. You could take it that way." Now, that is Dr. Holcombe, and you have the same thing when you come to the evidence of Sister Grant. This is with reference to Mrs. Penn : " Q. Does she very much resent the suggestion of suicide?—A. Yes, she resents the idea of her sister having been in the hospital under a charge of suicide; it upset her. Q. And she prefers some other explanation if she can get it?—A. She never said that to me. Q. Has not she conveyed that impression to you, that, if she can manage it, she will get some other explanation than the explanation of suicide? —A. Not exactly, she hasn't. Q. What do you mean by ' not exactly '? In substance, is not that the case?—A. Well, I think she was rather glad it was supposed to be an accident; she was very satisfied that it was an accident at the time. Q. She welcomes the accident theory?—A. At the time it was cleared up as an accident. Q. What exactly do you mean by the expression that ' at the time it was cleared up as an accident '?—A. At the time of Mrs. Merrett's death or thereabouts; I can remember myself reading in the newspaper it was an accident." Now, you will weigh these two passages I have read to you, and you will consider whether you can exclude the view that what Mrs. Merrett said may not in a real sense have been suggested to her at a time when her mind was not in a condition to resist suggestion.

Addresses to the Jury.

Mr Aitchison

There is another matter to bear in mind. You remember that we were told by Nurse Innes, who also spoke to some kind of conversation, that she had seen in the Infirmary the statement of the evidence which Sister Grant was going to give. Well, I think you must take that fact also into your very careful consideration in determining what weight, if any, you are to attach to the evidence which has been led regarding the statements. Members of the jury, assuming the reliability of the statements, what really do they amount to? Taking the statements at their face value, what do they amount to, assuming them to have been made. Not to any affirmation of guilt, not even to any accusation against the accused. Taking them at their highest—and in saying this I may be putting it unfairly to myself—at the very highest the statements alleged to have been made by Mrs. Merrett amount to no more than the faintest and vaguest suggestion of doubt as to something having happened, and uncertainty as to what that something was. But as Professor Robertson told us that is precisely the condition of mind that might arise in the case of a head wound, whether accidentally or self-inflicted. Now, I think that that is a perfectly fair way in which to state the matter. Again I urge you to hesitate long, in a case of this gravity, before you attach weight to statements made in the circumstances which you have here.

Now let me go briefly to another matter. What about the conduct of the accused? There has been regarding this matter a good deal of suggestion, a good deal of innuendo, a good deal of insinuation. I confess I would much rather things were not insinuated; I would much rather they were said openly. Now, leave out of account for the moment all questions about the cheques and the bank account—I am going to deal with that later. What is the suggestion, I would like to know, that the Lord Advocate makes regarding the conduct of the accused in this matter? I confess I do not know what suggestion he makes. Is the suggestion that the accused's subsequent conduct was callous? Well, if it is, why do the Crown not say so and let us meet it openly and fairly? Is it the suggestion that the accused was dancing while his mother was dying? If that is the suggestion that is made, then I put it to you that there is not a shred or particle of evidence to justify it. Long before I was retained as counsel in this case I knew that the tongue of rumour, and of lying rumour, was busy regarding the accused, and I ask you, who are charged with the responsibility of deciding this case, to put out of your minds once and for all anything you may have heard regarding the accused. It is so tremendously easy to jump to hasty conclusions in a matter of this kind. After all, what are the facts? He was a stranger to Edinburgh. He had only been there a few months. He had practically no friends. Supposing he did go to the Dunedin Palais de Danse, where he had a friend in Miss Christie, why should not he go? In order to test the

John Donald Merrett.

matter aright, you must not test it as you would test it in the case of a person whose real home was in Edinburgh and whose friends were in Edinburgh. Why should not he go? What was wrong in his going? He had not a relative in the world. He had not a guardian in Edinburgh. The flat was empty. Where was he to go? What was more natural than that he should go and see Miss Christie, with whom he was on terms of friendship, and honourable friendship. Test the matter in this way. Think of an Edinburgh lad alone in London, who knows no one but a dancing instructress. Would not it be the most natural thing in the world that he should go to her and in confidence tell her of what had happened? Now, I mention that for this reason, that I think the Lord Advocate—unintentionally it may be—used an expression yesterday in the opening passage of his speech in which he said there was something about the conduct of the accused at the time from which you could draw an adverse inference. What is that something? There is not a scintilla of evidence of any callousness on the part of the accused. The evidence is all the other way. There was an expression used—I think it was in Dr. Holcombe's evidence—that the accused had asked on one occasion whether it was " still on the cards " that his mother would recover. Well, that expression may in a sense seem casual. After all, we are living in an age when every one is more or less casual in expression. It seems to me to be the very expression one would expect to get from a boy who had just come from a public school. And was it any more casual than Dr. Holcombe's reply that she had a " fighting chance "? Members of the jury, it is a small thing, but I have mentioned it because it may have occurred to you that the expression was casual, and that it rather indicated a want of feeling and sensibility. Do not forget that a boy at the age the accused was—and he was only seventeen and a half—is very apt to be ashamed of anything that looks like emotion, and if there is anything in his conduct at all to suggest that he was casual or callous, you will bear that in mind.

Now, may I just, before completing this question as to the conduct of the accused, deal in a word or two with the statements that the accused made? Members of the jury, the Lord Advocate was right when he said that he had made statements to twelve different people, that there had been ample interrogation. I am not concerned in the very least with minor discrepancies in the statements which the accused may have made, especially when we are depending again upon the recollection of witnesses, and I think I am well founded in saying this, that from first to last, from the morning he was interrogated in the house—I am not using the word " interrogated " in any sinister sense—but from the morning of 17th March, when he was asked in the house as to what had happened, right down to the last statement deponed to in this case, he has told, and consistently told, the same story, with one variation only, and it is a variation that points very

Addresses to the Jury.

strongly in favour of innocence. And what is it? You may remember that when one witness, Mrs. Hill, put it to the accused whether it was not possible that some one might have got into the flat and shot his mother, he would not hear of any such suggestion. Is that consistent with innocence or with guilt? Would not a man with a guilty mind have welcomed any suggestion that took suspicion from himself? But the accused would not hear of it. And there was another incident in the case, and it was Mrs. Penn who spoke to it. There was one other incident regarding a statement made by the accused, which seems to me to be tremendously significant, and it is this. I do not know whether you have noticed it, but while the accused first said suicide, he afterwards said accident. It is not unimportant to remember that he had learned that his mother was being detained, or would be detained, in the Infirmary on her recovery in order that she might be handed over to the police on a charge of attempted suicide. There is no doubt whatever that the authorities regarded the case originally as one of attempted suicide, and it seems to me a tremendously strong point in favour of the accused that on the one hand he would not have the idea of the injury having been caused by the act of a third party, and on the other hand, when he became aware that his mother was going to be charged with attempted suicide, although that might have exonerated him, if there was any guilt in his mind, he said this is not attempted suicide, this is accident. You will say whether that is more consistent with innocence or with guilt.

Members of the jury, when I am dealing with statements made by the accused, just a word regarding that remarkable interview in the Infirmary with Mr. and Mrs. Penn. I confess I am not surprised that the Lord Advocate does not lay any weight upon that interview. That was the interview at which Mr. Jenks was present. Who is Mr. Jenks? What is Mr. Jenks? and where is Mr. Jenks? I have a very strong suspicion that, if the Crown in this case had cared to follow up the clue of Mr. Jenks, they might have got something illuminating. I have often seen witnesses astonished in the witness-box. I do not think I ever saw any witness so astonished as Mrs. Penn when she was asked by his lordship who Mr. Jenks was. She was familiar with Mr. Jenks; but it had never dawned on her that anybody would ask her who Mr. Jenks was, and she took a long time to answer. Now it is a thing of significance in this case that two days or three days before the occurrence of 17th March Mrs. Merrett said to Mrs. Sutherland that she had had a hard, hard life, and that her husband had died in the Russian Revolution. Now, that is spoken to by Mrs. Sutherland. Then, I confess, I was mightily astonished when Mrs. Penn, the sister of Mrs. Merrett, is asked regarding Mr. Merrett, she should say he is not dead in Russia, but is alive in India! I should have liked, I confess, to have known something more of the family history, of what Mrs. Merrett

277

John Donald Merrett.

Mr Aitchison

meant by the hard, hard life, of what her worries about money matters were, and whether there was any one concerned with those money matters of whom we have not heard. And we have not seen Mr. Jenks, who might have known something of the family history and have enlightened us in these matters.

Now, members of the jury, let me come to the second charge, and I am taking it as part of the first as bearing upon the question of motive. The second charge is a charge of uttering. I want, if I may, to make it perfectly plain what the second charge is, because, if I may say so, I do not think it has been fully explained to you, and I want you to appreciate two things. I want you to appreciate, first of all, there is no charge of forgery against the accused in this case. Now, please appreciate that. The accused is not charged with having forged the signature of his mother. And the second thing I want you to keep clearly in mind is this, the accused is not charged with having misappropriated a single penny belonging to his mother. What he is charged with is uttering. Now, uttering, if one uses a non-technical term, just means passing. If I have a bad shilling and put it down on a shop counter in payment of some article I buy, I am not guilty of uttering, but if I have a bad shilling, and know that it is bad, and tender it in payment, then I am guilty of uttering. Similarly with a Treasury note, if I put down a forged note, not knowing that it is a forged note, I am not guilty of uttering, but if I put down a Treasury note, knowing that it is a forged note, then I am guilty of uttering. And, therefore—and this is matter of direction on law in which I know you will be guided by what his lordship tells you—it is essential to the crime of uttering that you should have guilty knowledge on the part of the person using the document. Now, remember that the accused is not charged with forgery. The Crown do not say he forged a single one of these disputed documents, nor is he charged with misappropriation. I am bound to say, with great respect, that I think there was misdirection in what the Lord Advocate said to you yesterday. The Lord Advocate was dealing with the 29 cheques. He was pointing out that they were traced, what he called " traced signatures," and then he said, " These two points are sufficient to establish that these are not Mrs. Merrett's signatures, and, as I said to you, it is not necessary to the Crown's case to prove who in fact actually did the tracing, whoever it was." Now, I agree with him up to that point, but then listen to this : " We do not need that in any way, but there can be no doubt that the accused either did it himself, or got somebody else to do it in collaboration with him." That seems to me to be a grave misdirection. Let me paraphrase what the learned Lord Advocate said. He said in effect the accused either committed the forgery himself, or got somebody else to commit the forgery in collaboration with him. With respect to the Lord Advocate, I do not think he is entitled to make any such observa-

Addresses to the Jury.

tion, but that is a matter upon which his lordship will no doubt direct you. The Crown, in my submission, are not entitled to ask you to *assume* that the accused forged these signatures. As I said before, the presumption of innocence is not a fiction in our law; if the Crown thought it necessary to prove that these signatures were forged by the accused they should have libelled it, and they have not done so, because when you go to the indictment you find that the indictment runs, "Such signatures being forged," but it does not say forged by the accused. The Crown cannot say by the accused, because they know perfectly well they have no evidence by which they could prove it. Now, the importance of that matter is just this, if you are not entitled to assume forgery against the accused—and I ask his lordship to direct you in law that you are not—then you cannot say he forged his mother's signature, and therefore knew he was dealing in forged cheques. You cannot say that; because if you say that, you are really assuming against the accused a criminal act with the commission of which he is not charged, and that you are not entitled to do. And, therefore, if you are going to bring home guilty knowledge to the accused, that he was dealing with forged cheques, you must find the guilty knowledge in something apart from the commission of the forgery itself. I think that is of importance, subject again to what his lordship will tell you. You cannot say, "We are unable to think of any one else who can have forged these cheques, and therefore it must have been the accused, and therefore he must have known." Of course, if you can argue in that way, there is an end of the case. But you cannot so argue, because he is not charged with forgery; and, therefore, again I impress upon you that you must find guilty knowledge independently of the commission of the act of forgery, if forgery was committed.

Now, members of the jury, was there forgery here at all? The Crown case for forgery stands upon the evidence of handwriting experts. It is a commonplace in our Courts of law that there is hardly any evidence so unreliable as the evidence of handwriting experts. It is evidence which must be received with the utmost caution, and that is not a partisan view. It is what our judges have said again and again, and said with good reason, that you must receive the evidence of handwriting experts with the utmost caution; and it does not make any difference at all that you are dealing here with what is called a peculiar type of forgery, forgery by tracing, because the imagination of handwriting experts can be just as active in one type of forgery, or alleged forgery, as in any other. I should just like, if I may, to read to you, as part of my speech, what is said by a very learned author in one of the classical works on the law of Scotland, Dickson on "Evidence," vol. i., second edition, sec. 409. Mr. Dickson says, "It is competent in Scotland both in civil and criminal cases to adduce engravers, writing masters, bankers'

John Donald Merrett.

clerks, and other persons whose attention is commonly directed to the examination of handwritings, and who have compared the writing in issue with genuine documents written or signed by the party. But the value of this evidence is very small; for, besides being subject to the same defects as the opinions of persons speaking from previous familiar knowledge, it arises from a forced acquaintance with the handwriting, derived from a few, even from selected specimens; while the examination is made solely with a view to giving evidence in favour of the party to whom the witness looks for remuneration. When one is subject to such biasing influences, his evidence on a matter of opinion deserves but little credit; for even with an honest witness the wish is apt to be father to the thought. This class of witnesses, accordingly, can generally be got to swear on either side of the case, in equal numbers and with equal confidence." And if you turn to Macdonald on " The Criminal Law of Scotland " you will find this passage—" The evidence of professional witnesses as to writings, although competent, is admitted by all the textbooks to be of little value."

Now, what is the evidence of Mr. Gurrin? Mr. Gurrin in his report fastened on the word " coincidence." It is a fine word, and when in cross-examination by Mr. Macgregor Mitchell upon the comparison of two signatures—it would have taken weeks to go through them all—when he is pointed to two signatures, and to fifteen or twenty very distinct dissimilarities in them, what does Mr. Gurrin say? He says, " Oh, that does not matter, you have still got the coincidence." Members of the jury, that won't do. I confess I should have liked to know what Mr. Gurrin's evidence would have been if we of the defence had said to him, " Look here, Mr. Gurrin, apply your mind to these documents and tell us what you find suggesting they are genuine." I should have liked to have seen his report if that question had been addressed to him. Certain questions were addressed to him by the Crown, but that question was singularly omitted. Mr. Gurrin started by saying that some twenty or thirty signatures which he got were genuine signatures. They are called " admittedly genuine "— admitted by whom to be genuine? The Crown have not proved that the signatures, which are the basis of Mr. Gurrin's report, are genuine signatures at all. I do not know whether they are genuine or not. There is no evidence as to whether they are genuine or not. In his report they are called " admittedly genuine." I do not admit they are genuine. The whole basis of Mr. Gurrin's report goes by the board. But as against Mr. Gurrin I would put to you the evidence of Mr. Kerr, the banker, and in this matter one honest banker is worth half a dozen experts. What does Mr. Kerr say about the matter? Mr. Kerr was asked by the Crown to examine these signatures, and Mr. Kerr is a banker of experience. It is quite true that at the close of his evidence, in answer to a question by the Court,

Addresses to the Jury.

" Have you experience of forged cheques ? " he said, " No, my lord." That is why I attach weight to his evidence. People who live in an atmosphere of forged cheques are very apt to find them when they do not exist. What does Mr. Kerr say ? I showed him No. 29. " Q. We are told by experts that that is a forgery. As a banker of experience do you see anything at all about it to suggest forgery ?—A. No." What does the Lord Advocate say about that ? Mind, it is his own witness. The witness says, " No." " Q. Would you look at it under a magnifying glass. [The witness was handed a magnifying glass with which to examine the cheque.] Do you see anything about that alleged forged signature to suggest to you as a banker of experience that it is a forgery ?—A. No. Q. Would you have any hesitation at all in cashing that cheque ?—A. No hesitation." Every cheque with a questioned signature was passed here by a banker, and yet we are asked to take it from Mr. Gurrin, with his binoculars and his microscope, that they are all forgeries. " Q. Is it the case that you have been asked by the Crown "—now listen to this ; I am not going to let the Crown run away from it—" Is it the case you have been asked by the Crown to examine a large number of what are called questioned signatures ?—A. It is the case. Q. Have you been able, after a careful examination of those questioned signatures, to pick out a single one that you as a banker are prepared to say is a forgery ?—A. No."

Members of the jury, in that state of the Crown evidence I submit to you the Lord Advocate is not entitled to say, " I will take Mr. Gurrin and I will leave the other evidence out of account." The other evidence is the evidence of a banker of experience, who says, " I have examined these signatures, and I do not agree. I cannot find any forgery about them at all." Of course, I need not tell you a handwriting expert has no doubt about it. There is nobody in this Court, there is nobody in the Parliament House, who ever knew of a handwriting expert who had doubt about anything ! I have got here a reference to a very celebrated case—the case of Adolf Beck. Adolf Beck was sent away for a long term of penal servitude, not merely on wrong evidence regarding identification, but on wrong evidence of handwriting experts. And do you think they had any doubt about it ? I am reading from Professor Glaister's " Medical Jurisprudence," p. 100—" A handwriting expert, employed by the Treasury to examine certain documents found in Beck's possession and to compare these with written documents given by the offender to the defrauded women, swore that he was ' perfectly satisfied ' that they were all in the self-same handwriting." He was perfectly satisfied ! The jury convicted, and Adolf Beck was sent to penal servitude, and then he received a free pardon for a crime he had not committed. Perfectly satisfied ! Members of the jury, I find it difficult in this case to get out of my mind this fact, that the name of the handwriting expert who led to the conviction of Adolf Beck was Gurrin—not

281

John Donald Merrett.

the present Mr. Gurrin. Out of respect to the present Mr. Gurrin we refrained from asking what relationship he bore to the expert who gave evidence in the case of Adolf Beck. In this case you have Mr. Gurrin on the one hand and Mr. Kerr on the other, and I submit to you that it would be hazardous, in the state of the evidence, to reach the conclusion that the signatures of these cheques are forged signatures. You have heard evidence as to what is called the double signature and the appearance of a line under the signatures, but the Crown did not think it worth while to make any chemical analysis of the ink of the signatures to see how far the solid matter might have separated itself from the fluid matter so as to give the appearance of double signature.

If the signatures are not forged, then that is an end of it. But what if they are forged? That will not entitle the Crown to a conviction of uttering. If you say they are not forged, you need not consider the matter further. But if they are forged, then you must consider are there any facts pointing to guilty knowledge on the part of the accused. In a few words let me tell you what facts inferring guilty knowledge are alleged by the Crown. First, it is said you have a sequence of cheques drawn in favour of the accused, John Donald Merrett. Well, what about it? The Crown do not say the accused misappropriated any money. They have had nearly a year in which to make investigations, with all the machinery of the Criminal Investigation Department at their back, and they have not been able to get any evidence of misappropriation on the part of the accused. I think they found out about the purchase of a ring that cost £2 10s. Well, that does not suggest extravagance to my mind. The next thing they found on is this—they say there is a suspicion arising from the fact that cheques were not drawn in properly numbered sequence, and arising from the fact that a bank book is found in the boiler room of the Dunedin Palais de Danse. Probably we all have cheque books, and if it is going to be evidence of crime that we do not always write our cheques in the proper numerical sequence, I am afraid all of us would be more or less suspect. The evidence regarding bank books and counterfoils is all too vague to justify you drawing any conclusion at all. As regards the bank book being found in the boiler room of the Dunedin Palais de Danse, that seems to me to be in the accused's favour. What is the suggestion the Crown make regarding that? If the accused wanted to get rid of the bank book as evidence, surely he would have put it in the fire. But when you find the boiler room is a step or two down from the passage leading to the cloakroom in the Palais de Danse, surely the natural conclusion is that the book had dropped from his pocket as he went to the cloakroom, and that it had been kicked into the boiler room. The fact that it is left lying about casually favours innocence rather than guilt. Do not forget that the bank book shows that on 16th March money was paid into the bank by the accused. We have the entry, and we

Addresses to the Jury.

know from the pay-in slip it was by the accused, and he would have the bank book with him; and though he put it in his pocket and went on to the dancing hall, what possible inference can you draw from the fact that it was found there? If he were paying in money for his mother, and he *was* paying in, as the bank book shows, what inference can you draw from the fact that he had the book in his possession, and it was found later in a place of amusement to which he was in use to go?

The only other element of suspicion from which you are asked to draw an inference of guilty knowledge relates to a motor cycle. The evidence on that matter strikes me as singularly unconvincing. It is quite true to say that the cheques which the accused paid to the Rossleigh Company were subsequent in date to Mrs. Merrett's going to the Infirmary. I think they began about the 23rd. But, in order to draw any adverse inference against the accused you would need to exclude a great many possibilities which the Crown have not done. You have got to exclude the drawing of cheques in blank for one thing. There was an instance I put to one of the witnesses in the box where he said everything pointed to a cheque having been drawn in blank. But also you would need to exclude this—the possibility that Mrs. Merrett may have arranged with the Rossleigh Company that her son was to get a new cycle for an old second-hand cycle he had. The Crown have not excluded that at all. They have called one man from the Rossleigh Company. They have not called the manager. They have not called any of the numerous other assistants, and they have put the case in the position that you are asked to draw a conclusion that the 22nd March was the first time the motor cycle was ever mentioned to the Rossleigh Company. Well, we do not agree with that, and we say that the Crown are not entitled to draw any such conclusion.

There were some trifling points about cheque counterfoils. You will not attach any importance to where these things were found. I should think it is extremely likely that Mrs. Merrett may sometimes have written in one room, and sometimes in another. That is the substance of the Crown case on this charge, and my submission to you is that it is altogether insufficient.

Now, let me put to you on this part of the case these points for your consideration. We have heard a great deal about Mrs. Merrett being a good business woman, and you are asked to draw this conclusion, that because one book is produced in which it appears she made certain entries the Crown take it for granted that it was the only book she kept—and because you do not find certain other entries in that book, you are to conclude that she had no transactions other than those to which the entries relate. I have here Crown production No. 171. It is a letter which was put in evidence, although its contents were not taken. It is a letter written by Mrs. Merrett from the Waverley Hydropathic, Melrose, to her banker, and it began thus: " Dear Mr. Rooker,

John Donald Merrett.

Mr Aitchison

I think you must feel like giving me up in despair. Many apologies for so stupidly sending my cheque unsigned." Well, that does not strike one as good business, and yet she was made out to be a very good business woman. It is a small incident, but it just illustrates how careful you have to be before you jump to conclusions in a matter of this kind. Even if the case for the Crown were strong upon this matter, a conclusive answer is furnished, or at any rate such an answer as is more than sufficient to turn the scale in favour of the accused, in two letters under the hand of Mrs. Merrett. I refer to the letter of 4th March, 1926 (No. 175 of the productions), and the letter of 12th March, 1926 (No. 176 of the productions). Now, this letter of 4th March is a significant letter. Mrs. Merrett is writing from 35 Palmerston Place, and she writes : "Dear Mr. Rooker, Would you kindly give instructions for my bank book to be made up to date and sent to me here at 35 Palmerston Place. Lately "—now, this is of importance—" lately, I have had to pay out one or two rather, for me, large cheques, and am anxious to know what amount stands to my credit." Now, just consider that. Here is a woman who, according to the Crown, kept such a careful note of everything she did that she knew exactly how her affairs stood. " I have just paid out one or two rather, for me, large cheques, and I am anxious to know what amount stands to my credit at the bank." Why did not she know, if she was the business woman we are told she was? But the real significance of the letter is this. We have got the bank book, and what do we find? We find when you come to the bank book (production No. 11a) that the large cheques drawn out are not cheques drawn payable to her, but cheques drawn payable to the accused. Now, that is tremendously significant. Why is she writing on the 5th of March to her banker saying she has had to draw out one or two large cheques if, as is suggested, she did not know that these were cheques made payable to her son Donald? How can the Crown argue that she did not know that these cheques were being drawn on her account? They cannot say that. It is impossible, having regard to the letter, to say that. But if Mrs. Merrett knew of the cheques, you will see that the whole foundation of the Crown case is destroyed. There is another and more significant letter. There is the letter of 12th March, 1926, and this is a letter signed by Mrs. Merrett, and the letter runs thus : " Would you kindly send me a new bank book," and so on. " I wrote and asked for my pass book some few days ago." Now, remember she wrote from Palmerston Place. This letter is written on 12th March from Buckingham Terrace. " I wrote and asked for my pass book some few days ago, but as yet I have not received it. Would you kindly forward it to my new address at your earliest convenience." Now, we know she had changed her address. We know there was an arrangement under which letters were either to be sent on from Palmerston Place to Buckingham Terrace, or to be called for. It is in evidence, I think, that some

Addresses to the Jury.

letters were called for. Then, listen to the postscript : " My pass book has just arrived from my old address, where they have had it some few days. It is quite in order." Members of the jury, that letter is signed by Mrs. Merrett, and the pass book which had just arrived was the pass book from the Midland Bank which was made up to the 4th or 5th March. If that pass book was in order, and if Mrs. Merrett said it was in order, she gave her approval, and her sanction to the operations on her account right up to the 4th March, and that covers the larger part of the alleged fraudulent operations of the accused upon her account. Well, how does the Lord Advocate get round this? The Lord Advocate gets round it by saying that that statement about the pass book having arrived and being in order is put in in the form of a postscript. Members of the jury, to my mind that is one of the strongest points in favour of the genuineness of the letter. If the letter had not been genuine, do you imagine for a moment that the writer would have put in a postscript? If it had been intended to mislead the bank do you think the writer of the letter would not have put it in the body of the letter? And there is another thing that very strongly suggests it is perfectly genuine, and it is this, the writing of the postscript is at a slightly different angle from the writing in the body of the letter. We had it from Mr. Gurrin, if I may found upon the evidence of a handwriting expert, that you could not draw any inference from the writing of the postscript being at a different angle, because when you examine the specimens of the accused's handwriting you will find he sometimes writes at one angle and sometimes at another. The very fact that it is at a different angle seems to me to be strongly in his favour. If he were adding a postscript after the letter was signed by his mother in order to mislead, I should have thought that he would have taken care to see that the post-script was written in the same way as the body of the letter, and at the same angle, so as not to arouse any suspicion in the mind of the bank. The fact that you find him writing at a different angle is strongly consistent with innocence.

Now, ladies and gentlemen of the jury, that is the case upon the second charge, and I submit to you, with great confidence, that it is not proved. I submit to you that if you analyse the evidence upon the second charge it entirely fails. Of course, if it fails, you are not only bound to acquit the accused of the second charge, but you cannot take it into consideration at all as bearing upon the question of motive in the case of the first charge. That is why I have examined the evidence on this charge at some length. Supposing for a moment I assume that you are against me on charge two, then my submission would be—and I revert now to charge one—that you ought not to draw from that any inference which would justify you in finding the accused guilty of murder under charge one. Uttering may be a serious crime, but it is a long, long way from uttering to murder. And

285

John Donald Merrett.

Mr Aitchison

while the Crown might be entitled to suggest it gave motive, still I put it to you that it would be hazardous in the extreme, even if you were against me upon charge two, to say that because the accused uttered, therefore he committed murder. That is why in opening my address to you I made a protest against the placing of the two charges in one indictment. Such a conjunction is perilous to fair judgment; it is fraught with grave danger to justice when the issue involved is one of life or death.

Members of the jury, there is a matter I must now deal with. I have said nothing so far about the medico-legal aspect of the case, about the evidence of the medical jurists as to the inferences to be drawn from the wound, its site, its direction, and the absence of blackening at the point of entrance. In the state of the evidence I feel convinced that you must very clearly be in my favour on that matter. Professor Littlejohn and Professor Glaister have conceded that, so far as the site of the wound is concerned, and so far as the direction of the wound is concerned, these are consistent alike with suicide and with accident; and on that matter I want nothing better than what was said by Professor Littlejohn in his first report before we come to his revised version. In his post-mortem report, dated 5th April, he says this : " So far as the position of the wound is concerned, the case is consistent with suicide. There is some difficulty in attributing it to accident, although such a view cannot be wholly excluded." Very well, we should be grateful for so much, and I think Professor Glaister in substance really takes the same view. I think you would be impressed by the evidence of Mr. Churchill, whom I called yesterday, the gunmaker from Leicester Square, a man of very large experience, who is often called into Charing Cross Hospital in cases of accident with firearms. You could not but be impressed by the demonstration he gave us of how a person holding the pistol at the right temple might instinctively avert the head at the very moment of pulling the trigger, so as to give you the angle and direction of the wound which you find here without in any way putting the hand into a strained position. I think if you try an experiment for yourselves you will find that if you suddenly avert the head the result is to put the weapon at an angle to the longitudinal line of the head and at the same time you can get the hand back a distance of 3 inches from the head without any movement of the hand at all. On the evidence of Professor Littlejohn and Professor Glaister, 3 inches back is all I need. Now, speaking purely as a layman, I should have thought that there was nothing more likely than the view spoken to by Mr. Churchill of the instinctive aversion of the head. There is a classical instance of the power of instinct—I do not know where I read it; I have tried to find the reference, but am unable to do so. It is told of a man who one night in Paris went down to the Seine to take his life, and at the very moment he was about to plunge in he noticed on the sleeve of his coat a little whitening,

Addresses to the Jury.

or whitish material, from a wall, and before he took the plunge that was to end his life he paused to brush it off. That is a very striking illustration of the power of habit and the power of instinct. Instinct is strong in life, and instinct is strong in death. Instinct is as strong in the suicide as in any other person. With a woman of a highly strung emotional nature, such as Mrs. Merrett was, if, in a moment of impulse she put that pistol to her head, is not it the very likeliest thing that at the moment of pulling the trigger her head would be instinctively averted, so that you would get the wound exactly in the position and with the exact direction that we have in this case?

Then, members of the jury, what about the absence of blackening? It is on this that the medical theory of the Crown is based. It is consistent in their view with a shot fired at a distance of more than 3 inches, and is inconsistent with a shot fired at a distance of 3 inches or less. Now, you have heard the passages from the textbooks which I put to the experts for the Crown upon this matter. They seem to me to be summed up—I am not going to detain you by reading them in detail—but they seem to me to be summed up in the passage from Taylor, which is a book of very great authority, at page 540, where that learned writer says, " The matter may be summed up thus : if there are marks of powder or burning, the weapon was not more than a foot away on firing. If there are no marks, it is impossible to tell how far off it was, for one negative upsets any number of positives in this instance." Now, you will not leave out of account the evidence that the wound had to be washed, and thoroughly washed; that pressure had to be applied to it to remove the coagulated blood ; and that in conveying Mrs. Merrett to the Infirmary the wound might easily be subjected to a certain amount of friction; and it is the evidence of Sir Bernard Spilsbury—of whom I will say just a word or two in a moment—that that friction and the pressure that would be required to remove the coagulated blood from the wound in the ear were sufficient to remove any sign of blackening, or, at any rate, to remove blackening to such an extent that it could not have been detected without very careful examination by means of a hand lens. We know that a hand lens was not used. In this connection I think I am entitled to represent to you what Professor Littlejohn says in his own book at page 120—I always marvel at the way experts forget what they write in their learned treatises. He says this : " With a sponge the blackening of the smoke and any blood would be wiped off." Now, that is simple, and that is our evidence. How can you, in a case of this kind, draw any adverse conclusion against the accused upon so slight a circumstance as that upon which the Crown founds?

I need not remind you that in this case we have had the great and learned assistance of Sir Bernard Spilsbury. I do not dispute that Professor Littlejohn and Professor Glaister are men

287

John Donald Merrett.

Mr Aitchison

of eminence, but I do not hesitate to say that there is no name in Britain, there is no name in Europe, on medico-legal questions, on the same plane as the name of Sir Bernard Spilsbury; and I am certain that you cannot have failed to be impressed by the moderation and restraint and fairness, and by the complete absence of partisanship, displayed by him in the evidence which he gave in the witness-box yesterday. Standing the evidence as it does, I claim that on this, the medical aspect of the case, it is emphatically in my favour.

Members of the jury, I am not going to develop the theory of accident. I content myself with saying this—surely it is a platitude that with firearms accidents occur in the most unexpected ways. I demur entirely to the view put forward by the Lord Advocate that the Crown must succeed unless I prove that the mother of the accused knew about the pistol. It does not seem to me to matter very much whether she knew beforehand or not. Everything points to her knowing beforehand. The firearms certificate had been taken out, and the usual official inquiries had been made. It is in evidence that they had contemplated going a holiday about Easter. I am not going into it in detail. It seems to me to be a relatively unimportant point. Members of the jury, you may say suicide is unlikely. Well, unfortunately, one's experience of human life teaches us that suicide sometimes occurs in the case of people who are least suspected of having any suicidal tendency at all. If suicide is unlikely, is homicide less unlikely? If you come to balance the human probabilities in this case, is it more unlikely that Mrs. Merrett in a moment of impulse should take her own life than it is that her son should take the life of his mother? You must judge of that; but, speaking for myself, it humbly appears to me that the probability of suicide, on the facts of this case as we have them, is nearer the truth, or the probability of accident, on the facts of this case as we have them, is nearer the truth, than the probability of murder.

Now, members of the jury, I am done. You may say to me in conclusion that there are many things you would have liked explained in this case. So be it. I would only say this to you : there are greater things in life than loyalty to one's own life, and there is no greater loyalty in life than loyalty to the memory of one's mother. And why do I say that? I say that because I want you to be on your guard in this case when you come to consider your verdict—I want you to be on your guard against saying, "Why not this, and why not that? We would have liked light on this, we would have liked light on that." Members of the jury, do not forget there are people—and, thank God, there are people—who would rather go to their death with their lips sealed than that they should speak a single word that would reflect upon the name of a mother—a name which is incomparably the greatest name in all the vocabulary of our human life. I leave the case there. Judge with truth and judge with insight.

Addresses to the Jury.

Mr Aitchison

And I beseech you, if you have not got all the explanations you would have liked, do not jump to conclusions. There may be reasons which you do not know and of which you can know nothing. I need not remind you, members of the jury, of what your verdict means to the accused, who has undergone the ordeal of these trying days. Do not forget that he is without the guidance of a father, who should have been his guardian and his mentor as he was passing from boyhood into manhood. You have seen some of his relatives—and his mother is in her grave. But you have got to send him out into life; and I say to you, with the utmost respect, that if you send that lad out into life with a verdict of not proven, with a verdict that implies a stigma on him, upon the evidence that has been led in this case, then I say to you that you take a tremendous responsibility upon your shoulders. Members of the jury, I claim from you with a clear conscience a verdict of not guilty upon both these charges. Give him, by your verdict, a reputation up to which he will have to live for the rest of his life; and I will only say this to you, as one who has been much and intimately in contact with him during these last few days—and it is my final word—send him out from this Court-room this afternoon a free man with a clean bill, and, so far as I can judge, he will never dishonour your verdict.

The Lord Justice-Clerk's Charge to the Jury.

The LORD JUSTICE-CLERK—Ladies and gentlemen of the jury, in this anxious case, whatever its upshot may be, I think you will agree with me that the Lord Advocate has conducted the prosecution with that scrupulous fairness, and even, where the public interest admitted of it, generosity, which accords with the best traditions of the Crown Office. And you will also, I am sure, agree that the defence has been conducted with an adequacy at once undeniable and complete.

Now, the evidence must be fresh in your minds, and the speeches of counsel—eloquent, exhaustive speeches—are still ringing in your ears. If the case were an ordinary one, I should feel absolved from the necessity of a detailed examination of the evidence, or from comment upon it. But the case, as you will long ago have recognised, is by no means an ordinary one; on the contrary, it is quite extraordinary. Just consider for a moment. There are two charges against the accused, a charge of murder and a charge of uttering—charges serious and diverse in their character. As regards the former, the charge of murder, while punishment for other crimes may vary, for that crime, if proved, the law knows but one punishment, and that is death. Again there is the relationship between the accused and his alleged victim—the relationship of mother and son. Cases of alleged

John Donald Merrett.

The Lord Justice-Clerk

matricide are, fortunately, rare in the annals of Scottish crime. Again, there is the comparative youth of the accused, eighteen years or thereby. As regards the second charge, the charge of uttering, that it is a grave charge, having regard both to its inherent quality and also to the amount involved. Now, you will agree with me that the cumulative effect of these considerations is to show that this case is one quite exceptional in its character and in its gravity, and that your responsibility is correspondingly increased. You will therefore bear with me, if I endeavour to help you to the best of my ability in the discharge of your onerous task.

I propose to deal with the charges in the order in which they appear in the indictment. The charge of murder comes first. I do not for a moment forget that the second charge has an intimate bearing upon the first, as the Lord Advocate very properly reminded you, and I shall refer to it from that angle later. On the threshold of the case, one fact strikes my mind, unchallengeable and significant, and that is that the charge of murder brought against the accused is an afterthought on the part of the Crown. Do not misunderstand me. That consideration is by no means conclusive one way or the other. Though the charge is an afterthought, it may none the less be a correct afterthought. But that it is an afterthought appears to me on the evidence to be manifest. At the time of the occurrence which we are investigating, the Crown, after inquiry through its officials, were satisfied that they were dealing with a case of attempted suicide, not a case of homicide. Indeed, it appears that a charge of attempted suicide against Mrs. Merrett was formulated, or, at any rate, contemplated by the Crown authorities, and that, in respect of that charge, she remained under detention in the Royal Infirmary during her illness.

Now, there are certain obvious consequences which follow from the, I was going to say, belated character of the charge, but I will say which follow from the afterthought from which this charge results. Precision regarding (a) the circumstances which surrounded the alleged crime, and (b) the statements of the alleged victim of the crime before her death—absolute precision with regard to these matters is now unattainable. I take two examples which illustrate that proposition. In a case which is deemed from the outset to be one of murder, an exact record of all matters relating to the issue, and in particular relating to the state of affairs at the *locus* of the alleged crime, is always preserved, and is generally beyond question or dispute. Here we do not yet know whether the pistol which did the deed was found, after the tragedy, by the victim's side, or on the bureau in the sitting-room. Mrs. Sutherland says it was on the bureau when she first entered the room after the occurrence. Constable Izatt, who was examined for the Crown, says that he saw the pistol picked up from the floor beside Mrs. Merrett's body by Constable Middlemiss; and

Charge to the Jury.

The Lord Justice-Clerk

Constable Middlemiss, who picked up the pistol, is not certain whether, when he did so, he picked it up from the floor or lifted it from the bureau. He told me, in answer to a question which I put to him, that he included in his report made at the time a statement where the pistol had been found. We have not got that report. The position of the pistol may not be conclusive one way or the other, but none the less it is important, and the state of the evidence regarding it is highly unsatisfactory—I had almost said deplorable.

Then as regards the statements made by the alleged victim, instead of having a deposition sworn before and taken by a magistrate, we are remitted to a series of alleged statements by Mrs. Merrett, made to a variety of persons, under varying conditions, of which no note was taken at the time, and which, even if accepted, are, as we shall see, casual, conflicting, and ambiguous. The result is that precision with regard to vital matters—which is desirable, if not indeed essential, in a murder charge—is here entirely lacking.

There are four possible theories to account for Mrs. Merrett's death : suicide, accident, and homicide, either by the accused, or by an outside person. When I use the word homicide in that connection I mean murder. I quite agree with what Mr. Aitchison said, that the true inquiry to which you have to direct your minds is whether it is proved beyond reasonable doubt that the accused murdered his mother. While that is so, it seems to me that a convenient way of looking at the case is to examine the evidence and see how it stands with regard to these four possible theories. The last of them, homicide by an outsider, may safely and at once be disregarded. The accused himself said to Mrs. Hill that he made no suggestion of that kind. There is no suggestion from any quarter that any person, other than those of whom we have heard in this case, had anything to do with what occurred in that room that morning. Let us then consider the remaining theories. Unless the Crown has excluded, as Mr. Aitchison put it, the hypothesis of accident or suicide as a reasonable explanation—not a possible explanation, but a reasonable explanation—then no doubt the accused would be entitled to your verdict. There are these two competing theories. The case for the Crown is homicide, in other words murder, by the accused. The case for the defence is suicide or accident.

It is trite to say that the onus is upon the Crown to prove beyond reasonable doubt that the hand of the accused fired the fatal shot. Mr. Aitchison asserted that; the Lord Advocate admitted it. According to the law of Scotland every man is presumed to be innocent until he is proved to be guilty. The onus is not upon the defence to prove innocence; the onus is upon the Crown to prove guilt. These are rudimentary topics, and I almost apologise to you for reminding you of them, but in a case of this

John Donald Merrett.

The Lord Justice-Clerk

gravity it is well to have plainly before one's mind the funda-
mental principles upon which the operation of our law is based.
Therefore the question in this case is, has the Crown discharged
the onus which rests upon it of proving the guilt of the accused?
How does the Crown seek to discharge the onus which, by the
admission of the Lord Advocate, rests upon it? So far as I can
see, from four sources which may be conveniently and, I think,
accurately compartmented. I shall explain in a moment what I
mean by the convenient divisions which I propose to adopt.

First, the Crown proposes to discharge that onus by evidence
of what happened at the flat. Secondly, by evidence of what
happened at the Infirmary. Thirdly, by evidence of what happened at the University (I shall explain that in a moment); and
fourthly, by what happened in relation to the statements and
conduct of the accused. The first source is the oral evidence of
those who were at or near the spot at the time. The second is the
statements made by Mrs. Merrett, or alleged to have been made
by her, in the Infirmary before she died. The third is the expert
testimony regarding the appearances presented by the wound, and
the inference to be drawn from these appearances, and the result
of experiments made at Edinburgh University. And the last is
the statements and conduct of the accused.

I shall deal with these theories in the order in which I have
stated them. First, the Crown relies on the oral testimony of
those who were at or near the scene of the alleged crime. There
were only three persons in the flat at 31 Buckingham Terrace on
the morning of 17th March, and one of them has since died. These
three were Mrs. Sutherland, Mrs. Merrett (who made no statement there), and the accused. I turn first to the evidence of Mrs.
Sutherland. She was put in the box by the Crown as the Crown's
first witness. You must inquire whether her testimony advances
or retards the Crown case, or whether, as a possible alternative,
it is merely neutral. She told the Lord Advocate that she was in
the kitchen of the flat when she heard a shot, a scream, a thud, but
saw nothing, and that she remained in the kitchen until the
accused came through and told her of what occurred. But, then,
as you have been reminded, her attitude on that matter has not
always been the same. Have you any doubt that, on the morning
of 17th March, shortly after ten o'clock, Mrs. Sutherland told
Inspector Fleming and Sergeant Henderson that she heard a shot,
went into the lobby, saw Mrs. Merrett fall, and saw a revolver
fall from her hand. Inspector Fleming says so quite distinctly.
Sergeant Henderson, a witness on the Crown list, examined by the
defence, confirms his evidence. Mrs. Sutherland's denial that she
may have said so is so faint as to amount in substance to an
admission that she did. She admits that she may have said so,
but she adds that she was " mixed " at the time. Inspector
Fleming, on the contrary, says that she was not agitated, and

292

Charge to the Jury.

that he saw no reason at the time to doubt the accuracy of the statement which she made to him; and in that he is confirmed by Sergeant Henderson. Remember, ladies and gentlemen of the jury, the quality of the statement attributed to Mrs. Sutherland. It is detailed. It is circumstantial. It comprises three statements of fact: first, that she went into the lobby; secondly, that she saw Mrs. Merrett fall; and thirdly, that she saw the pistol fall from her hand. Assuming some excitement on Mrs. Sutherland's part, you will ask yourselves the question whether she could inadvertently, by reason of agitation, have been betrayed into making these three grave misstatements, as she now calls them. Was any temporary confusion adequate to explain that triple misstatement of fact, as she now describes it? And, in considering this question, you will not forget that she had already, before she saw Henderson and Fleming, made a statement inconsistent with that which she made to them, to Middlemiss. Fleming and Henderson both stated that what Mrs. Sutherland said was volunteered by her, and was not in reply to questions put by them. Moreover, it is noteworthy that, to some extent at least, her statement to them coincides with the statement made by the accused to Fleming on the 30th March: that he saw the maid in the hall. It is true that Mrs. Sutherland withdrew the statement made to Henderson and Fleming in conversation with Constables Gibson and Watt on Sunday, 21st March. It is also true that she adhered to that withdrawal to Fleming on 30th March. What, then, are you to make of it? Can you rely on Mrs. Sutherland's evidence? Again, have you any doubt that, on the evening of 17th March, she made a statement to Dr. Rosa which left on his mind, although he does not profess to be able to give the details, the impression that she was in substance an eye-witness of what happened? If you think that Dr. Rosa is completely mistaken in his view, you are entitled to adopt that attitude, and you will disregard his evidence; but, on the other hand, having regard to the fact that, directly he read of the arrest of the accused, he felt uneasy as to his duty on the matter, took advice, and ultimately made the statement, which he gave us in the witness-box, to the advisers for the defence, you may find it difficult to disregard his evidence as unworthy of credence. It contains some passages—for example, the passage with regard to false teeth—which it is very difficult to believe he either invented or imagined, and yet Mrs. Sutherland denies that she made any such statement to him. If the statements to Fleming, Henderson, and Rosa were in fact made, it is for you to consider whether these statements in themselves may not be destructive of the Crown case. It is for you to say whether these statements, if made, and if true, do not indicate a plain case of suicide, and nothing but suicide. Moreover, you will bear in mind that the statement made to Henderson and Fleming to a certain extent fits in with the statement of Constable Izatt that he saw Middlemiss pick it up from beside Mrs. Merrett's body, and with the evidence which you

293

John Donald Merrett.

have before you to the effect that there was blood upon the weapon. Even if Mrs. Sutherland's later statement be accepted as true, you must consider whether, if it does not retard the Crown case, it advances it in any way. It merely amounts to this : that she saw nothing. You will have to consider, in short, whether her evidence, whichever view you take of it, is either not helpful to the Crown, or disastrous to the Crown.

I feel bound to add at this stage that it appears to me that the police evidence with regard to what they saw and what they did at the flat is loose and hazy in its character. Watt and Gibson, who went there to interview Mrs. Sutherland on 21st March, seem to have thought that they were there to see whether she adhered to the statements which, *inter alios*, she had made to Middlemiss. The position with regard to the pistol, and the position with regard to the letter to which the Lord Advocate referred, but which was not taken possession of by the police at the time, seems to me unsatisfactory, inconclusive, and perfunctory. but that is for you to judge. Therefore, taking leave of this first branch of the case, the question which you have to ask yourselves is—Mrs. Sutherland being the only witness whom you have had examined before you regarding what took place at the flat that morning—whether her evidence advances the Crown case, or retards it, or is neutral, and neither advances nor retards it.

I now pass to the second compartment of the case, namely, the statements alleged to have been made by Mrs. Merrett in the Infirmary. I ruled that these statements were admissible in evidence. But that does not abate my regret that you have not before you a sworn, authentic, and complete statement made by Mrs. Merrett to a responsible officer by way of deposition. To whom were these statements in the Infirmary made? They were made, so far as my recollection goes, to seven persons in all. And I am afraid I must ask you for a moment or two to attend with some care to the precise character of the statements. There is, first of all, Sister Grant. To her a statement was made on Thursday, 18th March, and the statement was to this effect : that Mrs. Merrett was sitting writing at the time of the occurrence, when suddenly a bang went off in her head like a pistol. Sister Grant said, " Was there not a pistol there? " Mrs. Merrett said, " No, was there? " in great surprise. " Donald was standing beside me, waiting to post the letter, I think." Sister Grant added that Mrs. Merrett was quite clear mentally when she made the statement, and that she said substantially the same to Dr. Holcombe. In cross-examination, Sister Grant admitted that an accident to the head may leave a patient without clear recollection of what happened, and that she was not certain whether Mrs. Merrett said, " Donald was beside me " or " was standing in the room." She thinks it was the former, but she did not remember the exact words, and took no note at the time. Well, with regard to that evidence, accepting it for the moment, you will ask your-

Charge to the Jury.

selves how far it carries the Crown in the direction of the estab-
lishment of the charge. Then we have Dr. Holcombe, to whom a
statement was made by Mrs. Merrett on the same evening, Thursday, 18th March. The statement was to this effect. She was
sitting down writing letters. Donald was standing beside her.
She said, " Go away, Donald. Do not annoy me." The next she
heard was a kind of explosion, and she remembered no more. Now,
Dr. Holcombe said to me that Mrs. Merrett at that time was in
full possession of her faculties, and fit to answer his question
which elucidated the statement, namely, " How did it happen ? "
On the other hand, in cross-examination, he said he made no note
of the conversation at the time. He admitted that she may have
said, " Donald was standing in the room," not " standing beside
me," which might make a very considerable difference, you may
think, to the value of the evidence. Dr. Holcombe said he could
not swear which was the form of words used by her. He, like
Sister Grant, admitted that in head injuries the memory
may be a blank with regard to what happened at and before the
time when the injury was inflicted. Again, you will ask yourselves, even assuming the statement to be accurate, how far does
it carry you ? Then there is Nurse Innes. She had an interview
on the Thursday night with Mrs. Merrett. She substantially confirms what Sister Grant said with regard to the conversation which
then took place. In cross-examination, she said, " Donald was
standing beside me " was the statement made by Mrs. Merrett,
but she admitted that she might have been mistaken with regard
to the precise words used. She was, however, almost sure of
them. And she also said, as Mr. Aitchison has to-day reminded
you, that she had discussed with Sister Grant the precise words
used by Mrs. Merrett on that occasion, and saw and read Sister
Grant's statement to the police. She added that Mrs. Merrett
seemed quite clear in her mind from the 17th to the 25th. Then
comes Mrs. Hill. Mrs. Hill saw Mrs. Merrett on the morning of
Friday, 19th March, and said to her, " You have had a fall."
Mrs. Merrett said, " No, I have not had a fall. I was sitting
writing a letter, and a pistol went off under my ear." She did
not see or handle the pistol, so she said. She said there was not
one there. And Mrs. Hill says she was quite clear mentally. In
cross-examination, Mrs. Hill admitted that no note of the conversation was made by her at the time, that she was not certain
of the exact words used ; and she also said, in reply to a question
put by Mr. Aitchison, that Mrs. Merrett never insinuated that her
son shot her, or indeed connected her injury with any one.

Then you come, after an interval of about a week, to the
interviews with Mr. and Mrs. Penn. They saw Mrs. Merrett,
after their arrival in Edinburgh, on Wednesday morning, 24th
March, between ten and eleven o'clock. Mrs. Merrett said to them
that she doubted if she had had a fall, as she had been told, and

295

John Donald Merrett.

substantially made the same statement, "I was sitting at the table writing, when a sudden explosion went off in my head, as if Donald had shot me." Mrs. Penn said, according to her evidence, "That would be impossible." Mrs. Penn added that Mrs. Merrett was clear in mind, but was suffering greatly. A good deal was suggested in cross-examination by Mr. Aitchison, and said to you in his speech, with regard to the animus alleged to exist on the part of Mrs. Penn against the accused. Well, of that you are the judges —whether such an animus existed at all, or whether it is a mere figment of imagination. It is true, on the one hand, that, according to Dr. Holcombe, Mrs. Penn pretty nearly insinuated that Donald had something to do with the tragedy. On the other hand, you will judge whether, on a fair view of the evidence, there is anything proved to you, upon which you can rely, to the effect that Mrs. Penn had any prejudice whatever against the accused. Mr. Aitchison's observations on that matter seem to me to be a little less than just. But of that you are the judges, not I. Mrs. Penn took no note of the conversation at the time, but she said the words used by Mrs. Merrett were burnt in upon her mind, which is not surprising. She also said, in reply to me, that she thought at the time that it was impossible that the accused had anything to do with what happened, and her conduct at the time would seem amply to demonstrate that proposition, for she took him to live with her for two months in the flat at 31 Buckingham Terrace after Mrs. Merrett died. As regards Mr. Penn, there is very little in his evidence which deals with this matter. He heard Mrs. Merrett say, so he thought, that she heard a deafening noise in her head. "Apart from that," says Mr. Penn, "I heard nothing from Mrs. Merrett, and cannot swear to anything else she said." Then, finally, you have Nurse Grant. She was present at the conversation between Mrs. Penn and Mrs. Merrett on Wednesday, 24th March, and her account of it is this: "There was a sound like a pistol or gun shot in my head. Did Donald not do it? He is such a naughty boy." In cross-examination, Nurse Grant said that Mrs. Merrett was suffering a lot of pain at the time; it was the day before delirium supervened. She said that she did not hear Mrs. Penn say to Mrs. Merrett, "That is impossible," or anything like that. She said that Mrs. Merrett did not say, "As if Donald had done it," and added that she would have remembered that if it had been said. Now, it seems to me quite a fair illustration of the hazard of relying implicitly upon exact language deponed to by witnesses after a space of so many months, when you find that with regard to the words, "It is impossible," which Mrs. Penn depones to, Nurse Grant says they were not used, and that the words which Mrs. Penn depones to, "As if Donald had done it," were not used, and, further, that the words used were words not spoken to by Mrs. Penn at all: "Did Donald not do it? He is such a naughty boy." So it would appear that, on one important matter, Nurse Grant does

Charge to the Jury.

The Lord Justice Clerk

not confirm Mrs. Penn, and that on another important matter, Mrs. Penn does not confirm Nurse Grant. You will consider whether the difference between them does not go a little further than that, and whether, so far from not confirming one another, they go the length of contradicting one another.

Let me pause here for a moment and look back on the Infirmary episode. The Crown says that the statements alleged to have been made by Mrs. Merrett in the Infirmary are at any rate inconsistent with the theory of suicide. The Crown further points out that the evidence depicts Mrs. Merrett as a bright, cheerful person, with, to use Mrs. Hill's phrase, " a keen grip on life and all it contains "; and the Crown goes on, very naturally and justifiably, to say that, in these circumstances, no adequate motive for suicide has been suggested. Now, with regard to the statements in the Infirmary being inconsistent with the theory of suicide, I think you will probably, having regard to what I have already said, be disposed to examine these statements with care and to accept them with caution. Professor Robertson, than whom there is no more eminent alienist in Scotland, doubts if these statements or any of them can be relied upon. He thinks it consistent with his view of the case that Mrs. Merrett at the time she made them was in a state of what is known as altered consciousness. He can neither affirm nor deny that, but he suggests it as a reasonable possibility, and his doubt with regard to the reliance which can be placed upon these statements applies with added force to those which were made by her on the eve of delirium, namely, those made to Mrs. Penn and Nurse Grant the day before delirium supervened. Professor Robertson's view is that almost inevitably the attack on the Thursday must have been preceded by certain mental disturbances on the previous day. I am not aware of any evidence of the same quality which can be set against that testimony, but you will judge. Dr. Holcombe, who was asked about this, rather demurred to his competence to deal with it, and said it was more a matter for experts than for him. Professor Littlejohn, if I remember rightly, said he would be disposed to rely upon the testimony of doctors and nurses, who were there at the time, with regard to Mrs. Merrett's mental state. So, ladies and gentlemen of the jury, the questions which I invite you to put to yourselves, before you leave the Infirmary branch of the case, are these : First, were the statements imputed to Mrs. Merrett made by her at all? Second, can you be sure of their complete accuracy as reproduced more than ten months after the event? Third, if made and accurately reported, can they be implicitly relied upon, having regard to her mental condition as conceived by Professor Robertson? And, lastly, accepting them as accurate, and accepting the view that her mental state was such as to render the statements intelligible and reliable, how far do they advance the Crown case, which is one of murder?

And as I have referred to the question of suicide, and the

John Donald Merrett.

The Lord Justice-Clerk

Crown view of it, let me add a word on that topic before I pass
from this stage of the drama. As regards motive for suicide, I am
afraid that you can only speculate. It is true to say that none has
been disclosed in evidence; it is also true to say, I think, but you
will judge, that none of any weight has been suggested in argument.
No doubt Mrs. Merrett said, before the episode of the 17th, to
Mrs. Sutherland that she had had a hard life, but that does not
carry you very far. On the other hand, you will consider, as men
and women of the world, whether motive for suicide is usually
either suspected or disclosed. Does a suicide, in your experience,
or from your reading, broadcast his intention to commit suicide, or
announce to anybody that he proposes to do it? It is said that
the place and the time of the occurrence are not consistent with the
idea of suicide, and there is a good deal of force in that view.
On the other hand, as was suggested by Mr. Aitchison, was it not
an equally unlikely place for homicide? Were the circumstances
not such as to exclude the one theory just as much as the other
theory? My comment, for what it is worth, upon these statements alleged to have been made in the Infirmary, before leaving
them, would be this : so far as I know, but you are the judges, no
one who heard these statements made at the time thought that
they attributed or involved the guilt of the accused. The Crown
certainly did not, otherwise he would have been arrested. If those
statements are of so unequivocal a character as the Lord Advocate
attributed to them, is it not a fair question : why, if they involved one inference and one only, did the Crown stay its hand?
Ask yourselves this : are you being invited to draw an
inference of guilt, from these statements which no one at the
time drew? Consider, further, whether the statements may accurately be described as ambiguous, inconsistent, inconclusive, not
upon oath, not noted at the time, not testified to at the time.
All these vices would have been avoided by a sworn deposition.
I am afraid I do not share Mr. Aitchison's view with regard to
the duty of the police in this matter. I am not disposed to
attribute any censure to the police in respect of their alleged
supineness in taking a deposition from Mrs. Merrett. No suspicion
of crime attached to any one, unless on the part of Mrs. Merrett
herself—I mean the suggestion of attempted suicide—no suspicion
attached to any one present at the time with regard to the
occurrence. It was accepted on all hands that the case was one
of suicide. Now, as far as my experience teaches me, it is only,
generally speaking, in a case surrounded by suspicion of
crime that such a deposition as was desiderated by Mr. Aitchison
is taken. I should have thought that the view of counsel for the
defence would have been, not so much to blame the police for not
taking a deposition, as to affirm that the absence of a deposition
was the best proof of the innocence of his client as regarded by the
police at that particular juncture. But these, ladies and gentlemen of the jury, are matters for you, and I do not for a moment—

298

Charge to the Jury.

The Lord Justice-Clerk

I have no right to—dogmatise regarding them; I merely submit to you, for your final consideration and adjudication, the observations which I have made.

I now proceed to consider the third branch of the case, which relates to experiments made at the University by learned professors and lecturers : the evidence in the case which deals with the appearance of the wound, the experiments made regarding it, and the inferences to be drawn from these experiments. On the one hand, you have Professors Littlejohn and Glaister, both men of great eminence and fairness, and their evidence deserves, and I am sure will receive, your most careful consideration. But in approaching it you must ask yourselves this question : in any attempted reconstruction of a crime is the proceeding not notoriously difficult, and is there not a danger that the conditions as they originally existed may not be accurately and fully reproduced? May some factor which was essential, or may have been essential, not be omitted? But, with that caution in your minds, consider very carefully what Professor Littlejohn, in the first place, said. Professor Littlejohn wrote two reports. In the first report he declined to rule out either accident or suicide as accounting for Mrs. Merrett's death. In his second report he in fact rules out both those theories. He said, in reply to a question which I put to him, that the sole reason for the difference in the conclusion which he reached on these two occasions was the absence of blackening around the wound. His reasoning was this : no blackening, therefore not a near wound, therefore not an accidental or a suicidal wound, therefore a wound inflicted by an outside agency. Such is the logic. I do not think, having regard to what the Lord Advocate said and omitted to say, that you need trouble very much about the direction of the wound, or any inference to be drawn from its direction, as excluding the theory of suicide. Professor Littlejohn in his first report said that, so far as the position of the wound was concerned, it was consistent with both theories, accident or suicide; and in the witness-box he adhered to that view. His statement, made in answer to a question I put, was entirely to the same effect, namely, that he was proceeding upon blackening, not upon direction. Sir Bernard Spilsbury and Mr. Churchill both expressed the view that the direction of the wound is consistent with either theory. The chief objection suggested to the theory of suicide from the direction of the wound, as I recollect it, was that it would involve a constrained position of the arm in firing. Well, you will consider whether that objection was not met or neutralised by the exceptionally simple suggestion which has been made, that a sudden and instinctive aversion of the head by the person who was going to fire the pistol would naturally account for the position of the wound, without any constrained position of the arm. No, ladies and gentlemen of the jury, I think, after Professor Littlejohn's evidence, you must take it that the case for the Crown on this matter depends upon

John Donald Merrett.

the absence of blackening, and in substance on nothing else. Professor Littlejohn admitted that, given a close discharge—say, within 3 inches—suicide or accident would be quite possible; but he thinks they were not possible, because he holds there was not a near discharge, and he reaches that conclusion because there was no blackening. On the question of blackening two subsidiary questions arise. The first is, on the evidence, was blackening there, and, if it was not, is its absence conclusive one way or the other? And the second is, assuming that blackening had originally been present, may it have been rubbed off? On the first question, the textbooks, so far as I followed Mr. Aitchison's questions, indicate that there may be no blackening, and yet you cannot safely infer how far off the pistol was at the moment when the shot was fired. With that view Professor Littlejohn is in disagreement. With that view Sir Bernard Spilsbury agreed. Accordingly, on this matter you have a direct conflict of skilled testimony. You must, however, bear in mind the experiments which were made. Mr. Aitchison cited a passage in Taylor, a well-known volume, in which he says, "If there are no marks, it is impossible to tell how far off it (the pistol) was, for one negative upsets any number of positives in this instance." But then, in the very next paragraph, I find this, "It must be finally reiterated and emphasised that no general rule can be laid down. Experiments must be done with the weapon or with cartridges or loading similar to those which have been alleged to have been used." Now, the experiments were made in this case with the very weapon, with ammunition which admittedly corresponded, if it was not identical, with that which was employed at the time; and these experiments are undoubtedly in favour of the Crown view. Accordingly, on that first question, without disregarding the results of the experiments made in Edinburgh, which are far more important than those made in London, you must very carefully consider whether these experiments, whatever the general rule may be referred to by Taylor in his book, indicate that, in the use of this pistol and this ammunition, blackening is found. But, of course, that is not an end of the matter on the question of blackening. Blackening may, according to one view of the evidence, have been rubbed off. Professor Littlejohn says it may be partly rubbed off but not completely; and therefore he differs profoundly from Sir Bernard Spilsbury—to whose evidence I should imagine you would be disposed to attach the very greatest weight—who says that you could remove substantially all the blackening by rubbing, leaving traces which could only be detected by a lens. It is true that Dr. Bell, Dr. Holcombe, and Nurse Innes saw no blackening. On the other hand, that there was rubbing and washing is indubitable. And you must also ask yourselves this question : whether the suggestion put forward by Sir Bernard Spilsbury, to the effect that it was almost inevitable that, before Mrs. Merrett reached the Infirmary in the ambulance, there must have been wiping of

Charge to the Jury.

that wound, is well founded or is not. Then you have Professor Glaister, of whose evidence I would only say this, that you must remember that in his report he states, in January of this year, that he is unable to exclude the possibility of self-infliction of the wound. And in his evidence he said two things which I noted. One was this : you can never exclude any question as to suicide or accident, so long as you do not know the facts and circumstances. Do you, in this particular instance, know the facts and circumstances, or do you not? And he further referred to the whole matter, at another stage of his evidence, as being problematical.

These are the most important points with regard to the expert evidence on this matter, and you will say whether you find yourselves in a position to accept the testimony with regard to absence of blackening, and with regard to the possibilities of rubbing, which was given you by one set of experts, and to reject that which was given by another set of experts. I do not think that the evidence of Professor Littlejohn and Professor Glaister, on the one hand, and that of Sir Bernard Spilsbury and Mr. Churchill on the other, is susceptible to reconciliation on these vital points. But that is a question upon which you will judge. If they are irreconcilable, Professor Littlejohn was asked, if experts differ, what are we to do? And his reply was, " I don't know." You, ladies and gentlemen, if you think, on a review of the evidence of the two experts on each side, that they differ on vital points, have to decide what you are to do with regard to that matter.

I now come, on this branch of the case, to the last compartment of evidence, which relates to statements by and the conduct of the accused. It appears that he made a series of statements to at least a dozen of people as to how the accident occurred, and you will judge whether in these statements there was any substantial variation. My impression is that there was not. But that is for you to say. There are several statements made by the accused to which attention might be drawn. One may have struck you, which Sister Grant attributed to him, namely, this : " If my mother gets better, don't tell her, as I don't want her to know anything about it." You will judge whether that is not an ambiguous statement. You will judge whether it carries you any way. Then with regard to the statement to Mrs. Penn, " If you like, I will confess," I shall say no more about it, because the Lord Advocate, with great moderation and very properly, invited you to disregard it, as having no substantial bearing upon the issue which you have to try. There was the statement to Mrs. Sutherland, which, she says, was to this effect : that he (the accused) had been wasting her (his mother's) money, and she was worried about it and " quarrelled " him about it. Again, you will consider whether Mrs. Sutherland is to be relied upon in retailing that statement, and also whether it helps to advance the Crown case. There was also a statement made to

John Donald Merrett.

Inspector Fleming, on which the Lord Advocate founded, and which I do not detain you by retailing. You will judge of its value. The Lord Advocate thought that Inspector Fleming should have attached more importance to it than he did. It was a statement with regard to his mother's knowledge of his possession of the pistol. Well, an experienced detective officer apparently attached no importance to the statement at the time, and you will judge how the evidence stands with regard to the matter. It is, I agree with the Lord Advocate, of great importance to reach a safe conclusion on the topic of whether Mrs. Merrett knew or did not know of the existence of the pistol. On the one hand, you will judge whether the evidence disclosed any concealment by the accused of his possession of a pistol. There was the application for a licence for it, which resulted in at least two calls by the police at Palmerston Place, where the Merretts then were, in connection with that application. The accused told both Miss Christie and Mr. Scott that he had a pistol. It is for you to say whether you have any ground upon which you can reach the conclusion that his mother did not know that he had it. Inspector Fleming, who depones to the statement attributed to the accused, admitted that he was not quite certain of what he said. The accused, if you believe the statement he made to the police, definitely affirmed that his mother not only knew that he had a pistol, but took it from him. You will have to review the evidence, and ask yourselves whether the evidence reveals anything which would justify you in reaching the conclusion safely that Mrs. Merrett was in ignorance of the fact which several other people knew, namely, that her son had a pistol.

As regards the conduct of the accused, I am not sure that Mr. Aitchison was justified in saying that the Lord Advocate insinuated that his conduct in connection with the Palais de Danse was callous. Certainly, no such statement was made in his address to you, nor do I think it can safely be inferred from an examination of the witnesses who deponed to the relations of the accused with that place of amusement. You may think that his obligations to his mother should have overborne his obligations to his " pal " at a critical time. That may well be, but we are not here as a Court of morals, we are not here to approve or disapprove of conduct, except in so far as it has a relevant bearing upon the commission of the crime with which we are concerned. And, therefore, you will consider whether anything which the accused did or omitted to do, at what I call a critical moment, can yield any safe inference with regard to the state of his mind in relation to his mother. There are certain points in connection with his conduct to which I feel bound to direct your attention, and which seem to me rather to point in the opposite direction. So far as I recollect the evidence, it is that not only was his mother attached to him, but that he was attached to her. Again, the shot was fired in the flat at a time when Mrs. Sutherland was there. It

302

Charge to the Jury.

might have been fired quite easily in her absence, had any one so desired. It was fired at a time not only when Mrs. Sutherland was there, but when the door of the sitting room was wide open, and any one in the passage, who took a couple of steps from the kitchen to the bathroom door, could see the chair, the table, and the bureau. It is in evidence that the accused was so upset at the time of the incident that he put his head on Mrs. Sutherland's shoulder, and she thought that he was going to cry. Then he made, according to her account, to take her hand, and said, " Let us go out. I cannot stand to look at it any longer." He helped to 'phone for the police. He wired for Mrs. Hill. Was all that acting? Was he, as Mr. Aitchison phrased it, a consummate actor as well as a villain, on the theory of the Crown? He left the pistol lying about. He admitted its possession and ownership, and that the pistol did the deed. He said to Mrs. Hill it was impossible that a third party could have done it. He visited the Infirmary frequently. He kissed his mother there. Was it the kiss of Judas? He stayed in the flat for two months with the Penns. Did Mrs. Penn harbour as her guest during those two months her sister's assassin? These are questions which you must consider with reference to the conduct of the accused, putting to yourselves the inquiry : was that conduct more consistent with that of an innocent than of a guilty person? putting to yourselves the question : is there anything in the statements or in the conduct of the accused which advances to any material extent the Crown case?

Now, reviewing the case so far as I have gone, I invite you to ask yourselves this further question : is the Crown claiming at your hands a verdict of murder against the accused upon evidence which they deemed insufficient even to warrant his arrest upon this charge? Unless I entirely misread the situation—but it is a matter of evidence and you will be the judges—the Crown had the evidence of Mrs. Sutherland, of the nurse and doctors at the Infirmary, of the Penns, and of Mrs. Hill before them in the month of April, and also the various statements attributed to the accused. They had the result of Professor Littlejohn's experiments before them in August, although his formal report was not written until January. Still there was no arrest. The arrest took place, I think, on the 2nd or 3rd of December. It followed upon Mr. Gurrin's report, which was dated in November. Ask yourselves this question : was *that* the new factor which induced the Crown, who had hitherto abstained, on all the other information it possessed, from arresting the accused, to proceed to do so? Did the Crown come to the conclusion that they had now discovered a motive for the crime which had till then been lacking, and which in their judgment warranted a step which they had hitherto abstained from taking? These are matters which you will consider, and on which I offer no opinion at all, but regarding which you are well entitled, and indeed bound, to form an opinion.

John Donald Merrett.

The Lord Justice-Clerk

Let me say two things before I pass, as I naturally do at this stage, to the second charge. The first thing I want to say is this : proof of motive to commit a crime, however important—and it is often supremely important—will not atone for the absence of sufficient evidence to prove the commission of that crime. And the second is this : you must ask yourselves whether the motive suggested is at all commensurate with the crime suggested. In other words, are you to infer that, because of this theory—I am merely putting it as a hypothesis—are you to infer that, upon the theory that the accused had been uttering false documents, and felt certain that the truth would out, and that his mother would come to know of it—is it a safe inference from that to reach the conclusion that he would therefore kill his mother sooner than that she should discover his perfidy? Well, that is a matter of common sense and experience. I merely formulate it as one of the many questions to which you have to find an answer.

Now, let us come to the second charge. You must bear in mind precisely what that charge is. No doubt you have heard a great deal about cheque books, cheques, pay-in slips, bank books, and bank accounts, and it is all enveloped in a certain atmosphere of suspicion. But you, ladies and gentlemen of the jury, must keep your eyes steadily upon the charge which is made. What is it, and what is it not? Mr. Aitchison was quite right when he said that the accused is not charged with forgery; he is charged with uttering. What is uttering? It means feloniously using a forged document, and, when I say feloniously, I mean knowing it to be forged. The accused is charged with having uttered 29 cheques, 12 on the Clydesdale bank and 17 on the Midland Bank, knowing them to be forged. Three questions arise with regard to the second charge, and three only. The first is : has the Crown proved that these 29 cheques were, in point of fact, forged? Secondly, has the Crown proved that the accused presented them for payment? Thirdly, has the Crown proved that, if he did, and if they were forged, the accused knew them to be forged when he presented them for payment? Accordingly, the first question you have to consider, on this branch of the case, is whether the Crown has made out that these cheques, or a substantial number of them, are forgeries. If the Crown case fails on that point, you do not need to consider points 2 and 3 at all. If they are not proved to have been forged cheques, then that is an end to the second charge.

How stands the evidence? You have the evidence of Mr. Gurrin and of Mr. Smith. Now, it won't do simply to jeer at the evidence given by those two gentlemen as being that of experts in handwriting. It is true that the evidence of experts in handwriting, like the evidence of all experts—and two at least have been called for the defence—requires to be carefully examined. But it is treating the matter too lightly—and you cannot so treat it— simply to say, "The evidence of handwriting experts! No

Charge to the Jury.

reliance is to be placed upon it.'' You must go into the matter much more fully than that. The evidence comes from two gentlemen, one of whom in England, and the other of whom in Scotland, has had wide experience in dealing with documents of a questioned character. They both find in these 29 cheques certain features which in their view are inconsistent with the genuineness of these cheques. In the first place, they have detected, or they think they have detected—and it is for you to say whether their evidence is reliable—a very extraordinary feature of those cheques—namely, a double signature—a signature below, upon which is superimposed, not so much by way of writing as, to use the word which both these witnesses employed, by painting, a second signature. It is the sworn testimony of both those gentlemen that they find that feature. You will judge, but it seems to me to be quite an extraordinary feature in every one of the 29 cheques. Are both witnesses suffering from a hallucination in that matter? Are they completely mistaken? When they say they saw two signatures, are you in a position to affirm that they could only have seen one? That is not the only ground upon which they proceed. They proceed further on the marked similarity in the mechanical formation of the letters contained in the signatures alleged to be those of Mrs. Merrett. And in that connection, of course, you will bear in mind Mr. Macgregor Mitchell's skilful cross-examination, and what it elucidated. Ask yourselves whether, while these differences—fifteen or twenty—brought out in cross-examination interfere with the general proposition that, in the mechanical formation of the letters, there is an unusual and suspicious resemblance. The third feature upon which the experts for the Crown found is the contrast between a certain stilted and halting formation of the letters in the cheques in question and the ordinary free and flowing hand which Mrs. Merrett employed in the genuine cheques. For these three reasons both experts are agreed that these cheques are forged. They have given you their reasons. You heard them. You saw the witnesses, men of experience, corroborating one another; and, while you will bear in mind their cross-examination, you will also bear in mind that there has been no counter skilled evidence on this matter adduced by the defence. That is not due to want of ability on the part of the advisers of the defence. Neither, I imagine, is it due to want of resources on the part of the defence to provide that evidence, if it were obtainable. On this matter all the evidence is one way. It is for you to judge whether, because of the undoubtedly skilful character of the forgery—if it be a forgery—the mere fact that a bank clerk was tricked into passing the cheques as genuine has any bearing at all upon the question whether they truly are genuine. For myself I am not disposed to attach so much importance to the second and third features, to which I have alluded, as I am to the first, namely, the double signature. But with regard to that you will judge, not I. Put to yourselves, then, the question whether

x

John Donald Merrett.

these cheques, for one or more of the reasons alleged by the witnesses adduced by the Crown, whose testimony is uncontradicted by any corresponding witness for the defence, in point of fact are not genuine cheques; and whether you are entitled to reach the conclusion that, whoever forged them, they were not signed by Mrs. Merrett.

The second question is whether these cheques were presented to the bank by the accused as genuine. Probably the best evidence of that is his own endorsement upon the cheques. You heard the evidence of the tellers. All those 29 cheques were payable to him, and were endorsed by him. All were honoured by the bank upon that endorsement. Have you any reasonable doubt that the accused presented those cheques for payment? I should think you will have none. And, indeed, I do not understand that any question was raised by the defence that, be the cheques genuine or be they forged, they were presented by the accused for payment and were paid upon his endorsement.

You now come to the third question : did the accused know that these cheques were forged? Direct evidence on a topic such as that is generally, if not always, unavailable. You are investigating the state of a man's mind. The matter is usually one for inference from the surrounding facts and circumstances of the case. The Lord Advocate has founded on a large number of these, which, in his view, plainly involve that the accused knew all about these cheques, and that his course of dealing with them is inconsistent with the view that he thought they were genuine. I merely remind you of the heads upon which the Lord Advocate founded, without going into any details, and what I understood him to represent as facts and circumstances which inevitably, if unexplained, yield only one reasonable conclusion, namely, that the accused cannot be freed from knowledge of the forgery, assuming them to be forged. The accused had an allowance of 10s. a week. So he told the police. You find him purchasing, on the 8th of March, a motor cycle for a sum of £28. There is no evidence that his mother paid for that motor cycle. How was it paid for? There is no trace of it, either in her account book or in the accused's account book. Mr. Aitchison suggested there might be a second account book. That is a mere suggestion, of which there is no evidence. There is no trace in the accused's book of the bookings-out of Miss Christie at 15s. or 30s.; no trace of the cost of the rings which he gave her. Where did the money come from? Again, there is a second motor cycle, a racing cycle, purchased late in March, for which payments to the extent of £70 or thereby were made by the accused to Rossleigh. Again, where did the accused find the £70 with which to make these payments? Further, the 29 cheques said to be forged are the only cheques, out of a hundred or more produced, in which he is the drawee. The 29 cheques are not drawn in sequence, as Mrs. Merrett's cheques generally were. There are counterfoils missing. There

Charge to the Jury.

is mystery attaching to the cheque books. Did Mrs. Merrett use the third Clydesdale Bank cheque book at all? Where is the fourth cheque book? None of the 29 cheques is entered in Mrs. Merrett's account book. As regards the pass books, the Clydesdale Bank pass book was not at the bank after 13th March. Where was it? Did Mrs. Merrett see it? Where was it found? In the boiler house at the Palais de Danse. As regards the Midland Bank pass book, it appears to have been sent from Bournemouth on the 5th of March. Did Mrs. Merrett ever receive it? Who wrote the postscript on the letter of 12th March, and why was it written? It was written by the accused. Why, you will judge. An overdraft was arrested at the Clydesdale Bank. How? By whom? Transactions took place at the Clydesdale Bank long after Mrs. Merrett was in the Infirmary. These are at least some of the facts and circumstances upon which the Crown found in saying that it is impossible to acquit the accused of guilty knowledge, assuming these cheques to have been forged. Ask yourselves whether these incidents do or do not, taken in cumulation, prove that the accused knew all about it. Do they or do they not raise a presumption of guilty knowledge on his part so strong as to demand explanation? It is for you to judge whether any explanation worthy of the name has been tendered with regard to these devious and suggestive dealings. Mr. Aitchison made suggestions about blank cheques. They are only suggestions. What you require—what you probably would desire in this connection—would be not so much speculation as substantive evidence. Mr. Aitchison commented on the Lord Advocate's statement in addressing you yesterday with regard to the forgery by the accused. The statement to which objection was taken was as follows. The Lord Advocate said, "We do not need that in any way, but there can be no doubt that the accused either did it himself or got somebody else to do it in collaboration with him." Mr. Aitchison said, "You are not entitled to assume forgery against the accused." That is perfectly true, but—and this you will take from me, and if I am wrong in the law which I lay down I shall be corrected elsewhere—though you are not entitled to assume forgery against the accused, there is no reason in law why you should not, on evidence which has been accepted without objection, and having regard to the course of dealing revealed by that evidence, reach the conclusion that the accused knew that the cheques were forged, either because he forged them himself, or was privy to it. In short, you may regard any reason which the evidence reveals as proving guilty knowledge on the part of the accused. And I certainly cannot exclude from your consideration that evidence, probably the best evidence, from which a conclusion can be reached, merely because the crime of forgery is not charged in this indictment. You are obviously not entitled to consider the evidence from the point of view of establishing a charge of forgery, which is not made. You are not, however, invited to use the evi-

John Donald Merrett.

dence for that purpose by the Crown, but for quite another, namely, as evidencing the state of his mind. And the state of his mind can be put beyond all doubt if you are satisfied, as you are entitled to be upon the evidence, that the hand that forged the cheques or instigated their forgery was the hand of the accused. So, on this branch of the case, ladies and gentlemen of the jury, you must review the facts and circumstances to which I have referred, and put to yourselves this question : do these facts and circumstances, or do they not, in the absence of any proper explanation, sufficiently establish guilty knowledge on the part of the accused that these were forged cheques? If you think the cheques were forged, that they were presented by the accused, and that he knew they were forged, then it will be your duty to convict the accused upon the second charge.

That, ladies and gentlemen of the jury, is the whole case. The task of counsel, faithfully and adequately performed, is complete. My task, faithfully and, I hope, adequately performed, is also discharged. It is now for you to shoulder your task. The question you have to consider is not whether you suspect, or believe, or think that the accused is guilty of either or both the crimes charged. The only question—I end as I began—the only question is : has the Crown satisfied you beyond all reasonable doubt that the accused committed either or both of these crimes? Mathematical precision in such matters is unattainable ; it is a question of common sense. But, if any reasonable doubt exists in your minds with regard to either charge, the accused, in accordance with our traditions, is entitled to the benefit of that doubt. If you are not satisfied that the Crown has made out its case, then, according to the view which you take of the evidence, you will find the accused not guilty of either or of both charges, or find either or both charges not proven. If, however, you are satisfied that the Crown has proved its case with regard to either or both charges, then, unpleasant though your task may be, I doubt not that, bearing in mind the oath which you have taken, you will faithfully and fearlessly perform it.

The jury retired at twenty-five minutes to five. On returning at half-past five—

The CLERK OF JUSTICIARY—Members of the jury, what is your verdict?

The FOREMAN OF THE JURY—The verdict under the first charge is not proven, by a majority, and under the second charge, uttering, guilty, unanimously.

The verdict having been recorded and read over to the jury—

Lord KINROSS—My lord, I move for sentence on charge two.

Charge to the Jury.

The LORD JUSTICE-CLERK—Have you anything to say, Mr. Aitchison?

Mr. AITCHISON—No, my lord.

The LORD JUSTICE-CLERK—John Donald Merrett, you have been found guilty, by a discriminating verdict of the jury, on the second charge only. The charge is serious in its quality—presenting cheques which the jury hold you knew to be forged. It is also serious in its extent, the amount involved being £457. I have before me a certificate from the Prison Commissioners to the effect that you are unsuitable for Borstal treatment. I have no option, therefore, but to sentence you to a term of imprisonment. In respect of your youth, I shall restrict that sentence to one of twelve months' imprisonment. That is the sentence of the Court.

[*To the members of the jury*]—Ladies and gentlemen of the jury, I am now in a position to discharge you. I desire to thank you for the services which you have given to the State in a very anxious, responsible, and prolonged case. Arrangements will be made with the view of exempting you from further jury service for a term of five years.

The Court then rose.

APPENDICES.

APPENDIX I.

FIRST MEDICAL REPORT BY HARVEY LITTLEJOHN, M.B., PROFESSOR OF FORENSIC MEDICINE IN THE UNIVERSITY OF EDINBURGH.

Edinburgh, 5th April, 1926.

I certify upon soul and conscience that by instructions of the Procurator-Fiscal of the county of Midlothian, on Thursday, 1st April, in the mortuary of the Royal Infirmary, I examined the body of Bertha Milner or Merrett.

The deceased was a well-nourished and apparently healthy woman of about fifty years of age.

There was a perforating wound of the antihelix of the right ear, less than a quarter of an inch in diameter, and behind this a larger wound which passed into the skull immediately posterior to the meatus or external entrance of the ear. These wounds were healthy in appearance.

With these exceptions, there were no recent marks of external violence.

On removing the skull cap, the brain membranes were found to be inflamed and infiltrated with purulent matter. The brain was uninjured, but embedded in the bone of the base of the skull, close to the *Sella turcica*, there was a nickel-plated bullet of small calibre. The direction of the wound, judging by the external wounds and the position of the bullet where found, was horizontal and slightly from behind forwards, the bullet lying about an inch anterior to the external wound.

The various organs of the chest and abdominal cavities were normal and healthy. Both ovaries and the appendix had been removed by operation at some previous time.

I am of opinion that death was due to meningitis, the result of a bullet wound.

There was nothing to indicate the distance at which the discharge of the weapon took place, whether from a few inches or a greater distance. So far as the position of the wound is concerned, the case is consistent with suicide. There is some difficulty in attributing it to accident, although such a view cannot be wholly excluded.

(Sgd.) HARVEY LITTLEJOHN, M.B.

APPENDIX II.

SECOND MEDICAL REPORT BY PROFESSOR LITTLEJOHN.

Edinburgh, 13th January, 1927.

I certify upon soul and conscience that the post-mortem examination made by me on the body of Mrs. Bertha Merrett showed that the bullet had entered the skull through the right ear in a direction from behind forwards at an angle of approximately 120 degs. to a line drawn longitudinally through the middle of the skull. The deceased having survived for fourteen days after the injury, there were no indications at the post-mortem examination of the distance at which the weapon had been discharged, such as injury to the surrounding skin from the action of flame of the discharge or of particles of unconsumed powder driven into the skin, appearances which are present if the discharge has taken place close to the skin, that is to say, within three inches. On this point I made careful inquiry from

John Donald Merrett.

Dr. Holcombe, the house surgeon who examined her and dressed the wound on her arrival at the Infirmary, and he stated that there was only a redness around the wound, and no indication of blackening or tattooing by ingrained particles of powder.

I received the automatic pistol from the Procurator-Fiscal, and with it and similar cartridges to those sold to J. D. Merrett by Mr. Stott, of Hardy's, Princes Street, and which I obtained from Mr. Stott on 6th August, I have made experiments by firing the automatic pistol at a piece of white cardboard.

The automatic pistol is marked " King. Made in Spain." Its total length is $4\frac{1}{4}$ inches. The distance from the trigger to the butt is $2\frac{1}{8}$ inches, and the muzzle projects $1\frac{1}{4}$ inches beyond the finger placed on the trigger. Considerable force or pull on the trigger is required to discharge the weapon. I found this pull to be about 6 lbs. The cartridges which I obtained from Mr. Stott are " Eley Smokeless Cartridges " .25. The bullet is nickel capped and weighs 3.27 grammes (about 50 grains).

Experiment I.—The discharge at a distance of half an inch from the object caused intense blackening around the bullet entrance, measuring $1\frac{1}{4}$ inches in diameter. Outside of this there was an area $2\frac{1}{3}$ inches in diameter of darkening by smoke and a large number of discrete particles of powder embedded in the cardboard.

Experiment II.—Distance of 1 inch. An intense blackening three-quarters of an inch in diameter, and outside of this radiating lines of blackening involving an area of $3\frac{1}{2}$ inches in diameter.

Experiment III.—Distance of 6 inches. A few particles of ingrained powder.

Experiment IV.—Distance of 9 inches. Showed nothing except the hole produced by the bullet.

Experiment V.—Distance of 12 inches. Showed nothing except the hole produced by the bullet.

Experiment VI.—Distance of 3 inches. No blackening, but numerous particles of ingrained powder over an area of $1\frac{1}{2}$ inches in diameter.

Experiment VII.—Distance of 1 inch (with cotton wool). A ring of intense blackening and diffuse blackening 2 inches in diameter, tattooing 1 inch in diameter; no singeing.

Experiment VIII.—Distance of 3 inches. Ring of blackening two-thirds of an inch in diameter, and tattooing one quarter of an inch.

Experiment IX.—Distance of 2 inches. Diffuse blackening 3 inches in diameter, and tattooing three-quarters of an inch.

On Wednesday, 8th December, 1926, in the Forensic Medicine Department of the University here, I made further experiments along with Professor Glaister. These closely corresponded with the above in all particulars.

From the foregoing experiments it is evident that, if the discharge took place with the muzzle at a distance of 3 inches or less from the skin, there would have been definite evidence of such a near discharge which Dr. Holcombe would have recognised if present. This evidence would not have been removed by the blood or by the washing of the wound, but would have remained for many days.

The discharge must therefore be assumed to have taken place at a greater distance than 3 inches from the head.

314

Appendix II.

In considering the question of a possible accidental discharge of the pistol by the deceased, I am of opinion that this is not easily conceivable when one considers (1) the position in which the pistol must have been held, viz., behind the ear and not less than 4 inches from it; (2) the angle at which it must have been held, with the muzzle pointing forwards; and (3) the considerable force required to discharge it.

Intentional self-infliction is in my opinion equally inconceivable.

The suicide, as a rule, leaves nothing to chance. He holds the weapon close to his head in a natural position and fires at the temple or side of the head in front of the ear. The wound always shows the characters of a " near " discharge.

In the present case the discharge was not a near one. The wound was in a very unusual position, while the direction, considered along with the distance of the discharge, indicates that the hand and arm must have been in a strained position—a most unlikely circumstance in a would-be suicide. With the weapon held in such a position, the person could have had very little knowledge of what part of the head he would hit, also a very strong point against self-infliction.

From these considerations I am of opinion that suicide was in the highest degree improbable.

The direction of the bullet wound, the position of the wound, the distance at which the discharge took place, all point to the weapon having been fired by another party.　　　　　(Sgd.) HARVEY LITTLEJOHN, M.B.

APPENDIX III.

MEDICAL REPORT BY JOHN GLAISTER, M.D., &C., PROFESSOR OF FORENSIC MEDICINE IN THE UNIVERSITY OF GLASGOW.

University of Glasgow,
10th December, 1926.

DEATH OF MRS. BERTHA MERRETT.

I hereby certify that by instructions of William Horn, Esquire, Procurator-Fiscal, Edinburgh, I have carefully considered certain information given to me relative to the death of Mrs. Bertha Merrett, late of 31 Buckingham Terrace, Edinburgh, and I have examined and experimented with certain productions which are referred to in the case of John Donald Merrett.

The information given me includes the following facts :—That on 17th March, 1926, John Donald Merrett and his mother, the now deceased Mrs. Bertha Merrett, occupied a flat at 31 Buckingham Terrace, and while alone in the sitting-room of the flat, the deceased Mrs. Merrett received a gunshot wound in the head; that Mrs. Merrett soon thereafter on the same day was removed to the Royal Infirmary, Edinburgh; that Mrs. Merrett died in said Infirmary on 1st April, 1926, the cause of death being certified as basal meningitis following a bullet wound in the cranium; that a statement regarding the nature of said injury to the head of the deceased at the time of her admission to said Infirmary was made by Dr. Roy Stanley Holcombe, house surgeon in said Infirmary; and that a post-mortem examination of the body of the deceased was made by Professor Harvey Littlejohn on Thursday, 1st April, 1926.

I was furnished with a copy (1) of the statement of Dr. Holcombe, house surgeon, and (2) of the report by Professor Littlejohn of the post-mortem examination.

John Donald Merrett.

I further certify that on 8th December, 1926, within the Forensic Medicine Department of the University of Edinburgh, Professor Littlejohn demonstrated to me the situation and direction of the wound in the skull and the position of the bullet when found by him at the post-mortem examination; that I was shown by him the automatic revolver and the said bullet connected with the case; and that then and there we made jointly certain experimental observations with said automatic revolver and cartridges referred to in the case.

The question to which I am asked to devote my mind is : how and by whom was the said head injury of the deceased produced?

There are three points demanding attention before answer can be made to this question, viz. :—

1. The appearances of the wound externally on the head of the deceased at the time of her admission to the Infirmary;

2. The direction of the wound in its entirety, as discovered at the post-mortem examination by Professor Littlejohn;

3. The foregoing points in relation to the probable distance from the head of deceased the muzzle of the revolver was at the moment of firing the weapon to produce the injuries to the ear and head as found; and, arising out of these,

4. The mode of causation of the head injury relative to the answer to the question whether said injury was or was not self-inflicted.

Question 1.—The appearance of the wound externally on the head of deceased at the time of admission to the Infirmary.

Mr. Holcombe, house surgeon, who dressed the wound, describes it as " a small, well-defined wound no bigger than the circumference of an ordinary slate pencil, there being little destruction of tissue at site of the entrance of the bullet; there was a redness about the edges of the wound, but there was no blackness or tattooing of ingrained particles of powder, so that there was nothing about the appearance of the wound to suggest that a gunshot had been fired close to it."

Professor Littlejohn describes the external wounding as seen by him at the post-mortem examination on 1st April, 1926, as follows :—" A perforating wound of the antihelix of the right ear, less than a quarter of an inch in diameter, and, behind this, a larger wound which passed into the skull immediately posterior to the meatus or external entrance to the ear."

Professor Littlejohn, in answer to my question, explained that the words " behind this " were intended to convey the meaning that this larger wound was nearer the skull bone than the smaller wound, and not that it was further back on the head than the smaller wound.

Since it has been my experience of examinations of a large number of shooting cases—accidental, suicidal, and homicidal—that whenever the muzzle of the weapon at the moment of firing is close to the part struck, there is always some blackening or tattooing of the skin around the wound, my attention was arrested in this case by the absence of any such blackening or tattooing. It is noteworthy that this tattooing is always most marked when the cartridges used contain gunpowder as the explosive, due to the unconsumed particles of gunpowder being lodged in the skin.

Examination of the cartridges which are used with the automatic revolver in this case proved them to be 0.25 Eley cartridges, the contained explosive being cordite.

In order to determine definitely whether the cartridges used in this automatic revolver would demonstrate their effects upon parts at different distances, Professor Littlejohn and I resolved to make the following experiments :—

Using the automatic revolver and the cartridges in this case, we fired at white paper sheets mounted on cardboard at different distances.

These experiments were made by us on 8th December, and I have written on each the measured distances from the paper at which these shots were

316

Appendix III.

fired, and each of the results has been signed by Professor Littlejohn and myself.

Six shots were fired; one each at the following respective distances, viz. :—Half an inch; 1 inch; 2 inches; 3 inches; 6 inches; and 12 inches.

Examination of these results shows as follows :—

No. 1. *Weapon fired at distance of half an inch* (8th December, 1926). *Observation.*—Around the wound or puncture in the paper there is an area of blackened deposit measuring 2 inches in diameter, with dark stellar rays proceeding outwards from the principal blackened area. Individual specks of tattooing are not easily visible to the naked eye, but are readily visible by hand lens.

No. 2. *Weapon fired at 1 inch distance* (8th December, 1926). *Observation.*—Around the wound there is a series of discrete blackened marks, and outside of these is an area lighter than in No. 1, but of the same stellar form, measuring $2\frac{1}{4}$ inches in diameter. Individual specks of tattooing are not easily visible to the naked eye, but are readily visible with hand lens. This exhibit shows evidence of some scorching of the paper around the puncture.

No. 3. *Weapon fired at 2 inches distance* (8th December, 1926). *Observation.*—Around the puncture the area of blackening has become considerably reduced in size, measuring only about 1 inch in diameter. Individual specks of tattooing are now visible to good eyesight and to slight magnification.

No. 4. *Weapon fired at 3 inches distance* (8th December, 1926). *Observation.*—The area of blackening around the puncture is still further diminished in size, the diameter now being nearly half an inch. Individual specks of tattooing are visible to the naked eye.

No. 5. *Weapon fired at 6 inches distance* (8th December, 1926). *Observation.*—All blackening around the puncture has now entirely disappeared. A few individual specks of tattooing are visible to the unaided eye.

No. 6. *Weapon fired at 12 inches distance* (8th December, 1926). *Observation.*—All blackening around the puncture has entirely disappeared, and individual specks of tattooing have also disappeared.

I produce these experiments as part of this report.

I was shown further a similar series of experiments previously made by Professor Littlejohn with the same revolver and cartridges, and at the distances respectively as in those experiments above stated. On comparing these experiments with those made jointly by us, the results were found to correspond even to detailed particulars.

We conducted further experiments with skin, using the same revolver and cartridges.

Shots were fired at the distances of (1) Half an inch, (2) 1 inch, and (3) 3 inches respectively, against skin.

The effects on the skin were similar to those produced on the paper-cardboard, fired at the same respective distances.

Question 2.—The direction of the wound in the skull of deceased as ascertained at the post-mortem examination by Professor Littlejohn.

Professor Littlejohn's report bears that the larger wound externally nearest the skull bone " passed into the skull immediately posterior to the meatus or external entrance of the ear, the brain was uninjured, but embedded in the bone of the base of the skull, close to the *Sella turcica* (of the sphenoid bone and so called because of its likeness to a Turkish saddle), there was a nickel-plated bullet of small calibre. The directions of the wound (in the skull), judging by the external wound and the position of the bullet where found, was horizontal and slightly from behind forwards, the bullet lying about 1 inch anterior to the external wound—that is, the direction was at an angle approximately 120 degrees to

John Donald Merrett.

a line drawn longitudinally through the middle of the skull from before backwards."

Professor Littlejohn demonstrated to me on specimens of the human head —wet and dry—the line of traject of the bullet and the position in which he found the bullet.

We agreed that while the main direction of the wound in the skull was horizontal, it also showed a slight upward inclination from the point of entrance into the skull to the point where it was found embedded.

The slight upward inclination was probably due to the position of the head of deceased at the moment when the bullet entered the skull; for example, if deceased's head had been then slightly bent on the neck looking at an object below the line of vision when sitting or standing, that might give the slightly upward inclination present. But while this is so, it is of importance to note that the direction was from behind forwards.

The reason why in this case the brain of the deceased was found to be uninjured becomes clear, because the line of traject of the bullet was entirely within the more or less solid bony structures of the base of the skull until its point of arrest.

Careful examination and measurements of the bones composing the base of the skull show that if a line be drawn across the head from the centre of the bony entrance of one ear to the bony entrance of the other ear, and a measurement is then made from that line to the point in the base of the skull where the bullet lay, the distance will be found to be 1 inch in front of that line, and, since the wound in the skull of deceased— that is, the wound of entrance—was immediately behind the opening into the right ear, it follows that the angle at which it entered to a line drawn from front to back in the middle line of the skull is in the neighbourhood of 120 degrees.

I have measured this angle and corroborate Professor Littlejohn's finding.

In view of the facts (1) that the main direction of the bullet in the skull was horizontal and slightly upwards, and (2) that from the point of entrance to the point where the bullet was lodged, the direction was from behind forwards, the question has now to be answered, if possible, could such a wound be self-inflicted?

Question 4.—Whether said injury was or was not self-inflicted?

In order that the wound found in this case or one approximating to it could be produced by self-infliction, a person would have to place his body, his head, and his right arm and hand in a very constrained, unnatural attitude and position; in fact, to do this, the elbow of the arm and the hand would require to be strained further back than the shoulder, and the shoulder itself pulled much backwards.

My experience of suicidally inflicted wounds by shooting into the head is, that suicides commonly adopt the easiest and the most certain position to effect their object. Indeed, a suicide usually shoots into the temple of the head, or, when into other places, into the forehead, and in other instances into the roof of the mouth.

If the facts (1) that there was no blackening or tattooing of the skin around the wound, and (2) the direction of the wound in the skull was horizontal, slightly upwards, and actually from behind forwards, be now conjoined, as they were in this case, one is forced to the following conclusions, viz. :—(1) That the muzzle of the weapon was at the very least 4 inches, and, much more likely, between 6 and more inches from the head at the moment of firing, and in view of the facts mentioned is not compatible with a self-inflicted wound when the weapon is held commonly near the part to be struck; and (2) that the direction of the wound in the skull found in this case implies the abnormal use of the hand and arm to produce the wound by self-infliction.

318

Appendix III.

Opinion.—Taking all the facts of the wounding in this case, while I am unable to exclude absolutely the possibility of the production of such a wound as in this case by self-infliction, the improbabilities so outweigh in my mind the possibilities that I have come to the conclusion that the head injury which caused the death of Mrs. Merrett was not self-inflicted.

These are attested on soul and conscience.

(Sgd.) JOHN GLAISTER.

Note.—I have signed the labels attached to (a) the automatic revolver, (b) the bullet found in the skull of the deceased, and (c) have also signed the productions Nos. 1 to 6 sent herewith as part of the foregoing report. I have also initialed the box of Eley 0.25 cordite cartridges with which productions Nos. 1 to 6 were made.

(Intd.) J. G.

APPENDIX IV.

EXCERPTS FROM REPORT BY GERALD FRANCIS GURRIN, F.R.M.S., ON SIGNATURES PURPORTING TO BE THOSE OF BERTHA MERRETT TO CHEQUES ON THE CLYDESDALE BANK, LTD., GEORGE STREET, EDINBURGH, AND ON THE MIDLAND BANK, LTD., BOSCOMBE.

1. I have had submitted to me by the Procurator-Fiscal for Midlothian, Edinburgh, a number of documents for examination, falling into the following three classes :—

Class I.—Documents bearing signatures '' Bertha Merrett '' which are in dispute;

Class II.—Documents which bear undoubted signatures of or are in the handwriting of the late Mrs. Bertha Merrett;

Class III.—Documents in the handwriting of or bearing signatures of John Donald Merrett.

2. The documents have been each given an identification number, and are as follows :—

Class I.—Questioned Documents.

Twenty-three cheques drawn on the Clydesdale Bank, Ltd., George Street, Edinburgh, on the account of Mrs. Bertha Merrett.

. . . .

Thirty-three cheques drawn on the account of Mrs. Bertha Merrett at the Midland Bank, Ltd., Boscombe.

. . . .

Class II.—Undoubted Writing and Signatures of Mrs. Merrett.

Sixty-one cheques drawn on the account of Mrs. Merrett at the Midland Bank, Boscombe, and one slip signed '' Bertha Merrett.''

. . . .

Seven cheques drawn on the account of Mrs. Bertha Merrett at the Clydesdale Bank, Ltd., George Street, Edinburgh, payable to Mrs. Sharp.

. . . .

Three pay-in slips for the account of Mrs. Bertha Merrett at the Clydesdale Bank, Ltd., George Street, Edinburgh.

. . . .

John Donald Merrett.

130. A notebook titled " Accounts—J. D. Merrett."

131. An application for firearm certificate (Firearm Form 1), dated 10th February, 1926.

132 to 141. Ten pay-in slips on the account of Bertha Merrett with the Clydesdale Bank, Ltd., George Street, Edinburgh, dated respectively : Feb. 4, Feb. 8, Feb. 15, Feb. 18, Feb. 24, Mar. 3, Mar. 4, Mar. 13, Mar. 16, Mar. 18, all of 1926, signed " J. D. Merrett."

142. A faint-ruled sheet of paper headed " 3rd June, 1926," bearing the words " Bertha Merrett " written six times by John Donald Merrett in the presence of police officers, the last two instances of the name being intended for reproductions of his mother's signature.

3. I am informed that the documents scheduled above in Class II. may be relied upon as being in the undoubted handwriting of the late Mrs. Bertha Merrett.

4. My instructions are to examine the signatures to all the documents in Class I., and to report to the Procurator-Fiscal upon their genuineness or otherwise; also, if I find that any of the signatures in Class I. were not written by the deceased Mrs. Merrett, to ascertain, if possible, whether any of them were produced by the writer of the documents in Class III.

5. Certain specific questions have been put to me which I will set out at a later stage, together with their answers, but for the moment I desire to deal generally with the documents, with the methods of examination and the results obtained.

6. The first step in an examination of this kind is to study the un-doubted signatures with the object of familiarising oneself with the peculiarities of the writer. Accordingly I have taken the documents in Class II., which consist of the sixty-one cheques on the Midland Bank, Ltd., and one slip, Nos. 57 to 118, the seven cheques drawn on the Clydesdale Bank, Ltd., in favour of Mrs. Sharp, Nos. 119 to 125, and the three pay-in slips Nos. 126 to 128.

7. I have thoroughly familiarised myself with the details of construction of these signatures and with the general appearance of them upon the various types of paper. The one outstanding feature, apart from the formation of letters, into which there is no need to go, is the speed and cleanliness of their execution, there being no sign of hesitation or patching up and the signatures being blotted promptly after execution, so that only a thin film of transparent ink is left upon the paper.

8. With this knowledge I turned to the documents in Class I., consisting of fifty-six cheques, twenty-three on the Clydesdale and thirty-three on the Midland Bank. These were arranged in such fashion that only the signatures were visible to me, and it was not until after my examination was complete that I saw the writing in the bodies of the cheques, the names of the payees, &c. I found that, so far as the design of the questioned signatures was concerned, they corresponded quite well in the majority of cases with the signatures in Class II., but two things struck me as peculiar with regard to them, the first being an appearance of solidity or heaviness in many of them, a feature quite foreign to the undoubted signatures, and the second a remarkably close similarity in the formations and positions of the letters between a number of these questioned signatures themselves.

9. As both these features are of a suspicious nature, I proceeded to investigate the cause and made a thorough examination of the ink strokes comprising each of the fifty-six questioned signatures with a powerful microscope. I found that in the case of twenty-nine of these signatures the heavy appearance was caused by the fact that a double signature existed. First there was an outline consisting of deep violet strokes either of carbon impression or very soft pencil, then over this outline was an ordinary blue ink outline which followed the violet strokes fairly closely from beginning to end of the signature. There were many places in these twenty-nine sig-

Appendix IV.

natures, however, where the ink stroke had not completely covered the violet outline and the latter could be seen protruding either at the ends of strokes or even alongside such horizontal lines as the crossings of the " t's." Even where the ink strokes covered the violet outline the latter could be seen quite clearly on the paper through the film of ink. The outline was traceable on the signature only and not on the underline to the signature, with one exception, namely, the cheque identified as No. 5. In this case the outline is traceable throughout the underline. In order that the condition of these twenty-nine signatures may be appreciated I have made enlarged photographs of two of them, and reproductions are attached to the fly-leaf of this report. Their numbers are 50 and 53. In No. 50 the violet outline can be seen running from beginning to end of the signature almost without break. It is represented by the thin dark strokes appearing sometimes on one side of the ink strokes, sometimes on the other, and sometimes crossing from one side of the stroke to the other. In at least three places the violet outline is seen protruding below the ink strokes, namely, at the base of the first downstroke of the capital " B," at the base of the loop which forms the lower right-hand portion of the capital " B," and at the base of the second small " r " of " Merrett."

10. In the signature No. 53 a similar outline can be followed throughout the signature, and it is clearly seen that there is no such outline in the underline.

11. The photographs, of course, do not show the complete difference in colour between the blue ink and the violet outline, but this can be quite clearly seen under the microscope. The presence of an outline of this kind is entirely inconsistent with genuineness, and points to the signatures having been reproduced from a genuine model by one of two methods. The first is for the paper or cheque upon which the reproduction is to be made to be placed first on the table covered with a sheet of carbon paper and the model or genuine signature placed upon the top of the carbon. The model is then gone over with a dry point or a fine pencil and an outline made on the cheque form by the carbon paper, this outline being subsequently inked over. The other method is for the paper or cheque form upon which the signature is to be reproduced to be placed over the model, the two then having a light placed behind them (for example, both being placed on a window pane), and the model being lightly traced over with a pencil on the cheque form which is upmost. This outline is subsequently inked over. In the present case either of these two methods might have been employed. In order that there can be no possible doubt, I have examined every one of the seventy-two undoubted signatures of the late Mrs. Merrett in Class II. and all the remaining twenty-seven cheques in Class I., and have not found indications of violet outline in any single case.

12. I will now turn to the second suspicious feature I noticed in the signatures under examination, namely, the close similarity between some of them. In order to test this I took a tracing of one of the signatures at random, which happened to be No. 10, and superimposed it upon all the fifty-six signatures in turn. I found that it corresponded almost exactly with the outline of the signature in the case of sixteen of the cheques, so that seventeen of the cheques are almost exactly alike. A second tracing was made of a slightly varying form, in this case the cheque taken being No. 52. I found that this outline corresponded with the signatures in ten other cases, so that there were eleven drawn upon this basis.

For convenience I have called these two tracings Model A and Model B. Neither of these tracings coincided with any of the undoubted signatures in Class II. or with any of the signatures in Class I. (the questioned signatures) which I had found to be clean and straightforward. These two models, therefore, accounted for twenty-eight of the twenty-nine signatures bearing traces of carbon. The signature with which neither of them coincided was No. 5, and this I have called Model C. It is well known that no two genuine signatures are ever exactly alike so far as the size and proportions of the letters are concerned and their positions relative to one another.

John Donald Merrett.

In this case, so far as the signatures corresponding with Models A and B are concerned, the agreement is far too close for the signatures to be genuine. This would be the case if only two signatures corresponded to this extent, but here we have eleven in one case and seventeen in the other, and it can only mean that these two groups of signatures were reproduced from two genuine signatures. As to Model C, the presence of the violet outline shows that it is a reproduction, but evidently the model has only been used once so far as the documents before me are concerned.

13. A table of the twenty-nine signatures which I have found to be defective, showing which model was used for each signature and upon which bank the cheque was drawn, is given on page 13.

14. We therefore have it that in each of twenty-nine of the fifty-six signatures under examination two conditions are present, either of which is inconsistent with genuineness, and that the remaining twenty-seven are clean and straightforward. These twenty-seven I have compared with the undoubted signatures of the late Mrs. Merrett, and found agreement between them.

15. I now answer the questions which have been put to me. The questions and their answers are as follows :—

Question 1.—Whether in my opinion any of the Clydesdale Bank cheques bear signatures which are not the genuine signatures of the deceased Mrs. Merrett, and, if so, which of them?

Answer.—In my opinion twelve of the cheques on the Clydesdale Bank do not bear genuine signatures of the deceased Mrs. Merrett. They are—

Feb.	2, 1926.	No.	5	for	£7	7	0
,,	3, ,,	,,	6	,,	2	13	0
,,	5, ,,	,,	7	,,	3	3	0
,,	13, ,,	,,	10	,,	10	0	0
,,	17, ,,	,,	11	,,	5	0	0
,,	20, ,,	,,	12	,,	10	10	0
,,	22, ,,	,,	13	,,	5	8	0
,,	27, ,,	,,	15	,,	4	2	6
Mar.	2, ,,	,,	16	,,	8	6	0
,,	4, ,,	,,	17	,,	5	0	0
,,	6, ,,	,,	18	,,	10	0	0
,,	11, ,,	,,	21	,,	15	15	0

Question 2.—Whether in my opinion any of the Midland Bank cheques bear signatures which are not the genuine signatures of the deceased Mrs. Merrett, and, if so, which of them?

Answer.—In my opinion seventeen of the cheques on the Midland Bank do not bear genuine signatures of the deceased Mrs. Merrett. They are—

Feb.	8, 1926.	No.	34	for	£15	0	0
,,	9, ,,	,,	35	,,	5	0	0
,,	11, ,,	,,	36	,,	8	0	0
,,	15, ,,	,,	38	,,	15	0	0
,,	18, ,,	,,	37	,,	10	0	0
,,	24, ,,	,,	41	,,	20	0	0
Mar.	3, ,,	,,	45	,,	15	15	0
,,	8, ,,	,,	47	,,	30	0	0
,,	13, ,,	,,	48	,,	25	14	0
,,	15, ,,	,,	49	,,	22	10	6
,,	16, ,,	,,	51	,,	30	0	0
,,	18, ,,	,,	52	,,	30	0	0
,,	20, ,,	,,	54	,,	25	0	0
,,	23, ,,	,,	50	,,	30	0	0
,,	24, ,,	,,	55	,,	30	0	0
,,	26, ,,	,,	56	,,	30	0	0
,,	27, ,,	,,	63	,,	28	9	6

Appendix IV.

Question 3.—Whether, assuming I am of opinion that some of the signatures of the cheques are written by some one other than Mrs. Merrett, I am able to form any opinion from the handwriting of J. D. Merrett as that appears in Class III., that the signatures were written by J. D. Merrett?

Answer.—In cases of free-hand copying of a genuine signature it is possible, in spite of the close adherence to a model, for some features of the writer's own peculiarities to appear in the signature produced. In cases of traced forgery, however, such as appears in the twenty-nine signatures in this case which I do not believe to have been written by Mrs. Merrett, the models have been accurately traced, and there is practically no possibility of the writer's peculiarities becoming manifest. My reply to the third question must therefore be that there is nothing to enable me to form any opinion as to whether the twenty-nine signatures which I do not believe to have been written by the deceased Mrs. Merrett were written by J. D. Merrett.

Table of Cheques found not to be Genuine.

. . . .

Seventeen spurious signatures reproduced from Model A.
Eleven spurious signatures reproduced from Model B.
One spurious signature reproduced from Model C.
Tracings of Models A, B, and C are upon page 16.

16. Having answered the specific questions put to me, I have examined the cheques for any other feature which might throw light generally upon the matter and have grouped the results under five headings as follows :—

1. The twenty-nine signatures all show clear indications of carbon outline;
2. Twenty-eight of the twenty-nine are clearly reproduced from two models;
3. All the twenty-nine cheques are payable to J. D. Merrett;
4. Not in the case of any of the twenty-nine was the body written by Mrs. Merrett.
5. In the remainder of the cheques (*i.e.*, those which I believe to be genuine) there is no instance of the body having been written by any other hand than that of Mrs. Merrett.

17. I have not dealt with the question of whether the bodies of the twenty-nine cheques were written by J. D. Merrett, as I rather gather from my letter of instructions that there may already be some evidence of fact upon this question.

18. There is one point connected with the specimen of J. D. Merrett's handwriting No. 142 which may have some significance. This is the document written in the presence of the police officers, and I notice that when asked to write in imitation of his mother's signature he produced two slightly varying forms of her signature so far as the capital " B " and the capital " M " are concerned. It is curious to note that these two forms of signature are precisely the forms used for producing the bulk of the signatures which I consider to be spurious, or, in other words, they correspond with Model A and Model B. Of course, if at the time this specimen was produced J. D. Merrett had before him two of his mother's signatures and was deliberately copying them, this point could have no substance.

19. If it is desired that I give evidence in support of the opinion above expressed, it will be necessary for me to have an opportunity of photographing the signatures which I have found to contain evidence of reproduction and also a number of the undoubted signatures and of preparing the necessary comparative diagrams for the proper demonstration of the facts to the Court. If the opportunity of so doing is afforded me, I shall be prepared to support my opinion upon oath.   (Sgd.) G. F. GURRIN.
Dated this 4th day of November, 1926.

John Donald Merrett.

APPENDIX V.

Excerpt from Report by John Michael Geoghegan, Chartered Accountant, Edinburgh, on Mrs. Merrett's Account Book and Banking Transactions.

. . . .

Mrs. Merrett kept accounts with the Midland Bank, Boscombe, and the Clydesdale Bank, Edinburgh. The former was her principal account, and she kept the Clydesdale Bank account in credit by drawing cheques on her Midland Bank account whenever necessary.

Mrs. Merrett recorded in her book her transactions with the Clydesdale Bank showing the sums paid into the bank, the cheques drawn from the bank, and the balance from time to time remaining at her credit.

The transactions so recorded by her do not agree with the transactions recorded in the copy bank account, in respect that in the copy bank account there are cheques drawn from the bank and sums paid into the bank which do not appear in Mrs. Merrett's book.

	£	s.	d.
The balance in the Clydesdale Bank as recorded in Mrs. Merrett's book at 13th March, 1926 (the date of the last entry), is	10	9	0
to which add—adjustment for error in summation in Mrs. Merrett's book on 1st March, 1926, - - - - -	0	0	3
	£10	9	3
Deduct adjustment for erroneous entry in Mrs. Merrett's book— a cheque dated 8th March, 1926, No. 2335, being entered as £3 7s. 6d. in error for £7 3s. 6d., - - - - - -	3	16	0
	£6	13	3

In order to agree this figure with the balance shown in the copy bank account it is necessary to give effect to the following transactions appearing in the copy bank account, but not in Mrs. Merrett's book :—

I. *Sums paid in—*

Date. 1926.	Pay-in slip signed by	Amount.		
Feb. 8.	J. D. Merrett,	£10	0	0
,, 15.	J. D. Merrett,	13	0	0
,, 18.	J. D. Merrett,	5	0	0
,, 24.	J. D. Merrett,	10	0	0
Mar. 3.	J. D. Merrett,	7	7	0
,, 13.	J. D. Merrett,	8	14	0
,, 16.	J. D. Merrett,	25	0	0
,, 18.	J. D. Merrett,	17	0	0
		£96	1	0

II. *Cheques drawn—*

Date. 1926.	No.	In favour of	Amount.					
Feb. 2.	2011	J. D. Merrett,	£7	7	0			
,, 3.	2016	J. D. Merrett,	2	13	0	£13	3	0
,, 5.	2015	J. D. Merrett,	3	3	0			
,, 13.	2330	J. D. Merrett,	10	0	0			
,, 17.	2329	J. D. Merrett,	5	0	0	25	10	0
,, 20.	2340	J. D. Merrett,	10	10	0			
,, 22.	3602	J. D. Merrett,	5	8	0			
,, 27.	3605	J. D. Merrett,	4	2	6			
Mar. 2.	3606	J. D. Merrett,	8	6	0	48	11	6
,, 4.	3608	J. D. Merrett,	5	0	0			
,, 6.	3609	J. D. Merrett,	10	0	0			
,, 11.	3607	J. D. Merrett,	15	15	0			
						£87	4	6
						£8	16	6

324

Appendix V.

On 4th March, 1926, there is entered as paid into the
bank in Mrs. Merrett's book £25; on the same date
there appears in the copy bank account as paid into
the bank £20; the pay-in slip is signed by J. D.
Merrett,

Difference, - - - - - - - - 5 0 0

3 16 6

Balance in the Clydesdale Bank at 18th March, 1926,
as shown by the copy bank account, - - - - £10 9 9

Mrs. Merrett also recorded in her book her transactions with the Midland Bank showing the sums paid into the bank, the cheques drawn from
the bank, and the balance from time to time remaining at her credit.

At 1st January, 1926, the amount shown in Mrs. Merrett's
book as at her credit with the Midland Bank is less than the
amount shown in the copy bank account by £39 5s. 9d., but as at
26th January, 1926, Mrs. Merrett corrected the figure in her book
to agree with the bank's figure, and at 4th March, 1926, the date of
the last entry in her book, Mrs. Merrett shows at her credit with
the Midland Bank the sum of - - - - - - £373 15 0
Add adjustment for error in summation in Mrs. Merrett's book
on 16th February, 1926, - - - - - - - - 1 0 0
Adjustment necessary to make the figure in Mrs. Merrett's book
at 26th January, 1926, agree exactly with the figure in the bank's
books, - - - - - - - - - - - - 0 2 4

£374 17 4

The following cheques appear in the copy bank account and
the bank pass book as drawn from the bank, but do not appear in
Mrs. Merrett's book, and if these cheques are deducted from the
above figure the balance at Mrs. Merrett's credit in the bank's
books at 29th March, 1926, is obtained.

Date. 1926.	No.	In favour of	Amount.
Feb. 8.	73960	J. D. Merrett,	£15 0 0
,, 9.	73955	J. D. Merrett,	5 0 0
,, 11.	73950	J. D. Merrett,	8 0 0
,, 15.	73942	J. D. Merrett,	15 0 0
,, 18.	73945	J. D. Merrett,	10 0 0
,, 24.	73953	J. D. Merrett,	20 0 0
Mar. 3.	73952	J. D. Merrett,	15 15 0
,, 8.	73959	J. D. Merrett,	30 0 0
,, 13.	73949	J. D. Merrett,	25 14 0
,, 15.	73951	J. D. Merrett,	22 10 6
,, 16.	73954	J. D. Merrett,	30 0 0
,, 18.	73956	J. D. Merrett,	30 0 0
,, 20.	73957	J. D. Merrett,	25 0 0
,, 23.	73958	J. D. Merrett,	30 0 0
,, 24.	76541	J. D. Merrett,	30 0 0
,, 26.	76542	J. D. Merrett,	30 0 0
,, 27.	76543	J. D. Merrett,	28 9 6

£370 9 0

,, 15. Cheque book, - - - 0 5 0

370 14 0

Balance in bank as shown by copy bank account on
29th March, 1926, - - - - - - - £4 3 4

The sums paid into the Clydesdale Bank which are not recorded in

John Donald Merrett.

Mrs. Merrett's book were all paid in on the same dates as cheques (not recorded in Mrs. Merrett's book) were drawn from the Midland Bank.

The cheques drawn from the Midland Bank on these dates are in each case for larger amounts than are paid into the Clydesdale Bank; in some cases the pay-in slips show that the proceeds of these cheques were partly paid by the bank in cash over the counter and the remainder credited to Mrs. Merrett's account.

In Appendices Nos. I. and II. to this report I give statements showing the particulars of all cheques charged against Mrs. Merrett's account in the books of the Clydesdale Bank and the Midland Bank respectively; it will be seen that the numbers of the cheques in favour of J. D. Merrett, which are not recorded in Mrs. Merrett's book, do not follow in the same sequence as the numbers of the cheques which Mrs. Merrett did record in her book; the cheques in question seem to have been written out in a different part of the cheque book from that which would naturally have been used.

Mrs. Merrett recorded in her book her personal expenditure under various headings, and the amount of that expenditure between January and March, 1926, is as follows :—

House rent, food, meals, &c., - - - -	£100 10	8
Dress and clothes, - - - - -	15 8	10
Travelling, - - - - - -	6 18	5
Stamps, notepaper, books, newspapers, and magazines, -	5 13	3
Doctors, dentist, medicine, hairdresser (self and Donald), -	3 6	2
Charities, collections, and extras, - - -	2 9	3
Household requisites, - - - -	13 12	7
Donald's expenses, - - - - -	52 10	7
	£200 9	9

Add—Cheque drawn on the Midland Bank dated 2nd March, 1926, in favour of Robert Anderson and not entered in Mrs. Merrett's record of her expenditure, -   25 0 0

£225 9 9

I find that the amount Mrs. Merrett drew out of the bank during the period January to March, 1926, exclusive of the cheques in favour of J. D. Merrett, which do not appear in her book, was £231 4s. 9d., made up thus—

Cheques drawn from Midland Bank, per page 6, - -	£237 18	0
Less balance in Clydesdale Bank at 13th March, 1926, as recorded by Mrs. Merrett, per page 2, - - -	6 13	3
	£231 4	9

Mrs. Merrett's statement of her expenditure as contained in her book corresponds very closely therefore with the amount which she recorded in her book as drawn from the bank.

She has left no record whatever in her book of the application of the cheques drawn from the bank in favour of J. D. Merrett, nor any record that such cheques were actually drawn by her.

The cheques drawn in favour of J. D. Merrett and not entered in Mrs. Merrett's book amount to—

On Midland Bank, per page 6, - - - -	£370 9	0
On Clydesdale Bank, per page 5, - - -	87 4	6
	£457 13	6

Reported by

(Sgd.) JOHN M. GEOGHEGAN, C.A.

13 Albany Street,
Edinburgh, 28th December, 1926.